ENGLAND IN CONFLICT, 1603–1660

Kingdom, Community, Commonwealth

DEREK HIRST

William Eliot Smith Professor of History,
Washington University in St Louis, USA

A member of the Hodder Headline Group
LONDON • SYDNEY • AUCKLAND
Co-published in the United States of America by Oxford University Press Inc., New York

First published in Great Britain in 1999 by
Arnold, a member of the Hodder Headline Group,
338 Euston Road, London NW1 3BH

http://www.arnoldpublishers.com

Co-published in the United States of America by
Oxford University Press Inc.,
198 Madison Avenue, New York, NY10016

The advice and information in this book are believed to be true and
accurate at the date of going to press, but neither the author nor the
publisher can accept any legal responsibility or liability for any errors or
omissions.

British Library Cataloguing in Publication Data
A catalogue record for this book is available from the British Library

Library of Congress Cataloging-in-Publication Data
A catalogue record for this book is available from the Library of Congress

ISBN 0 340 62501 5 (pb)
ISBN 0 340 74144 9 (hb)

1 2 3 4 5 6 7 8 9 10

Production Editor: Rada Radojicic
Production Controller: Priya Gohil
Cover design: Terry Griffiths

Composition by Scribe Design, Gillingham, Kent
Printed and bound in Great Britain by MPG Books, Bodmin, Cornwall

What do you think about this book? Or any other Arnold title?
Please send your comments to feedback.arnold@hodder.co.uk

Contents

Foreword

A narrative history no longer needs the apologia that might have seemed appropriate a generation ago, since we have become more attuned to the cultural significance of narrative structures. But the rationale for the dates chosen to frame a narrative history needs to be clear, lest writer and reader slide into unthinking assumptions that the contingent – a death long anticipated in this case – is the determining. To end a narrative in 1660 makes some sense, for few episodes have been brought to such insistent formal closure as the republic: one of the first – and most futile – measures of the restored monarchy was to deny that the immediate past had ever been. The attempt to close one chapter and open a new is symbolised too by the establishment that year of the new science in the Royal Society. But to open in 1603 seems either to capitulate to the unthinking choices and monarchical biases of previous generations, or to imply that there was something peculiar to the Stuart style of rule that made of it a high road to civil war and revolution.

A guilty plea might be entered to both charges. English historiography has long been shaped by dynastic changes approximating to the turns of centuries (1399, 1485, 1603, 1688/1714), and there is not much sign that those convenient organising devices are losing their magnetism. After all, we need organising devices – provided that they organise rather than determine our thoughts. 1603 proved a turning-point in England's political history, in the sense that a road was not taken. The wars of the last two decades of Elizabeth's reign had severely strained the English polity; in particular, the Irish war that began in 1594 necessitated unremitting expenditures in a time of considerable socio-economic disruption. To avert pressure for political and religious concessions in return for parliamentary grants of supply, Elizabeth sold lands and resorted to various quasi-fiscal devices, novel in appearance and often corrupt in practice. The consequence was a growing public cynicism, and an outpouring of protest in her last parliaments. The coincidence of her death in March 1603 with peace in Ireland, to be followed in 1604 by peace with Spain, freed the incoming regime of James Stuart to confront the crown's plight. James's failure to use peace to reform, and his promotion of many of those who had implemented or defended high-handed measures in the 1580s and '90s, made the early decades of the new century the testing-time of the establishment he had inherited, with civil war the – by no means inevitable – outcome.

There was more to the turn of the century than changes in political style. One emblem of the demise of the late-medieval polity was the occurrence in 1601 of what proved to be the last aristocratic revolt, that of the Earl of Essex. More fundamental was the changed shape of that polity. For a century and a half, England had been fairly self-contained, its dependencies in France lost, and its hold on Ireland vestigial; in 1603 not only did all Ireland come under its power, but the Stuart succession brought Scotland too into uneasy association. England's embattlement in the Elizabethan years had contributed to the formulation of a fierce chauvinism just as England's isolation was about to come to an end. What gives a tragic, and chaotic, character to the years 1603–60 is their determined and often violent probing of the new British realities. This book is, however, not a British but an English history. There is scope for both, but since many aspects of England's story bore scant reference to Scotland and Ireland, and since in those that did the initiative all too often came from England, to start with England has some appeal.

The recognition that a British frame contained and constrained events in England is one measure of what must distinguish a history of the seventeenth century written in the 1990s from one written fifteen years ago. As I wrote *Authority and Conflict: England, 1603–1658* (1986), I was working in a context very different from today's. The English historical scene of the early 1980s was shaped by revisionist challenges to long-standing assumptions that the struggles between crown and parliament were part of the story of progress. Not only have we been able in the intervening years to gain the perspective of distance on those controversies about the nature of politics, English historians have been reminded as well that a story of progress is harder to sustain when English history reverberates in the experience of Scotland and Ireland. Nor can assumptions of progress, and of the sufficiency of the old interpretive conventions, easily withstand questioning by the historians of women, whose increasingly richly layered work has been the other great historiographic development of recent years.

England in Conflict is therefore not merely a second edition, expanded and extended, of *Authority and Conflict*. The outline of the earlier work is still visible, and some of the judgments remain, though sharpened in the light of recent scholarship. But new understandings of a world that did not fit readily into the triumphalist English story have required a broad reconceptualisation. While the world beyond England's borders and on the other side of the bed and hearth has been brought into clearer view, a world of beliefs, about the body, the role of ritual, community, honour, is steadily being uncovered. Such discoveries have recast our sense of the past; even when they do not show up explicitly in the text they have made this book very different from the one it supersedes.

Although the results of others' work do appear in the text, their names do not. The author of a broad work such as this, which incorporates both original research and the fruits of others' labours, incurs considerable debts. Such debts are the greater in that the publisher's distaste for footnotes precludes any acknowledgement in the text. Nor can the bibliography make adequate amends to the many scholars whose work has been plundered: I can only assure them they have my gratitude.

My greatest debt, for everything, is to my wife, Lori; and our children also deserve my thanks, for while without them this book would have been finished earlier, life would have been a lot less. . . .

Derek Hirst
St Louis, Missouri

|1|

The body politic

The body politic formed the binding early-modern myth. All members of society were bound in an organic whole, whose well-being was at heart collective. Such doctrine, preached relentlessly from the pulpit and acknowledged in proverb and ballad, was two-edged. It required that those above recognise the needs and claims of those below: the monarch should respect and favour the nobles, local elites should protect and benefit their inferiors. And inferiors were expected to know their place. The rhetoric of order abounds in anatomically specific tirades, like that of Menenius in Shakespeare's *Coriolanus* against the political aspirations of plebeians, the big toe of the state; but on the other hand, food rioters insisted that the body must be fed. While the metaphor proscribed dissent, which was inconceivable within a body, the same metaphor also encouraged the imagination of drastic medical or physical remedies – purgation, amputation – against corrupt members.

We should not therefore exaggerate the inherent authoritarianism of the polity so imagined. As we shall see, the king possessed the commanding heights of central government, and was appointed to many offices in the localities; but the being of the polity lay beyond him. Just as its origins lay beyond human memory or artifice, so the political community had its own capacities. Parish worthies apportioned poor relief or arranged seating in the church; the gentry leaders of Sussex in 1640 levied men for the king's disintegrating service though there were no officers to receive them; and committees of parliament-men began to run the country in 1640–1. Many of the actions of the body needed little direction from the royal head.

In the body politic all relationships were politically charged, and social subordination necessarily entailed political subordination. The Cheshire gentleman William Davenport reminded his heirs of those tenants who had not followed his wishes in the civil war, so that they might impose sanctions – the expectation is as noteworthy as the rebellion. The legal responsibility of the master of the household for domestic servants and apprentices may seem rational enough in a society with a high birthrate and no police; more startling is the assumption of the participants in the army debates at Putney in 1647 that servants would vote with their masters. But the body that was political was not only powerfully normative; it was also gendered, and breaches of propriety always excited alarm. Wives who murdered their husbands did not risk being hanged as felons but rather, convicted of petty treason, being burnt at the stake. Less dramatic gender transgressions earned retribution that now seems similarly disproportionate, but which reflected the fundamental importance attached to right order. A wife who domineered over her husband might provoke her neighbours to enact a potentially violent shaming ritual and duck her in the pond. Equally important, the neighbours sought the humiliation of the husband who had failed to keep his wife in order.

The assumption that gendered or sexual misdeeds undermined political order because they threatened the whole had its corollary in the conviction that political deviance went hand in hand with behavioural transgression. This explains the quite remarkable 1620s taste for obscene ballads on the hated and reputedly bisexual Duke of Buckingham, or a generation later for bodily scandals that might delegitimate the republican leaders. The Civil War battle-standard, 'Cuckold we come', thus went far beyond mere cavalier fantasy. 'Family values' were part of the order of Creation, enjoined by the fifth commandment, and of the state. The display of domesticity in the portraiture of Charles I was not intended to be simply personal.

Only by registering the force of the body politic as ideal and ideology, and of the patriarchalism that gendered that body, can we understand the resilience of the early-modern polity, and also its turbulence. Fecundity was part and parcel of the legend, and the excitement that greeted the accession to the English throne in 1603 of a king with children, after two generations of barrenness, suggests the assets possessed by an adult king, even one who happened to be a foreigner. Contrariwise, the horror unleashed in 1649 when the body politic was decapitated always bedevilled the new republic's attempts to root itself, until horror and republic alike were obliterated in the executions and the corporeal delights of 1660. Despite the periodic misery of the poor, and despite the availability of legends of better times in a mythic past or future, villagers and townspeople alike overwhelmingly accepted their lot, and the privileges of those above them. The latter, of course, subscribed to a similar vision; but the ideal was not empty, though there were many rack-renters and exploiters, and the Earl of Salisbury's house at Cranborne, Dorset, was spoiled by his tenants at the outset of the Civil War. Abundant funeral sermons, not all of them the work of sycophantic toadies, portrayed gentry patrons as benevolent landlords and supporters of the poor.

King, court and patronage

Of the political character of the king's body there could be no doubt. When the king died all commissions terminated, all officers' charges came to an end; but then, in one sense, the king never died, for the king was the government, and a successor reigned from the very moment the old king was alive and dead. The convention that the king could do no wrong expressed not only a legal prejudice in favour of the king but also that conviction Thomas Hobbes so vividly reflected in the famous frontispiece to his *Leviathan* (1651): the king embodied the realm. James I provided another version when he insisted to his first English parliament that he was the husband and the isle of Britain his wife. Nevertheless, even this narrow reading of the metaphor could be challenged, as Charles I's parliamentary opponents showed in the Civil War when they pulled apart the king's two bodies, personal and political, and claimed to be fighting against Charles Stuart in defence of the king's office. But outside that time of trouble the person of the monarch focused the majesty of the state: the royal portrait on the coin of the realm was no mere emblem but a fundamental political statement.

The king's body centred the nation's political life not only symbolically and formally but also in practice. Where the king was, there was his court: his home, his place of entertainment, and his place of business. Old-fashioned and sprawling in its architecture, Whitehall palace formed the largest royal court in Europe. And the early-Stuart royal household was, fittingly, the largest institution in the country: with its 2000 or so employees and their families it actually formed one of the half-dozen largest communities in the country, hugely affecting London's economy. In the ceremonies and privileges of court life contemporaries read the political auguries – who's up, who's down; through those ceremonies a king might reconfigure a whole political culture, as Charles did when he systematically reduced access. More obviously, court ceremony projected the splendour and hierarchy of rule for audiences both large (for the pageantry of James's official entry into London) and small (for the elaborate royal dining arrangements, on which the favoured might gaze). Kings could also shape culture by the assertion of their personal tastes, and not only through the Italian paintings that Charles prized. James's generosity, and his boundless curiosity, certainly contributed to the intellectual and cultural vitality of a reign that saw the commissioning of the architecturally innovative Banqueting House at Whitehall, as well as court sponsorship of work by Shakespeare, Francis Bacon, Ben Jonson and John Donne. In turn, Charles's delight in his family setting, and his liking for idealised Platonic renderings of harmony and affection, challenged the protestant heroic style that had been so prominent in Elizabethan and early-Jacobean projections of the elite world. But since government emanated from the king, the royal court was most obviously the place of politics.

Court politics turned on the king's ear, and access was the prime objective. The informal ways of James VI's Scottish court brought a measure of openness, sometimes shading into chaos, to the rigidities of the Elizabethan inheritance; but Charles carefully policed the traffic through the galleries of Whitehall. In such policing lay the influence of the king's intimates in the privy and bed chambers. Lobbying and caballing in advance of privy council meetings, solicitation and counter-solicitation of those close to the king or other great personages in hopes of some material suit, all hinged on the chance to persuade. And since the forms of influence to be brought to bear, direct and indirect, were legion, the numbers involved in court politics might be correspondingly large. They included of course the king's friends and servants, some of them high-ranking nobles like the Earl of Pembroke or the Anglo-Scottish Duke of Lenox, others personable intimates. Amongst the servants can be included the political (as opposed to the middle-ranking legal and financial) office-holders, and around these clustered assorted hangers-on, those hopeful of office or favours, and servants of the king's servants. Foreign agents and representatives were also part of the court, a politically unfortunate fact when most European diplomats and exiles were Roman Catholics. The court's floating membership might run into the hundreds, and Charles's rule-book and the serjeant porter tried with varying success to impose decorum and order.

The court was not only amorphous; centred as it was on service to the King's person, it became a world of intensely personal quarrels over honour, as well as more material rivalries. Although there were insufficient jobs for all the aspirants, rewards for the few top jobs in those pre-bureaucratic days could be enormous, and the Earls of Salisbury and Suffolk, Jacobean lord treasurers, built palaces on their profits. The competition therefore waxed hot. Those with access acted as brokers and charged for their favours; and patronage and reciprocated benefits were the rules of the game. Not surprisingly, a large literature on the corruption and expense of court life developed, not all of it the work of losers like Sir Walter Raleigh and John Donne.

The court was more than just a place where pigs plunged their snouts into the trough. Those with policies to forward had to go to the same sty, ensuring that the court encompassed ideological as well as personal differences. Identifiable groups of courtiers in the 1620s, especially those surrounding the third Earl of Pembroke, backed the Protestant cause and war with Spain; others, most notably the Earls of Middlesex and Arundel, urged peace and financial retrenchment. Such divisions, which historians once thought factious, are now recognised to have lessened estrangement in the country. The anxious puritan appalled by James's pacific ways in his last years, and outraged by signs of religious backsliding, might find consolation in access to Pembroke or the Earl of Warwick. But the outcome of the court Charles created, which allowed the airing of only a single viewpoint, was incomprehension in the country, and a dangerous alienation.

The court offered practical as well as ideological contacts to the country. The mayor seeking relief for a town devastated by fire, the gentleman seeking local office, the widow seeking wardship of her son, all had to find a friend at court, usually someone with local ties, to smooth their way. The fragile hopes of the outsider are reflected in the judgment of the mid-century colonial projector, Thomas Povey, that for success, 'Words [must] be so luckily placed, as to be able to please.' The emphasis on 'placing' there makes it clear that more than sycophancy was involved. The courtier, possessing a country house and far-flung relatives and interests, needed to demonstrate his standing by his following, by his ability to do favours; so he might be pleased to respond to some at least of those who addressed him. Historians used to assume alienation, but though ridicule of bumpkins and parasites abounds in correspondence and poetical effusions, neither court nor country could survive alone.

Patronage was the essential ligament of this world of personal connection and favour. Candidates for jobs were found amongst the dependants of those with influence. The existence of a spoils system does not mean that early-modern morality was inferior to our own; rather, the personal nature of government meant that just as the king enjoyed the rewards of his position, so should his servants. These turned to their friends when appointing subordinates, for partisan loyalties had not yet displaced lineage ties; politics was furthermore a dangerous game, and the headsman's axe claimed Sir Walter Raleigh and the Earl of Strafford even before civil war broke out. If merchants used younger brothers as their factors abroad, why should not politicians turn to those with personal reasons for loyalty, assuming they were also competent? Such considerations were of course reinforced by the natural human emotion of pride: politicians like to have followings. The rules of the game were enduring, and were not abrogated by the fall of the monarchy. The town worthies of Leeds urged the election to parliament of one army officer in 1654 because General Lambert was his patron, 'and he strikes with great hammer'!

The ties of patronage rested on reciprocity, not unthinking submission. Charles's favourite, the Duke of Buckingham, expected his clients to protect him against impeachment, but beyond that they could and did give him conflicting advice. And if inferiors were to show deference their superiors must show generosity. When James's lord treasurer, the Earl of Suffolk, was disgraced for corruption in 1618 he soon found himself isolated locally when his neighbours realised he could do nothing for them. The dictates of hierarchy were far from straightforward, and superiors might be drawn in their inferiors' wake. Thus, Sir Thomas Wentworth recognised the capacity of his Yorkshire followers to pull him into disputes in the 1620s. And followers could even shape how a patron projected himself on the national stage: the Duke of Buckingham's employment of John Packer, a staunchly puritan patronage secretary, surely reflected others' concerns and not his own. But reciprocity was jeopardised by the accession of a king as incapable of understanding the role of favours as he was effective at provoking ideological confrontation. Charles's austere temperament led him throughout his career to expect unquestioning submission, not talk of a quid pro quo. When the Earl of Suffolk tried to bargain over a post the king retorted, 'Where is your obedience?' The scant support noblemen and even courtiers and councillors gave Charles in 1640–2 reflects his frigidity. As the disappointed Earl of Arundel (who was to leave the country to avoid the fighting) remarked, 'It is an ill dog that is not worth whistling.'

The king's government

Not only did the king control the distribution of office and favour, he also determined policy. To some extent the latter stemmed from the former. When James carefully balanced a pro-Spanish with an anti-Spanish secretary of state for most of his reign, he ensured that policy would not lean heavily in either direction, and thus reinforced his hopes of acting as Europe's peacemaker. Conversely, Charles's one-sided appointments to bishoprics after 1628 changed the character of the church of England. But the king's control over the formulation of policy was also more direct. Despite historians' jibes at James's devotion to hunting and young men, his servants could never take him for granted. Not even the alliance of Prince Charles, the Duke of Buckingham and parliament could hurry the king into war against Spain in his last, allegedly declining year. And Charles, in his turn, steadfastly refused to disclose his foreign policy to his councillors in the 1630s, or to consult either his Scottish or his English councils over his catastrophic Scottish policy until it was too late.

To enable him to govern the country the king had certain prerogatives, recognised at law. The royal prerogative was a blend of powers and rights that included sole control over foreign policy, regulation of overseas trade and of the coinage, pardoning of criminals, and (although there was dispute over this, since some demanded statutory and others scriptural warrant) regulation of the church. Looming over all these was the king's duty to take, as he alone saw fit, emergency action to preserve the state; it was this 'absolute prerogative' that was to be the focus of so much tension in the reign of Charles I. The king's power of government was indicated most clearly by his ability to issue proclamations that reinforced, or filled gaps left by, the less flexible instrument of statute: proclamations promulgating measures against epidemics are an example. Unless statutes specifically provided, proclamations were not enforceable in the common law courts; nevertheless, the king's possession of quasi-legislative as well as executive – and, as we shall see, judicial – functions warns against thinking in modern categories of separated powers.

The king needed advice and assistance, and this he could take from whomever he chose. Historians have made much of the problem of counsel, for whether the kingdom was well or ill governed must hinge on the counsel received by a king who ruled. But though in both England and Scotland Charles formally relied on his privy councils, the proper organs of government, he did not thereby gain any guarantee of independent counsel since he alone controlled membership. In England the council ranged in size from fifteen at the end of Elizabeth's reign to over forty in Charles's. It included the great officers of state, like the lord treasurer and the two secretaries of state, as well as leading officers of the royal household, like the lord steward and lord chamberlain, as befitted a government centred on the person of the king. James's council sometimes heard lively debates, especially over finances in 1615 and foreign policy in 1623–4, but these seem to have been rarer in Charles's reign after the heart-searchings over finances and 'new counsels' in 1627–8. At the start of the reign Charles declared his council 'the representative body of king and kingdom'; but when his subjects observed Buckingham's dominance, some responded cynically that 'all the king's council rode upon one horse'. Charles's residence in England meant that he was never as isolated and uninformed as he was of Scottish affairs, but his aversion to disagreement was such that by 1640 parliament seemed even to some privy councillors the essential alternative source of counsel.

An uncounselled king does not mean a king with full freedom of action. The body politic's blurring of public and private ensured that in an important sense government was 'private', and not quite the king's – many offices at what might be called the administrative if not the policy-making level were effectively freeholds. In the localities appointments normally reflected local political realities; at the centre too the king possessed less control over his administration than might be imagined. Office-holders recruited their own servants and expected payment from the public in fees and perquisites rather than from an appropriate salary. Even senior 'political' figures like the two secretaries of state received only £100 per annum each in salary, which they supplemented to an appropriate level through fees. A further 'unbureaucratic' feature of government lay in the sale of administrative offices and 'reversions', or future appointments.

The customs, which were of critical importance to royal finances, similarly blurred the distinction between 'public' and 'private'. At the opening of James's reign the king's ministers replaced direct administration with a 'farm', or lease, of the collection to merchant contractors, thereby confessing their inability to manage large-scale undertakings. Farming was variously attractive. It guaranteed fixed sums of revenue instead of an unpredictable flow; it gave courtiers an opportunity for manipulation and bribery when arranging the lease (thus, the Earl of Salisbury received £6000 from the successful syndicate in 1604); but most important of all, the customs farmers could be cajoled into providing credit, the most urgent need of all governments.

A consideration of royal finances might underscore the 'private', or patrimonial, nature of government. Government was the king's own in a formal sense since, in theory, he paid for it and the subject, again in theory, did not. Kings were expected to 'live of their own', to which end they enjoyed certain 'ordinary', or recurring, revenues. These came from fines and from residual feudal dues, from the customs, as well as from the ancient crown lands. Direct taxation (the subsidy, plus some lesser taxes) was viewed as an extraordinary and usually wartime affair, and had to be granted by parliament, on the maxim that subjects' property was their own. But the ancient convention of patrimonial and self-sufficient government was not sustained in practice. For example, the royal prerogative of purveyance, the right to pre-empt supplies in the market at below-cost prices, amounted to a covert subsidy equal to around one-quarter of James's regular revenues; and fees and bribes to officials were probably equivalent to 40 per cent of the regular royal revenues. Perhaps 80 per cent of the sustenance of the head of this polity came straight from the pockets of its members. Had this arithmetic been available to James's first parliament, proposals for the establishment of regular fiscal support for government might not have been so disconcerting.

The small scale of peacetime government helped delay the challenge posed by royal quasi-fiscal practices to the convention that kings only took from their subjects in limited circumstances. The central administration was exiguous even by contemporary European standards; indeed, it was probably smaller under Charles I than the royal government of the single French province of Normandy. What we might term the central executive consisted of up to ten clerks of the council, and the two secretaries of state, with perhaps fifteen clerks under the latter. Charles did attempt to improve executive performance by appointing a series of overlapping council sub-committees, and when the administrative burden mounted under the stress of ship money in the late 1630s he encouraged reforms in the filing of council papers. Nevertheless, individual ministers, the council collectively, and even the king himself, ended up handling trifling complaints from individual petitioners. While such busy-ness intensified the irrepressible tendency to delay, it did underscore the patriarchal nature of monarchy.

The lack of a bureaucracy limited the sources of information open to the central government. 'Policy' tended to be merely ad hoc responses to whatever petitions from interested parties landed on ministers' desks. Except in the most urgent of matters, like Laudian church reform and ship money, consistency was lost in a fog of ignorance and amid the often conflicting cries of vested interests. The perpetual shortage of funds increased the difficulties, since not until the so-called 'financial revolution' of the 1690s could governments tap long-term credit and thus afford the luxury of formulating policies. Furthermore, the governing myth imposed its own constraints, for the essence of the body politic was health; and this implied stasis, not dynamics.

Parliament

A favourite phrase applied by its devotees to the parliament at Westminster was 'the representative body of the kingdom'. Parliament embodied the kingdom, and the king was therefore a member; indeed, up to the outbreak of war most commentators assumed that the king constituted one of the three estates in parliament. Put more practically, parliament was the king-in-parliament; the two houses were anciently the king's great council, and included most of his privy councillors. Parliament's meeting depended on the king's will: he called it into being – usually when he needed money – and dissolved it as he saw fit. Parliament was therefore a meeting-ground, a place for the doing of business, both royal and private, and was not a point of conflict; indeed, it could not be in a body politic. Had conflict been what parliaments were about, kings would have seen little value in them; and when conflict came to outweigh the doing of business kings did see little value in them.

Talk of harmony and business seems to jar with the historical record. Parliaments only sat for about four and a quarter years between 1603 and 1629, and the 1620s abounded in gloomy predictions that England would shortly follow its neighbours in seeing 'the last of parliaments'. These predictions certainly reflected the impatience of some councillors, and of Charles I himself, with the carping and the distractions from normal governmental business that parliaments occasioned. But such predictions also reflected an awareness that parliament's practical value was in question. Its legislative record was spotty in the extreme. Contrary to Tudor norms no statutes emerged from the meetings of 1614, 1626 and the spring of 1640, and only a tax grant from that of 1621. James looked to his first parliament for a legislated union of England and Scotland, and Charles in 1628–9 sought parliamentary ratification of his collection of tonnage and poundage, a form of customs levy; but otherwise they turned to parliament only for money.

Fruitlessness was, however, not the same as aimlessness, since others besides the king's servants could take the initiative. Thus, in 1621 the Commons surprised James by quickly voting supply to advance what they thought should have been his foreign policy. Parliaments may have been events, but they were also an institution, possessing some continuity in personnel, in business, in their records, and most of all in their memory and sense of corporate identity. The growing sophistication of the Commons' committee system is too easily dismissed as freeing windbags to be loquacious. Careful committee-work allowed the house to time the progress of its supply bills; it then sometimes used the power of the purse to extract concessions, most notably in the shift towards war in 1624 and in the passage of the Petition of Right in 1628. Granted, the efforts in parliament in 1628–9 to alter Charles's religious policy failed miserably; and despite repeated efforts the Commons failed to persuade the crown to abandon impositions, its new levies on foreign trade. Yet the constructive nature of the Commons' aspirations are evident in the balance successive houses struck in 1621 and 1624, inveighing first against the corruption of monopolists and then passing an anti-monopoly bill in 1624 that, to the crown's relief, carefully left room both for corporations and the protection of new inventions.

The Commons' growing sense that they, rather than the two houses together, represented the nation probably owed less to the strategies of fiscal and legislative politics than to ties to the localities. MPs spent much time on local concerns: on the deepening of the River Ouse or the setting of a new light on Dungeness. While these rarely contributed to a common agenda they did strengthen consciousness of the threads tying parliament to kingdom, and thus contributed to an ideology. Such ties were rooted for the most part in a deep identity. MPs fixed their gaze firmly on their constituencies because they were usually local men, and only part-time MPs. They spent most of their lives looking to their harvest or their caseload as JPs, and as often as not sought their seats in a local competition for status rather than with any clear sense of national purpose. They then hurried home as fast as they could, or as fast as London's delights would let them. The costs of life in the capital gave them all the more reason to do so: as Sir Simonds D'Ewes observed gloomily in 1642, 'We all know that by our attendance here we are few of us savers.' Symptomatic of the performance to be expected of such amateurs was their reluctance to reverse the steady slide in the yield of the parliamentary subsidy, or to pursue bills to reform the antiquated militia in the 1620s. Congenital back-benchers and local bigwigs were unlikely to seek eagerly to involve themselves in government or to increase the burdens on their neighbours. Significantly, the only MP who was systematically committed to increasing taxation in order to refurbish the state was John Pym, the great manager of the Long Parliament – and he seems the only real carpetbagger in the Commons. Averse to putting down local roots, he lacked a 'country' to defend against the centre.

Yet parliament-men did know enough, and feel themselves sufficiently part of a single body politic, to assert themselves when the crown's demands seemed threatening or its servants outrageous. Localism was not myopia, for lines of communication from the capital steadily penetrated the furthest recesses. The growth of London and its economy, and the expanding business of its law courts, ensured a steady stream of visitors from the regions. It has been estimated that one in six of the population found their way to the capital at some time in their lives, and these might take or send news and views back home. Additionally, wealthy gentlemen increasingly commissioned newsletter-writers, proto-journalists, to keep them informed, while clerical networks maintained their own correspondence. At the close of parliamentary sessions in the 1620s, the Suffolk minister John Rous regularly bustled across to hear the news from a returning MP. The scandalous ballads suggest that some of the news percolated downwards; so does the widespread rejoicing at the return of Prince Charles and Buckingham without a Spanish bride in 1623, and the delight at the assassination of the duke in 1628. Such political interest and arousal communicated itself to parliament-men both during session, in letters, and at election time. Although the majority of MPs emerged unchallenged at the hustings as a result of discreet negotiations among the local gentry, this did not make them unrepresentative of or insensitive to their neighbours. Furthermore, the larger and more prestigious and populous constituencies were particularly likely to be contested. Yorkshire and Somerset were fought out repeatedly between 1604 and 1640; and borough constituencies, even when perhaps electorally tame, often had a sufficiently strong sense of identity to correspond with their representatives in London. MPs testified repeatedly to their anxiety to satisfy their localities.

The strengthening ties between the Commons and the country could not but affect the upper house of parliament, the House of Lords. Although the Lords contained a preponderance of royal supporters – in the privy councillors and prominent courtiers, and among the twenty-six bishops (over one-sixth of the total members in the 1620s) – the Commons set much of the political pace. With the exception of 1624, when foreign policy dominated the agenda, the main business confronting parliaments throughout the pre-war years was fiscal, constitutionally very much the Commons' preserve. The upper house did not on the whole adjust well to the development. The role of individual peers as royal servants, great patrons or indeed political managers cannot be denied: thus, the Earl of Pembroke's clients dominated the Commons' foreign policy debates of 1624 and the attack on Buckingham in 1626. But historians' claims for a 'crisis of the aristocracy' find some justification in the corporate capacity of the Lords. The peers' acquisition of a judicial capacity in the 1620s as a forum for impeachments and a sort of appeals court provided some institutional solace, though the appeals role was virtually to overwhelm the Lords in business in the 1640s. The diminution otherwise of the Lords' role is surely emblematic of the growing complexity of the polity. In 1614 the Commons agreed to proceed quickly with some bills 'to find the Lords something to do'; and in 1624 one jaundiced gentleman noted accurately how few public bills came from the Lords any more. Most remarkable of all, at one point in the troubled session of 1628, peer after peer rose to move for an adjournment on the grounds that their thin house had not 'any business to do until the Commons shall send [some] up to them'.

The House of Lords' growing sense of itself as a broker between king and Commons offers a rather ambiguous comment on the ideal of organic harmony. Charles's attempt in his Answer to the Nineteen Propositions to appeal to the peers as war loomed in 1642 by stressing their role as a 'screen or bank' between crown and people suggests how uncomfortable that posture had become. The Commons always sought co-operation with the Lords, yet when in 1628 the peers tried to placate the king by softening the Petition of Right the lower house brushed aside their reservations. More generally, as Lord Chancellor Ellesmere testified after James's first parliament, the peers were at a disadvantage in conference encounters with a lower house that contained so many leading lawyers. Only as political crisis in the Long Parliament lessened the worth of legal argument, and money ceased to be the overriding issue, did the Lords for a while regain their old prominence. When in 1641 attempts to conciliate and co-opt failed, and more radical initiatives followed, the majorities in the two houses found themselves on a collision course.

If the two houses were so unproductive of legislation, why did parliament bulk so large in governmental as well as popular estimations? Part of the answer is straightforward. When kings lived so much from hand to mouth, they could ignore no addition to their revenues, and the taxes granted in 1606 in particular, and in 1624 and 1628, were substantial. Some claimed, and others have claimed since, that parliamentary subsidies were not worth all the labour and the concessions, most especially in the restraint the crown showed over impositions after 1610. Nevertheless, the council in its intensive revenue debates in 1615 and in the winter of 1627–8 could think of few alternatives. The ideal embodied in parliaments was the unity of king and people: each, acquainted with the concerns of the other, should come together in common purpose. All agreed that a king's strength lay in the love of his people, and conciliar assertions to this effect were not necessarily empty piety. One councillor, Sir Thomas Edmondes, confided in 1621 that 'Abuses were grown to such a height of ill as the kingdom had been undone, if we had been much longer without a parliament.' While some were sceptical, councillors had had much the same upbringing as had other MPs in assumptions of harmony. Despite its financial limitations, James did not treat as contemptible the Commons' declaration of support in 1621 for his efforts in Europe. The courtiers and councillors who in the crisis of 1639–40 hoped for a rapprochement with the nation in parliament were therefore scarcely turncoats.

An emphasis on conflict has been the main historiographic legacy of the study of early-seventeenth-century parliaments. Yet procedure within parliament aimed less at divisions than at unity, consensus, 'the sense of the house'. Until 1641 divisions in the Commons were fairly rare. They were no more frequent between Commons and king, and William Hakewill, an outspoken critic in 1610 of the royal fiscal policy of impositions, observed that MPs were 'all of counsel with the king and commonwealth indifferently'. But few parliament-men even in 1640–1 foresaw parliaments acting as constant counsellor. They left that role to a privy council that was broadly based, they might hope, but still the king's. Instead, drawing on members' local knowledge, parliaments must present abuses to the king for rectification and, if necessary, remonstrate against corrupt councillors and royal servants.

The Commons were therefore by no means self-confidently aggressive. They passed over royal slights to their privileges in 1621 and 1624 and got on with business, even voting taxes in unpromising circumstances. Procedural uncertainty or unease sometimes threw them, and the Lords too, into long periods of uneasy silence. The rate of absenteeism, from both houses, was high, and only a few dozen members 'speechified', to use a later expression; the reticence of country gentlemen and merchants may have made the house easier to influence than we think. But it is as misleading to focus exclusively on the deference and petty-mindedness of the Commons as it once was to portray members as incessantly hungering after power, or steadfastly voicing high principles. There were variables. Commitment to England's ancient constitution was well-nigh universal, but commitment to godly ideals and a vision of the popish enemy was not. The crown found it much easier to deal with the likes of Sir Edwin Sandys, Sir Robert Phelips, or Sir Thomas Wentworth, whose anti-Catholicism was less visceral. Conversely, it found itself increasingly boxed in as anti-Catholic fervour surged in the 1620s. But the prevailing calculus in the Commons was never simply localist and anti-Catholic. Preference for local business may have undermined the Commons' effectiveness, yet the inadequate grants for war in the 1620s, which had such fatal consequences, stemmed also from a fully conscious conviction that the war was not the right war and that it was being mismanaged. However aware parliament-men were of their duty to aid and counsel the king, they also knew that they had to 'speak for their country' – and that phrase comprehended both neighbourhood and nation.

The position of parliament-men, situated as they were at that point where the body politic writ large encountered the person of the king, seemed to ensure ambivalence. Spokesmen at the centre for their localities, they had to explain and implement royal policy as local magistrates and leaders of their communities on their return. A deeper dilemma lay in England's problematic inheritance of what has been called a 'double majesty', though it might as well be called the dual manifestation of the body politic. On the one hand stood the king as embodiment of the realm, the focus of a fairly coherent theory of kingship and authority, guaranteed in the last resort by his 'absolute prerogative'. On the other stood the wider community, focus and source of an equally powerful theory of law, rights and custom, articulated and defined not just in the law courts but also in parliament. Both demanded respect and allegiance, and harmony was presumed, yet political circumstances drew them apart. As the Rev. Nathaniel Ward in Massachusetts put it ruefully in 1647, 'He is a good king that undoes not his subjects by any one of his unlimited prerogatives: and they are a good people, that undoe not their prince, by any one of their unbounded liberties.'

Most MPs were realists and recognised that the well-being of the whole sometimes required even benevolent rulers to take extraordinary measures. But kings could not be left unchallenged when they asserted those measures as their inherent right, when they sought, that is, to make a permanent political reality of their claim to embody the body politic. In the interests of doing business, the Commons early in 1621 ignored piece-meal affronts to their privileges; but when James in December openly tried to control debate they dug in their heels. Similarly, reactions to imposi-tions (which many MPs realised had been levied by Elizabeth), to the royal power of arrest in 1627–8, and later to ship money, indicate that gentle-men and lawyers saw a crucial distinction between powers that were tacitly acknowledged and powers that were publicly asserted.

The central courts

The ancient justification of kingship lay in justice, the administration of *meum et tuum*, what's mine and what's yours. James, as so often, rendered vividly physical his understanding of the royal body politic when he declared that the law lay in his own breast, that he was 'lex loquens, a living, a speaking law'. He took seriously his role as the fountain of justice. Not for nothing did his funeral sermon talk of him as Britain's Solomon. At least until the crisis in the courts of 1616 his council intervened frequently, as a sort of supreme arbitrator, at all stages of litigation; and James later installed a cleric, John Williams, to head the equity court of Chancery as custodian of the king's conscience. James's conviction that kings were the source of law found support from several high-flying clergy and also his first lord chancellor, Ellesmere.

Reflecting the primacy of justice, early modern government was divided into an overlapping series of courts. Even the privy council was also a law court of a kind, as were the councils in the north and in Wales. In the Star Chamber, privy councillors sat with the judges to police a wide range of governmental concerns, as well as dangerous breaches of the peace. But justice was always subject to the pressure of litigants and petitioners, whose allegations of riot dragged star chamber into property disputes. Its business increased probably tenfold between 1550 and 1625.

The other leading courts – Chancery and the great common law courts of King's Bench and Common Pleas – were no less the king's, and their judges no less protectors of the king's peace. They were 'lions under the throne', as James called them; and in successive constitutional test cases they inclined strongly towards the crown. Thus, all the opinions in the

1637 ship money case recognised that in emergencies the needs of the kingdom, defined by the king, superseded the rights of the individual. The crown was after all more than merely the symbol of national unity, and medieval baronial pretensions had been struck down in the courts as much as on the battlefield. Chief Justice Hobart was no innovator when he opined in 1623 that in the courts 'everything for the benefit of the king shall be taken largely, as everything against the king shall be taken strictly'. But as politics became more polarised the judges were often left holding the ring. This was an unfortunate development when they were the paid servants of the king: thus, a standard career pattern was for the attorney general, the king's chief legal officer, to succeed to a judgeship, even as chief justice or lord chancellor. Parliament impeached for treason in 1641 all but one of the surviving common law judges of the 1630s, in tribute to their intimate association with the king's will.

Far from being reducible to some political scientist's analysis of function, the law courts and judges were full participants in the living confusion of the polity. The agenda of courts and judges certainly reflected the needs of the crown; but since the income of officials as well as lawyers came from fees, each court adapted its procedures to attract litigants. As competition with the ecclesiastical, equity and regional conciliar courts grew heated in the early seventeenth century, King's Bench and Common Pleas launched volleys of 'prohibitions' against them, banning further proceedings. Since the common law courts were formally superior they usually won unless the privy council intervened. The bitter rivalry between King's Bench and Chancery came to a head in 1616, provoking James into a broad assertion of his custodianship of the law even while he selected less contentious judges.

The delight of the judges and lawyers at the increase in business was not generally shared. The case-load of King's Bench quadrupled between 1560 and 1580, and doubled again by 1640; the other courts were not far behind. Delays mounted alarmingly, encouraged by the common law's preoccupation with procedural technicalities. The lawyer-MP Edward Alford, admittedly a hostile witness, reported in the parliament of 1621 that the average duration of cases in Chancery, the leading equity court, was twenty-three years; but his comment, that three years should be enough, damned the common law courts too. The calculation of fees by the number of pages in documents invited prolixity and abuse. The twice-yearly exodus from Westminster of the judges on their assize circuits through the counties to hear both criminal and civil business did divert some pressure from the central common law courts. With two days for each county, the assize judges seem to have averaged about one civil case every twenty minutes, and an overworked trial jury might hear a dozen criminal cases in succession. The system was clearly creaking.

The proliferation of litigation speaks to popular demand, and to the involvement at law of others besides the king and the lawyers and substantial property-owners. Such involvement arose not just from the complexity of the land market after the dissolution of the monasteries, but as well from an accelerating commercial life and the difficulty of resolving disputes as population density and mobility grew. It has been estimated that the rate of civil litigation at the start of the seventeenth century was the highest in English history; and the overwhelming bulk of business originated outside the gentry. A telling instance of social pressure comes from the main London church court. Over a half of the business of the consistory court of St Paul's in the early 1630s came from women, often newcomers to their neighbourhoods, whose sexual honour had been slandered during some neighbourly or commercial dispute. Their concern with sexual reputation is as revealing as the fact that they eagerly resorted to formal means to vindicate themselves: but if they were to participate in society they had to be deemed honourable. All the evidence suggests a huge demand for the law, and in all regions. The pre-war duchy of Lancaster court dealt with around 2000 bread-and-butter cases a year, as did each of the provincial councils at York and Ludlow; and in the 1650s northerners petitioned eagerly for the restoration of the regional conciliar tribunals that had collapsed in 1641. Despite the law's mystification in obscure forms and archaic languages, acquaintance with the law, and not simply as victims, was widespread. Law reform of course had a huge appeal to radical groups in the revolution; but ordinary villagers were sufficiently knowledgeable to use the law skilfully against an assertive state in the 1630s and the 1650s alike.

Local government

The body politic needed regulation and magistracy. As a growing population brought new social problems, 'stacks of statutes' drawn up by the Tudors and their parliaments shaped a response in the generation or so on either side of 1600. Not only relief of the poor was required, but moral reform, and the suppression of sin.

Fear, and not just godly zeal, or even altruism, shaped the activist programme. At assize courts in the south, and also in the northwest, prosecutions for property offences, and executions, rose to a peak in the 1620s. The economy was under strain, thefts almost certainly increased, and punishment reflected the usual calculus of deterrence and revenge. Yet the vagrants, and the women convicted of bearing bastards, who were whipped until their backs were bloody, surely did not pose a threat sufficient to warrant their fates; nor did the luckless handful of Oxfordshire men tortured and executed in 1596 for projecting a rising against the gentry. The disproportion suggests what has been called a 'moral panic'. Those who channelled the law's violence were sufficiently alarmed by the social stress, and occasional protest, in the bleak times of the generation or so after 1590 to doubt the very coherence of the body politic.

Order was, in the last resort, preserved in the villages. Country magistrates were often thin on the ground: in the extreme case of Amounderness in Lancashire one justice of the peace governed more than 7000 people. We may wonder how dangerous such disproportion really was, for late-medieval field-rotation agreements and parish collections show everywhere a large capacity for self-regulation. Even in perhaps the most untraditional settlement, Whickham, a site of precocious industrialisation, immigration, and potential disorder in the developing Durham coalfield, conventional family patterns and the cultivation of kinship ties lessened the chance that the world would ever be turned upside down.

The magistrate therefore did not stand alone between order and chaos. Social discipline might be well maintained by an alliance of squire and parson in villages with a resident gentleman; such discipline was likely to be tighter in those areas, usually in the central belt of the country, where boundaries of manor and parish more or less coincided. Many manorial courts still possessed considerable vitality: the large Staffordshire manors of Cannock and Rugely sent only a handful of cases to the county's courts around the turn of the century, for the manor courts wielded jurisdiction over misdemeanours and petty debts. Hierarchy is evident too in the Gloucestershire manors of Farmcotte and Postlippe where a 1608 census recorded that five-sixths and more of the men were employed by a single gentleman.

Such concentration of power was rare. Perhaps half of early-seventeenth-century settlements, largely in the uplands and woodlands, lacked a resident gentleman. It was to these areas, with their available waste land and their prospects of varied non-arable livelihoods, that surplus population was drifting. The demographic upsurge was felt too in the towns, and above all London, as immigrants flooded to the alleys of the inner parishes and to suburbs beyond the walls. Municipal officials were no more equipped to deal with such changing conditions than were the distant county magistrates and the often non-resident clergy of the wood-pasture zone. By the 1630s and '40s, therefore, informal oligarchies of better-off householders and sometimes lesser gentry had everywhere emerged, often constituting themselves as select vestries in the parishes. Seizing the opportunity presented by the poor relief acts of 1597 and 1601, these vestries asserted social discipline. The process has been closely studied in a variety of communities: the London suburbs of Southwark and Havering, Terling in Essex, Whickham, and Keevil in Wiltshire. Churchwardens and overseers of the poor withheld charity from the disorderly, and jurymen presented the stubbornly wayward to the appropriate secular or ecclesiastical court, as householders (by no means all of them puritan) used petty political power to buttress the order from which they benefited.

The extension into the parishes of a sterner vision of order left the petty (or parish) constable exposed. Often selected by rotation from among the householders, the constable was the last link in the chain stretching from privy council to people; he was also the one with whom the better sort had to deal in their efforts to reform or purge the 'good neighbourliness' of alehouses and village dancings. Too zealous a constable risked all the usual scatological or sexual abuse, and might be beaten up after his year in office; too indulgent towards his neighbours, he risked prosecution. Indeed, though there is abundant evidence of constabular efficiency, prosecutions at quarter sessions for slackness abound in periods of crisis. The constable who harried the poor widow for trying to feed her family through an illicit alehouse broke all the conventions of neighbourhood and community. Political change too strained the norms of reciprocity, and refusals of office increased in the later 1630s, when the collection of ship money caught the constable between the wrath of council and sheriff on the one hand and the sometimes violent resentments of villagers on the other. The dilemma became most painful with the soaring levies of the civil war, during which not a few constables fled or were murdered. It can best be felt in the lament of one Wiltshire constable, scrawled on an order from a local garrison commander: 'Woe is me, poor bastard.'

No less sensitive to pressure was the justice of the peace, or JP. Although unpaid and involving duties that could be onerous to the conscientious, the post attracted no shortage of candidates, for it manifested a gentleman's membership of the county's elite. It also brought local power, the ability to protect friends and strike at enemies in innumerable petty ways. The most obvious of the JP's functions was his role as lay judge, attending at the county's quarter sessions court to try a wide range of cases (though capital felonies were increasingly dealt with by the assize judges on circuit). Acting alone, the JP took depositions and evidence, bound over suspects in preparation for the sessions, and acquired certain summary powers (for example, to fine swearers) under the new regulatory legislation. As well as a criminal court, quarter sessions were an administrative forum, where JPs were called upon to set local rates for bridge and highway repair, or settle inter-parochial disputes about responsibility for the upkeep of bastards.

As with the parish constable, so with the justice of the peace: the members of an organic polity were not always disposed to innovate. Some JPs, such as the Bacons in Norfolk and the Lewkenors in Suffolk, enthusiastically pursued the Calvinist vision of a godly commonwealth, and combined fierce moral correction with a disciplined charity; but the privy council came to doubt the ability of the JPs as a whole to cope. Gentry competition for honour drove up the numbers of county JPs past the limits of effectiveness. When the Northamptonshire commission, an extreme case, rose from 43 in 1562 to 113 in 1616, individual JPs often assumed others would do the work. The council's concerns were even sometimes shared in that stronghold of the gentry, the House of Commons: one lawyer MP in 1614 claimed that of the 300 statutes requiring enforcement by JPs, 'few of them knew fifty of them'. In a crisis magistrates might respond energetically, as in 1629–31 when economic disaster drove the

Essex JPs to investigate both supply and demand, checking the amount of grain stored in barns and the acres still to sow, and seeking from the constables information on the sizes of local households; they then apportioned grain to the weekly markets. Too often, however, magistrates clung to custom; and custom was fertile ground for the rating disputes that regularly disrupted local administration.

The council slowly felt its way towards using the assize judges on their circuits to bind the localities closer to the centre. From the late 1580s the judges riding circuit were regularly 'charged' with the needs of government. They were to keep a tight rein on jurors (suspected not merely by the council of corruption), to galvanise the JPs, and report on performance. Increasingly, the judges required action of the JPs, chiefly concerning the poor. The council attempted to formalise these requirements in the years after 1605. As always, consistency was lacking, and attention in the 1620s swung between economic and military crises. Nevertheless, peace and renewed economic crisis in 1630 brought a new flurry of activity when the council dispatched its celebrated books of orders of 1630–1 into the counties for general enforcement.

The council's efforts furthered a new formality in local government. To ease the pressure of business, the 1605 orders had urged two or more JPs to meet informally in their neighbourhoods between sessions to bind over, take sureties, and oversee the petty regulation of the parishes. Such ad hoc 'petty sessions' had in fact already emerged in many counties as conscientious JPs responded to all the tasks confronting them; the strident insistence on petty, or 'monthly', sessions in the 1631 book of orders was largely superfluous. In a more important development, the compulsory parochial collections for the poor rate required by Tudor legislation were by 1640 everywhere established, under pressure of economic adversity and conciliar exhortation. The containment of the poor, and the increasingly capable maintenance of local order in a time of considerable local stress, suggest therefore the flexibility of the polity.

The history of the militia evidences the same tension between a general preference for old ways and the desire of a few for reform. In the wartime crisis of the 1580s a hierarchy of command shaped itself to local realities. The senior resident peer in a county usually served as lord lieutenant, assisted by three or four leading gentlemen as deputy-lieutenants and others as junior officers. The militia itself was the local body politic in arms. Gentry reluctance to put arms in the hands of 'the meaner sort' ensured that the main element, the trained bands, comprised the 'discreeter' householders, or their sons. But community control exacted a price in inefficiency. Although the peace of 1604 offered opportunities for reform of the technologically outmoded Tudor requirements, local foot-dragging obstructed the council's efforts to second experienced sergeants to the county forces. At Westminster, reforming legislation fell victim to the inertia of council and parliament-men alike.

Military and constitutional issues intersected, since the militia was left dependent on the royal prerogative. That prerogative, especially in military matters, carried weight, and by the end of the 1610s the council had cajoled the counties into equipping the trained bands with expensive muskets. But in the warring 1620s the uncertain status of the militia proved debilitating, for by then the crown was striving to raise money as well as arms by its prerogative. Deputy-lieutenants everywhere came to regret their lack of unquestionable 'compulsive' powers, and England became a military backwater. Many gentlemen did substantiate their traditional chivalric claims by short periods as volunteers for continental belligerents; younger sons, and those without a patrimony, became mercenaries. The future parliamentarian captains-general, Essex and Fairfax, are examples of the one, and those supreme professionals George Monck and Philip Skippon of the other. But it was fortunate that Europe's great powers, Spain and France, were too distracted in the 1620s to seek to chastise Charles for his newfound belligerence.

Deputy-lieutenants directed their bitterest complaints at unco-operative urban magistrates. These in turn insisted either that they were unfairly rated by rural neighbours, or that their charters exempted them from county jurisdiction. Such complaints expose the complexity of pre-modern politics: within the greater body politic were lesser 'corporations', each more or less self-regulating, and with no clearly demarcated relations. Towns were by no means as purblind as their jurisdictional rivals sometimes claimed. Larger centres like Bristol had wide-ranging interests whose protection dictated the cultivation of sophisticated links with Whitehall; but dignity had also to be protected, so Bristol's corporation in the 1610s fined its citizens who took suits to the central courts. Overlapping jurisdictions spawned jealousies, not only between towns and counties but also between towns and another enclave, cathedral closes. Corporations had to be on their guard. The town clerk of Warwick urged all towns to beware the gentry, who used towns only 'as they do their stirrups to mount to their horse'; and the days of the church triumphant in the 1630s brought many challenges to the charters of cathedral cities. Even without the stimulus to political consciousness sometimes claimed for capitalism, townsmen had reason enough for the congenital insubordination so many commentators alleged.

Towns were usually enclaves of intense government as well as of self-government. Certainly, some industrial settlements, such as the Essex new draperies towns of Coggeshall and Braintree, were unincorporated and had to rely on an often unsympathetic neighbouring JP. But most towns had their own officers who regulated all areas of life, from prices in the market to the precedence of wives. The crown sought to buttress the forces of order against expanding urban populations by strengthening the powers of urban magistracies; and oligarchies duly entrenched themselves behind the closed doors of the often splendid town halls erected in the century after the Reformation. But urban populations as a whole were not depressed into an under-class. The poor immigrants lodged in alehouses and tenements may indeed have experienced authority primarily as victims. But the urban freemen, those free to practise a trade, who often comprised a half of a town's adult male inhabitants, had a wide range of minor offices in ward, parish and trade guild open to them. It has been estimated that one in ten of the city of London's adult males was serving at any one time in some post.

Such a civic education undoubtedly helped foster the urban 'independence' Clarendon deplored. The drift to oligarchy sometimes generated deep resentments: thus, the dispute between the Leeds clothworkers and the merchant corporation eventually merged with the politics of civil war and revolution. Nevertheless, the authorities need not have worried that in the towns they faced either a 'many-headed monster' or incipient republicanism. In all the larger towns the burgeoning powers of the aldermanic elites were buttressed by merchant and craft guilds that bound male workers into inter-generational – and hence usually stabilising – networks of masters and their apprentices. London, which had the most poor, also had in the City proper the most developed poor-relief system in England, with doles, almshouses, charitable apprenticeships and subsidised education. To maintain the effectiveness of London's system, parish officers, acting under the direction of the oligarchic select vestries that took over a majority of the City parishes in our period, kept regular and detailed lists of their neighbours, whether householders or lodgers. In Ipswich, constables went the rounds of alehouses hunting absentees from Sunday services, and in town after town godly magistrates and ministers joined to exert a moral discipline, above all in the thoroughgoing regime instituted at Dorchester after the town fire of 1613 had seemed to threaten God's judgment.

Political thought

The English polity was full of ambiguities. In one sense the government was the king's, though in the localities it was the domain of the magistrates, constables, and churchwardens. Accordingly, broad and narrow readings of the body politic – like prerogative and liberty – were expected to overlap and support one another. But by 1628 the lawyer and MP Robert Mason could inject a note of doubt as he reflected on the Petition of Right: 'The next word is "trusted", which is very ambiguous, whether it mean [a king] trusted by God only as a conqueror, or by the people also, as kings which are to govern by laws *ex pacto* [made by agreement]. In this point I will not presume to venture.' More usually, what the modern mind sees as contradiction the early-modern deemed reinforcement, '*concordia discors*', harmony in discord.

At his coronation, James I took an oath to protect the laws of England. The oath preceded the acclamation, with its cries of 'God save the king,' and the ceremonial symbolised the consensual nature of monarchy. Yet monarchy was also part of the natural order – Shakespeare's plays resound with analogies of fathers, lions, eagles. And kingship was divine: Christ had acknowledged Caesar, while God had directly commissioned King Saul and David. The words of David, psalmist and king, comforted James VI and I as he meditated upon kingship and tutored his subjects in its merits, not least in the fiercely patriarchalist catechism *God and the King*, published by royal command in 1615. The homily on obedience, the church's main political formulary, declared the message equally broadly. John Pym, who was soon to shape parliament's civil war cause, was not merely complimentary when in 1640 he extolled the king, 'the fountain of justice, of peace, of protection; . . . the royal power and majesty shines upon us in every public blessing we enjoy.' The royalist battle standard in the civil war, with its scriptural injunction, 'Give Caesar his due', appealed to deep habits of reverence.

Kings were irresistible, virtually every articulate Englishman agreed until late in the 1630s, and most far beyond that. But kings were not tyrants. Paraphrasing David, James reminded parliament in 1610 (and parliament-men long remembered) that though kings were as gods, like God they moved in orderly ways. God kept His promises to Israel, observed His own laws, though of course He could not have been coerced into doing so. And so England's king would observe England's laws.

Whatever the political theology, the business of governing was governed by law, whose language was history, moderation. Although James repeatedly stressed the origins of law in royal grant, and in his great confrontation with Sir Edward Coke in 1616 pronounced it treasonous to elevate the law above the king, he also observed of the common law, 'No law can be more favourable and advantageous for a king, and extendeth further his prerogative.' Indeed, time after time, the courts upheld royal powers. They may of course have been encouraged in this by the 1616 dismissal of Coke (the first of a judge in over thirty years), and the silencing in Charles's reign of three other senior judges. But principle too pulled towards the crown. Although in 1623 Chief Justice Hobart maintained, 'The prerogative laws are . . . the law of the realm for the king, as the common law is the law of the realm for the subject,' in fact the crown steadily argued the coherence of royal prerogative and subjects' rights within a framework of law.

Critics of royal policies spoke as pointedly as Hobart when they housed under the law both prerogative and 'the liberty of the subject'. That term seems to have emerged in 1601. From Thomas Hedley in the 1610 debates on impositions to Coke in the Petition of Right debates in 1628, they contended that the law bound all, king and subject alike. To Coke, the law arose from the customs and enactments of the community through the ages, and was infused with a transcendent rationality. As the crown stretched its money-raising powers, lawyers in the Commons, and in the courts too in Bate's case in 1606 and in the ship money case, used general theory and ancient precedent to argue what amounted to the subject's absolute right to property. Paradoxically, they presented this as strengthening the crown: men confident of what was their own would 'love' their king and thus be more easily governed. They would also fight more bravely: 'No property, no valour', as Sir Nathaniel Rich, the Earl of Warwick's cousin, put it in 1628. The claim reflected the interdependence of the body politic.

In the last years of Elizabeth's reign a very different strain of thought crystallised. Elizabethan presbyterianism (that is, anti-episcopal puritanism) had appealed to parliament and aristocracy for support, and against it some churchmen and officials urged the royal supremacy in church and state, and an imperial monarchy responsible only to God. With such thinking Richard Bancroft, whom James appointed Archbishop of Canterbury in 1604, was closely associated, and so was James VI of Scotland, as his *Trew Law of Free Monarchies* (1599) showed. A succession of bishops and their advisers argued not simply the divinity of kings but a practical politics of that doctrine: subjects had an absolute duty to supply their king with money since, as Bishop Montaigne of London put it in 1622, 'what we have is not our own'. Roger Manwaring and Robert Sibthorpe, who caused such a storm in the forced loan crisis of 1627–8 by preaching that consent was not needed when kings levied supply, did not stand alone.

The House of Commons was the source of grants of taxation by consent, and alarm there led to the drafting in 1604 of a defence against the 'daily' growth of royal power. Although not presented, the Apology's assertion that the Commons' privileges were immemorial was frequently and feelingly quoted in the 1620s. A clearer indication that underneath the hymns to reciprocity divergent visions were emerging came in December 1621, in the affair of the Protestation. A royal ban on further debate of foreign policy drove the Commons to insist, as the Apology had done, on the immemoriality of their privileges. Against the claim that a part of the body did not owe its being to the head, James reacted in a piece of high theatre. Seated in full council, he solemnly tore the Protestation from the Commons' journal.

The cult of law and history rested, as James was made to realise by the debates of 1604 and 1607 on union with Scotland, on a profound conviction of the peculiar excellence of English ways and English liberties. The common law's distinctness from the Roman Law practices of Scotland and the continent was not simply the cry of chauvinists, though in 1628 Sir Edward Coke proudly trumpeted Britons' separation from the world. Some lawyers, above all John Selden, were distinguished comparative scholars; and most parliament-men by the 1620s knew enough to express a plausible concern at continental developments. The Somerset squire Sir Robert Phelips may have erred in his historical judgment, though not in his sense of politics, when he declared in 1625, 'We are the last monarchy in Christendom that yet retain our original rights and constitutions.'

History and common law, powerful though they were, scarcely encompassed English political ideology. The siege mentality of late-Elizabethan protestantism contributed hugely to the conviction of English exceptionalism, while the increasingly divided world of early-Stuart churchmanship gave a harder edge to the zeal of Calvinist activists. But though England might stand alone, Europe exercised an influence. It was from his comparative researches that Selden derived his arguments for the historical origin of all institutions, arguments that he advanced most systematically in his inflammatory *History of Tithes* (1618), challenging clerical claims of divine right. A more direct import from France was the new thinking about the state that came with Jean Bodin's *Six Books of the Republic*, translated into English in 1606. The polemical implications of Bodinian thinking were by no means one-sided, and Henry Parker in 1642 advanced a clear case for parliamentary sovereignty. Nevertheless, some thought the continental drift clear. James looked to the example of contemporary European monarchs when justifying his fiscal impositions in 1610 and 1614, while Charles rationalised his fiscal demands by the fashionable plea of 'necessity'.

Political models were also, and more influentially, drawn from the classical past. While the early-Stuart kings eagerly invoked the imperial figure of Augustus, Renaissance humanism had also shaped a sense of the commonweal, and of the duty of the magistrate and counsellor to foster it. The works of Cicero, a republican exponent of public service, remained staples, and not just of the grammar-school curriculum. A humanist sense of the cycles and patterns of history led two aged ex-Elizabethans – the great antiquarian William Camden, and Fulke Greville, Lord Brooke – in their disillusionment at what seemed moral and political decay, to found England's first history lectureships at the universities. Their aim was to disseminate classical examples of virtue and service.

Implicit in the humanist vision lay an aristocratic political order. Thus, Greville wrote the *Life* of the Elizabethan Sir Philip Sidney, the supreme embodiment of an active protestant nobility, while Thomas Hobbes acted as mentor to the Earl of Devonshire. Indeed, these years, with their new thinking about kings, witnessed something of a cult of chivalry and nobility. Nobility was not just nostalgia, though the abolition of the House of Lords in 1649 provides a harsh backdrop for the romance posturings of Sir William Davenant's unfinished epic, *Gondibert* (1651). The Earl of Arundel was certainly enamoured of ancient chivalry, but he was, as well, bitterly averse to the rule of favourites, and preoccupied with vindicating the continuing role of a highly schooled nobility. The Earl of Bedford and John Pym may have been merely pragmatic in their search in 1640–1 for medieval precedents for aristocratic controls over a king, but the taste of the Sidney family, or of Henry Parker and others in Lord Saye's circle, for classical republican ideas suggests a more far-reaching ideology of aristocratic virtue.

The instability of late-sixteenth-century Europe introduced an uneasy dimension to such classicising thought. Continental theorists of the state were drawn to Tacitus's analysis of the violent dynamics of Roman empire. The English avant-garde quickly saw the point, and among the earliest users of the the phrase 'reason of state' were the poets Ben Jonson and Thomas May. Classical scholarship provided psychological insight as well as state theory, since those stoical Romans, Tacitus and Seneca, who had exposed the corruptions of empire, also offered mordant comment on those who ruled. The English genre of country-house poems – at its height in Jonson's 'To Penshurst' – speaks to the popularity of their persuasion to virtuous retirement. But the Tacitean practice of demythologising rule – as in Jonson's dark Roman play *Sejanus*, or the horror-strewn *Revenger's Tragedy* – proved dangerously attractive in a world filled with corruption and overweening favourites. Sir John Eliot was jailed in 1626 for likening Buckingham to Sejanus; the comparison invited an angry Charles I to read himself as Sejanus's master, the flawed emperor Tiberius.

That confrontation in 1626 highlighted the general assumption that the health of the polity lay in virtue. The obverse was the conviction that tensions, ills, arose not from structural problems, which were inconceivable in the organic world of the body politic, but corruption. Cries of corruption brought down Lord Treasurer Suffolk in 1616, Lord Chancellor Bacon in 1621 and Lord Treasurer Middlesex in 1624, and swelled the attack on Buckingham in 1626–8. These catastrophes probably resulted less from the proliferation of misdoings than from a generalised political unease that was automatically personalised. Whatever the cause, conspiracy theory abounded. Charles in his proclamation dissolving the 1628–9 parliament blamed 'the malevolent dispositions of some ill affected persons'. Dissident subjects habitually denounced 'evil counsellors'. Rather than admit that reform of the law was necessary when law had failed to protect liberty and property, in 1641 the Commons accused the judges of treason.

Suspicions of conspiracy might be counter-productive rather than simply unproductive. On one level, Jacobean MPs denounced corruption and extravagance at court and overlooked the genuine financial problems that Salisbury tried to bring to their notice. More fundamentally, the assumption of conspiracy, which was at its most damaging in the church, sapped the trust essential to the working of any body politic. When 'fears and jealousies' became the mainstay of polemic in 1641, 'the ill humours of the body' were impervious to the work of the sovereign physician, the king-in-parliament.

To close with rampant ill humours might imply the inexorability of the surgeon's work that came in 1649. We would do better to conclude with the deluge of petitions to king and parliament in the spring of 1642, that testified so vividly to the belief in harmony and balance. But such assumptions offered little guidance when king and parliament did divide: the individual then stood alone with his conscience, as Philip Hunton observed bleakly in 1643 in his impressive *Treatise of Monarchy*. It was an alarming conclusion, and the Kent gentleman Henry Oxinden prayed for some 'omnipotency', some authority more unqualified than 'king-and-parliament' and 'fundamental law', to draw him off. To answer such prayers Thomas Hobbes was to write his *Leviathan*.

Performance

The remorseless decline of the subsidy (the tax granted by parliament that fell mainly on lands) suggests the polity's dangerous decrepitude. Until 1635 direct taxation came rarely, fell lightly, and fell on few individuals. The crown's failure to tax helped drive it to disreputable or dangerous courses. The fiscal slide brought some compensations, for in the long term both economy and social order benefited from the smallness of the slice carved out by the state. But if consumers were left with money in their pockets, or at least bread on their tables, the state was the loser.

The crown could collect money. In 1626–7 over the forced loan, and in the 1630s with the early ship money writs, the council geared itself up unprecedentedly, and overawed opposition. But in the familiar field of the subsidy the council followed ancient ways. Yields lagged miserably, as assessors and collectors made no attempt to adjust for the impact of inflation or to tax new owners as land changed hands. The average assessment of seventy Sussex gentry families dropped from £61 to £14 between the 1540s and the 1620s, though the intervening period had been one of inflation, and of prosperity for the landed sector. By the early seventeenth century probably only 10 per cent of households in the nation were assessed. In consequence, the yield of a subsidy fell from £137 000 in 1559 to £55 000 in 1628; in real terms, allowing for inflation, this was about one-fifth of the 1559 level.

The English government was in consequence driven perilously close to what has been called 'functional breakdown', the inability to do what it and others expected, above all in the crucial field of war. Parliamentary taxation, whose major purpose had been to pay for war, dwindled just when changing technology and tactics were making wars more expensive. One official calculated that the 1625 Cadiz raid cost four times as much as Drake's 1587 attack on the same port. Military change also eroded the critical distinction between peace and war. The medieval expedient of conscripting merchant ships for naval purposes proved ineffective at Cadiz in 1625, and that failure argued for peacetime expansion of the royal navy as a precaution. The convention had been that the customary royal revenues should pay for peacetime costs; but, as some councillors realised early in James's reign, there could be no such easy distinction in Ireland, where war had cost £1.8 million in the 1590s. Troops and therefore funding were constantly needed.

The problem can be exaggerated. Although the mystique of kingship centred on war and diplomacy kings did not have to fight, as James recognised from the start, and Charles too after 1630. Furthermore, a different sort of war in the 1620s, and above all, a naval war against Spain, would certainly have attracted more parliamentary support. It might indeed have challenged modern assumptions, based on ramshackle performance in that decade and 1639–40, about England's congenital incapacity. Nevertheless, the new realities of war made some realignment essential. The divergent approaches reflected familiar ambiguities. Lord Treasurer Salisbury's solution, in the abortive Great Contract of 1610, implied a closer binding of the polity: abandoning medieval conventions, he sought more regular parliamentary funding of the ordinary needs of government. Charles, after experiencing another war and the resentments inspired by James's notorious profligacy, at the end of the 1620s took the opposite course of exploiting the implications of the royal personification of the polity. He therefore tried variously to raise money from his subjects outside parliament. The eventual solution might have gone either way: closer parliamentary involvement with, if not necessarily in, government, or a crown financially independent of parliament.

The material stresses were complicated by an abiding ethos of common law, statute, and consent, hardened now by awareness of the rise of royal power in Europe. This was no crusading dynamic, but it did shape the way in which events and actions were viewed, and therefore helped determine responses. Reform, which necessarily meant innovation, became a sensitive subject. Reform became especially sensitive when attempted by monarchs with a taste for theories of divine-right monarchy, or an increasingly evident taste for novel ways in religion. The suspicion that greeted the Great Contract, the failure of the 'benevolence' of 1626, and the problems besetting ship money in its later years, point to the ideological limits under which governments operated.

Loyalties

The eventual English outcome, a monarchy rooted in parliament, was scarcely inevitable. The achievements of Richelieu and Mazarin in France showed what could be achieved when a nation faced a credible external threat. The Stuarts' misfortune may then have been that the winding down of hostilities with Spain coincided with the growing economic importance of Mediterranean trade routes, and thus of Spain. The old focus of fear and animosity therefore dwindled. Antichrist was, for its part, too much a partisan concern; and relations with France and the Dutch, soon to be tense enough, were not yet capable of sustaining a national cause that would require and justify extraordinary action.

The absence of an agreed enemy allowed localism, which governments interpreted as mere obstructionism, free rein. Many gentry families had ancient local roots, and had acquired a powerful sense of place. Probably a majority of gentry married within their counties – over 70 per cent in relatively isolated Kent and Lancashire, perhaps 30 per cent in Essex and Hertfordshire. And local loyalties informed national life. Oxford and Cambridge colleges had regional affiliations, while informal county dining associations met fairly regularly at London inns. Yet stability can be exaggerated, for only 18 per cent of the gentry families in pre-war Warwickshire originated before 1500. The horizons of the greater gentry, the county leaders, were rarely bounded by the county: the East Anglian cousinage linking the Rich family in Essex with the Hampdens in Buckinghamshire and the Cromwells in Huntingdonshire could be matched elsewhere.

Though quarter sessions helped consolidate county consciousness among the gentry, the county was not always a natural unit. The sessions, and the grand juries at assizes, were often likened to county parliaments. But apart from the assize court and parliamentary elections, which themselves connected Westminster and county, there were no countywide meeting-grounds in large counties like Yorkshire, Lincolnshire and Sussex, which had separate quarter sessions for their different regions. In Norfolk and Warwickshire the sessions rotated regularly from town to town, attracting different groups of gentry to each. County solidarity was there-fore often less than is sometimes imagined. The Huntingdonshire author-ities' refusal to cross county boundaries to aid nearby Essex in the invasion scare of 1625 has become something of a benchmark of localism. In fact, endemic local rivalries, particularly those between county and town, often gave the privy council the chance to mediate and thus to insert itself.

Local ties anyway competed with other loyalties. A polite education could not help but reduce introversion, and polite educations were becom-ing widespread: in 1636 84 per cent of the JPs in a sample of six counties had attended either a university or an inn of court, or both. Political or religious allies might lodge together when attending parliament, or recom-mend suitable ministers, or marriage partners, to each other. Assize judges regularly reminded the localities of Whitehall's claims; and always there were litigants returning from the law courts and carters bearing news as well as goods to alert even home-bodies to the wider world. The effects of bad roads can be exaggerated: although in 1607 the council's letters ambled at 2 mph towards a king away hunting, rumour could travel fast: over fifty miles in a night in the Irish scare of 1641. National issues may have been refracted for local eyes, but illumination still occurred even in distant Cheshire, where Sir Richard Grosvenor delivered a rousing election address in 1624. Maps of England were as popular as were county maps, and a Frenchman, or a Scot, was infinitely more a foreigner than was someone from beyond the county line. Far from being opposite poles, nation and locality had overlapping claims on all politically conscious individuals, and detailed studies of probably the two best-documented county figures, Sir Thomas Wentworth in Yorkshire and Sir Robert Phelips in Somerset, have shown how intense were the connections of centre and locality. The ambitious gentleman had to propitiate both his neighbours and the 'great ones' at Whitehall if he were to gain the due rewards in prestige and power. The most telling comment on the relationship of the political centre in the royal court to the country at large came in 1642, when both split down the middle.

Every localist ultimately acknowledged the supremacy of the nation state. While towns might brandish their charters and privileges, they knew that these originated in the grant of the crown, and might be revoked. England was in fact precociously centralised. Not only were the economy and the main transport routes increasingly focused on the metropolis of London; the long tradition of royal government had habituated subjects to obedience. A single legal system, centred in the capital, and a single representative institution, parliament, intensified national consciousness and national loyalties; and they stood in sharp contrast to the patchwork-quilt of jurisdictions and institutions in the slowly evolving nation-states of France and Spain, still more The Netherlands. A powerful ideological boost to the claims of the state came from the spread of early-modern humanism, indoctrinating the gentry in the duty of service to the common-wealth. Those loyalties were crucially reinforced by the newfound belief, from which many Englishmen drew a sense of common purpose rivalling that of Spaniards of the Reconquista, that England was God's elect nation. The English government may have creaked and stumbled, but so did all European governments; and in some respects the English record was striking. The most challengeable, and challenged, of the government's fiscal measures, the forced loan of 1626–7, and ship money until 1638, achieved remarkable yields by European standards. By such measures, the English polity semed healthy enough.

A growing sense of English identity, trumpeted in the history plays of Shakespeare, the travel accounts collected by Richard Hakluyt, and the legal writings of Sir Edward Coke, came (not altogether coincidentally) as English contacts with others were intensifying. It was not just geography that made Shakespeare's realm increasingly a part of Britain, in ways that then and now have resisted categorisation. While the accession of James Stuart of Scotland to the English throne brought the southern kingdom into new proximity to its northern neighbour, the crushing, in Elizabeth's last days, of the great Gaelic revolt in Ireland finally opened the whole of that land to English rule. Not for the last time, the metropolitan kingdom did not know quite what to do with empire. On the one hand, the absence of any sustained Protestant evangelism allowed the Counter-Reformation at last to make its mark on Irish parishes in the 1620s, thus adding fierier religious hostilities to the old ethnic, cultural and economic tensions. On the other, colonisation and economic exploitation came easily. The movement of settlers, from England and Scotland into Ulster after 1607, from the southwest into Munster in the 1620s and '30s, made for more substantial ties between the islands. Both James and Charles occasionally hoped for closer integration of Ireland in a widened English polity, and the appearance at Whitehall in the 1630s of an Irish Gaelic courtier, the earl of Antrim, was a sign of what might have been. Both kings certainly dreamed (mostly vainly) of Irish revenues. But others contrasted the obduracy of Ireland's religion and culture with England's pretensions there, and its effective military control; and they hungered to make a reality of Westminster's sovereignty, in a way that could only provoke the majority of Ireland's inhabitants.

Scotland's was to prove an equally uncomfortable throne for an English king. In material terms, Scotland had even less to offer England than did Ireland, since there were no lands open to confiscation, and scant trade to exploit; and to kings with limited interest in war, the Europe-wide reputation of both Scots and Irish as mercenaries meant little. But the grandeur of ruling multiple kingdoms meant much; and anyway, Scotland was James's home. Accordingly, he sought the closer integration of the political establishments of his two ancient kingdoms, though he faced the generally successful resistance of both. Absentee rule of Scotland from Whitehall certainly provoked Scottish resentments, and English jealousies too as James favoured his old cronies. But it was the accession of Charles, patently English, with an English king's unconcern for Scottish ways, that brought fatal provocation. With few exceptions, Charles's English subjects had neither quarrel with, nor interest in, affronts the king offered to the Scots; nevertheless, he left himself an inadequate base in Scotland with which to counter any Scottish protest. Crisis to the north was therefore likely to be felt south of the common border; and England and Scotland had alike experienced innovations in rule and religion.

Scotland and Ireland manifest a phenomenon common to much of Europe in this period. Everywhere outlying provinces and kingdoms, often acquired by dynastic accident, protested against increasing subjugation and exploitation by the core state of a dynastic empire. The gathering revolt in Scotland in 1637–40 and the Irish cataclysm of 1641 mirror near-contemporaneous events in the Spanish Habsburg dominions of Portugal, Catalonia, Naples, and also in some of the French crown's less unified provinces. The troubles stemmed in part from Charles's more activist foreign policy in the later 1620s, that led him to impose new burdens on jealous kingdoms drawing few benefits from his rule, and often to ignore local customs and immunities in so doing. But there were ideological stresses too, the consequence of the early Stuarts' taste for seeing in themselves the whole body politic. Influenced by Renaissance principles of uniformity and symmetry, Charles strove to reduce all to a single, and largely English, pattern. Disaster ensued from his blithe assumption that though he cast few glances north and west he could shape both religious practices and patterns of landholding by command. Whatever English hostility to ship money, and whatever John Pym's political skill in 1640–1, the underlying resilience of the English polity ensured that the Stuart monarchy fell first at Scottish and Irish fences.

And if Charles Stuart's British nemesis provides a corrective to Anglo-centric assumptions, we may find Britocentrism itself inadequate. England was and is part of the British Isles, and the British Isles were and are part of Europe. Europe's Thirty Years War helped shape Calvinist militancy in Scotland as well as England, even before Scotland's Calvinists repeatedly disrupted English alignments. The coincidence in 1637 of Charles's abandonment of ties with Scotland's 'auld ally', France, and the outbreak of the Scottish troubles might be merely coincidence. But the coincidence of Charles's failure in the spring of 1640 to gain Spanish aid, and his resentful collapse into the uncomfortable embrace of parliament as he confronted the Scots, suggests complex geopolitical connections. These are confirmed by the crisis in the spring of the following year, when the reluctance of parliament and the City of London to aid him against the Scots saw him play a Roman Catholic card: the financial denominations he tried to write on that card were variously papal and Irish. England's prevailing metaphor may have been the body politic, with its implications of sufficiency and closure; but that body had some very intrusive neighbours.

Yet British and European contexts should not obscure the English frame. The collapse of Charles's government in a composite British monarchy experiencing fiscal strain and religious division may seem unsurprising in the unsteady Europe of the seventeenth century. England's progression towards revolution, on the other hand, was peculiarly English. European contemporaries certainly thought it so, and the more worthy of explanation for all that.

|2|

The holy and the unholy

Visions of the church

The church existed to minister to the people. Modern commentators often assume that religious commitment was a matter of broad political commitment, of social need, of habit; but they thereby discount the experience and aspirations of countless individuals, whose piety and zeal burn through the surviving pages of meditations and advice, prosaic journal and lyric verse. For such people, the Church – or more often the church or congregation writ small, the local site of worship, ritual, fellowship – might dwarf in importance even the home.

Yet the church of England was an expression of the polity. Most educated contemporaries subscribed to an erastian account of the relations of church and state, and endorsed the claim that the state (there were disagreements as to whether the king alone or king-in-parliament) should determine the frame of the church. But Richard Hooker, the church's greatest apologist, gave that claim a very different force when he argued in the 1590s that the church was the soul of the body politic: since all were by law members, church and state were different names for the same body. Compulsory attendance was reflected in hierarchical seating arrangements, and in the widespread practice of almost corporate communions by the whole parish three times a year. The king governed the whole, and was far from alone in mingling secular and ecclesiastical roles. In its turn, the church insistently enjoined obedience – the general stress on the fifth commandment was reinforced by regular prayers for those in power and place.

There was another story, more urgent and less comfortably organic. It derived from the Old Testament, and told of God's dealings with a chosen people. That account, of captivity and turmoil, served to explain and legitimate the church's beginnings in the sixteenth century and its anxious survival. The ensuing vision could be intensely dynamic: in the *Acts and Monuments*, better known as the *Book of Martyrs,* the Elizabethan John Foxe had saluted the godly prince, the new Constantine, leading the church militant into battle with the Roman Antichrist. His was to prove one of the most influential of all early-modern works.

Contemporaries therefore abhorred, and in the early 1640s sometimes attacked, those Roman Catholic recusants or protestant sectaries who separated themselves from the church. Not only did dissidence mean disunity, challenging the very corporateness of the polity; it also signified disloyalty. The century before 1650 brought assassination plots and religious war to the British Isles as well as to Europe; the horrors besetting Germany, Ireland, France, as well as petty village squabbles, were clear to see. The human capacity for error made differences in conscience unavoidable, but whatever the inward conscience the unity of the whole demanded uniformity of practice, of worship, of allegiance. This lent itself to blunt political assertion. James I famously insisted 'No bishop, no king', and stressed the symmetry and interdependence of hierarchy in church and state; and a defeated Charles I in 1646 prized his power over the church as highly as the sword. But had hierarchy and power alone driven that reciprocity, and not divine injunction too, it would scarcely have commanded such commitment.

At all levels, the church was part of the early-modern fabric. The Bishop of Durham was at least nominally the fount of temporal authority in the county palatine of Durham, and every bishop and every dean (the head of the cathedral clergy) wielded local authority, dispensing hospitality, administering estates, and also, usually, serving as JP; the dean and cathedral chapter of Salisbury governed a quarter of that city. The bishops sat (as they still do) in the House of Lords, and some were active courtiers. The hierarchy of church courts had jurisdiction over laity as well as clergy, not only in matters clearly pertaining to religion and morality but also in probate and marital litigation. Defamation cases, which might be vital business in days before impersonal credit-ratings, also came before the church courts. The church courts were certainly an instrument of social control; but they reflected as well an ideal of community, for their final sanction was excommunication, which brought expulsion from the sacrament of communion and, in theory at least, from the life of the community. A strong case can be made for the courts' vitality and effectiveness before the Civil War, but their hold varied according to the accused's stake in the community. Young people, the poor, and poor women in particular, having less need to worry about the social stigma and less money to pay the fees, were less moved. Over a half of those cited before the church courts for moral causes failed to respond and were excommunicated for contumacy, for fornication was widely thought 'but a trick of youth'. At any time, perhaps 5 per cent of the population was excommunicate, however briefly.

The church was of course not primarily an instrument of control but a provider of spiritual solace, and as such its role had changed considerably in the generation and a half before 1600. The pre-Reformation priesthood reconciled the essentially receptive congregation to God through sacrament and ritual. Protestant reformers attacked ritual for inculcating passivity and idolatry, and for encouraging the people to look for mediators between themselves and God. Demanding a 'lively faith' of the individual who faced God alone and for whom the only mediator was Christ, they insisted that the cleric was above all to expound the gospel, not to administer the sacraments. Their clergy became ministers of the Word, not a priesthood; preaching was to provide 'the ordinary means to salvation', the instrument for awakening the requisite faith in the people.

From Archbishop Toby Matthew of York, who preached a sermon a week for forty years, down to humble curates in the countryside, the ideal of the preaching pastor took hold. By 1640 over three-quarters of the clergy had university degrees, more in the south-east, fewer in the north and west; the proportion had doubled since 1600. Educational advance was buttressed by widespread efforts to improve preaching. Leading pastoral practitioners from William Perkins at the start of our period to Richard Baxter at the end urged their colleagues to translate their highly formal university learning into terms suitable to a popular audience. And there were formal means to help them, like the 'lectures by combination', in which neighbouring ministers preached, or lectured, usually in monthly sequence, in local market towns, and then criticised and discussed the performance.

Exposition of the Word was central to godly worship, but its exponents recognised the magnitude of their task. John Foxe had dreamed that the printing press would swiftly complete the work of reformation, but even he combined graphic woodcuts with his stirring text. Other godly ministers and printers learned to counter protestantism's latent iconophobia by co-opting the forms of popular literature – woodcut, moral tale, ballad, murder narrative, even romance – to reach out to new audiences. The drama of sin and redemption was repeatedly enacted in the vivid scaffold narratives clergy of various stripes drew from the lips of the condemned. The classic work at the intersection of godly and popular culture was of course John Bunyan's *Pilgrim's Progress* (1678). But the most important address to 'mean apprehensions' was the question-and-response format of catechism. From Luther and Calvin at the very beginning of the Reformation, evangelists came to value the catechism's simplicity and aids to memory as they sought to tailor their message to the ignorant. Probably half a million copies of the official prayer book catechism had been dispersed by 1600, while the combined sales of its wartime successor, the *Shorter Catechism* of the Westminster Assembly, and of the hundreds of different catechisms by clergy of the stature of William Perkins, John Owen, Henry Hammond, probably ran into the millions. The Jacobean

Stephen Egerton's *Briefe Method of Catechising* alone went through at least forty-four editions by 1644. Even works aimed at a more literate audience, such as Arthur Dent's hugely successful *Plain Man's Path-way to Heaven* of 1601, responded in their dialogue form to the pressures of oral discourse.

Evangelists met a mixed response. On the one hand, countless of the godly practised 'household religion', recapitulating at home the preacher's argument in feats of memory and reconstruction, often with the parents catechising children and servants. Lodewijck Huygens, a Dutch visitor to London in 1651–2, was struck by the presence at sermons of innumerable adult note-takers, ready to venture forth to exhort their households. But outside those godly citadels lay not merely the earthy materialists characterised by Dent, nor the 'children in years and children in understanding' addressed by so many catechists. Evangelists encountered as well another vision of the church, focused less on the individual and family than the community, that had survived and expanded in the decades since Elizabeth's accession. The theologically protestant church of England had dispensed with a mediating priesthood, but a modified liturgy (or order of service) and ceremonial had been left in place in the 1559 *Book of Common Prayer*.

The partly reformed church did what its predecessor had done for centuries. It provided parishioners with the physical setting in which might be found a form of holiness, the symbols of a unifying worship, and simplified rites of passage – baptism, marriage, burial. The church claimed to embody a community that was ritual as well as social. The ideal was of course just that, an ideal, and never met. But that organic vision of the church appealed to countless parishioners who, from the turn of the century to the Restoration, litigated and fought for the inclusive and familiar prayer book. One critic gave its power grudging recognition when he derided it as 'the only book of the world' in popular estimation. The rituals it expressed were held no less dear, and it was no accident that one round of the Second Civil War was sparked by the suppression of Christmas in Kent.

Stresses and strains were inevitable. The growing professional competence, the university qualifications, the theological learning of a reformed clergy, as well as their tendency to intermarry, distanced them from their parishioners, and often contributed to a background resentment at clerical 'pomposities'. Anticlericalism could become more pointed in cases of absenteeism and non-performance, offensive both to those prizing the awakening sermon and those seeking the solace of ritual and sacrament. The evangelising role adopted by so many of the clergy could cause open conflict in the parish. As ministers who opposed ceremonial took it upon themselves to castigate sinners and assert a godly discipline, they provoked not only the manifestly unregenerate but also those who clung to the vision of community affirmed in parochial ritual. John Murcot's vindictive sermon on the death of a Cheshire parishioner who had defied him

over local festivities, and the angry response of the 'rabble rout', illuminate the tensions.

The material church

Despite the succession of two sincere churchmen as kings, the obstacles
to either vision, reformist or organic, were legion. Not least, attendance
lagged. Patriarchalist biases meant that householders were assumed to be
the vital core of the parish, who would instruct their families: thus, the
churchwardens of Allhallows the Great, London, were in 1615 instructed
to fine absentee householders. While some schools mandated attendance,
the absence of most children, and perhaps young servants too, especially
women, must have been widely accepted. The physical impediments to
attendance were sometimes overwhelming. The huge parish of Whalley in
Lancashire, covering 180 square miles and including almost forty separate
townships with some 10 000 inhabitants, was exceptional, but many other
parishes in the north were simply too big. In wooded areas, scattered
settlement complicated the long walk to church, and left the sprawling
parishes in the Sussex and Kent Weald, for example, prone to religious
dissent and to irreligion. Towns suffered as well, for demographic change
had not respected medieval parish boundaries. The single parish church
of burgeoning Sheffield, or of Jacobean Leeds, could scarcely hold either
town's several thousand inhabitants. Too many people lay outside the
reach of the church, a fact that helps to explain the appeal of wandering
missionaries, whether Baptist or Quaker, in the revolutionary years.

The church's physical problems that so hampered its spiritual provision
were compounded by its participation in the mundane world. The church
was dominated in important ways by lay property-owners; though the
largest was the crown, the most numerous were the local gentry. The
Reformation had brought a partial lay take-over of the church's material
resources, above all of its patronage. Laymen controlled almost three-
quarters of the advowsons, or rights of presentation to parish livings, in
Somerset, while the Earl of Warwick owned rights over twenty-two
livings, chiefly in Essex. Most patrons did not demand crude sycophancy
of their appointees, nor practise outright simony, or sale of livings: but
they rarely adjusted stipends to inflation. Archbishop Whitgift calculated
in 1584 that only 600 parish livings, out of over 9000, could support
learned clergy, especially clergy with families. Probate evidence suggests
that clerical living standards gradually improved, and where a minister
possessed the glebe land attached to the parish church he might farm
comfortably as a yeoman, as that voluminous diarist Ralph Josselin did
at Earl's Colne in Essex. Where the minister also possessed the 'great'
tithes, those on his parishioners' arable produce, he might in an era of
rising agricultural productivity and prices be a rich man; indeed, the

rectory of Wigan in Lancashire was one of the wealthiest estates in the county. Senior cathedral clergy were also wealthy. But parochial poverty was widespread, especially in the four-ninths of livings whose revenues were left 'impropriate' to laymen by the accidents of the Reformation. The elaborate church surveys carried out under the republic show many livings valued at scarcely more than a day labourer might earn: thus, fifty-one Lancashire curates earned less than £15 a year. All the primates of the early-Stuart church campaigned energetically, with the support of both kings, to rebuild church finances, and to revalue and renegotiate leases of church property; and most churchmen, of whatever doctrinal leaning, believed the duty of the laity to pay tithes divine in origin.

Yet it would be misleading to accentuate the negative. As at most times, observers of the church were prone to jeremiads over the failings of fallen mankind; but they could also find reasons for optimism. The increasingly competent ministry in the parishes found reinforcement in a spate of printed works catering to an increasingly literate audience. Discipline advanced, as moralist legislation put new weapons in the hands of the local alliances of magistrates and ministers, and as a well-intentioned king James fostered a fundamentally harmonious church.

Identifying puritanism

If churchmen of all stripes agreed that there was still work to be done, what of puritanism, the call for further reform that has so vexed modern historians? Reacting against the claims of those who have seen in the rise of puritanism a prime cause of the English Civil War, several modern scholars have observed the anachronism of the modern term 'puritanism', with its implications of system; indeed, they maintain that it is little safer to talk of 'puritans', for although there is contemporary warrant here, it was a term of abuse. Zeal-of-the-land Busy in Ben Jonson's *Bartholomew Fair* fits, indeed shaped, the caricature: extremist, hypocritical, disreputable. So to call a minister or gentleman a puritan is to use the word in a way few would have understood until the Laudian years. Yet some words are too useful to abandon, and provided that we remember it is no party label 'puritan' can serve to characterise a person manifesting at least some of a cluster of attitudes. And as a descriptive convenience 'puritanism' too has its advantages: it can denote a cast of mind or broad commitment – though not a formal creed or programme.

The distinctions between Jacobean puritans and non-puritans, are matters of inflexion and emphasis. Prior to the rise of what is generally known as Arminianism in the 1620s and its triumph under Archbishop Laud in the 1630s, the theology of the English church was largely Calvinist, stressing an omnipotent God's foreknowledge of all things, and the inefficacy of the will and works of sinful man in attaining salvation. The

Calvinist bishop John Davenant was rightly perplexed at Laud's hostility to predestination: 'Why that should now be esteemed puritan doctrine, which those held who have done our church the greatest service ... I cannot understand.' The strength of the pre-Laudian consensus is remarkable: all James's archbishops drew their divinity from John Calvin's Geneva, as did James himself, and the university establishments were largely Calvinist. Theological common ground helped dampen other conflicts. Like many other Calvinist bishops – Matthew of York, Montagu of Winchester, Lake of Bath and Wells – George Abbot, Archbishop of Canterbury from 1611 to 1633 and a fierce enemy of separation from the church and its discipline, accepted considerable non-conformity in ceremonials from those who shared his anti-Catholicism.

The bishops' complaisance in turn helps explain why their government of the church was so little at issue in James's reign. Elizabeth had crushed the presbyterian challenge, and there were few who joined the Mayflower Pilgrims in separating from the ungodly whole in pursuit of the true church. After all, in the matter of preaching the bishops were on the right side. They too saw it as the vital means to awaken saving faith; most supported lectures by combination, and many earned widespread respect for their own herculean preaching. They were 'fit to be made examples for all ages', as the parliamentary martyr Sir John Eliot declaimed nostalgically in 1629.

Distinctions may be problematic before the later 1620s, when the rise of Laud and the Arminians made issues clearer, and the Thirty Years War made them more urgent; yet distinctions remain. People tended to be called 'puritans' when their protestantism did not centre on prayer book and church building, and when they visibly applied their faith to their daily lives. So Richard Baxter's father was derided for his piety as he distanced himself from the festive culture of his Shropshire neighbours. The characteristic stress of such puritans was on a 'lively', an 'experienced', faith. 'Godliness' meant what has come to be called 'experiential Calvinism' – internalising and living out a creed to which 'the common sort of protestants' paid at best formal observance.

Logically as well as doctrinally, all centred on salvation. Calvin's intensification of the protestant doctrine of justification by faith alone, his emphasis on the inscrutability of an omnipotent God who granted saving faith at will and unbeknownst to the recipient, generated not only the doctrine of predestination but also widespread perplexity. Since election or damnation lay in the hand of God alone, the fate of the soul became a matter for theological dispute and often agonised concern. Explaining why morality still mattered, William Perkins, the greatest English Calvinist theologian, amplified in the 1590s the theology of covenant. God covenanted with fallen man through the New Testament's offer of grace, while the elect covenanted with God to strive (however ineffectually) to obey the law of the Old. Although Christ's sacrifice offered grace, the chosen still had to struggle incessantly with sin in order to avail themselves of it. But the covenant left unanswered the burning question of who was saved. Conformist Calvinists, such as Bishop Lake, who confronted the pastoral needs of the church, tended to argue the pointlessness of further inquiry since God's choice was unknown. Undaunted, many Jacobean theologians, and even the king himself, debated whether the elect could ever fall from grace, and the relationship between election and Christ's atonement for the sins of humanity. The dazzling court preacher of the 1620s, John Preston, was not alone in constructing masterpieces of harmonics, that some might think evasion, to reconcile individual responsibility and Calvin's God of power; but John Milton may have had the last word when he consigned *Paradise Lost*'s fallen angels to an eternity debating God's eternal decrees.

Formal teaching probably had less impact than did obfuscation. Most catechisms taught beginning Christians an implicitly universalist message; and many godly pastors modified their academic stress on God's will to suggest that, although works availed nothing with God, a godly life might testify to election, since only grace granted by God could generate a proper hatred of sin and love of God. Perkins for one had sought to hearten his audience. Though, he warned, 'it is an hard thing for a man to search out his own heart', self-examination might both steel faith in action and bring some 'assurance' that the soul stood right towards God. The diaries that were so much a puritan product chronicled those self-examinations and godly strivings. In 1656 John Beadle even produced a guide to the keeping of such records, *The Journal or Diary of a Thankful Christian*.

The Thirty-Nine Articles, the church's formulary of faith, insisted that the doctrine of election could be 'full of sweet, pleasant and unspeakable comfort'. The will of Sir Francis Hastings, in early-Jacobean Somerset, suggests how this might be. Hastings's God, 'in his foreknowledge, and before I was to work either good or evil, hath chosen me to be his child and predestinated me to eternal salvation'. Most ministers tried to guard against assumptions of security by insisting that God would always hold the key, and therefore the believer's status must remain in doubt. The godly duly strove all the more for assurance through discipline and action. A myriad works of practical divinity offered guidance. But despite the availability of Perkins's *How to Live, and That Well,* or Bishop Lewis Bailey's *The Practice of Piety*, insecurity could breed the despair to which John Bunyan's spiritual autobiography, *Grace Abounding unto the Chief of Sinners*, attests. To salve such despair Richard Baxter and countless other clerical 'physicians of the soul' counselled the godly that the very lack of confidence could be a sign that God was with them. They offered as well a scripturalism more insistent than the focus on Christ crucified so characteristic of non-puritans like John Donne or George Herbert, or of Aemilia Lanyer and those other women writers who found inclusion through the suffering Christ. 'Study the scriptures, much meditate in them day and night,' Preston reassured, 'And thou shalt find this, that grace will follow.'

Preston's account of the way to grace is non-institutional, even individual. St Paul, the all-important authority for protestants, had urged 'edification' through the church. Conformist Calvinist clergy, like the Calvinist King James, interpreted that to mean the institutional church God had approved and the state had ordained, the source not just of the sacraments and ceremonial prized by Catholics and Laudians alike, but as well of 'practical' sermons on the application of scripture to the individual. Others understood by 'edifying' something active: extempore prayer, study of scripture, repetition of sermons in godly fellowship. The aim was conversion, and many preachers worked heroically, catechising and counselling their flocks. Thus awakened, godly neighbours then associated informally, often enough with the parish minister present: a community within the community of the parish. 'Our society', Josselin called those at Earl's Colne who strove to make good the deficiencies of a parish church that also included the ungodly. The Jacobean church therefore offered room to those who sought active participation, but yet remained loyal to the ideals of national church and national reformation.

Godly fellowship challenges claims that puritanism centred on an appeal to the individual conscience. As Oliver Cromwell forcefully reminded comrades in his approximation to a gathered church in the army in 1647, 'Thus far as we are agreed, I think it is of God.' There was here an ideal of community fully as powerful as that cherished by the devotees of the prayer-book church: but the community of the godly was, like the visible church of the godly, independent of place. The godly London woodworker Nehemiah Wallington, crossing parish boundaries in London in search of sustenance, was a world away from George Herbert, delighting in the meeting of his flock within the parish church.

As Wallington's conduct suggests, and as Charles and Laud suspected, puritans' ecclesiastical loyalties were conditional upon reformation. The church was God's; and when Antichrist was loose in the world, working his will from Rome, appeals to unity were not enough. Thanks to John Foxe, who had built a national apologetic around Antichrist, an apocalyptic potential lay deep in the protestant mainstream, waxing and waning with the political climate and the prospect of catastrophe for the protestant faith. But the resulting anti-Catholicism was not merely xenophobia, and nor was it a minority commitment. On the one hand, the universal nature of the foe drew from puritans an insistence on the need for international protestant solidarity; on the other, even King James could agree that the pope was Antichrist. For James, however, this was an intellectual and political, not a lived, commitment. Although the Gunpowder Plot of 1605 gave Antichrist firmer shape in his mind, he saw Satan in the Jesuits, working against kings and nations. Others, whom we may call puritans, applied the apocalyptic scriptures to their lives and discerned a struggle within the nation as well as without; they therefore demanded an end to the ceremonies inherited from the pre-Reformation, popish, church. The pope's hand was detected everywhere. The Calvinist lawyer William Prynne was not alone after 1649 in attributing the execution of Charles I to an Antichristian Jesuit plot to discredit protestantism.

If apocalypticism and millenarianism were the moods of inflamed minds, providentialism – the belief in God's responsibility for all events – offered a blueprint for everyday. God had turned his back on one sinful nation, and the Jews' successors as God's chosen must learn from that history to eliminate sin. Godly discipline was not just a matter of public decency, or even of the glorification of God; it would also determine national survival. The Long Parliament's closing of the theatres was part of its war effort. And comfort was available. Since the God of the Old Testament punished sin in this world as well as the next, scrutiny of events might offer a guide to His purposes. The world was, in the title of the book by Oliver Cromwell's tutor Thomas Beard, *The Theatre of God's Judgements*, and many were the puritans who chronicled in their diaries God's 'providences', their escapes from danger or catastrophes afflicting neighbours and nation, in order to determine God's purposes. The teleology of history, like the portentousness of monstrous births and lunar eclipses, ranked among the great clichés of the age; but a certain sort of protestant does seem to have internalised the calculations to an extent that could be disconcerting. The Lancashire minister Henry Newcome was able to distinguish between 'bye', 'ordinary', 'particular', 'special', and 'extra-ordinary' providences in his affairs in the mid-1650s, while Simonds D'Ewes in 1622 saw 'the retrograde growth of beans' as a portent. Only humility could restrain the morally dangerous temptation here to exalt worldly success or, as defeated royalists pointed out, the spiritually dangerous temptation to overlook the story of Job, scourged by God for no apparent reason. In time Cromwell came to read divine punishment of his and the nation's sins into the failure of his 'western design' against Spain, just as he had seen God in his victories.

Puritanism in the world

'Experiential' protestants inwardly applied, or internalised, a widely shared body of doctrine. Personal yearnings and temperament ultimately determined who would be a puritan and who would not, and the distribution of godliness across the social spectrum, and within families, underscores the randomness of the spiritual variable. Undeterred, many scholars have argued that socio-economic or socio-cultural factors affected the distribution of puritanism. From Ben Jonson's exercises in ridicule, through civil war historians like Clarendon and Lucy Hutchinson, with her scorn for the 'worsted stocking men', to modern Marxists, claims for the urban and industrial correlates of zeal have been heard. More recently, an ecological variant has been advanced: in the southwest, the middling sort in the wood/pasture zone of scattered settlements and rural handicrafts were allegedly more inclined towards puritanism than were villagers in the arable and sheep-corn areas.

Puritanism took root and spread where the seed was sown and nurtured. As with Richard Baxter's father, and John Bunyan, who seem to have come to their faith in relative isolation, Bible-reading and the consumption of even a few godly works could lay a foundation for zeal. But the recommended progression from catechism to Bible did not always breed spiritual heroics. It took a godly minister, often working with the support of a local gentleman or town corporation, to drive home the awakening message; better, it took a succession of godly ministers to foster a sustaining fellowship. Local studies have suggested the importance of clerical succession in the development of puritanism, at Terling in Essex, Barnstaple in north Devon, or Manchester. They have also suggested its importance in puritanism's failure to develop in the 'dark corners of the land' in the northern uplands and Wales, whose impoverished parishes rarely saw a qualified preacher, let alone a succession. The possibilities are apparent in the saga of Anthony Nutter, whose congregation in Leicestershire included the family of George Fox the Quaker and whose later congregation in Yorkshire included the family of James Nayler, the other great Quaker leader.

While the variation of commitment among country parishes may therefore indicate merely the serendipitous effect of patronage, some broader patterns emerge. Huguenot silk-weavers in Kent and Flemish lace-workers in south Devon suggest the role of artisan refugees from Europe's religious wars in inclining the areas where they settled towards puritanism. The many puritans in the textile regions of the Stour valley in East Anglia, the West Riding of Yorkshire, and southeast Lancashire suggest a broader alignment. And commercial, manufacturing and port towns everywhere – Northampton, Coventry, Birmingham, Ipswich, Hull, Dorchester, Taunton, above all London – gained a reputation for puritanism.

Godly ministers and patrons were renowned for their interest in market towns as centres for persuasion and dissemination. And handicraft workers had more opportunity for reading and reflection than did arable farmers. But to explain the puritanism of manufacturing areas we need to supplement clerical itineraries and the higher incidence of books and literacy by reference to factors of community and cohesion. The medieval guilds and religious fraternities had provided both comradeship and a sense of exclusiveness, and their disappearance after the Reformation left a large gap. The characteristic puritan modes of address – 'brother', 'sister' – suggest that godly fellowship, with its psalm-singing and processions to sermons, provided a substitute, one that was all the more valuable in towns, where so many inhabitants were newcomers, uprooted from the community of their villages. The footloose John Bunyan's yearning to be part of the godly community in Bedford provides a poignant example.

The conviction of contemporaries, and many modern historians, that puritanism was concentrated among the middling sort has been strongly contested. Without question, there were many poor people among the godly. But local studies suggest a resolution. In socio-economically stable Cambridgeshire, dissent seems to have grown rooted in particular families; as branches of these prospered or failed, zeal came to span the social spectrum, becoming integrated in the neighbourhood. Yet in areas of mobility and change, such as Havering to the northeast of London, nearby Terling in Essex, or the wood-pasture zone of the southwest, there seems no doubt that below a crucial section of the elite, puritans did come largely from the middling sort. There were both push and pull factors: on the one hand, the doctrine of providence, and the insistence on striving, might mean little to the poor, who were overwhelmingly victims of circumstance; on the other, property-owners hungered for discipline.

But did discipline require puritanism? In the crisis years around 1600 the worthies of the safely manorialised sheep-corn village of Keevil in Wiltshire, whose festive and ritual community of alehouse, village green and parish church had survived, punished fornicators and drunks. Social discipline was, in other words, not synonymous with puritanism. But in manufacturing centres like Taunton or Gloucester, disciplinarians also targeted swearers and sabbath-breakers. Where the culture of neighbourliness was already under stress, puritanism offered a very different version of order. Bible, sermon, and moral constraint constituted a frontal assault on the old patterns of communal culture. The scale is most apparent in the zealous reshaping of Dorchester by its worthies after the 1613 fire. Only such a confrontation, heightened by the apocalyptic pressures of anti-Catholicism, can account for the storm kindled by James's 1618 book of sports, authorising various Sunday pastimes, and its reissue by Charles in 1633. In traditional villages and manor-houses in Lancashire or Northamptonshire (not inhabited entirely by clowns and debauchees), the book of sports had widespread support; but to the godly London turner Nehemiah Wallington, or the publicists William Prynne and Henry Burton, chronicling the fate of sabbath-breakers, it marked the advance of Antichrist.

Such cultural tension might be thought the origin of civil war, and certainly when war came its most powerful clarions were anti-Catholic zeal on the one hand and an anti-puritanism asserted as the defence of community on the other. Yet puritans were no mass movement, bearing down a reactionary king and state church. The conviction of the godly that they were few, a remnant, bears remembering. Nor was the road from zeal to wartime parliamentarianism always direct – Edward Lord Montagu, Ralph Brownrigg (promoted to a bishopric by a desperate Charles I in 1641), or the godly neutrals encountered by Richard Baxter in the West Midlands in

1642, all remembered that the Bible enjoined earthly obedience. The clergy may have sought to change the world, but their dream was of a godly discipline, not individualism, and they co-operated closely with the lay elites to this end. In Dorchester under its pastor John White, in Ipswich under Samuel Ward, and also in the Massachusetts Bay colony of John Winthrop and John Cotton, as intimate a local alliance of church and state existed as that between king and bishops: the ministers urged on the magistrates the duty to punish sin, and they urged on the people reverence to their godly superiors. Meanwhile, noblemen and gentlemen like Lord Robartes and Sir Walter Earle in the southwest, Lord Saye and Richard Knightley in the Midlands, the Earl of Warwick and Sir Nathaniel Barnardiston in East Anglia, valued order as much as they valued godliness. All these dreamed of a hierarchical, as well as a religious, commonwealth, and in their intensive reading found scriptural and historical models, from David to Constantine, of the godly prince. The language of divine kingship came from them as well as from James VI and I; in their turn godly commoners looked reverently on the great patrons, despite their sometimes unpuritanical lives.

Nevertheless, a puritan political challenge was not simply a response to Charles's and Laud's new policies. For puritans, the magistrate did not simply exist, to the twin ends of justice and protection, in the world as it was; he had to act to make the world as it should be. He had to show 'a holy violence in the performance of all duties', as the puritan minister Richard Sibbes put it. Like all their contemporaries, experiential Calvinists knew that worldly power was both divine and natural in its origins; but unlike others, they also knew that it was conditional (though the godly lords, Saye and Brooke, were dismayed to find, when they contemplated flight in the mid-1630s, that the puritans of Massachusetts Bay were not wedded to the heritability of authority). The exercise of power had ultimately to be measured against the Antichrist. As sheriff before the 1624 Cheshire election, Sir Richard Grosvenor urged on all, MPs and voters alike, constant vigilance against the popish threat.

Archbishop Laud's conviction that puritans endangered the state as well as the institutional and ceremonial church he revered thus had plausibility. Not least among the Calvinist seeds of change was the Bible. The editors of that version of the Bible that was compiled during defeat and exile in Geneva in the 1550s observed, in the Old Testament's margins, the duties of kings and the fate of royal sinners. And, they offered another marginal suggestion: the classic New Testament justification of obedience, Romans xiii.10 ('Let every soul be subject unto the higher powers'), applied merely to the 'private man'. They discreetly passed over the duties of the lesser magistrate, be he godly nobleman or parliament-man. The Authorised Version of 1611 offered some competition, but the Geneva Bible remained popular throughout the period, and generations of readers were thus introduced to a vision of conditional monarchy. Cromwell's scriptural citations show its influence.

The consequences of such a creed became apparent as tensions mounted with the outbreak of the Thirty Years War in 1618. Since all were alike responsible to God, negligent superiors did not excuse inferiors' inactivity. When royal policy seemed to take England dangerously close to the Catholic camp, the lesser magistrate might be called upon. Preaching at the Norfolk assizes prior to the 1621 election, Thomas Scott urged electors even to ignore the Lord Lieutenant if the cause of true religion demanded it. Preaching to the Coventry militia company that year, Samuel Buggs prayed that godly parliament-men would save the nation; by the end of the decade Sir Richard Grosvenor even urged Cheshire jurymen to present their landlords, if Catholics, for punishment. Such action was within the law, if unusual. Others' expressions went further, and at least two godly members of the political elite, Thomas Scot, MP for Canterbury, and the young Simonds D'Ewes, confided to their diaries their longings for a rebellion; the unsympathetic Norfolk clergyman John Rous noted similar talk in the parishes in 1627–8. In the excitement of the early 1620s, and the near-despair in puritan circles later in the decade, we can already see the powerful ambiguity of puritanism: a proffer of discipline, but also a demand for personal commitment and responsibility to God in a polarised world. The importance of the figure of the Antichrist in precipitating action from this mixture is clear in the attempt of a group of puritan aristocrats to conduct their own anti-Spanish foreign policy through the Providence Island Company in the 1630s. It is clear too in the decision of Nehemiah Wallington's friends among the London godly, fearing an assault by papists and privy councillors from the Tower of London, to go armed to church in the summer of 1640; and in the lynching of a Catholic officer by Somerset troops headed for Scotland that summer. Experiential Calvinism was not simply an instrument of social control, for that creed also encompassed the anti-Catholic violence that broke out in the industrialised Stour valley in East Anglia in the summer of 1642. In such events lay the seeds of radical departures in the 1640s – and the seeds too of a reaction towards the king as the source of order.

Puritans saw themselves at war with the world, and the world reciprocated. When Thomas Hooker, whose lectureship at Chelmsford in Essex Laud suppressed in 1630, was about to leave for New England he comforted himself that God would require of the unregenerate in his audience 'an account for all thy abominations, nay for all thy speeches against the people of God, upon thy ale-bench when thou didst toss them to and fro'. Puritans sought to discipline their neighbours, and Richard Baxter's account of the rabbling of godly ministers in the Welsh borderlands on the eve of the war suggests the social costs. The war confirmed that puritans had earned the hostility of a surprising number of ordinary parishioners who were devoted to the religion of the Prayer Book, as well as of the 'good fellows' of the ale-bench, whose culture and whose popular pastimes they had sought to extirpate.

Anti-Calvinism

Calvinism may have been orthodoxy in the early-seventeenth-century English church, but it was no monopoly. As theologians in late-Elizabethan Cambridge pursued with scholastic rigour the intricacies of God's decrees, they sparked a reaction. From the outset, politics and theology went together. Even before the Laudian triumph, Lancelot Andrewes, James's favourite court divine (who became Bishop of Winchester in 1619), pointed insistently to the alleged populist tendencies of puritanism as he exploited the king's concerns for order and discipline. The Calvinists, of course, behaved similarly, suppressing debate at Cambridge in the 1590s, and regularly denouncing as popish writings and sermons that seemed to open the door to human free will.

Underlying the anti-Calvinist polemic was a coherent vision of the church and of religious life. Puritans tended to follow Foxe in defining the church on earth as the faithful, and accordingly located the church of the long pre-Reformation centuries underground, among the persecuted. But Andrewes and his allies and heirs, above all Richard Neile (who succeeded to the major see of Durham in 1617) and Laud, lacked confidence that they could identify the faithful, or that Christ had enjoined them to do so. Convinced that the church on earth was the expression of Christian society, rather than the preserve of the elect, they asserted the historical, even apostolic, succession of the institutional church from antiquity. Calvinist bishops like Abbot and Lake might applaud the claims for episcopal dignity, and themselves talked of 'mother church', but (and James agreed with them in this) episcopacy was for them a matter of royal institution, not apostolic succession and divine right; nor did they share Andrewes's delight in corporate and corporal worship. The anti-Calvinists' distaste for what they saw as the cold intellectualism of puritan sermon-going found its apogee in the clerical poet George Herbert's pastoral ideal, *Priest to the Temple* (1633).

To label Jacobean anti-Calvinism is harder than to outline it. The Laudianism of the 1630s was certainly its direct heir, but the appearance of anti-Calvinism predated Laud's hegemony. 'Arminianism' (after the Dutch anti-Calvinist theologian Arminius) has often been suggested, but the direct influence of Arminius only becomes visible in the 1620s. Anyway, the anti-Calvinists' commitment to ceremony is as striking as their theological conviction that Christ's sacrifice was universal. Many scholars have claimed that the later term 'Anglican' is anachronistic; but we may see in Andrewes or in Herbert something that can usefully be called proto-Anglican, in their recognisably protestant yet non-Calvinist theology and their devotion to ritual, symbol, and inclusiveness.

The gradations of anti-Calvinism, from Laudian aggression to Herbert's peaceable ritualism, underscore the variety of religious life in early-seventeenth-century England. Indeed, anti-Calvinism was by no means always anti-puritanism. Prominent in the mid-century revolution were groups such as Levellers, General Baptists, above all Quakers, that seemed to emerge from a puritan milieu, yet emphatically did not hold to Calvinist teachings on grace. Pastoral pressures, and in particular the need to reach parishioners who found the doctrine of election incomprehensible, had contributed to a steady modification of Calvinism. Even in England, with its state–church and its unusually narrow and powerful university establishment, by no means all developments flowed outwards from the centre.

And in the parishes, the vitality of prayer-book worship reminds us that not all was theological controversy. Even for intellectuals the attractions of polemic sometimes palled. By the 1630s the sterility of the doctrinal battles, and the confusion brought to the church by the diverse attempts to establish godly rule, generated an impressive reaction against controversy. In despair at the arid disputes, a group of scholars (including Thomas Hobbes) gathered at Great Tew, the Oxfordshire estate of Lord Falkland, who was eventually to become a very unhappy royalist; there they aired what appear to be distinctly humanist views. Their distaste for formal theological systems that could never be verified until God made all things clear, and their preference for a charitable way of life, was to come to seem increasingly attractive.

Catholicism

The importance of anti-Catholicism in the puritan dynamic suggests that we cannot understand protestants without considering Catholics. Not only was much protestant doctrine worked out in polemic with Catholics, but protestant reformism was part of an evangelical drive affecting all of Europe. Both protestant and Catholic reformers faced a largely uneducated people given to beliefs and practices that sixteenth-century system-builders often considered heterodox. Like their protestant counterparts, Catholic bishops strove to improve clerical performance, and similarly encouraged catechising and devotional literature for the laity. Some of these works even found a market among English protestants who at first lacked their own tradition of pietism to fall back on: the youthful Richard Baxter, for one, profited from 'Bunny's' *Resolutions* – the work of the Jesuit Robert Parsons.

Indeed, the parallels between puritanism and Catholicism are striking. The displacement of the formal structure of the Roman church left English Catholicism fully as focused on the household as were its foes: thus, the Blundell family in Lancashire instituted a constant round of catechising and moral and social exhortation. And in the engagement with the established church we can see similarities. Conformist puritans participated, however reluctantly, in the ritual of church life, while nonconformists like Thomas Hooker or the Mayflower group took their discontents to the point of flight or outright separation; on the other side, 'church papists' were those whose political loyalty or caution drove them to occasional participation in protestant communion, while outright recusants withdrew wholly, and others migrated to religious orders across the Channel. In both groups too the roles of lay patrons and clergy were fundamental. If the godly preacher was needed to instil experiential Calvinism, so the priest was essential to the Catholic community locally; and while protestant gentlemen acted as patrons, the Catholic elite protected chaplains from informers and prosecution. The clusterings of puritans and Catholics in the countryside therefore reveal not so much deference to landlords' preferences as the participation of lay elite, clergy, and people in the making of the religious map. Such participation crossed the gender line, for while legal norms and office-holding make it difficult to assess women's role in the established church, less orthodox groupings, with a weaker footing in the law, had less power to restrain women's spiritual strivings. Not only were devout women on both sides of the confessional divide, such as the puritan Lady Joan Barrington and the Catholic Magdalen, Lady Montague, sometimes bolder as patrons than politically cautious males. Like the Bristol separatist leader Dorothy Hazzard, or Mary Ward, who almost established a new Roman Catholic order in 1618, they also found in religious heterodoxy one area where they could assert themselves.

Shared approaches to the problems of Christian life were nevertheless drowned in the noise of controversy. To proselytise for Rome was not only an act of political disobedience to the royal head of the established church of England; it also breached unity in a way that puritan nonconformity, even outright separatism, did not. For it seemed to urge obedience to a foreign enemy that had tried to depose Elizabeth. But although Catholic priests risked execution for treason, and lay recusants who obstinately stayed away from church risked potentially heavy fines, the penal laws, like other early-modern statutes, were for extraordinary, not continuous, use. The Gunpowder Plot in 1605 pushed James into a flurry of executions, but he sought political loyalty, not extirpation. The persecution under which twenty-five priests died in the years to 1618 was balanced by inclusion, in an attempt to extract a strict oath of allegiance from Catholic priests and laity alike, and in tolerance for prominent Catholics like the Earl of Worcester at court. To the dismay of many protestants who had their eyes on the Thirty Years War, there were no more victims until the excitement of 1641–6, when another twenty-four suffered, with a last two in 1651–4. A similar story can be told of the laity: few families were ruined by fines, for prominent Catholic families were generally accepted locally, or had friends at court to protect them: thus, the Vavasours, with an income of £2000 per annum, paid around £40 per annum to the crown. But pressure for enforcement, of these as other penal laws, came from hungry courtiers and others. The main punitive years were therefore the 1630s, despite the number of prominent Catholics at Charles's court. In general the godly republic brought a relaxation, though with some local variations.

Why then was anti-Catholicism so potent? As James assumed, lay Catholics were, after the Gunpowder Plot, far more loyal to the crown than to the pope. Many clung to Catholicism from sheer cultural conservatism, seeing in their faith continuity with their ancestors and in its adhesion to hierarchy a glowing contrast with protestant fractiousness. Catholics in the countryside were unlikely rebels. But protestant fears stemmed not simply from Catholics' past, their adherence to Rome, and their breach of unity. The binary early-modern worldview, structured around poles of good and evil, fostered assumptions that if God faced the Antichrist, the godly too had their counterparts, whose inversions and perversions corrupted the body politic. The Gunpowder Plot, the assassination of Henri IV, and then the horrors of the Thirty Years War, proved the point. And this when the numbers of English Catholics were growing, from around 30–40 000 recusants in 1603 to perhaps 60 000 by 1641. They remained few in proportion: in Yorkshire, a more Catholic county than many, recusants probably never numbered more than 2 per cent of the population. But they compensated by their prominence. Around 10 per cent of the peerage in 1641 was Catholic, and, fatally for Charles, there were unknown numbers of Catholics at court; worst of all, the number of priests soared from 250 in 1603 to over 700 in the 1630s, while the number of the Jesuits, the most feared, quadrupled. The Catholic Reformation was taking root in England; but to alarmed protestants it seemed that the Counter-Reformation was striking home.

Witchcraft

The century after 1570 saw England, Scotland and much of the rest of Europe caught up in a witch hunt whose basic dimensions are fairly clear. Although fewer than 600 were executed in England for witchcraft, that tally dwarfed the total of Catholics dispatched under the penal laws. The English figures were in turn dwarfed by the 1500 witches executed in Scotland, whose population was one-fourth of England's. The identity of the condemned is as as striking as the number. Although witches could indeed be of either gender, over four-fifths of those condemned, in both countries, were women. Most people believed that supernatural powers were real, and were available; but they were also taught from various sources that women were weaker, and more susceptible to the devil's wiles. Witch-beliefs thus reinforced, and were fed by, a variety of other prejudices.

The stereotype of the witch as the ugly old woman provides part of the explanation of the hunt, and of the character of its victms. A high proportion of English witch trials arose from the withholding of charity. A pauper requesting aid from a neighbour was rebuffed, and responded with curses. Some mishap turned the householder's guilt-feelings into a conviction of injury, and then into an accusation of *maleficium*, the evil deed on which most English witch trials centred. Protestant teachings on work, and a new commercialism, worked to undermine traditional community by impeding the flow of charity, leaving elderly widows, often marginalised, and dependent on the goodwill of their neighbours, particularly exposed. But, as an interpretive model, the failure of charity has important limitations. In many trials there was little social disparity between accuser and accused; nor does the charity argument wholly encompass Thomas Dekker's play *The Witch of Edmonton* (1619), where the witch's curse is the dramatic counter to male tyranny.

The witch hunt seems all too clearly the unacceptable face of patriarchalism. The gendered nature of prosecutions across Europe reflects a deep misogyny, and a willingness to channel that misogyny into violence against aggressive or transgressive women in a time when religious, political and socio-economic change seemed to anxious men to encourage transgression. The risks run by outspoken women are evident in the accusation of witchcraft against the visionary Anna Trapnel in 1653. Equally unmistakable is the growing sexual animus. Previous theorists had located the witch's mark (the teat at which the witch's familiar sucked) anywhere on the body; but the 1630 edition of Michael Dalton's *Country Justice*, the essential magistrate's handbook, advised that it was to be found in the genital area.

Yet misogyny alone cannot explain the witch hunt, for women were heavily involved, not only as matron searchers for the mark, but also as witnesses, and complainants. The participation of so many women in proceedings that victimised women may suggest their absorption in the dominant values of society. But it points too to the sources of power, and also the divisions, within local communities. Two areas that fell very much under women's control were the preparation of food, and childbirth. It is surely no accident that many of the accusations started here, with rumours vented by women jealous or fearful of the power of other women, rather than among men suspicious of women wielding power of any kind. But men dominated the formal proceedings. And for the men of the locality the witch sometimes served as scapegoat, allowing the source of disharmony and pollution to be cast out – many of those who fell victim to the 'witchfinder-general' amid the dislocations of wartime can be put in this category. Other cases resulted from long-running and complicated disputes, in which one faction or another seized any weapon that was to hand. And here gender bias could prove crucial. Only a readiness to objectify the woman can explain why a power-struggle in Rye between butchers and brewers could be resolved by a witchcraft charge against Anne Taylor, the wife of the leading butcher.

Feud, misogyny, the failure of charity: all were major contributors, yet none was peculiar to the years of the witch hunt. The role of the elite was crucial. Religious change and conflict, in England as elsewhere, encouraged contestants to bid for the moral high ground of purification and reform: encouraged by the new protestant clergy, parliament in 1563 and 1604 provided for the trial of witches in the secular courts, and toughened the penalties. The role of such ideological competition and vindication is still clearer in the appearance of the witch hunt in Scotland in 1591-2, in the aftermath of civil war, and in its bloody continuance in the troubled 1640s.

The state put machinery in the hands of local persecutors, but the impetus came from the intellectuals. The clergy in particular had imbibed continental theories of devil-worship and the heightened neo-Platonist tendency to populate a polarised world with angels and witches. Even the generally tolerant Sir Thomas Browne argued in his *Religio Medici* (1643) that to deny the existence of witches was to deny the existence of God. The influence of the new thinking in England is evident in the 1604 statute's emphasis on diabolism and also in the doctrine of the witch's mark, both absent from late-medieval popular witchcraft beliefs. The clerical quest for evidence of thorough-going satanism then merged with popular jealousies, with suspicions of local 'wise women' and 'cunning men' who provided remedies of various kinds, with resentment of assertive women, to create a volatile mixture.

The new theories emerged full-blown in the Lancashire scare of 1633–4, and above all in the campaign of Matthew Hopkins, the 'witchfinder-general', in East Anglia in 1645–7. Hopkins, who occasioned 200 accusations in six months in 1645 and at least 28 deaths, used to be thought un-English in his preoccupation with devil-worship, and in his rigour. But the Lancashire cases, those in East Anglia, and another wave in Kent in the early 1650s, suggest that local hatreds could have laid England as open as south Germany, Scotland, or Salem, Massachusetts, to a major witch scare.

But there were significant differences between England and other jurisdictions. The common law's presentment jury allowed popular concern with *maleficium* to predominate over more dangerous influences unloosed by the inquisitorial practices prevailing on the continent and in Scotland. Furthermore, the abnormal centralisation of the English state gave professional, and often sceptical, judges on their assize circuits considerable control over proceedings. As early as 1600 the judges were ensuring the acquittal of perhaps 60 per cent of the accused, and their impact increased once King James made his doubts clear. Only the civil-war stoppage of the assizes afforded Hopkins his opportunity in 1645. The contrast with Scotland is striking. There, once the royal theologian James VI had set proceedings in motion in 1591, his later misgivings were unable to restrain the local dignitaries, whose gusto often matched that of Matthew Hopkins.

|3|

The politic society

A traditional economy?

The economy of early-seventeenth-century England and Wales was an economy under pressure. In the century up to 1640 the population almost doubled, from less than three million to over five million. As striking was the demographic distribution. If we define towns as those settlements with populations greater than 5000, then the urban population increased from perhaps 5.25 per cent of the whole in 1520 to 13.5 per cent in 1670. The most spectacular growth occurred in London, which had around 50 000 inhabitants in 1500, and some 475 000 by 1640, making it a genuine metropolis, the largest city in Europe let alone in England.

Growing pressure on the market in the adverse climate of the 'little ice age' that set in from around 1550 brought a rapid rise in prices, since farming techniques changed only slowly. The price of the leading grains had by the end of the 1640s risen between eight- and ten-fold from their level in 1500, with rents marking a parallel path; and though wages had risen too, in real terms these had halved over the previous century. Emigration was one natural response. At first the poor looked for work and subsistence in nearby or even distant towns, but eventually many drifted as squatters to woodland areas, and beyond. Almost 2 per cent of the English population emigrated in the 1630s, and again in the 1640s; by mid-century there were probably 50 000 English colonists in the Americas, and many more had perished there. Ireland was probably still more important as a safety-valve for a booming population in a sluggish economy. It has been estimated that as many as 100 000 English and Scots may have left for Ireland in the century of confiscation and settlement after 1589. Only when countless couples began in the 1640s to marry later, and have fewer children, did pressure on resources drop, at last allowing real wages to recover in the following decade.

Like its neighbours, England was therefore in 1600 far from a sufficiency in the necessaries of life. Widespread deaths from famine in the bleak years of the later 1590s were followed by renewed starvation in 1623 in the isolated northwest. The state of the weather was quite literally a matter of life and death: a bad harvest occurred on average every four years, and the poor yields reflected in a seed to crop ratio that was often as low as 1:3 or 1:4 meant that one failure often bred another as small farmers were driven to eat their seed-corn. The consequences for the labouring poor who in normal years may have spent 70 per cent of their income on rent, food and drink could be disastrous.

The effects of rainy summers were compounded as soaring food prices soaked up resources that would otherwise have been spent on manufactured goods. Falling industrial incomes then added to the misery of high prices. That conjunction accounts for the abnormal suffering in 1623 and the later 1640s, when the hungry took to the roads in alarming numbers. And of course bad weather reduced output as well as demand. Prolonged rain, or heavy frosts, halted work in the fields; fluctuations in water and wind prevented mills grinding, left cold Londoners without their 'sea coal' from Newcastle, and stinted water-intensive industries like tanning and soap-boiling. Much of the labour force had little prospect of year-round employment, so the ability of all members of a poor family to find odd jobs was crucial to survival.

Low productivity was endemic. Dismal hygiene and medical skills left average life expectancy at birth wavering in the mid-30s, though a fourteen-year-old who had survived the dangerous years of infancy could count on perhaps another forty years of life. Less than 50 per cent of the population therefore fell within the age-range of efficient work, from 15 to 50. The various ailments, from 'griping in the guts' to toothache, spawned by the dietary deficiencies common to all classes diminished efficiency still further. Incentives such as consumer goods or avenues for social mobility that might have spurred productivity were lacking. Leisure was therefore the rational choice for the labouring poor when good times did occur, and pulpits thundered vainly against idleness and drink. Indeed, in one week in 1632 carters carried into London over 30 per cent more malt, for beer, than bread-corn. Only the increasing variety and cheapness of consumer goods in the later seventeenth century could generate new habits.

Cultural barriers to economic expansion were legion. Lending money at interest, or 'usury', was discouraged in sermons and on stage; but borrowing too had its risks. Though the official rate of interest fell from 10 per cent to 8 per cent in 1624, borrowers faced large forfeitures for even the most technical of defaults on short- or long-term loans. The law, geared as it was to a landed past, hampered business in other ways, making scant provision in matters of fraud, liability, recovery, agency and partnership. Much can be inferred of official attitudes from the government's suspicion of the one significant labour-saving invention, the stocking-frame, developed late in Elizabeth's reign for weaving hosiery, which seemed likely to increase unemployment. Early-modern governments impeded business in various ways, for they tended to treat the economy as a source of plunder. Customs tariffs drew few distinctions between exports and imports, between manufactures and raw materials. Penniless monarchs gratified courtiers by granting them monopoly patents, which increased costs and diminished supplies.

The record of foreign trade seems to highlight the undynamic nature of the English economy. London's exports were in 1640 still dominated by textiles as they had been a century before: almost 87 per cent of the value of total exports came from cloth, with other manufactures providing a mere 2.3 per cent. And the textile trade was firmly in the hands of oligarchy. About half of London's exports, the traditional partly finished broadcloths sent to Germany and the Low Countries, were shipped by one company, the Merchant Adventurers; half of this trade was controlled by twenty-six men. The one significant sign of change was that, by 1640, re-exports, largely colonial products, amounted to 6.4 per cent in value of the capital's exports: this was a harbinger of England's profitable later role as Europe's entrepot. The main cloth export, broadcloth, faced growing competition in Europe: this old-established industry was handicapped by restrictive practices, by shifting patterns of sheeprearing which affected the quality of the fleece grown, and most important from 1620 by currency manipulations in the major market of the Baltic and north Germany that reduced English competitiveness. Though Spain and the Mediterranean provided a growing market for the lighter 'new draperies', and proved a valuable source of luxuries and spices, that trade was repeatedly disrupted in the decades after 1620 by political instability in war-torn Europe and ultimately in England too. Despite the short-lived boom that came with peace in 1604, the record of England's foreign trade was therefore one of recurrent crisis.

The newer branches of trade offered as yet little recompense. The East India Company, that was eventually to prove so lucrative, and that had shown such dazzling promise after its foundation in 1600, faltered in the 1620s. Dutch competition, at its most brutal in the Amboyna massacre of 1623, drove the company out of the Spice Islands (now Indonesia); its operations in India were of scant appeal yet to a non-tea-drinking people. And like the Levant Company (which traded to the eastern Mediterranean), the East India Company was handicapped by political problems at home. It was unpopular because in order to bring back its spices, silks and calicoes it exported bullion, and seemed to drain the domestic economy of its coin; and insolvent monarchs and courtiers regarded the Company as a rich cow to be milked. Only slowly would the re-export potential of its imports, and their capacity to change tastes in England, become apparent.

The westward trade was equally dispiriting. England's American colonies were not the Eldorado for which the Elizabethan explorers had hoped. Although 50 000 colonists had settled there by 1640, these offered neither a regular nor a wealthy market for English products; nor could their own products revitalise the English economy. Only the wholesale importation of African slaves from around mid-century transformed the faltering Caribbean tobacco economies into the labour-intensive sugar producers on which much of England's later re-export prosperity was to be based. The other tobacco-growing colony, Virginia, fared even worse for much of our period. The gentry and merchants who flocked to invest in the Virginia Company in James's early years had hoped for bullion, but these hopes soon evaporated along with the investments. Competition from the superior tobacco of the Spanish colonies, and ill-prepared settlers, brought the colony close to collapse in the 1610s and 1620s. It was only saved by the introduction of a better strain of tobacco, and by 1640 Virginia and Maryland (founded in 1633) were exporting about two million pounds of tobacco yearly. The northern colonies, the New England settlements established in the 1620s, proved still more disappointing economically. Although they are often thought to have been havens of conscience rather than enterprise, and quite different from the southern colonies, most of the early migrants were, like the Virginia or Caribbean settlers, driven by hardship, by over-population and depression in England. And hard soil and harsh climate meant that New England made a poor substitute for the riches of Mexico and Peru, or even for the Spice Islands lost to the Dutch. Nevertheless, in the 1630s signs appeared of the individualist enterprise that was eventually to build an empire piecemeal. In that decade, attempts to establish on Providence Island a bastion against Spain in the Caribbean faltered as English settlers pursued even to New England the dream of absolute private property that common lawyers were fast articulating, and turned away from southern shores where English planners sought to bolster landlords' rights.

The gloomy tone of so much economic writing is therefore hardly surprising. England seemed to have picked the wrong sites to build its empire; its main export, broadcloth, was losing ground; and in every area the Dutch, with their more advanced credit organisation and their far more effective shipbuilding techniques, were edging out English competition. The only exception was the Mediterranean, where the bulky Dutch fluits were ill-suited to withstand Barbary corsairs. The English response was characteristically defensive. Commerce ought as much as possible to be organised in great trading companies, like the East India or the Levant companies, where it could be regulated and protected. As much as possible Dutch ways should be emulated. And where they could not be emulated the Dutch should be excluded: that of course was the rationale of the Navigation Acts of 1651 and beyond. But for the moment, England's balance of trade seemed dangerously precarious, particularly in the 1620s. Any outflow of payments would mean an outflow of coin, and in a society without effective credit mechanisms a shortage of coin could bring economic activity to a stop.

Economic change

Historians' fixation with foreign trade has resulted more from the fact that the records are there, in the customs figures, than from its intrinsic importance. Although exports allowed the import, in return, of goods that helped London merchants make fortunes and eventually, as they cheapened, proved crucial in changing ordinary tastes, the export trade was dwarfed by an often highly localised internal economy that was probably at least twice as large. Even in Jacobean London half the aldermen, the merchant princes, were domestic traders. And in contrast to the faltering export trade, the internal economy was not only diversifying but growing considerably.

London was not the sole 'engine of growth', but its growing impact on the nation was the most obvious feature of internal development. The concentration of the sale of England's major export, broadcloth, at the single mart of Antwerp for much of the sixteenth century had elevated nearby London's role as the other axis of the trade. 'Outports' like Southampton and Boston had been overwhelmed by the competition, and increasingly the nation's commercial and financial activities centred in the capital, to considerable provincial resentment. London's dominance was growing still further. While the capital shipped 77 per cent of the country's new drapery exports in 1610, the figure had risen to 85 per cent by the 1640s. The anxieties of the southwestern ports drove bitter protests from MPs as peace with Spain in 1604 opened the prospect of London dominance of yet another trade route. Overall, the concentration of trade and resources helped generate economic advance. Wage-rates in the booming capital were double the national average, and as London drove its supply lines far up the east coast as well as deep into the Midlands it did much to stimulate growth. London's grain imports quintupled between the 1570s and the 1630s. Entrepreneurial farmers, especially the market gardeners in London's immediate hinterland, the coastwise shipping industry, Newcastle's coal trade: all owed much to Londoners' hunger.

The Newcastle region was by no means alone in its integration into an increasingly national economy. Progress should not be exaggerated. The costs and delays of inland transport, especially by road, meant that pastoral regions still grew grain for bread and beer. Outlying upland counties periodically had difficulty in sending taxes to London, especially in winter, since so little traffic went that way, and cross-country contacts by road were even more difficult – indeed, the average price of wheat in Devon late in the dearth year of 1631 was 50 per cent higher than in neighbouring Dorset. Nevertheless, growing specialisation in agriculture accounts for the fame of Cheshire cheese and Worcestershire apples. Transport ties to London were sufficiently developed for John Taylor's *Carrier's Cosmography* in 1637 to give details of carriers linking the capital with all regions. By the 1630s regular stage coaches linked London with major towns in the southeast and Midlands, and by the 1650s

Edinburgh and most major provincial cities had been drawn into the coaching network. More substantial connections appeared by mid-century, as inns along the scarp slope separating the Severn and Thames valleys allowed traders to join the hinterlands of Bristol and London.

A commercial economy had advanced further in England than in any other part of Europe save northern Italy and The Netherlands. The permanent retail shop slowly spread from London (and scattered outliers could even be found in the mountainous northwest by 1600), while brokers and middlemen traded in bulk in roadside inns. There are signs too of a critically important shift towards consumer values. Most sixteenth-century Warwickshire probate inventories listed livestock first, while a century later all began with an increasing variety of household goods. Even quite humble families increasingly cooked in brass instead of iron pots, ate off pewter instead of wooden bowls, and wore knitted stockings. The new commodity of tobacco, millions of pounds of which were being smoked by mid-century, spawned new demands, not just for the weed but for pouches, and the clay pipes that were being manufactured in Bristol by the 1640s. The rise of the 'new draperies' reinforced this shift in attitudes. Clothing for ordinary people up to the late sixteenth century was a household good: thick broadcloth garments endured, to be left to children in parents' wills. Even with a booming market in used clothes, the costs of clothing the ever-increasing number of bodies could have been ruinous, but from around the start of our period cheaper and lighter fabrics spread fast. Since these bays and perpetuanas could be highly coloured they also allowed the indulgence of fashion. The age of the consumer society, and of civility too, was dawning. By the 1650s coffee-houses began to appear in London and Oxford.

Change was occurring, though at a slow pace. The growth of London and the forging of a national economy were both cause and effect of developments in both agriculture and industry. In agriculture the gradual spread of new techniques was symbolised by a new vogue in handbooks, such as Walter Blith's *The English Improver* (1649). As the market expanded more attention was given to the crops and farming practices best suited to local soils: the growing popularity of 'convertible' or 'up-and-down' husbandry, alternating periods of arable and pasture, is evident across much of lowland England. More striking still is the way many farmers, small as well as large, converted to new cash crops like madder and woad for dye, to tobacco in the Severn valley, as well as to market gardening around towns. Although the full impact of the new crops was only to be felt after mid-century, when slackening demand encouraged farmers to raise productivity, England slowly outstripped much of the rest of Europe in its ability to feed and employ a growing population. Starvation in the crisis of 1623 was limited to the northwest; and thereafter, despite appalling hardship in the later 1640s, famine seems to have been more or less eliminated.

Industrial change was similarly piecemeal. Coal production in the northeast was certainly accelerating: thus, shipments from Newcastle rose from 33 000 tons in 1563–4 to 453 000 tons in 1633–4, with much of this expansion occurring after 1610. That expansion once gave rise to claims for an 'industrial revolution' in this period. But what is surely significant here is that coal's industrial uses were largely limited to glass-making (from 1612), the production of salt, and the manufacture of nails and other low-grade metal wares. Most of the demand came from London households, and household demand is the key to much of the industrial development of this period. So too with lead, whose production tripled between 1610 and 1630: most of the output went on London and provincial roofs. And the expansion of lead- and tin-mining was outpaced by glove- and lace-making and by the new draperies (all of which had benefited from the skills of immigrants from the Low Countries in Elizabeth's reign). By 1640 the value of new drapery exports was beginning to vie with the product of the traditional broadcloth industry. But most of the nails, needles and pins produced by the metalware industry in the West Midlands were for the domestic market, as were the shoes of Northampton, and the sedan chairs, musical instruments, wagon wheels, clothes and so much else made in London.

The household was the centre of production as well as consumption. Wage-earning was spreading in the larger coal mines of the northeast and, rather more contentiously, in the Derbyshire lead mines; but everywhere industrial production occurred in family workshops and in cottages. The entrepreneur, who might deal with few outside his own family in the textile areas of West Yorkshire or up to perhaps 500 in the new draperies of East Anglia, provided domestic workers with raw materials and sometimes even with tools; he then collected their product, usually paying them piece rates.

The prevalence of domestic production in textiles, in leather-working, in most branches of the metal industry, makes it impossible to measure economic distress. Cost-of-living figures measure prices in the market. Much of the population was engaged in both agriculture and industry: the small farmer whose wife and servant did some subsidiary spinning or stocking-knitting, the artisan miner with a small plot of land attached to his cottage, even Norwich labourers who did harvest-work in nearby fields in the 1630s, and gleaned after the harvest. The numbers of entirely landless grew, above all in London. But while real wages fell markedly, work was often available for the whole family. People therefore had to work much harder than their ancestors in 1500 to keep alive, but low wages did not cause total privation. The new industries proved critical here, providing considerable support for an expanding and otherwise probably unemployed labour force. It has been estimated that stocking-knitting alone provided year-round employment for 100 000. The diary of the Rev. Ralph Josselin shows graphically how the varied local economy of Earl's Colne preserved the poor in the bleak years of the later 1640s. Over a longer period such diversity helped England escape the horrors of starvation which hit Scotland and France in the later seventeenth century.

Social groups

Early-seventeenth-century England was not bound to the unchanging values of the soil. But though economic change supported a burgeoning population, it tended to subvert the corporate assumptions of the body politic. In medieval theory (if never entirely in practice), trade and industry had been safely confined to towns and to guild structures, while farming had been arranged around manors, where lords dealt with a collectivity of more-or-less neatly stratified peasants. But by 1600 industry was well established, and deregulated, in the countryside and still more the suburb; guilds and manorial courts were withering under pressure of the market and mobility; and English agriculture was headed towards its modern pattern of a small number of large farmers and large numbers of the landless.

Elizabethan and Jacobean social commentators reacted fearfully, increasingly dividing the populace not into tranquil rankings of status and occupation but into two blunt categories – 'the better sort' (a term that might include the gentry but more often was used for the minor local elites of town and village), and 'the meaner sort' or 'the vulgar'. Such terms of opposition and distaste underly the concern of parliament-men and preachers with discipline, and the increasing recourse in the first two or three decades of the century to capital sanctions in defence of property. As the wealthy townsmen of Manningtree in Essex complained in 1627, their poorer, alehouse-haunting neighbours were now 'so rustical that for the better sort it is almost no living with them'.

But by then another element could be heard: in 1620 a gang from Wooton Bassett in Wiltshire looking for a fight demanded, 'Where were the middle sort of men in Tockenham?' Indeed, the novel category of 'the middling sort' was to become a prime component of social analysis of the civil war. Royalists and parliamentarians alike saw the king's supporters clustered at the two ends of the spectrum, while the middling sort (independent small farmers, craftsmen, traders) seemed drawn towards parliament, and puritanism. The emergence of this group into view in the early seventeenth century undoubtedly signals the immiseration of 'the poorer sort', from whom they were now increasingly distanced; but it also signals the crystallisation of a stratum that probably contained between a third and a half of all households. That stratum, increasingly literate and certainly litigious, had considerable socio-economic, cultural, and political significance.

The early seventeenth century thus saw the beginnings of a reorientation of society, towards groupings that would eventually yield themselves to class analysis. Yet status groups, and most of all the titular nobility, remained the first concern of all social commentators. The peers usually had rent rolls of over £3000 pa, and influence to match. Compared to the proliferating nobilities of France and Spain they were few, less than sixty in number in 1603, rather more than twice that a generation later. Nevertheless, they did not form a caste. English noblemen were taxed, they could marry commoners, and engage in trade. The demands of blood, lineage and land were further confused when the early Stuarts ennobled great merchants and financiers, Lionel Cranfield, Earl of Middlesex, and Baptist Hickes, Viscount Camden. But the nobility did not need new blood to teach them that status was empty without money. The fourth Earl of Bedford was perhaps the greatest property speculator of his day, and even noblemen as conservative as the Earl of Devonshire eagerly exploited the mineral resources found on their estates. Such entrepreneurial peers provide a warning against any simplistic dichotomy between 'feudal' and 'capitalist'. They also help explain how the values and goals of so many noblemen could overlap with those of parliamentarians in the City and House of Commons in the 1640s.

The peers had on the whole recovered well from the temporary financial difficulties caused by the inflation of the late sixteenth century. They had extensive landholdings, and this was a period of fierce land hunger. As tenancies came up for renewal, they raised rents, and entry fines for new tenants, sometimes to dramatic effect. Successive Earls of Pembroke far outpaced the inflationary curve through their estate policies. By 1641 the peers were richer than their predecessors had been in 1558, and many of them had built lavishly in the new fashions. There was, however, a price to pay. As landlords, and particularly absentee landlords, rationalised their holdings, they risked the resentment of their tenants and the loss of political influence. The determination shown by the Earl of Newcastle's 'whitecoats' in the Civil War was rare among tenants.

That the relative position of the aristocracy had changed is evident in the different forms taken by the civil wars of the fifteenth and seventeenth centuries. Nevertheless, the stress should fall on the word 'relative'. The peers had grown richer; but so too had other groups. The combined income of the five richest peers may have been less than £75 000 per annum, when the total income of the untitled gentry in pre-war Kent alone probably ran close to three times that figure; at the same time non-landed, urban wealth increased dramatically, and both literacy and religious division grew apace. Society was growing less hierarchical, and the position of the peerage was affected. Morale may also have suffered from the crown's sale of titles in the 1610s and 1620s, which increased the number of earls, for example, by 141 per cent. And fashion accelerated the change. The coach, fast-spreading among the elite from the middle of James's reign, points to tastes not just for luxury but also privacy. Privacy was symbolised too in that long-drawn architectural shift from the medieval great hall for hospitality to the polite entrance hall that was complete by the Restoration. Privacy of course challenged the very concept of a body politic in which all relationships were politically charged.

Yet the adulation shown in print and in public demonstrations during the 1620s for protestant stalwarts like the Earls of Pembroke, Essex and Southampton suggests little fall in the prestige of the aristocratic order as such. That adulation certainly suggests a conviction that hierarchy and place ought to be contingent on service; nevertheless, noblemen on the eve of the Civil War were scarcely in crisis. The demise of the House of Lords in 1649 owes almost everything to political rather than to social change.

The next tier down the pyramid was occupied by the gentry, of whose aggregate wealth there is no doubt. Historians estimate that the early-seventeenth-century gentry made up between 2 and 3 per cent of the populace, and owned perhaps 40 per cent of the land. Yet their identity was and is notoriously indistinct. Commentators agreed that gentle birth and way of life were essential; but what was that way of life, when in 1642 one-third of those deemed gentlemen in Yorkshire had less than £100 per annum, while two had over £4000 per annum? A plausible solution is to divide the status-group of gentlemen along economic lines. We would then distinguish parochial gentry, whose estates were limited to a single parish or settlement, from county gentry, whose lands spread more widely, and in turn from the greater gentry, such as the Yorkshire-man Sir Thomas Wentworth, whose estates might fall in several shires. Since this was still a basically landed society, the degree of land holding had the appropriate political consequences: the more land a gentlemen held, the higher he might rise in local government and politics.

Ultimately, to be a gentleman was to be thought a gentleman by one's neighbours. The newly rich, buying an estate and aping gentry ways, might very soon be thought gentlemen: as Sir Thomas Smith, an Elizabethan commentator, concluded, 'Gentlemen be made good cheap in England.' The contrast with France or Spain, where the connection between land and commerce was far more tenuous and where status was much more a matter of descent, was important both for England's socio-political and its economic development.

The relative ease of access to gentility meant that the numbers of gentry increased fast in a period when both the profits from land and the population as a whole were multiplying. There were for example seventy-eight more gentry families in Lincolnshire in 1634 than there had been in 1562, and over England as a whole gentry numbers probably tripled between 1540 and 1640, from around 6000 to perhaps 18 000. In this sense at least it is possible to talk of the 'rise of the gentry', one of the old subjects of historians' controversy. But gentility is not reducible to the economics of production or even of consumption. It involved descent, declared in the increasingly ornate tombs with which gentry families flaunted their status, and in the genealogy through which gentlemen proclaimed their pedigrees.

And it involved as well a way of life that extended beyond leisured pursuits to include, many argued, a care for the commonweal. While Ben Jonson's 'To Penshurst' displayed the ideal of the non-exploitative landlord, the rioters who destroyed the Midlands enclosures of Sir Thomas Tresham in 1607 offered a warning to gentlemen who oppressed their neighbours.

Shading away gradually from the bottom ranks of the gentry were the yeomen, who can best be characterised as large farmers of up to perhaps 100 acres (depending on soil type). Like the gentry, the yeomen were on the whole getting richer, as the profits of those producing for the market grew. The evidence is again visible in the buildings, and also in probate inventories, which show increasing domestic comfort, with pewter and sometimes even silver utensils replacing wood, and with glass in the windows and cloth 'hangings' to keep out the draughts. Though he might grow rich and acquire comforts, the mark of the yeoman was to shun the cultivated idleness of his superiors. And below the yeomen on the lower rungs of the landed hierarchy clustered the hard-pressed husbandmen, small or marginal farmers with perhaps twelve to fifty acres. Beneath these proliferated the cottagers and labourers, whose lives grew more miserable as prices rose.

Changes were occurring at this level as well as at the top. The degree to which English farming has ever been 'peasant', or largely egalitarian and subsistence in character, can be exaggerated, but detailed local studies have found that at the beginning of our period many communities were closer to the stereotyped peasant cluster of near-subsistence farms than they were at the end. While 'fielden', or arable, areas already contained many large capital-intensive farms employing landless labourers, in most regions significant numbers of husbandmen still worked the land, with no large pool of the landless beneath them. Half a century later conditions were changing. Continued population growth drove the burgeoning poor to areas where they could find living room and livelihoods, particularly to the towns and to woodland regions with sufficient waste land where they could erect squatters' hovels. While the core of yeomen and husbandmen in the swelling villages of the forest of Arden in Warwickshire, or in Myddle in Shropshire, remained relatively stable, a new class of landless paupers, comprising about one-third of the population, had appeared below them by mid-century.

In many fielden villages too an agricultural proletariat was forming. Although the lords of the manors could often restrain immigration, and the proliferation of the poor that accompanied it, they could not check all economic forces. Thus, in Orwell, Cambridgeshire, the disastrous harvests of the late 1590s and the continuing difficult conditions in the new century combined to wipe out many marginal farmers, polarising the inhabitants into rich and poor even more effectively than did the expansion downwards of the populations of the woodland and urban zones.

Throughout the arable belt, the spread of commercial farming, coupled with inflation, encouraged landlords to put pressure on marginal small-holders unable to pay rents per acre that might seem economic to the larger farmer producing for the market. In 1600 between a quarter and a third of England's rural populace were labourers, but by 1700 that fraction had risen to around a half.

In the long run, social polarisation probably helped to pacify agrarian England. The growing wealth of the yeomen, often the purchasers of the lands of failing husbandmen, tied them closer in values to their gentry superiors than to their inferior neighbours. And since they drew with them many of the rural craftsmen, few local worthies remained who were willing to give a political lead to the agrarian poor. Although the more slowly polarising forest regions of the southwest and the fenlands of eastern England saw extensive disturbances in the 1620s and 1630s, the countryside after 1650 was far less troubled by popular disturbance than it had been in the previous century. Nevertheless, the alarming reality was the relative and absolute growth in the numbers of the poor.

Social reorientation and differentiation were no less evident in towns. Immigrants who flooded to the suburbs outside the walls broke down the regulated pattern of absorption into the urban body: thus, early-Stuart London took nearly 4000 apprentices a year, but swallowed just as many newcomers who did not seek that traditional entry. Indeed, London had some of the same powers of attraction, in its casual labouring jobs, charity and crime, as the modern third-world megalopolis. The literature of the 1590s abounds with visions of a pullulating urban underworld of pickpockets and prostitutes, and Jonson's Jacobean dramas extend the dramatisation of the capital's low-life, suggesting something of a frontier ethos.

Distortion at the bottom, of which London's was clearly an extreme case, was widespread. But urban populations were filling out in more ways than one. Testifying to the presence of new resources, and new attractions, were the sons of gentry and professionals who increasingly gravitated into the higher-status merchant guilds: in London, but also in Bristol and Newcastle, offspring of the elite constituted an ever-increasing proportion of the seventeenth-century apprentice population. But whatever the economic benefits, such an intake brought new stresses, and from the end of the sixteenth century magistrates complained that apprentices were aping gentry fashions and showing a new disrespect for their elders. Nevertheless, even London retained the traditional characteristics of the trading town. Despite some immense fortunes like those of Cranfield and Hickes, most City merchants were no richer than parochial gentry. And though suburbs went largely unregulated, within the walls the City's guilds, great and small – Haberdashers, Grocers, Fishmongers and the rest – still dominated commercial and political life. Those seeking to trade needed to join, while the City's government meshed with the senior officers of the richer guilds.

London's role as social and political capital was becoming as important as its commercial and industrial dominance. While the law courts attracted an ever-growing procession of litigants, royal administration brought a flood of suitors to the City and to its twin, Westminster. As the nation's leaders beat a path to London, a service sector developed to cater to their expensive tastes. Gentry sent their sons to the inns of court, London's equivalent of a law school, for a year or so to acquire polite ways as well as a smattering of legal knowledge; after 1650 their daughters increasingly attended polite boarding-schools in the suburbs. Amusement centres like the Spring Gardens flourished; and by the Restoration, as the coach made travel easier for women, the beginnings of the London 'season' for polite society were apparent. A 1632 government census found almost a quarter of the peerage, and 250 of the gentry, resident in London without good reason. Indeed, by mid-century cosmopolitan aristocratic and gentry families, like the Pelhams of Sussex, had begun to purchase town houses: for them London visits were no longer dictated by litigation or political needs. Covent Garden, developed by the Earl of Bedford to the designs of Inigo Jones, pioneered the development of fashionable squares in the less smoky west end. The upshot was that the city increased not just in numbers but also in riches: by mid-century, while it contained one-twelfth of the nation's population it also contained one-eighth of the assessed wealth.

London was not yet megalopolis, and it was still possible to walk from end to end of the metropolis in a morning. But it was growing fast, and the smoke pollution was such that on a clear day in January 1652 a Dutch visitor to St Paul's cathedral was unable to see the nearby Tower from the roof. Paupers huddled in squalid tenements, behind the fashionable quarter in the west, in alleys and yards hidden by merchants' palaces in the City, and in some sections of the poorer east. One building in the relatively prosperous City parish of St Michael, Cornhill, had over ten inhabitants to a room in 1637. It was in the suburbs that the real boom occurred: in Southwark, there were said to have been 3000 workers in the leather trades alone in 1619, and by mid-century the population of the eastern suburbs was probably 50 000. Nevertheless, across the metropolis most housing was occupied by single families. Open tracts like Moorfields still dotted the landscape, and to the south and east Southwark and Stepney were genuinely separate communities, with their own neighbourhoods and networks.

Other towns stayed closer to their ancient roots. The 'poet' John Taylor, visiting the cathedral city of Winchester in 1623, reported 'almost as many parishes as people within its walls'. Contemporaries recognised some 800 market towns, but the claims of many to urban status seem suspect. Apart from London, only Norwich had over 20 000 inhabitants, with the other provincial centres of Bristol, Newcastle and declining York exceeding 10 000. London and the provincial centres were clearly genuinely urban, with a wide range of specialised occupations: Bristol in particular was finding new prosperity in the Atlantic trades. Elsewhere, Northampton had its leather-workers, fast-growing Birmingham its metal-workers, Leeds its clothiers and Wigan its pewterers. But most towns should be thought of as rural service centres, contrasted with their hinterlands not so much occupationally or socially as in density and administrative structure. In third-ranking towns with a population of 5000 or more, such as Worcester or Exeter, streets were likely to end in open country, orchards dotted the 'townscape', and dungheaps and wandering pigs were common traffic hazards. In such settlements, as the activation of Dorchester after the 1613 fire showed, the language of community still had power to move; but elsewhere economic change and the widening of markets and horizons began to challenge that identity. The political troubles within London, Bristol, Leeds, around mid-century cannot be detached from a growing sense of the inefficacy of corporate ideals and controls.

The steady transformation of the domestic economy is evident in social diversification. Not only were a range of new trades appearing in the biggest cities; the professions (the law, medicine, the church) were beginning to complicate the social hierarchy. Professionals grew in number even faster that did the gentry. At least twenty-two physicians practised in the prosperous cathedral city of Canterbury between 1603 and 1643, while the number of attornies active in the counties of Devon, Hertfordshire and Warwickshire quadrupled between 1580 and 1640. By mid-century the proportion of lawyers in the population stood at twentieth-century levels. Those numbers rested on robust demand: 70 per cent of litigants in the main common law courts in 1600 came from outside the landed elite. And those numbers not only reflected national prosperity; professionals amassed private resources and established themselves locally. Attornies in particular entered the urban elites: in Northampton, the proportion of the town's wealth held by professionals rose to one-tenth by 1640, from nil around 1600.

But social diversification by no means represented a challenge to traditional values. While 'professional' qualifications became increasingly necessary, inherited connection was almost as important to success in a profession as it was to land-owning families. The legal dynasties – the Bacons, the Whitelockes, the Finches – are notorious. They are matched amongst the clergy, and the tomb of the wife of the Jacobean archbishop Mathew of York could proclaim her close relation to two archbishops and five bishops. More generally, one-quarter of the Jacobean incumbents in the diocese of Exeter had succeeded to their fathers' church livings, giving another meaning to the legal fact that such livings were accounted freeholds. Landed society and professional society interpenetrated at every level. Younger sons of gentry looked for advancement, and their numbers amongst the clergy doubled between 1600 and 1640. Conversely, successful lawyers bought landed estates; the greatest of them, Sir Edward Coke, held enough acres to gain election to parliament for two separate counties in the 1620s. The leading clerical dignitaries were also landed magnates, and, lower down, the ordinary country minister was often a working farmer too, on the glebe lands attached to his living.

The social claims of the professions were, however, by no means wholly accepted. Many were the complaints against upstart and grasping lawyers. Indeed, it has been estimated that only a half of those called to the bar were sons of gentry. The protests swelled to a crescendo in the revolutionary years, with calls for the abolition of the whole profession. The clergy too were in social terms something of an anomaly, since despite their rising educational standards, their aspirations to status did not match their material rewards. Bishops still sat in the House of Lords, but they married their children into gentry families. Some said they were lucky to do that when Archbishop Laud was the son of a Reading clothworker and Archbishop Neile of York the son of a London tallow chandler: 'excrementa mundi' [the world's excrement] Lord Brooke called them on the eve of their fall. Similarly, although the parish minister might be addressed as a gentleman he was usually no richer than a yeoman, despite the efforts of benefactors from Laud to Cromwell to improve his lot. It is not unlikely that the hostility to clerical pretensions that ran strongly in the 1640s and '50s drew some of its fire from such discrepancies.

One further group, comprising half the population, was of and yet not of the prevailing hierarchy. Unlike their menfolk, women were identified in formal documents not by occupation but by their marital status. Symbolic subordination was affirmed at common law, since the military origin of land law meant that, except as widows, women in their own right could neither hold land nor proceed at common law. Only in widowhood did women achieve a measure of independence, with control over property or, in some towns, the right to practise their husbands' trades. But such rights were severely qualified. The widow usually received only 33 per cent of the family resources that the widower would have received. The case of Oxford, where only twenty-two widows traded in their own right between 1500 and 1800, and Bristol, where women comprised around 2 per cent of apprentices bound between 1600 and 1645 suggest something of women's occupational plight.

Economic realities bore out the biases of the law's presumptions. Of course, among the middling and meaner sorts women always played a central role in the domestic economy. They helped on the farm or in the shop, and they managed the household. In London, in particular, countless women had jobs outside the home; but, as in later centuries, these were overwhelmingly in the low-paid support sector, in catering, cleaning,

care-giving. At harvest-time, when men and women worked in compara-
ble jobs, women's wages averaged between one- and two-thirds of men's.
The deaths of perhaps 85 000 men in combat in England's civil wars from
1642–51 created an acute labour shortage that probably brought some
partial amelioration, but if so it was short-lived and, of course, offset by
loss. Broader trends were similarly mixed, and scholars dispute whether
women gained from new employment opportunities in a diversifying
economy, or lost as production began to shift outside the home.

Even in the more formal world of the law, women were by no means
helpless. As we have seen, in the London ecclesiastical courts they formed
a majority of litigants. More generally, the equity courts of chancery and
requests offered considerable relief to women in a matter of crucial
concern, their rights to inheritances and to property settled on them at
marriage. It has been estimated that in 1600 about 40 per cent of litigants
in these courts were women. Furthermore, the growing prosperity of the
'middling sort of people' – merchants, craftsmen, yeomen – meant that
more men made wills, and in due course many of these appointed their
wives executrix. These legal developments contributed to the relative
freedom, by European standards, of propertied English women by the
eighteenth century: in the seventeenth century visitors from abroad were
often struck by the social latitude women had negotiated for themselves,
most particularly in their ability to go to the alehouse.

Nevertheless, the formal subordination of women was intense. Among
the elite, primogeniture (inheritance by first-born males) ensured the exclusion of many women from most estate matters. The Wentworth family's
estate was built on an heiress's fortune, but his father's advice to Sir
Thomas Wentworth, future Earl of Strafford, rings with assumptions of
female inferiority. Such assumptions derived from convictions about the
weakness and imbalance of woman's body, and therefore mind; but they
drew also on a prejudice that went deeper than the story of Eve. The
prevalence of the phrase 'the Whore of Babylon' as an alternative to
'Antichrist' speaks beyond a hatred of Rome to an unease about female
sexuality; so too does the fact that sexual slander of men ('whoremonger',
'cuckold') drew its force from their failure to control female sexuality.
Accordingly, shaming rituals, such as duckings or 'Skimmington rides',
directed at turbulent wives occurred over a wide area of England, and may
have been increasing as the perception grew that gendered authority was
threatened. Thus, around 1600 the borough of Nottingham began to duck
turbulent women, instead of fining them. The witch charge provided a
final sanction.

The dominant male may have had his own insecurities: the proliferation in James's reign of tracts like *Haec vir* ('this man-woman'), satirising
the effeminacy of courtly and cosmopolitan standards, suggests as much.
The male was nevertheless taught not to compensate through callousness.
Preachers and moralists like William Gouge instructed wives to obey, but

they urged husbands to cherish – their emphasis on companionate marriage may not be unconnected to the fact that unlike their pre-Reformation predecessors they were themselves likely to be married. Evidence in diaries of emotional reciprocity and the sharing of decisions is buttressed by countless wills that made the widow the executrix. And among the elite many were the wives and mothers who acted informally as brokers for their menfolk, securing favours, or support at election time. The redoubtable Anne Clifford, Countess of Dorset, was even capable of defending her inheritance against husband, king and privy council. Nevertheless, even such figures only acquired a political capacity in exceptional circumstances: the roles of Lady Brilliana Harley and the Countess of Derby during the Civil War sieges of their absent husbands' houses, and the many royalists' wives who pleaded their husbands' cases before the parliamentary committee of compounding, are examples. Most telling is the case of the Levellers, who advocated a remarkable degree of democracy in the 1640s. While women figured prominently in their demonstrations, and while Elizabeth Lilburne, wife of one of the Leveller leaders, was prominent in the movement in her own right, the Levellers stopped short of demanding political rights or legal reforms for women.

The prominence of women as religious patrons and religious activists, both in England and elsewhere, surely owes much to their exclusion from other stages. The practice of piety was almost the only legitimate way for women to assert themselves on the same stage as men. Yet such activity was not usually mere compensation: writings as diverse as those of Aemilia Lanyer and Margaret Fell the Quaker suggest the importance of the doctrine of Christian equality and, still more, of the conviction that women presented a particularly human – because vulnerable – accessibility to Christ. The spreading belief among the protestant sects at mid-century that God spoke directly to the individual, of either sex, and that those to whom God spoke might participate fully in the church, underlay the large role of women in groups like the Quakers. The fierce male reaction the sects provoked can be at least partly understood from the fact that Quakers wrote almost half the works by women published in the 1650s.

Subordination scarcely tells the whole story. Whatever the lawyers' formularies and the theologians' treatises, in everyday practice women had what has been called their 'separate sphere', which was tacitly removed from male intervention. Women controlled the purchase and preparation of food, and all matters relating to childbirth. These activities had their own rituals; and though, like 'churching' (the ceremony through which women were readmitted to the church after childbirth), these sometimes intersected with the male domain, they centred and affirmed female networks. It is no accident that our word 'gossip' arises from the (ecclesiastical) status of godparenthood that itself of course originates in a new birth. Nor is it an accident that, though gossip as social control can bind men as well as women and children, gossiping is often thought of as a gendered activity.

Education

It is tempting to think of education in nineteenth-century philanthropists' terms, as a means to social mobility and betterment. And indeed, such terms are not inappropriate. The legend of Dick Whittington celebrates urban opportunity, and the legend retained its allure. Early-Stuart Bristol drew apprentices from thirty counties, who were enticed by the prospects apprenticeship offered to the young male who could pay an entry premium that ranged from a few pounds to several hundred, depending on the status of the trade. The association of learning with godliness ensured that for the lucky few among the poor other avenues opened. Many notables piously paid the school or university fees of clever boys from the locality. In Dorset there were both county and town collections for this purpose. Others were willing to pay for themselves.

The growth of the professions stemmed from the pressure of those who would be upwardly mobile as well as from the demand of the wealthy for their services. The university sector best reveals the extent of the surge, for a larger proportion of English male adolescents received tertiary education than was to be the case again until the twentieth century. Student numbers at the two universities of Oxford and Cambridge may have tripled between the mid-sixteenth century and the 1620s, to upwards of 1000 entrants a year (the graduate totals were much smaller). Most of the students were sons of clergy, merchants, yeomen and artisans, and many were supported on the 500 or so scholarships established in the philanthropic wave between 1560 and 1640; others worked their way as servants. And such people overwhelmingly sought jobs.

Social mobility should not be thought inherently destabilising, for the economy was expanding. Between a half and three-quarters of the graduates became clergy, and Thomas Hobbes certainly saw in an assertive clergy the seeds of revolution. But that was because of what they taught rather than because their elevation necessarily challenged a landed hierarchy. Benefactors and parents undoubtedly assumed that the training in which they invested would reinforce rather than subvert socio-cultural values. The apprentice was accordingly assigned to his master's household, though that situation was not without its stresses, as the apprentice group-culture, the periodic apprentice riots against the London brothels, and Nehemiah Wallington's unease when he had apprentices in the house all suggest. The universities' cultural appeal is clear in all those students of gentle birth (at least one-third of the intake by the 1620s) who were sent to acquire civility, learning and godliness. The humanists' insistence that the gentry be educated for their station in the commonwealth did not always pay off. Many gentlemen emerged with a mere smattering of Latin tags, doubtless to the relief of Hobbes, who believed classical learning fostered classical republicanism. Nevertheless, the remarkably learned and concerned networks of gentry in pre-war Kent and Warwickshire suggest the role of the universities in civilising the local community.

Secondary education was similarly ambiguous. On the one hand, the proliferation of grammar schools, both endowed and private, seemed to point to social change, and thoughtful conservatives like Francis Bacon worried about the consequences of overprovision. There were around 700 endowed grammar schools by mid-century, and perhaps double that number of private schools, whose teachers depended wholly upon fees. By mid-century most towns possessed a small grammar school, some of the larger ones several: thus, most of the populace of Kent lived within ten miles of a grammar school. Schooling was therefore accessible to most people who could afford fees, which were often as low as £1 a year. Yet Bacon might not have worried had he considered the intense conservatism of the curriculum. Pious benefactors had sought to impart godliness and sufficient Latin learning to enable students to enter university and, by extension, to become clergy; although over the century mathematics and English composition crept in, their impact on the the grammar schools' curriculum was predictably slight.

Education at the lowest level, in the petty schools, may seem more geared to socio-economic change. Farmers needed to be able to read contracts, more and more artisans and traders had to confront bills and written instructions and, if they were wise, to cast accounts. The growing complexity of the economy, as well as the demand of protestantism for laity who could read the Bible, generated a wide demand for schooling: this was strong enough to enable one London teacher of writing to adults to afford a summer house in fashionable Greenwich. Over half the parishes in the poor Midlands diocese of Lichfield had schoolmasters for some time between 1584 and 1642, and most of England's population lived within walking distance of an elementary school. Literacy rates soared from the later sixteenth century, until by 1642 almost one-third of the adult male populace was literate, but the figures were patchy. Townsmen were around two-thirds literate: the higher the status and the greater the complexity of the trade, the more complete the literacy. And so in the countryside, while gentry were completely literate, cottagers and labourers were largely illiterate. The poor had less economic need for literacy, although religious pressures might move a minority.

Similar factors governed the education of women. Barred from the universities and grammar schools, their role as mothers of potentially godly children might still have justified schooling them to the level of Bible-reading, and preachers and moralists often urged this. Many did go to elementary schools; some, such as Lucy Hutchinson and Margaret Cavendish, future Duchess of Newcastle, acquired a superb education through private tutors and self-help. But education for women as much as for men was for a station in life, and most parents were reluctant to pay fees for little tangible benefit. Schools for daughters of the better sort were established in the course of the seventeenth century, especially around London – there were several in Hackney by mid-century; these certainly taught reading and the Bible, but they seem to have concentrated on polite accomplishments appropriate for gaining a husband. And though many literate country women are found arguing scripture in the Civil War period, women overall received as little schooling as did the labouring poor: the female literacy rate was probably only around 10 per cent by mid-century, although perhaps 30 per cent in London.

Order in the localities

If education did more to reinforce than to challenge the prevailing ideals of community, were there more insidious threats to an organic political community?

Among the elite the steady growth of a civil society proved a crucial stabilising force. The Tudors had attracted many local magnates into the orbit of their court, and James, with his extravagant tastes, eagerly followed suit. Equally significant was the culture of peace he promptly established, which deprived potential aristocratic trouble-makers of practice in their traditional arts. Though they might go abroad for training, young nobles learned the low value placed on their skills at home. Elizabeth's rebellious Earl of Essex, who had absorbed the civic humanist exaltation of the state and like other ambitious noblemen aspired to a national politics, in 1601 lamented the political displacement of aristocratic honour and estate. The warrior ethos scarcely disappeared. In a major turn-of-the-century dispute in East Yorkshire the ancient and martial Eures ridiculed the sexual honour and physical misshapenness of the court-connected Sir Thomas Posthumus Hoby; and in a 1614 proclamation against duelling King James deplored the desire of the gentleman to 'put himself upon proof'. Identity in the male community of honour may nevertheless have been growing divorced from warriorhood, for James was also convinced that the main occasion of duelling was now 'giving the lie' rather than allegations of cowardice. That cultural shift was obviously long term, and rooted above all in education, peace, and the pull of the metropolis. But the crown's sale of titles, of baronetcy after 1611, of nobility after 1615 (increasing the number of earls from twenty-seven to sixty-five by 1628) also complicated the account and increased the resentments of the ancient nobility. Those who bickered in the Lords in the 1620s about the meaning of honour must have reflected ruefully on the title, let alone the honour, purchased in 1616 by Lord Stanhope, recently pardoned for murder, twice indicted for sodomy, and excluded from the commission of the peace for his delinquencies. Civility was less contentious, and it found an appropriate emblem at mid-century in the decision of the parliamentarian general, Lord Fairfax, to remodel his country house at Nunappleton in Yorkshire as a town house. But as the events of the 1640s were to show, civic values were no guarantee of political quiet.

And if the elite were being schooled into order, their inferiors seem to have been little inclined to challenge them. Prosecutions for theft certainly rose in the hungry 1620s, but there were no significant outbreaks of brigandage, and nor was there any rising of the poor. Perhaps forty food riots forced themselves on to the attention of the central government in the whole period 1585–1640; and serious agrarian disturbances were limited to the Midlands in 1607 and the eastern fenlands and southwestern forests under Charles I. They were the result of local changes in land use, rather than of class resentments. The behaviour of the poor in such times of trouble is instructive of the essentially reciprocal nature of authority and subordination. Rioters displayed an intense awareness of patriarchal authority, first approaching a neighbouring magistrate to complain about what they saw as anti-social activity, whether by landlords or food traders, and only acting for themselves when rebuffed. Even then they neither challenged the social order nor attacked the rich as rich. Food riots occurred not in the areas of greatest suffering but where trading in grain gave provocation; moreover, rioters often handed over to local authorities the grain they seized.

We shall never know whether rioters were expressing their inmost convictions or skilfully exploiting the ideological limits of their situation when the ideal of benevolent authority was everywhere promulgated. Whatever the case, their combination of general deference and particular outrage against exploiters like Sir Thomas Tresham in the Midlands secured an appropriate response from the authorities. For the privy council balanced outraged denunciation of disorder with a surprising practical understanding. Proclamations and statutes condemning economic exploitation by the rich had proliferated in the 1590s crisis, and rioters accordingly claimed that the law was on their side: they merely demanded enforcement. The council responded appropriately, issuing wholesale pardons to the rioters in 1607 while fining several landowners in Star Chamber. Such response may have been economically irrational, for much of the Midlands was, and still is, better suited to pasture than the arable farming for which the rioters clamoured. But as affirmation of community it made sense. The relationships of superiors and inferiors were not therefore simply imposed, but negotiated.

Yet arbitrariness and imposition were not absent from the rule of the local elites. The mounting problems of poverty provide the test. In most industrial towns around half the population dwelt in what contemporaries recognised as poverty. If not actually on relief, they were permanently vulnerable to minor dislocation. In Sheffield in 1616 one-third of the populace was described as 'begging poor'. Godly ministers and magistrates insistently blamed dearth on sin, denouncing the tippling that occasioned so much disorder and the alehouses that ate up barley, the bread-corn of the poor (a 1644 survey that listed one alehouse for every twenty households in parts of supposedly godly Essex suggests that their hostility was not groundless). But the authorities took a more practical course as they extended the compulsory poor rate, established by statute in the later sixteenth century as private charity lagged, and levied it as a matter of course on householders in the gloomy years of the 1620s and 1630s. Official relief was a frail safety-net. Poor parishes often faltered under their own burdens, and had to hope (usually vainly) for aid from wealthier neighbours when crises occurred. A more serious deficiency lay in the contemporary concept of poverty, which focused primarily on the truly helpless, the aged and women with dependent children. These received niggardly pensions, and their begging from door to door was usually tolerated. Local worthies took much less notice of pauper householders, whose numbers increased as depression worsened: only reluctantly, and with strict requirements about proper conduct and the wearing of identifying badges, did they grant the occasional dole. In industrial areas town authorities and county magistrates were often compelled to go further, subsidising sales of grain to the poor or even, in the disastrous 1620s, setting up more ambitious programmes such as Salisbury's renowned municipal brewery. But here too, the proceeds were only distributed to the truly deserving: poor relief demanded moral discipline.

Not surprisingly, hearts hardened towards those deemed undeserving. The churchwardens' accounts for West Ham, Essex, referred laconically in 1652 to the burial of 'a poor woman that died in the cage'. 'Sturdy' migrants and pregnant girls likely to add further burdens to the parish poor rates were whipped back to their last places of residence, communities acting for themselves or with the aid of the county quarter sessions blocked the construction of pauper cottages, and often pressure was applied to prevent the poor from marrying and bringing more poor into the world. The summary powers vested in local officials by statute could be put to a variety of uses and abuses, all in the name of the community of payers to the poor rate.

It is therefore important not to idealise. An ordered community required work: in the troubled 1590s the better sort maintained stability in London not only through official controls but also through constant and nervous attentiveness, institutionalised through the parochial select vestries that steadily established themselves. Community was by no means always good-natured. Noseyness abounded in early-modern villages and towns, even in London, where Nehemiah Wallington's notebooks of the mid-century point to the survival of neighbourhood. Incalculable numbers had to endure the gossip and backbiting reflected in proliferating defamation

suits. But neighbourly interest might avert conflict. The frequency of litigation testifies to the intensity of parochial feuds, but many more prosecutions were averted locally. The costs of action when there was no public
prosecutor, the resentments inspired, and the reluctance of village worthies
to jeopardise the life of a neighbour (though not of a vagrant) unless he
or she were a persistent trouble-maker, made mediation and persuasion
the main guarantors of the local peace.

At a deeper level, an ideology of personal relationships underpinned the
stability of the whole. All were expected to recognise their place. The
courts might be used against the undeferential, but normally an insistent
conditioning prevailed. Villagers doffed their hats to the squire, addressing him as 'your worship', or 'your honour', terms that reflect a world of
values; he in turn might address a yeoman and his wife as 'good man and
goodwife Green', while the rest simply heard their names called. Such
distancing was, however, both softened and reinforced by paternalism,
which both parties sought to manipulate. As with all generalisations,
qualifications are needed. The alternative values of the market-place and
of contract were gaining ground, while assertive women humiliated at the
ducking stool might have questioned how far male domination was ever
softened. But magistrates and householders alike repeatedly had held
before them a patriarchal ideal that combined love with justice. There may
be a touch of nervousness in the all-encompassing declaration of the
puritan Richard Sibbes, 'The word "Father" is an epitome of the whole
gospel': after all, the fifth Commandment, 'Honour thy father and thy
mother', refers to both parents. But it was the most frequently cited justification of political obedience. Even that alienated figure, Gerrard
Winstanley, theorist of the proto-communist Diggers, accorded fathers a
large role in his *The Law of Freedom* (1652). Stress on parental, and
above all paternal, discipline seemed to make sense when around half the
population was under the age of twenty.

It was not only children who were subject to domestic rule. Household
and hierarchy were assumed to overlap and reinforce each other, and both
James and Charles enjoined nobility and gentry to forsake metropolitan
entertainments and maintain hospitality at home. The politically correct
entertainment took place there: as Sir Henry Wootton, ambassador and
architectural publicist, put it in 1622, the country house was 'the theatre
of hospitality'. Responsibility for that 80 per cent or so of the labouring
population who seem to have been servants during their youth meant that
even ordinary households were charged with political duty. In London,
before the annual May Day rowdiness, authorities reminded all fathers of
their responsibility as householders for the actions of their servants and
apprentices. Indeed, even though many never married, everybody was
expected to become part of a family, subject to its discipline; only widows
and widowers, and the gentry, could live alone without disapproval. The
'masterless man', the single independent male, threatened society's image

of itself as an organic whole, an interdependent family, and was denounced as the source of all disorder. Similarly, the 'loose and disorderly woman' – a term contemporaries applied to the unmarried self-supporting glovemaker in Leicester as well as the London prostitute – was to be forced into service, into a household. Ideology rather than widespread delinquency underlay such rigours.

Family life

Such fears were reinforced by the mobility of England's population. Demographers have suggested that almost 2 per cent of the provincial population must have moved to London each decade to allow it to grow as it did despite its appalling mortality rate. And while many migrants were the wandering poor, desperate for jobs or for relief, those slightly above them seem to have been not much more rooted. Even amongst the freeholding, and therefore more secure, families at Laxton in Nottinghamshire in 1612, over a half seem to have been on their holdings for less than two generations; in the Northamptonshire village of Cogenhoe over half the population disappeared and was replaced between 1618 and 1628. Mortality alone cannot explain such flux. Most people moved at least once in their lives, although for the most part movement occurred within a fifteen-mile radius. Then as now, the young were the most mobile. Young people left home to enter service, whether domestic or in husbandry. Almost two-thirds of the 15–24 age group were servants, while there were probably 20 000 apprentices in London at any one time. Service allowed parents to get surplus mouths away from the family table, and allowed the children in their turn to accumulate wages, or skills, with which to set up on their own. Marriage partners were thus found outside the village as often as in, and horizons expanded and news travelled.

   For most people certain fundamental aspects of life were little different from what we know today. Personal mobility aided personal independence. Status and inheritance were vital considerations to those who had something to preserve, and strong parental pressure was often applied to determine the marriage choice of offspring. The daughter of the fierce old lawyer Sir Edward Coke was probably not alone in being whipped at the bedpost into obedience; but the derision hurled by his neighbours at 'Whip-her-arse Dick', a worthy of Thaxted, Essex, suggests that most people recognised limits. Many wealthy parents allowed their children at least a veto over selections made for them, and where there was less to gain or lose there was less point in parental exertions. That is not to say that, for the poor, selection of a mate could be a matter of unsullied romance or lust. Sexual relations mattered then, as now, and around 25 per cent of brides arrived at the altar pregnant. But prospective partners needed to be sure of their mutual abilities to establish and maintain a home, and average ages at marriage were therefore relatively late for the bulk of the populace. Numerous local studies show ages of males at marriage in the 27–29 years range in the first half of the seventeenth century; in the years of hardship around mid-century the average age of women at marriage sometimes crept as high as 26, with predictable effects on eventual family size.

In normal times, perhaps 25 per cent never married, and that proportion undoubtedly increased during the Civil War. Family formation was therefore scarcely more subject to physiological determinism than it was to parental control. It is easy to imagine that before modern contraception birthrates ran close to the biological maximum. But late marriages allowed England, like her continental neighbours, to escape the 'poverty trap' of near-maximum family size that has held back other regions. The planned spacing of children was clearly difficult, particularly for the elite who put their children to wet-nurses and thus avoided lactation's restraint on fertility; yet through late marriage, sexual abstinence and a variety of contraceptives and abortifacents, the population around mid-century contrived to limit its growth. Smaller family sizes, coupled with the growing agricultural flexibility generated by the increasingly market-orientated economy, then permitted some improvement in English living standards in the later seventeenth century.

The relative rarity of extended families worked to the same end of preserving living standards. The nuclear family was very much the rule. Surviving listings suggest that household size averaged around 4.5, though nobles and gentry might have dozens of servants under their roofs. Not only did relatively few grandparents survive to be supported in old age; among the poor, children departed early for service. But there were tensions that differed from our own within these small households. The English pattern of inheritance for land, like that of most of western Europe, was broadly primogenitive. There were regional variations, and partible inheritance was fairly common in non-fielden regions, especially among poorer farmers; but on the whole eldest sons were likely to remain on the family holdings, while younger sons and daughters received a portion of the family's possessions and an entry into service or apprenticeship. The pressures of primogeniture were particularly strong amongst the gentry, since considerations of status demanded that estates remain intact. Not for nothing did the Digger Gerrard Winstanley take the hapless younger brother as his metaphor for the poor of the earth. Most of these were left with 'what the cat left on the maltheap', as one put it bitterly. They had to make their own way in the world with an annuity grudgingly given by their elders, an opening into the professions, an apprenticeship or (increasingly important when too few new occupations were opening) a sea passage as an emigrant. The eagerness of apprentices and servants to escape through Bristol to the hard life across the Atlantic in the 1650s speaks poignantly to the circumstances they were leaving.

Mortality rates ensured, however, that even at home advancement often came earlier than it does today. The youth of some civil war commanders is striking: John Lambert was only 40 when his career ended at the Restoration.

The intimate landscape is nevertheless familiar. Too much has been made by historians of one alleged consequence of low life expectancy, and that is the coolness of relations within the family. Despite the likelihood of any child's early death, parents were scarcely averse to investing emotional capital. Diaries and letters suggest that, just as many marriages seem to have been built around affection and respect, so those qualities were not absent from relations between parents and children even amongst the gentry, where convention demanded a certain distance. Writing of her young son to her absent husband, that parliamentarian stalwart Lady Brilliana Harley reported that he was 'as merry as his little soul can be, till he is asked where you are, and then he makes some moanfull tune'. However much more frequently it happened than today, the death of infants could still prove devastating: on the death of one of his young children, Sir William Brownlow noted, 'I was at ease, but thou O God has broken mee a sunder and shaken me to pieces.' The death of parents might be equally felt. While his father's death allowed Nehemiah Wallington to achieve at last a closer access to God, the formidable Lady Ann Clifford mourned the death of her mother all her life. Assumptions that personal relations were distant sit ill with evidence that then as now much mental distress originated in family tensions. When Sir Robert Filmer read authoritarianism out of patriarchy he had to contend with legions of those who recognised within the family a powerful and reciprocating web of affections.

Social strain and political crisis

Little emerges from a survey of the economic and social characteristics of seventeenth-century England to suggest that civil war and revolution stemmed from socio-economic change. The social structure was by no means unstable, and social animosities seem to have been rather greater in, for example, 1549 than a century later. Many were hungry in 1642, and ready to seek their futures in arms, but it was not the hungry who took the political lead, nor even (at a higher social level) the younger sons and the dispossessed.

Nevertheless, social stress in the early seventeenth century was connected to the passions of civil war. It led some among the elite to suspect the hand of Antichrist and others to clutch more violently at hierarchical controls. Beyond the elite, the tensions born of social change and economic polarisation merged dangerously with the fears and resentments that swirled around the puritan campaign to reform the land.

Whatever the idealisations (present as well as past), settlements were not communities, and the mutual animosities of the godly and the good fellows were waiting for the chance to spill over. Petty local broils, and all the acts of intimidation or precaution, when reported in the capital formed part of the calculus of national politics.

More obviously, a changing economy and social structure shaped, even if they did not cause, the political upheaval. The economic dominance of the great landowners diminished as the commercial sector grew in strength; similarly, their political influence lessened as society diversified. If the Civil War and its outcome did not resemble the baronial wars of the thirteenth or fifteenth centuries, then the divergence must in large part be traced to the emergence of a less hierarchical society and to new political forces. London in all its transformations provided fertile ground for change, with its burgeoning and inadequately regulated suburbs, its increasingly self-confident tradesmen linked both to the new world of the Atlantic colonies and a broadening hinterland, and its presses printing food for thought. Above all, the spread of news and opinion in an increasingly integrated market and polity made of this a very untraditional world. It might not fit readily with purists' visions of hierarchy.

|4|

Peaceable kingdoms,
1603–1620

The succession of James VI of Scotland to the throne of Elizabeth in March 1603 linked all the kingdoms of the British islands for the first time. James saw in this remarkable circumstance the seeds of a wider and deeper peace, but his subjects' thoughts were narrower. In Ireland, the Nine Years War that had broken out in 1594 was giving way to a weary and resentful truce; in Scotland royal authority was growing as the Reformation struggles receded, but the prospect of rule by a king drawn southwards to London alarmed many. England too was a site of apprehension, and not just at the arrival of a foreigner: the realisation that the Tudor dynasty would die with Elizabeth had led many to stockpile weapons. The rejoicing that greeted James on his triumphal journey south was therefore tinged with relief; James read that celebration as testimony to his own preparations, to the assurances he had scattered wholesale, and, most of all, to God's goodwill towards him, His lieutenant on earth.

James's most important assurance was the promise of change he brought. An adult male, married (apparently amicably enough to Anne of Denmark), with two sons and a daughter, he offered England at last a king, fecund, with a secured succession. Indeed, fecundity seemed the watchword, and its appeal is clear in the poets' anticipations of his victory over the injustice, grudging and corruption of Elizabeth's last, war-strapped, years. Revelling in his newfound wealth, and recognising far better than did Elizabeth the importance of patronage, James showered largesse on those who rushed to meet him: in 1604 he spent the equivalent of nearly 20 per cent of the crown's regular revenues on jewels. He often spoke later of the perpetual 'Christmas' of his early years; but as a foreigner and first of a new dynasty he had to engender loyalty. And while James's yearning for the peace of Christendom was eventually to perplex many, the peace he promptly made with Spain in 1604 delighted tax-payers.

Despite a plague epidemic that devastated both London and the provinces in the summer of 1603, the political auguries seemed good. James's rigorous upbringing had left him with a taste for learning whose fruits were seen in the books he wrote, on kingship, on witchcraft, on tobacco. Some at least of his subjects were impressed. But however attractive he found book-writing, book-keeping yielded pride of place to hunting, and on occasion (most obviously at the end of the 1621 parliament) James allowed the chase to disrupt business. Nevertheless, he practised the arts of personal rule, unlike the ageing Elizabeth, who had increasingly withdrawn from business, if not from ceremonial. He had spent his years north of the border wary of an over-assertive Scottish nobility, and had learned to divide and rule, to separate intransigent Scottish presbyterian clergy from noblemen frustrated at new restraints. With some justice James prided himself on his 'kingcraft' when he reminded his English subjects that he was no mere novice, for he always sought to balance factions in a way that Elizabeth had lately failed to do.

Success in the containment of faction was no foregone conclusion, for the stakes were high. In court Lord Cobham and Sir Walter Raleigh were outmanoeuvred in the race for promotion by an alliance headed by Elizabeth's factotum Robert Cecil, and then destroyed when they looked to Roman Catholic intriguers for aid. James left Elizabeth's chief officers in place; but he balanced Cecil (whom he rewarded for his help in the succession with the earldom of Salisbury) with the able but sycophantic Henry Howard, Earl of Northampton, and by restoring to favour the survivors of the Earl of Essex's faction that had been broken in 1601. And he frustrated English aspirants by surrounding himself with old Scottish friends as bedchamber servants. Such flexibility was on the whole to serve him well in his dealings with parliaments and with religious zealots.

It was the religious malcontents who impressed themselves on the king first. On the exhilarating ride south, James had been greeted with the 'Millenary' petition of (allegedly) a thousand godly ministers seeking reform. They found a not unwilling audience, for the king's three predecessors in England had all begun their reigns with a religious settlement; and he had already suggested that the Elizabethan church might be improved. Indeed, James's interest in reform cannot be doubted: he steadily refrained from plundering the church as the more cynical Elizabeth had done, and he occasionally sought to limit the non-residence of clergy. Nevertheless, his motives in summoning a group of bishops and puritan clergy to confer at Hampton Court in 1604 probably had as much to do with the delights of theological disputation as they did with reform.

The Hampton Court conference has become legendary as a confrontation with diehard puritans – not least because James, claiming to detect his more resolute Scottish presbyterian foes lurking behind craven Englishmen, went out of his way to tie episcopacy to monarchy, insisting 'No bishop, no king.' The reforms the representatives of the godly urged on him were scarcely the assault on the church, let alone the state, he alleged, for English presbyterianism had disappeared even before Elizabeth, and James's general conciliatoriness shows he recognised this. But though puritan radicalism extended no further than a demand for the tightening of Calvinist orthodoxy and the removal of a few highly visible 'popish' ceremonies, such as the ring in marriage and the cross in baptism, the bishops insisted on the integrity of their church.

And to the bishops' manifest relief, the king supported them. James's ideal lay midway between presbyterianism and Rome, and he wished to lessen neither the dignity nor the comprehensiveness of his church. His 'middle way', or 'via media', was clearest in Hampton Court's most famous product, the new translation of the Bible which appeared in 1611, gaining subsequent renown as the 'King James' or Authorized Version. James saw the new Bible as a counter to the sometimes radical marginal comments of the popular Geneva Bible; but the prose for which his new Bible is so celebrated borrows heavily from the Geneva version and from the Catholic Rheims translation.

Equally instructive is the disciplinary outcome of Hampton Court. James sought to include in his church not just the ceremonialists but also the zealous – provided all accepted the principle of royal and episcopal discipline. Alarmed by what the puritan petitioning occasioned by the conference revealed of lay and clerical organisation, on Archbishop Whitgift's death in 1604 James appointed to Canterbury another disciplinarian, Richard Bancroft, who eagerly promulgated the canons passed by the ecclesiastical convocation of 1604. But once dissident clergy had shown their loyalty by subscribing to the legitimacy of the doctrine and ceremonies the canons prescribed, James had little interest in coercing them into practical conformity. The road from Hampton Court therefore took only a few into the wilderness, first underground and then eventually to New England: perhaps eighty ministers, less than 1 per cent of the total parish clergy, lost their livings. And the promotion of Bancroft proved something of an aberration, for James, a 'godly prince', accepted the need for a preaching clergy. The succession of good Calvinists whose episcopal appointments followed Bancroft's explains why puritanism in any ecclesiastical sense figures so small as a grievance in the Jacobean parliaments, with even the purge of 1604–5 dying as an issue by 1614.

Of course, James's parliament-men were given other matters to ponder. If unity was the king's dream of the church, that dream drove as well the attempt to bring together the two British kingdoms which James laid before his first parliament in 1604. His prurient interest in Anglo-Scottish marriages suggests some personal motivations, as does his delight in the marital imagery of the body politic: James found deep meaning in the personal union of the kingdoms, and was convinced that the royal 'husband' must avert the charge of political bigamy. But his personal motto, 'Rex pacificus' (the royal peace-maker), points to a sense of mission, the bringing of unity and harmony. His own person provided the means to end the centuries-old enmity between the English and the Scots. Accordingly, he declared himself king of Great Britain, and redesigned the English coinage and maritime flag. And he looked to a parliament to institute the full union of which he dreamed – to whose difficulties his councillors had done little to awaken him.

The Commons had fewer qualms than the councillors, and voiced real fears for national identity: unification under the name of Great Britain would wreak havoc with all laws that referred specifically to England. The claim had legal plausibility, but the debates revealed as well considerable xenophobia. It did not help that MPs' prejudices were not only shared by courtiers jealous of Scottish rivals, but were also mirrored by equally apprehensive Scots north of the border. The English insults to his native land, to blue-bonneted inhabitants and beggarly and rapacious traders, angered the king, and he gave vent to his accumulated frustrations by castigating the Commons for finding fault with all his propositions, and for meddling too in his finances. Here he was on weak ground, and when a Commons' committee prepared a defence, the famous 'Apology', it aggrievedly pointed out that the financial discussions had been 'upon motion' of privy councillors.

Those financial motions had been Salisbury's, who had learned from the uncomfortable experience of trying to run the wars of Elizabeth's reign from hand to mouth that peace must be the occasion for reform. The problems were immediate and obvious. While Elizabeth had left a small annual surplus on her 'ordinary', or regular, account, this would scarcely cover the higher costs of the court of a king with a family, all of whom needed their own establishments: thus, wardrobe costs almost quadrupled between 1599 and 1608. But there were deeper ills. Elizabeth's reign had been marked by fiscal and administrative ossification, for her hard-pressed government had responded to inflation merely by cost-watching. While other large landlords capitalised on demographic pressures by multiplying their rent-rolls, the royal estates were left virtually unsurveyed, and their economic potential was thus unknown. One example will tell much of the story. In 1587 Elizabeth agreed to a long lease on some Bermondsey property for £68 per annum; when the lease finally fell in, in 1636, it was found to be worth £1071 per annum. Furthermore, in the period of rapid inflation between Mary's death and 1604 there was no revision of the book of rates, the artifical valuations at which customs were levied on imports and exports.

Short-term solutions had only soured the political atmosphere. The queen had attempted to limit expenditure by curbing her payments to servants, thus forcing them to turn to indirect means, to higher fees or bribery and extortion. Officials and courtiers had also milked the economy through royal grants of economic privileges. Articles in common use, such as playing cards, could be brought within a monopoly patent by a claim

* inflexibility

to a new method of production; similarly, enforcement of the regulatory, or 'penal', statutes that had proliferated in the Tudor period might be awarded to private parties. Attacks on governmental corruption mounted, culminating in the storms over monopolies in Elizabeth's last parliaments of 1597 and 1601.

Salisbury's hopes lay in the altered climate created by a new king and peace. Natural goodwill would be intensified as peace eased the fiscal pressure on the subject; and peace ought also to permit financial recovery, since customs would grow with trade, all the more so after the 13 per cent increase in valuations in the 1604 book of rates. While it is difficult to deduce a coherent programme from a series of initiatives spread over some years, Salisbury seems to have hoped to reinforce the broad political community of king and kingdom, or king-in-parliament, and so to facilitate lasting reforms.

The first, and most important, step was the attempt to sell off the ramshackle edifice of ancient rights that has been called fiscal feudalism – primarily purveyance and wardship. Purveyance was the system whereby officials bought up supplies for the royal household in local markets at fixed prices far below cost. The incidence was as inequitable as the opportunities for abuse were legion. The crown's profits were appreciable: around £30 000 per annum in 1604, rising to about £40 000 in the 1620s. But Salisbury was attracted by the greater administrative simplicity of regular parliamentary supply, for which the way seemed to have been prepared by the growing practice of 'compounding', or paying money in lieu of purveyance. Still more striking is his readiness to abandon wardship, the ancient right of the king to provide a guardian for the lands and heir of a feudal tenant who by reason of age or sex was unable to fight for him. As master of the court of wards, charged with selling control over the land and marriage of wards, Salisbury's own profits probably averaged about one-sixth of the almost £20 000 per annum that the crown gained from wards in the new reign. His new-built Hatfield House was a fitting memorial.

But though Salisbury was ready to subordinate his immediate self-interest, his understanding of the politics of fiscal feudalism was not widely shared. Wardship was certainly resented since it could, on an average of one generation in three, devastate an estate and, perhaps, bring an unwelcome marriage to an heir. But to the crown wardship was a tool of patronage, allowing the king, or Salisbury as master of the court of wards, to reward courtiers with grants of wards on favourable terms. Furthermore, it had enormous symbolic and ideological significance, emphasising as it did the king's benevolent overlordship of the nation, and the regal nature of the body politic; passage of the reform might tip the polity towards a more broadly conceived community. As the government's prolonged hesitation in 1610 was to show, the equation was difficult to balance in practical terms too. If parliament were generous, a larger and more regular revenue might be secured; but abandonment of wardship would severely limit the crown's patronage resources. And the Commons' attitude to regular taxation was scarcely propitious.

Financial reform had competition on the agenda, from the union of the kingdoms, from a host of private bills, and from unexpected developments. A government with a legislative programme had certain assets, besides the welcoming climate of a new reign. The usually loyal bishops in the Lords were reinforced by the goodwill of the secular peers, who as a group had benefited handsomely from James's generosity. Although it is misleading to talk of a government 'interest' in the Commons, since the quasi-freehold nature of many posts imposed few obligations of political responsibility on their holders, loyalty and gratitude were presumed. The privy council practised no direct electoral management; yet courtiers and office-holders made up between a quarter and a third of the almost five hundred members, thanks to the efforts of friendly magnates and the eagerness of borough constituencies to gain friends at court. The taciturnity of most members meant that energetic courtiers might have a disproportionate impact. But most courtiers were no more active than their country neighbours, and Francis Bacon, striving hard for promotion, too often soldiered on with whatever help Salisbury's unofficial contacts in the lower house could provide.

A chaotic opening to the parliament hinted at how little of an actual agenda there was. Disorganisation soon gave place to dissension when government lawyers sought by sharp practice to reverse the result of the Buckinghamshire election. James was not personally concerned in the attempt to rescue the losing candidate, Sir John Fortescue, a privy councillor: the local dispute had its roots in Elizabethan tensions, while Fortescue was no friend of the Scots at court. But the king reacted angrily when the Commons declared that they were the proper judge of elections. The theocratic claims of Scottish presbyterians had bred in the king a deep abhorrence of claims to autonomous jurisdiction, so he lectured the Commons on the origins of their privileges in the grace of earlier kings. Alarmed, the Commons concluded that that grace could be withdrawn, and their privileges lost. But though both king and Commons had voiced significantly discordant arguments of principle, neither was anxious to dig itself into a confrontation. The Commons' eager acceptance of the tactful compromise James eventually offered suggests that the episode is as important for what it says of the desire for harmony, as for the fact that the crown attempted no further challenge to the house's control over its own composition.

Once the storm passed, the Commons resumed business, and with clear support and encouragement from Salisbury in the Lords turned to consideration of purveyance and wardship. They soon faltered at the problem of compensating the king. Distant counties, suffering little from purveyance, were naturally reluctant to contribute equally with the south-east; and wardship raised similar difficulties, since not all estates were held by military tenure. When members appreciated that they were being asked to establish a permanent tax their feet grew colder and progress slower.

Peace in Ireland, and the peace with Spain that James eagerly established in the 1604 Treaty of London, might have been expected to still the worst of the material grumbling. But worries remained. Devotees of the international protestant cause lamented the desertion of England's Dutch allies, who were still embroiled with Spain. More serious, at least in terms of the parliamentary timetable, was the way the expected trade boom inflamed the jealousy of the provincial ports for London. The cloth industry welcomed the opening of the Spanish trade, which was to prove important to the burgeoning new draperies; but many sectors feared that London would take over the newly reopening market. The provincial members protested in language fully as organic as that of the defenders of chartered corporations – blaming the trading companies for their greed, they denounced the capital as 'a head too big for the body', that reduced the rest of the kingdom to poverty. The merchants' cries were echoed by gentry MPs responding to constituency grievances or realising that their own fortunes were bound up with the price of wool and the fortunes of the cloth trade. The provincial protests were able to secure some relaxation in the organisation of the Spanish trade in 1606; but they irritated a government convinced of the virtues of corporations and regulation, and whose credit was closely tied to the London merchants.

The Commons never presented their defence, their 'Apology', against the king's list of resentments, for James avoided trouble by closing the session. But the 'Apology' reveals much of the outlook of early-Stuart parliament-men. Earlier historians erred in believing that the Commons were embarked on a campaign of constitutionalist aggression. The main initiatives in the house came from 'above', and members grew localist and leaden-footed in face of reform proposals. The most renowned passage of the Apology is appropriately defensive: 'All experience shows that the prerogatives of princes may easily and do daily grow [while] the privileges of the subject are for the most part at an everlasting stand.' Yet however conservative the outlook, the Commons thought they knew where they stood. The Apology confidently asserted that the privileges of parliament, threatened in the Buckinghamshire dispute and by other slights, were essential to the liberties of the subject and the well-being of the kingdom alike.

Unity and harmony eluded the political nation in the 1604 parliament. But they were rediscovered the following year, for the Gunpowder Plot offered the protestant establishment a brutal reminder that the person of the king was their prime defence against the old enemy in Rome. The prospect of catastrophe in a time of peace was the more remarkable in that most English Catholics were thoroughly loyal to the crown. But a

handful of zealots and conspirators still looked abroad for aid in returning England to the Catholic fold. In their frustration at James's peaceful
succession some had engaged in the half-baked Main and Bye Plots; these
had little effect other than in hurrying Raleigh and Cobham to the steps
of the scaffold and in shocking the tolerant James into agreeing to new
sanctions against recusants – the spring of 1605 brought over 5000 convictions and fines. The peace with Spain came as a greater disappointment
to those who had looked to Madrid; alienated and alone, they turned their
thoughts to a 'sudden blow'. The opening of a new session of parliament,
scheduled for November 1605, seemed their chance to destroy the whole
persecuting political elite as well as the protestant king. Ironically, they
failed because they were not alienated enough, and in this they offer the
clearest example of the advantages of the politics of inclusion at court.
Some were fatally reluctant to see Catholic lords blown up with the rest,
and allowed the secret to leak out.

The Plot occasioned a new burst of persecution. Prosecution of course
failed to halt the growth of recusancy, but new sanctions enacted in 1606
made life more uncomfortable for the propertied who could be black-
mailed by informers, or who attracted the attention of needy courtiers.
And the Plot had one unlooked-for by-product. A statute of 1606 imposed
on Catholics an oath of allegiance denying the pope's claim to depose
kings. Catholic polemicists denounced this as an intrusion into matters of
faith, while the king contended it was merely civil. In the ensuing international controversy James developed more systematically the views on the
divine origins and responsibilities of kingship that he had adumbrated in
his long struggle with the Scottish presbyterians. The greater intensity after
1606 of his rhetoric of lieutenancy to God, which was soon to be set
unflatteringly against his inactivity in God's causes, can be traced to
the conspiracy.

The immediate result of the Gunpowder Plot was, however, a recasting
of James as the protestant prince, the new Constantine leading his nation
against the popish foe. The continuing celebration of 5 November showed
how much anti-Catholicism entered the fabric of national life. But anti-
Catholicism had to share with property its central place in the national
ideology. Despite the patriotic outpourings, in the parliamentary session
of 1606 a grant of supply only passed the Commons by a one-vote margin.
Nevertheless, the grant went through. The unprecedented supply of
£453 000 is all the more striking since the royal debt had nearly doubled
in the years of peace since Elizabeth's death, with little to show for it, and
little sign of future improvement. What moved MPs was not the attractions of Salisbury's reform proposals, for which they showed little enthusiasm, but the simple realisation of how vulnerable and how valuable was
the king's body.

English good feelings towards James did not, however, extend to
James's grand plan, or to his compatriots. The king's delight in the 1606

session of parliament rapidly dissipated in the course of the third session in 1606–7 when he was again rebuffed over the union. To some extent he brought his frustrations on himself by his extravagance, as he characteristically celebrated the 1606 parliamentary subsidy by giving three of his Scottish cronies £44 000 to pay off their debts. But to unite the kingdoms was to confront deep sensitivities on both sides of the border. In Scotland James's proposal for a commission to further the union occasioned an impressive flurry of papers urging Scottish identity, while to the south the common lawyers in the short-lived Society of Antiquaries dug deeper into England's past. The Commons baulked at even minor proposals, and in a wrecking move one prominent MP, Sir Edwin Sandys, disingenuously urged a 'perfect union'. The scheme's 'perfection' lay in its proposal for abrogating Scottish law in favour of what Englishmen saw as the incomparably superior English law; the fears for the common law would thus finally be laid to rest. James's initial reaction was to lash out, although once again he tactfully moderated his displeasure by closing the session with a prorogation (in effect, an adjournment called by the king).

The king's good grace owed something to his dangerous realisation that he did not need parliament to gain all his objectives. Soon after the prorogation the government brought a collusive action, the Post Nati case, in which the judges made a comforting legal reality of the unity of the body politic in the royal body physical. Their resolution, that birth in Scotland or any other territory owing allegiance to the king of England automatically conveyed naturalisation had little immediate effect, for those affected (the post-nati) were of course born in or after 1603; but it was to have huge bearing on the future course of the British empire.

With the long-term future secured, James ceased to press union in parliament, an institution for which his feelings were left permanently soured. His efforts, at least on the main island of his dominions, became more piecemeal. He still made a point of comprehending influential Scots in the emerging British polity through their places in his bedchamber. Of perhaps greater potential were his ultimately abortive attempts to bring the two churches closer together, by advancing episcopacy and ceremonial in Scotland, even as he in 1611 promoted the staunchly Calvinist George Abbot, the English chaplain to one of his Scottish allies, to the archbishopric of Canterbury. More immediately, he turned his attention to the peaceful settlement of the 'middle shires' of his British kingdom, the old trouble-spot of the Borders; and he pointedly reminded sneering Englishmen of the obedience of the Scots, who could be governed by a stroke of the pen from distant Whitehall.

Another outlying area, across the Irish Sea, proved more recalcitrant than the Borders. The great uprising of the 1590s, centred on the Gaelic stronghold of Ulster and led by Hugh O'Neill, Earl of Tyrone, had finally collapsed as Elizabeth lay dying. But though Tyrone was defeated his position was not destroyed; consummate politician that he was, he moved

Dorset=Sackville

to recover by appealing to the conciliatory James. Not for the last time a gap opened between the policy of the government in London and its agents in Ireland. James and Salisbury were eager to return to normality, and doubted the value of punitive anti-Catholic measures in the absence there of a viable protestant alternative; furthermore, the growing fashion for Gaelic mantles and hairstyles at court suggests a new dimension to the king's dream of a pan-British union. But the king's local agents remembered only the recent upheaval, and hungered for land and vengeance. English policy in Ireland therefore wavered, breeding uncertainty and insecurity in those it affected. In 1607 the two great Ulster chieftains, O'Neill and O'Donnell, Earls of Tyrone and Tyrconnell, fled to safety in Europe.

English officials were not inclined to look a gift horse in the mouth. The 'flight of the earls' offered a dramatic solution to the problem of Ulster, the most recalcitrant region of Ireland, since the local leaders, and major landowners, had gone. The government happily assumed that those who stayed were equally involved in conspiracy, and almost immediately plans were afoot for the systematic extension throughout Ulster of the device of colonisation, with loyal settlers from the mainland, that had been used piecemeal elsewhere since Mary Tudor's reign. By the middle of the next decade the new Ulster was emerging – divided into shires, subjected to English justice, with new ports established at Londonderry and Coleraine through royal coercion of the city of London. But the new planters' resources and numbers proved inadequate to meet the crown's demand that in the interest of civility and security the bulk of the native Irish be displaced from 'British' (that is, English and Scottish) lands. Colonisation in practice consisted of a veneer of 'British' protestant estate owners dependent on the labour and rack-rents of the Irish, with (by 1630) some 13 000 protestant small farmers, mostly Scots driven by poverty and drawn by proximity from the mainland. These were made yet more zealous in their presbyterianism by proximity to Irish Catholics. The troubled Ulster of the protestant supremacy was the first truly British enterprise.

Closer attention from London might, by restraining the greed and aggression of local officials, have made some difference. But like all English governments James's was infinitely more concerned with domestic than with Irish problems. And those problems, which were more than ever Salisbury's to wrestle with when he succeeded to the lord treasurership on the death of his ally the Earl of Dorset in 1608, became overwhelmingly financial.

Royal finances were far from doomed. A debt of the order of twice the ordinary, or regular, revenue was scarcely catastrophic had rational policies been followed; of these Salisbury still had hope. With Dorset he had initiated a long series of commissions to examine 'projects', or means of raising money through the exploitation of resources natural and otherwise; these had generally proved abortive in the absence of committed royal support and administrative means. Another road to the reduction of the debt was by way of the crown lands: surveys Salisbury ordered in 1608 almost quadrupled the crown's rents from its Yorkshire lands, and retrospectively damned Elizabeth's inertia. But since the interest on the debt was 10 per cent while the yield of land was commonly accounted at 5 per cent, sales seemed more promising, whatever the loss in patronage and political influence. The campaign of planned sale that Dorset began shortly before his death had by 1610 raised almost £450 000. Had expenditure fallen too the liquidation of capital combined with the 1606 subsidy would have more than eliminated the debt. But while sales, subsidy and other windfalls brought in £1 185 000 between 1606 and 1610, the debt fell in the same period by a mere £455 000, to £280 000, as the king forgot his periodic vows that no longer would every day be a Christmas. He can scarcely bear all the blame, for Dorset's family name, Sackville, was popularly and pointedly inverted to Fill-Sack; but there is no question that the pattern of carelessness the king established drove Dorset and Salisbury to the fateful decision to exploit the customs.

The prospect of a major breakthrough appeared with an internal dispute among Levant Company merchants. This invited the revenue court of the exchequer to decide in Bate's Case in 1606 that duties imposed for the regulation of commerce were an unchallengeable element in the crown's foreign policy prerogative. The potential of the decision was obvious, for if the crown claimed it was regulating trade it could impose any duties it wished. In the summer of 1608 Salisbury accordingly imposed new tariffs on virtually every import except basic foodstuffs, munitions and ships' stores. As the chancellor of the exchequer, Sir Julius Caesar, gloated, the day would be 'the most gainfull to the king and his posterity as any one day's work'. The 1608 impositions brought in about £70 000 per annum, and by the 1630s, after further additions, the yield of impositions ran close to £250 000 per annum. At stake now was the late-medieval balance between crown and parliament in which taxation for the king required the consent of the community.

Salisbury still hoped for a consensual settlement. Although by 1610 the king's ordinary revenues had risen to about £460 000 from their 1606 level of £315 000, the failure to reduce the debt warned Salisbury that any new war would destroy his gains. Technological change necessitated greater military preparedness, and there was always Ireland to secure. To what must have been Salisbury's delight, one of the judges in Bate's Case had challenged the convention that kings lived off their own resources in time of peace, and instead held that kings must have peacetime supply for the defence of their kingdom. The time seemed ripe for bargaining, despite the defeat of the earlier attempts to liquidate fiscal feudalism. But the atmosphere for Salisbury's far-sighted 'Great Contract' of 1610 was poisoned by the exploitation of Bate's Case. As the lawyer James

Whitelocke was to warn the Commons, if kings could levy impositions at will, 'Considering the greatest use they make of assembling of parliaments, which is the supply of money', there was little future for parliaments. Salisbury had fatally underestimated the degree to which the Commons would see the new customs revenues as a threat to their traditional role in granting taxation.

The Contract was the last attempt until the very different conditions of 1641 to restore the crown's finances through harmony with parliament. In tense negotiations in the summer of 1610 agreement seemed to have been reached. For £200 000 per annum James was to surrender wardship, purveyance and the much-resented use of informers to raise money on penal statutes; additionally, James separately indicated his willingness to forego any further impositions without parliamentary consent. In an attempt to incorporate the whole political community in the massive constitutional innovation of regular direct taxation for the upkeep of government, members of the Commons were told to consult their neighbours over the recess. But when parliament reassembled in November both parties had thought better of the bargain. The Commons attacked the Scots as the likely beneficiaries, and James demanded immediate payment of all his debts. Despite Salisbury's efforts, parliament was soon dissolved.

The causes of failure must be sought partly in the arithmetic. Many MPs were reluctant to subsidise what they saw as sheer extravagance: Sandys alleged that James's court cost four times as much as its French or Spanish counterparts, although James aptly complained that most of his audience had either had or asked for something themselves. Moreover, since only a section of the populace had been liable to feudal dues the proposal that a general tax should replace them was resoundingly denounced in the constituencies, while landowners were equally hostile to the alternative, a permanent tax on lands liable to feudal dues. On the other side, the basic operating principle by which the government staggered along was at risk, for the Contract made little provision for replacing the indirect pickings, from rich wards, by which courtiers supported themselves. Salisbury's determination to press on testifies to his sense of the gloomy future under an unthrifty king and to his awareness of the political risks in raising the disputed revenues further. But as some of the king's advisers realised, the Contract left too little margin for reducing the debt. Worst of all, it asked the king to sacrifice flexible revenues for a fixed income in an era of inflation.

The failure of the Contract did not, therefore, result from deep animosities. Despite the king's occasional outbursts against the Commons, he took seriously his rhetoric about his divinely ordained duty to preserve the ancient laws of the kingdom. Indeed, despite their very different styles, James was at first rather more of a 'parliamentary prince' than Elizabeth had been. In her last, wartime, years Elizabeth had been single-minded in her use of parliament, calling it for frequent but brief meetings to gain money. James on the other hand allowed three separate sessions of his long first parliament of 1604–10 to pass without a grant of taxes, and this was not wholly because he was rebuffed. The legislative record in fact reveals that parliament was playing a more positive role in the mundane regulation of the commonwealth under James than it had under Elizabeth. The frustrated interests that had gained an average of only thirty-three statutes from the queen's last three parliaments could triumph in the seventy-two acts of the 1604 session and the fifty-six of 1606. Indeed, until the Long Parliament of the Civil War, the total legislative achievement of James's first parliament was second only to the monumental Reformation Parliament of Henry VIII. The detailed work on the regulation of alehouses, draining of fenland and reformation of corporations tells an important story of community.

Nevertheless, reciprocated fears for the future underlay the practical problems disclosed in 1610. James repeatedly claimed that all property was held of the king as the ultimate lord, and that all laws and rights originated in royal grace. He was therefore an audience for those, such as Lord Chancellor Ellesmere and perhaps also the Earl of Northampton, who urged the indignity of bargaining away the rights of the crown, and who resented too the growing prominence of the Commons – at the expense of the Lords as much as of the crown – as money matters became central.

Ellesmere's apprehensions were mirrored in the Commons. Many MPs feared for parliament's future should kings receive as their due from their subjects the adequate annual revenue James now seemed to claim. Moreover, any bargain made might prove insecure, for the judges in Bate's Case had held, and James reiterated, that since prerogatives were for the good of the kingdom they were inalienable. Indeed, although James's practical politics were conciliatory enough, a thread of suspicion of the crown's discretionary power runs through the sessions of this long parliament. The causes are obscure, but in all probability men conscious of European trends towards princely power grew apprehensive as they noted James's interest in European theory as well as his Scottish background, with its civil law and weak Scottish parliament. They countered that the common law and the rights, especially to property, it protected were the ancient 'inheritance' or 'birthright' of Englishmen, fully as inalienable as was the crown's prerogative, and just as central to the identity and well-being of the kingdom. When impositions, which looked suspiciously like the excise taxes on which so many European princes had built, created the prospect of a potentially limitless non-parliamentary revenue, lawyer–MPs like Whitelocke, William Hakewill and Thomas Hedley proved capable of articulating long and coherent constitutionalist objections.

The failure of the Great Contract marked a watershed in early-Stuart politics. Salisbury's successors, like Cranfield in the years around 1620, merely worked within the limits of the prevailing system, vainly trying to give substance to the convention that the king's ordinary revenue sufficed for ordinary expenses. Nobody strove to build the new relationship with parliament that Salisbury had sought. Remarkably, neither was there much sign before the 1630s (and precious little even then) of any willingness to pursue his alternative, and contradictory, strategy, of purposefully exploiting the customs, and risking a breach with ancient convention. Salisbury's failure and his lack of support from the throne must have dampened the ardour of other would-be reformers. In the absence of such vision, the preoccupation of the crown's servants increasingly became the finances of survival.

The pursuit of 'projects' best exemplifies the short-term fixations of James's later years. Salisbury had of course during his primacy himself examined various schemes, but in the years after 1610 the attention devoted to projects intensified. Private individuals pestered courtiers, and courtiers the king, with such devices as schemes to improve the production of toothpicks and codheads for the benefit of all – and not least the projector – and the detriment of none. This seamy world on the fringes of court and City was brilliantly satirised by Ben Jonson in *The Devil is an Asse*. The discredit was unfortunately balanced by little gain for the king. The one exception was the invention in 1611 of the hereditary and saleable title of baronet. Status-hungry gentlemen eagerly paid the asking price of £1095, and by 1614 baronetcies had brought in over £90 000. But the penurious king and his courtiers could not resist the temptation to sell as much as could be sold. With the promise of a fixed number ignored, the market was soon saturated and by 1622 the price had fallen to £220. The crown's role as the fountain of honour was cheapened as wits poked fun at the vital concept of 'degree'; and cynicism about the great spread.

Divisions at court compounded the cash crisis. Salisbury grew more vulnerable, since he had angered James by dragging his revenue and prerogative on to the stage to no good end, and permitted attacks on the Scots. The Lord Treasurer's decline saw Northampton and his nephew the Earl of Suffolk, the leaders of the Howard family connection, challenge a looser group that comprised notably the Earl of Pembroke, Chief Justice Sir Edward Coke and the sternly anti-Catholic Archbishop Abbot, whose appointment to Canterbury in 1611 was eased by the assassination of Henri IV of France, which stoked anew James's fears of radical Catholicism. The growing factionalism hemmed James in. Salisbury's generally unlamented death in 1612 left the key offices of Lord Treasurer, Secretary of State and Master of the Wards vacant, but in his anxiety to avoid polarising the court James gave the Wards to a political nonentity and left the other posts empty, putting the treasury under a body of commissioners and announcing he would be his own secretary.

That declaration of personal monarchy came the more easily since it was at just this time that James became deeply attached to a favourite. He created the Scot Robert Carr Viscount Rochester in 1611 and then Earl of Somerset. Although the charming and cultivated Carr was no intellectual match for some of those he dealt with he did provide a valuable screen for his master: a favourite could be an asset for a monarch beset by suitors. But there was clearly more to the relationship than politics. James's taste for lively and handsome young men became, and still is, notorious. Throughout his reigns in both Scotland and England he committed himself to a succession of male intimates (Esmé Stuart, Carr, George Villiers); this probably stemmed not from the homosexuality that has often been alleged but from a socially accepted homosocial delight in physical fellowship (indulged for example on the hunting field), and a less socially accepted but still not necessarily homosexual taste for intimate intergenerational relationships. There were political consequences to the flaunting of the royal body physical and its desires. In the later years some contemporaries grew disturbed by the careful decking out of a handsome 'myrmidon' that went with each faction's bid for power; and James's occasional air of drunken incapacitation, acquired from the porphyria that affected his central nervous system, did not help the reputation of the court. But when the habitation of the body politic in the body of the king was so widely assumed, few questioned James's right to rely on whom, and however, he pleased.

The Carr years were nevertheless not happy ones for James. Not only would he not apply himself to business as his new regime of personal rule required; he was also unlucky in the pressures and scandals of a period of increasing financial and diplomatic stringency. The death of his promising elder son Henry in 1612 not only required an expensive funeral; it also unloosed waves of lamentation from those who had seen in the prince an aggressive protestant future. With royal resources dwindling, and political discipline loosened by the two-year vacancy in the greatest political offices, James's servants turned to self-help of the kind that had marred Elizabeth's last years.

The malaise increasingly voiced in newsletters and correspondence was compounded as, for the first time in the reign, ideological division began to overlay the court squabbles for patronage and perquisites. While Pembroke and Francis Bacon, the new Attorney-General, urged the politics of harmony and a fresh approach to parliament, Ellesmere joined Northampton and Suffolk in urging the lessons of 1610, and pointing to the concessions and frustrations that would be the price of any parliamentary grant. Differences on foreign policy also began to emerge, for Europe seemed once again about to descend into war. Bacon, the supreme political thinker, was as anxious as his master to straddle differences. But Pembroke, Abbot and their allies urged a return to oceanic voyaging, and to preparations for the war with Spain their Calvinist consciences told them was inevitable. The Howards' preference for peace probably owed as much to a proper sense of the cost of war as to the notorious crypto-Catholicism of several of their number.

James's hopes of acting the peacemaker of Europe inclined him towards the views of the Howards. Spain was overextended, involved on three continents, anxious for peace, and also impressively regal in its ways; conversely, the Dutch were republicans and dangerous trading rivals. In the early 1610s the king's pacific dreams became more urgent when a succession dispute over the strategic duchy of Cleves–Julich threatened renewed religious war in Germany. As always, James saw the royal body as the means to peace. He hoped to couple the marriage of his daughter Elizabeth to Frederick, ruler of the Rhineland Palatinate and leader of the German Protestant Union, with a marriage alliance between his son and a Spanish princess. The two hostile blocs would be brought together by Stuart progeny.

Zealous protestants therefore found little cause for rejoicing in the diplomatic implications of Elizabeth's 1613 wedding. They were already sunk in mourning for the death of Prince Henry, who, had he lived, might have led England down a very different road in the ensuing European struggle. They watched with alarm the arrival in 1613 of a new Spanish ambassador, don Diego Sarmiento, better known by his later title of Count Gondomar. The growing public exaltation of the memory of Queen Elizabeth, whose death had been little mourned, was an eloquent comment on the close friendship Gondomar built up with the king. But James, soon reassured by his successful mediation in 1614 of the Cleves–Julich dispute, was undeterred from his grand vision, and slowly allowed the Howards to fill some of the political void left by Salisbury's death.

The Howard years saw the nadir of Jacobean scandal and indebtedness. Northampton's religion and the high prerogative views for which he was notorious inspired distrust; worse, the manner of the clan's accession to power hardened the growing sense of the corruption of the body politic in all its facets. Irreligion, illicit sex, inappropriate gains, all went together. James's favourite, Somerset, fell for Suffolk's daughter, the rather tarnished Frances Howard, who was at the time married, in mutual unhappiness, to the young Earl of Essex, son of Elizabeth's tragic favourite. Hugely scandalous divorce proceedings on the grounds of Essex's impotence were eagerly followed in 1613 in manuscript newsletters in country houses across England, as James pressed and packed a tribunal of shame-faced ecclesiastics to bring in the right verdict. When Suffolk gained the treasurership in 1614, the palace he built for himself at Audley End, largely financed from official balances, drew from James the appropriate but alarmingly lax comment that it was too big for a king but big enough for a lord treasurer. Not surprisingly, the annual ordinary deficit under Suffolk grew to £160 000, and the debt mounted steadily.

But corruption and scandal always have to be set in context. The Howards were by no means the lackeys of Spain – several had fought with distinction in the Elizabethan wars, and their current readiness to join so many of their colleagues in accepting gratuities from the old enemy reflected on the parlous level of official salaries. Nor were the Howards altogether leeches on the public revenues. Lord Treasurer Suffolk was eventually tried for corruption, but as Bacon later found, official propriety was defined by politics, and partisanship made life difficult for office-holders. Furthermore, self-interest and faction accommodated other ideals. Northampton, himself an able administrator, sought like any politician to prove that he could benefit the king. Not only did he in 1613 introduce to James and to public life the former London merchant Lionel Cranfield, who was to become the leading reform figure of the next decade; he was also soon to preside happily over a commission to investigate corruption in a navy run by the cousin he hated, Charles Howard, Earl of Nottingham.

Northampton in power was not therefore some latterday Nero, fiddling while Rome burned. He participated eagerly in a reform commission to investigate the king's revenues in 1613, though like everybody else he found the scale of the problems daunting. Another new book of rates promised some relief, but the commissioners found themselves boxed in by politics: fear of the reaction of a parliament that most assumed must come deterred them from pushing too hard, and they listed raising customs duties 'to the highest value' under the heading 'Projects not likely to prove well'. Bankrupt of ideas and nearly bankrupt of funds, James drifted towards another parliament in the spring of 1614.

James's lack of enthusiasm for a parliament is apparent in his continuing reluctance to fill vacant offices. Not until a week before parliament did he appoint as Secretary of State the diplomat Sir Ralph Winwood, an aggressive protestant but hardly a front-rank figure. As ever, the king was balancing and combining the factions, since the other secretary, Sir Thomas Lake, was a Howard client. But James made his intention to maintain his own control clear when he chose a political lightweight and then left him too little time to prepare himself for his coming role as the crown's chief spokesman in the Commons. Those courtiers who had advocated a parliament had not convinced the king that they knew the road to long-term relief. Although Bacon had had some twenty years of Commons' service, and his ally Sir Henry Neville had been an ardent critic of the government in 1610, neither had any solution to the burning question of impositions, nor anything other than minor sops to offer to the Commons in return for supply.

The confusion at court is almost, though not quite, a sufficient explanation of the disaster of 1614. As usual, there was no conciliar campaign to pack parliament, and the composition of the Commons was much like any other. But with Northampton sinking into his final illness Suffolk and Somerset seem to have taken their court struggle against Pembroke, the parliament's leading supporter, into the chambers at Westminster. Rumours the pair encouraged in the newly assembled Commons that someone was 'undertaking' to manage the lower house seemed borne out when an isolated case of electoral intimidation by a councillor, Sir Thomas

Parry, came to light. Fears of an attempt to subvert and destroy parliament took vivid shape, and the hapless Winwood and the few supporters of the king's requests for supply lost control.

A contrite Neville eventually stilled the uproar over the 'undertakers' by pointing to the innocence of his own proposals, but the move to substantive business did not improve tempers. MPs deplored the relaxation in the laws against recusants that had come with friendship for Spain, and could not be deflected by Winwood's obvious sympathy for their protests. The cries that good laws without enforcement were pointless exposed the limited role of parliament in government – and many feared that that role might become still smaller as the government systematically exploited impositions. The old animus against the Scots as beneficiaries still ran strongly: £67 498 of the £90 688 James gave away in 1611 had gone to eleven Scotsmen, and though these figures were not available to MPs, none could miss Somerset's dominance. But the 1614 debates on impositions reveal not only jealousy but also some highly sophisticated political thought. One member took up the theme of inexorable aggrandisement glanced at in the 1604 Apology when he gloomily observed that there were 'three sorts of kingdoms: elective, successive, and tyrannical, and accordingly did each extend his [sic] prerogative'. In the heat of debate Sir Edwin Sandys spoke the unspeakable when, pointing to the ominous French parallel, he warned, 'Nay, so do our impositions increase in England as it is come to be almost a tyrannical government in England.'

Such outspoken criticism fitted ill with the assumptions of the body politic. The anguished minority in the Commons could carry with them neither the silent majority, nor the Lords, and parliament dissolved in confusion. The occasion and manner of that breach are as instructive as the alarm over impositions. When the Commons learned that Bishop Neile in the Lords had branded the Commons seditious for disputing something adjudged in Bate's Case a prerogative of the crown, thus alleging the estrangement of the members from the king, the ensuing storm over privileges developed the air of a moral panic. The angry king, left with no chance of supply from an 'addled parliament' that had done nothing, turned yet further against parliaments. It was fear of precisely this outcome that led a number of MPs at the end to urge their colleagues to overcome their exasperation at James's spendthrift ways, that he might once again be 'in love with parliaments'.

A concern to secure harmony governed the responses of the body politic to this setback. The king for his part appealed to popular sentiment. Pointing disingenuously to the Catholic threat, James demanded of all taxpayers as an extraordinary 'benevolence' the subsidy the Commons had allegedly intended to give. That the nation generally paid up underscores parliament's key function as the arena for debate and dissent – whatever an MP's conduct at Westminster, in his locality a gentleman had to submit to commands from 'above'. The alarm voiced in the 1614 parliament did not, could not, signal polarisation in the country.

No more did James's decision to sacrifice the parliament rather than impositions herald the advent of prerogative government. The decision could hardly be faulted financially, after the experience of 1610. Circumstances were, it is true, creating ideology, in the council as in the Commons. Ellesmere and Suffolk were pessimistic: the matter of right and power was involved in impositions, and Suffolk 'knew not how it could be salved'. But the council still prized harmony. In yet another hunt for revenue the councillors in 1615 agreed that restoration of the king's finances could only come through parliament, and to that end most urged concessions on impositions. Though the importance of impositions was apparent to all, the council shied away, as it had in 1613, from imposing provocative new customs duties. Instead, James plumped for the greatest 'project' of all, Cockayne's scheme.

Cockayne's scheme is a case-study in the complications and risks of the corporate economy. William Cockayne, a London alderman and Eastland Company merchant trading to the Baltic, sought to break into the lucrative Merchant Adventurers' trade in unfinished broadcloth without staking the large capital required by the company. He reinforced his bribes to courtiers and king with plausible arguments. If the labour-intensive and profitable finishing of cloth were done in England rather than The Netherlands, not only would employment and profits be generated, but the treasury could expect increased customs revenues on exports. Cockayne therefore proposed that the export of unfinished cloth be phased out; to ensure this, the projectors should take over the Merchant Adventurers' privileges. But the scheme rested on false assumptions of English domination of production. Although cloth exports had surged by 25 per cent since the 1604 peace with Spain, English broadcloth was a traditional and high-cost industry, facing competition in lower-wage areas of eastern Europe. By the end of James's first decade merchants were warning that the north European markets were clogged and that cloths were harder to sell.

The Cockayne syndicate was ill equipped to deal in such a market. Its real aim had been to take over the Merchant Adventurers' trade, not to establish a finishing industry. But it was under-capitalised and could not keep pace with the seasonal nature of wool and cloth production, as the more creditworthy Merchant Adventurers had done. Unemployment soared in the clothing counties as the new company failed to buy cloth. By late 1616 exports through London were one-third down on 1614, the Dutch were finding new suppliers, and the king's customs had fallen correspondingly. To widespread relief, the old Merchant Adventurers were re-established in December 1616, though at further cost in pay-offs, and consequently higher prices. Although by 1618 London broadcloth exports were back to their 1603 level, never again did they reach their 1614 heights. All believed in the propriety of government intervention to nurture the body politic, but the Cockayne scheme suggested some of the dangers.

of Carr
p. 93.

The saga of scandal was, unfortunately, not limited to the Cockayne scheme. In 1615 the Howard edifice began to crumble when the family's rivals, led by Archbishop Abbot and aided by the queen, introduced a beautiful youth named George Villiers to the king. James was willing to be distracted, for the old favourite had been taking their intimacy too much for granted. One Somerset supporter, sensing the likelihood of a change, punned bitterly, 'The cat has found a new tail to play with.' Soon the court broke out into a new factiousness at the very top, since the failure of the 1614 parliament coincided with Suffolk's acquisition of the treasurership and Somerset's of the lord chamberlainship, a post that controlled access at court. When a rumour was heard that Frances Howard's marriage to Somerset had been eased by the murder of the latter's disapproving secretary Sir Thomas Overbury, the unstable equilibrium at court broke. The difficulties of the pro-Spanish Howards allowed Raleigh's friends to secure his release from the Tower; meanwhile Secretary Winwood and Chief Justice Coke moved to destroy their enemies. Coke had proved his remorselessness in the earlier attack on Raleigh, and soon established a case against Frances Howard. Somerset parted bitterly from James in October 1615.

The following winter saw one of the scandals of the century go to trial. Somerset had threatened to expose James's dirty linen as well as his own, but his nerve failed, and an enormously relieved king commuted the death sentence on the couple. The outcome still went far to placate outraged prejudices, since Frances Howard's assistant, Mrs Turner, whose gender-transgressing fashions and assertiveness earned her notoriety as a witch, did not avoid the scaffold. There was an appropriate symmetry to a moment that saw the body politic out of kilter and the politics of the body gone awry.

The Somerset debacle plunged not just the court but the law courts into disarray. The king saw in Coke an excess of zeal that had brought scandal uncomfortably close, and Coke's rivals eagerly took the hint. Coke's ringing principles were interlaced with professional rivalries. Common lawyers in the central courts had long feared for their positions and their fees, since the precedents and procedures of the common law were often outpaced by a fast-changing economy, while business went to the more flexible equity court of Chancery. In order to reinvigorate the common law the judges not infrequently wrenched precedents and statutes out of context – a good example is Coke's use of Magna Carta to damn commercial monopolies in his comments on the *Darcy v. Allen* playing-card case of 1602. To justify such a bold approach, Coke and his colleagues articulated a philosophy of the 'artifical reason' of the common law. In a sophisticated version of the ancient notion that law was not merely custom but was also immanent in the universe, Coke argued that the common law, as law, embodied reason; the judges, skilled reasoners, could see in the profusion of cases coherence and underlying principles.

Chancery seemed to challenge Coke's determination, expressed both on the bench and in his immensely influential *Reports* and *Institutes*, to make sense of the maze of legal precedents and to give the common law coherence and certainty. The chancellor, Coke's enemy Ellesmere, keeper of the conscience of a king who was also the fountain of justice, dispensed equity – by now a fairly defined blend of discretion and common law rules. But Ellesmere seemed as ready to intervene equitably in common law cases as to act the king's mouthpiece, and some common lawyers saw him in almost apocalyptic terms, as the engine of prerogative, the ally of favourites and the enemy of law. The judges shared this mindset, and hurled writs of prohibition barring the rival courts from further proceedings in cases that could be tried at common law. When the ecclesiastical court of high commission had also been challenged, it was no wonder that Archbishop Abbot joined Ellesmere, and Coke's jealous rival, Sir Francis Bacon, when the chief justice over-reached himself in a direct attack on Chancery's jurisdiction in 1616.

The king had other reasons for impatience. The chief justice's fame lies in his passionate commitment on the bench to the supremacy of the common law. Repeatedly Coke had treated the crown's discretionary powers with some reserve, and had not been cowed when in 1613 James kicked him upstairs from the main civil court of common pleas to the more prestigious but less remunerative King's Bench. Coke's anxiety to preserve the judges' independence of the crown came to a head in the so-called 'commendams' affair over ecclesiastical patronage in 1616, where he refused to swear to consult the king beforehand in cases involving the prerogative. Coke's insistence that the law arose from the customs of the community over the generations, and not from the king's will, cost him his job. James, as suspicious of assertive common lawyers as he was of all independent jurisdictions, then lectured the judges at length on the grace of kings.

But the turmoil at court in these years showed how thoroughly the king's grace was articulated in the workings of faction. Although James aimed to preserve his own freedom of action, politics was, to those whom he sought to balance, an all-or-nothing business. In 1617 George Villiers cemented his position in James's bosom, becoming Earl and then Marquis of Buckingham. Coke found renewed hope, and whipped his teenage daughter into a pathetic marriage to the new favourite's unstable brother. Suffolk, who had managed to survive his own daughter's fall, needed no instruction in sexual politics. Seizing the opportunity presented by the king's absence on his 1617 visit to Scotland, the first since 1603, Suffolk's allies schooled and beautified the son of a client to catch James's eye. Some ridiculed them in their failure; but Buckingham concluded that he must break his rivals.

The fall of Suffolk before Star Chamber charges of embezzlement brought the reputation of James's court to its lowest point. Like any treasurer Suffolk had had abundant opportunities for taking bribes, since with the crown so deeply in debt creditors competed fiercely for reimbursement. But in accepting £1000 per annum from the officers of the army in Ireland who had vainly hoped that their troops might be paid he had gone too far. By 1619 a contemporary could note with relish that the Tower was occupied by a former lord chamberlain (Somerset), a lord treasurer (Suffolk), a secretary of state (Suffolk's client, Lake, who also fell in a massive sex scandal), and a captain of the gentlemen pensioners, or ceremonial attendants at court (Suffolk's son Lord Walden). It was no hard task for Buckingham to appear as the apostle of reform, and attract to himself those like Cranfield and Bacon who hoped to purge the worst extravagance and corruption. And despite all the earlier failed efforts at reform, James was not averse to helping Buckingham make the effort.

No sane king could allow scandal to tell the story of his reign, and James was a more articulate and self-conscious representer of kingship than most. We might see damage-control, or mere prejudice, in the instructions to London preachers in 1620 to denounce the transgressions of women. But such attributions of blame were part of a broader assertion of royal patriarchy in the troubled years of the later 1610s. The royal meditations on scripture that were published for general application in 1619 and 1620 reflect an ageing king's intimations of mortality; but they seem also to challenge the tawdry, debt-ridden world. Indeed, from the moment he appeared for the first time in the court of Star Chamber in the summer of 1616 to confront Coke's law and judgeship in the name of an older, and divine, law and judgeship, the king seems to have been reclaiming the high ground. Though he had long shunned her example, Elizabeth might have approved.

The royal return to Scotland in 1617 may have been a welcome visit to old friends, but it was also carefully staged, the large entourage designed to impress an audience in both kingdoms. James lost no opportunity to acknowledge the loyalty and obedience of his Scottish subjects, or to stress his care for them *in absentia*. And when on his return he encountered local friction in Lancashire between the godly and the festive culture of neighbourhood he used the occasion to issue the 1617 *Book of Sports* and to assert the crown as patron and nurturer of an orderly and compassionate community. But this did not mean that he was throwing in his lot with the anti-Calvinist ceremonialists in religion. Indeed, he took care to affirm his credentials as the maintainer of a reformed consensus in England, and the delegation he sent to Dort in The Netherlands for the great Calvinist synod of 1618–19 sided unambiguously with the party of orthodoxy.

The image of the royal patriarch seemed to acquire more than a veneer of reality in the aftermath of the Howards. International crisis played its part: thus, as tension grew after 1618, the council abandoned its long unconcern for the militia, and steadily pressed the counties to deploy the more up-to-date, and costly, musket. But the new activism was also mundane and domestic. An extensive pruning of the commission of the peace in 1616–17 promised more active local government; this the council sought in the following years to shape into a surprising practical paternalism by promoting county granaries and fashionable root crops. More successful was the council's bid to curb the use of paid informers. Protests in the Commons in 1610 against one of the worst sharks, Sir Stephen Proctor (who had been granted a patent to suppress blackmailing informers and had then gone into business on his own account), were reinforced by the council's anxiety to remove obstacles to the textile trade after the Cockayne fiasco. At the prompting of Bacon, who was always concerned about the government's image, official discouragement of actions brought by informers in the central courts soon spread. By 1619 actions by informers in the key court of the exchequer were at one-sixth of the level they had been at in 1613, and continued to fall thereafter. It is important to note that the parliamentary campaigns of 1621 and 1624, which eventually barred most informers from the central courts, reinforced and prevented the reversal of a policy the council had already initiated.

The political prospects were therefore bright as Buckingham consolidated his position in 1618–19. Even financial reform seemed possible. It was certainly necessary, for James had had to force London to lend for his Scottish journey of 1617; his default on both interest and principal ruined his credit in the City for the rest of his reign. By mid-1618 the debt stood at the record level of about £900 000. Embarrassment reinforced the king's good intentions, for it encouraged those at court who saw retrenchment as the only way to avert bankruptcy. The key to reform was Buckingham, who coveted a patriotic image and who yet had few of the patronage ties to officials that might deter him from stern measures.

Commissioners appointed for the navy when in 1618 the favourite replaced the ageing Nottingham as Lord Admiral uncovered a saga of laxity and corruption. At one point there had been a mere seven ships in commission, while contractors, desperate for payment, paid retainers to officials and in return marked up the price of their supplies sometimes by 3000 per cent. The decline from Elizabethan days owed much to James himself, who had twice refused to pursue Northampton's jealous complaints against Nottingham. But now, thanks in particular to the diligence of John Coke, a future secretary of state, the commissioners both cut costs and built more ships. The treasury was a larger problem, but a first step was to put the treasury once again under commissioners, in the belief that they were more likely to resist temptation than a single lord treasurer had been. In the royal household too, where Cranfield took over as Master of the Wardrobe in 1618, economies were achieved. By rigorous accounting, checking how many cuts of meat could be had from an ox and ensuring competitive pricing, the former merchant trimmed the waste significantly, and in the wardrobe reduced expenditures by more than half. The combined savings, at the treasury, in the navy and in the household, were probably in the region of £120 000 per annum.

It took more than a well-intentioned king and favourite to balance the books. Fundamental reforms were to elude even the revolutionary regimes of mid-century, for eliminating official corruption necessitated raising salaries, which in turn demanded a dramatic, and improbable, restructuring of government since long-term borrowing was impossible. The economist Keynes was undoubtedly correct when he argued that in many societies corruption is the most efficient form of taxation. But structural dilemmas were intensified by character flaws. Not only can the reformers' strength of will be doubted, since it was dangerous to attack the pockets or jobs of courtiers; the reformers were themselves subject to temptation. The disastrous showing in the wars of the 1620s of the ordnance (provisioners of artillery) was not unrelated to Cranfield's readiness to cease his investigations once he had extorted land from the officers. Equally, the attacks in the parliament of 1621 on the delays and expense of justice in chancery suggest how little Bacon the reformer had done in the court to which he had been appointed in 1617: the good intentions he trumpeted seem to have amounted to little more than self-righteous advice from the sidelines.

Most important of all, Buckingham in power did not regard attacks on patronage in the same light as he had when rising. Unlike Somerset, he was surrounded by a tribe of relatives, provision for whom was both expensive and disreputable: as Cranfield and Sir Edward Coke discovered, advancement required a marriage alliance with the favourite's family. Buckingham's goodwill had to be purchased in all appointments, sometimes at enormous cost – Sir Henry Montague, later Earl of Manchester, paid £20 000 to become lord treasurer in 1620. And while the sale of English, Scottish and Irish titles of nobility between 1615 and 1628 grossed about £350 000, the crown saw less than half of this: Buckingham received £25 000 from the sale of Irish peerages alone in 1618–22. Meanwhile, a new flood of monopoly patents testified to the king's anxiety to reward Buckingham's friends as well as his own.

A public sermon in the summer of 1620 to the assize judges in Norwich protesting at the extortionate ways of the court suggests the growing perturbation of the country. But it need not have led to crisis. A total royal debt that still hovered around double the revenues ought to have been manageable, if rational policies had been followed. And with officials of the calibre of Bacon, Cranfield, or John Coke at the admiralty, and with a dominant figure of Buckingham's energy and tactical skill, such policies were not beyond reach. There was little here to disturb either the body politic or the court. But events overseas were to confront James's dynastic and pacific policies with ruin.

|5|

Peace and war in masquerade, 1621–1629

Two kings of very different character ruled England in the 1620s, yet the decade has a fundamental political unity. That unity stems from the catastrophe unleashed in the summer of 1620 with the entry of Spanish troops into the Palatinate, ancestral home of James's son-in-law Frederick. Nemesis came to Frederick, and then to Europe, in the autumn when disasters in the Palatinate were matched by a crushing Imperial victory outside Prague, at the Battle of the White Mountain. Frederick and his English 'winter queen' fled into a life-long exile. The wars that followed devastated Europe; in England, they strained those assumptions of balance and reciprocity that had structured the Jacobean peace. Worse, the wars were interpreted by many as a vast conflict of religions, of the true against the false. A dangerous ideological element was thus injected into a body politic already rendered uneasy by financial innovation and corruption.

The fuse had been lit in Europe in 1618. In that year Bohemian protestants rebelled against their elected Habsburg king, the future emperor Ferdinand, and then invited the eager Frederick to accept their crown. The challenge was not one that the Habsburgs could ignore, but the key question was whether the king of Spain would go to the aid of his Austrian cousin: a twelve years' truce between Spain and The Netherlands was due to expire in 1621, and a German struggle could easily turn into a European one. The crisis elicited very divergent English responses. Eager to avert the horrors of a pan-European war for religion, James berated Frederick for his intervention; more practically, he expedited the quest for the marriage alliance with Spain that was to be the foundation-stone of his new world order of peace and harmony, and in pursuit of which he had executed in 1618 that long-condemned gadfly of Spain, Sir Walter Raleigh. There were soon rumours, at least some of which were well-founded, that courtiers were learning Spanish and their ladies converting to Catholicism in anticipation. Yet James the Scot was never able to understand how much the drift towards Madrid conflicted with the legacy of

the long Elizabethan wars, which had for many defined English patriotism as gut hostility to Spain and to Catholicism. Archbishop Abbot saw
the apocalypse in the gathering storm: 'The kings of the earth . . . shall
now tear the whore [Rome] and make her desolate.' As James's subjects
came to suspect that his friendship with Spain threatened both his daughter and his religion, incomprehension grew.

The catastrophe narrowed James's options as he had feared. Both
honour and family feeling demanded that he succour his children, but
retrenchment at home had not yet yielded enough to fund the diplomatic
efforts the crisis demanded, let alone any more forceful action. And parliament seemed, after the experience of 1610 and 1614, a poor source of
aid. But in the winter of 1620–1 he was driven, with manifest reluctance,
to turn once more to his people, in hope that pressure for war might yet
moderate Madrid. His unease about the domestic response to the apparent collapse of European protestantism was clear in his proclamation
against public talk of affairs of state.

King and people alike had other causes of concern, since England was
in 1621 slipping into the deepest depression of the century. Currency
manipulations in the Baltic states had drained English currency at the same
time as they contrived to overprice English goods abroad. Shortages of
coin, when credit facilities were so primitive, increased both bottlenecks
and hardship as people found themselves without the cash to pay for
goods, even while falling exports increased unemployment. Any demand
for taxes in these circumstances was bound to create alarm inside parliament and out. To avert a storm, the always-prescient Bacon urged James
to surrender some of the most objectionable monopoly patents, particularly those, such as Sir Giles Mompesson's patent for licensing inns, that
trespassed on the local authority of JPs; but James declined, remembering
the damage done by pre-parliament undertaking in 1614 and forever reluctant to surrender anything that smacked of the prerogative. He would
instead trust to his powers of persuasion.

There was little in the public mood to suggest to James his confidence
might be misplaced. The crisis in Europe had impressed itself on propertied circles sufficiently for nearly £90 000 to be paid as a 'benevolence'
(or free gift) in late 1620 for the support of English volunteer forces in
the Palatinate. And while Thomas Scott's sermon to the Norfolk assizes
before the elections suggests growing anti-Catholic fervour, the elections
were generally quiet. Such rivalries as were fought out were overwhelmingly local – underlining once again the importance of parliament itself as
the stage for debate. But the local governors who sat in parliament had
to pay heed to those below them on whom their influence rested, all the
more so in a time of depression. If even the freeholder voters of metropolitan Middlesex preferred local gentry candidates to privy councillors
on the grounds of the inaccessibility of the latter, the suspicion of distant
Yorkshiremen that secretary of state Calvert might be too unresponsive to

local interests is hardly surprising. The Howard years had not been without effect.

Nevertheless, the parliament of 1621 was certainly open to persuasion. The king began auspiciously, recounting the plight of his family, and warning the houses that if he were to secure peace he must prepare for war, though he and his servants soon clouded the matter by talking of a costly land campaign into Germany. The Commons responded with alacrity to part of the message. The two subsidies (about £140 000) they eagerly voted were unprecedented at such an early stage in the session, and though they were not the blank cheque of which he dreamed, they pleased the king. The money would help cover immediate costs, and underwrite efforts to persuade Madrid that there was support for war. The Commons were also conciliatory when they turned, at the king's equally conciliatory invitation, to investigate the depression. They recognised, just as had the council in its revenue debates of 1615, that impositions could wreck a parliament, so they avoided the question. Instead, they found a ready answer for the shortage of money in the doings of patentees and monopolists.

The hunt for scapegoats is always an appealing solution to intractable problems; the early-modern scapegoat had the additional attraction of providing a natural cause for disorder in the body politic. Patentees were in one sense agents of prerogative power, but they also symbolised corrupt self-interest; courtiers and officials could accordingly display their care for the commonwealth by pursuing Mompesson, and eventually the luckless Bacon too. Indeed, every initiative in the attack on the patentees, which has often been seen as a stage in the growth of parliamentary control over the executive, came from within the court. Thus, it was two privy councillors, Cranfield and Sir Edward Coke (the latter appointed to the council in order to generate political goodwill), who directed the complaints on to the 'referees', the king's legal and financial officers who had approved the patents. Not incidentally, they thereby led the hunt after their private rivals, Lord Treasurer Mandeville and Bacon. The attack on the patentees indicates disquiet at the way the country had been governed, but scarcely a division between 'government' and 'critics'.

The king's part in the fall of his lord chancellor is instructive. Bacon perhaps paid the penalty for being always and gratingly right; but he also suffered for James's conviction of the moral, rather than the partisan, character of the political world. The king's belief in the divine origins of the justice he and his servants administered disinclined him to intervene when Cranfield and Coke urged that Bacon had accepted bribes on the bench. Similarly, a commitment to harmony led the king to congratulate Coke for discovering the judicial powers of the Lords that were to destroy Bacon. What was to be refined in later cases as the process of impeachment, unknown since 1450, thus emerged under the guidance of a privy councillor and with the blessing of the king. But a politics of morality might be two-edged. James's replacement of the politically ineffective Bacon as head of Chancery with John Williams, Bishop of Lincoln, can be read as the replacement of one conciliator by another; but the appointment to Chancery of the first clergyman in generations also hints that the king's conscience might outweigh the niceties of the law.

The first session of the 1621 parliament therefore fits easily into no simple story, whether of consensus or of conflict. Its outcome was, however, to lay the groundwork for the latter. James gave little sign during the summer of concern for Europe, but instead spent heavily on jewels. More alarmingly, in his concern to avoid a religious war he replaced as secretary of state the aggressively protestant Sir Robert Naunton with the Roman Catholic Sir George Calvert, and promoted the crypto-Catholic Sir Francis Cottington to Prince Charles's secretary; the new lord keeper, Williams, was also a known opponent of war. Such developments go far to explain the cries of perplexity so often heard in the following years.

Perplexity abounded as members reassembled for what was to prove the brief and unhappy second session. During the recess they had been reintroduced to local discontents; they had also read a fresh wave of newsletters about the sufferings of the Palatinate and the king's children, even while they brooded on the promotions at court. When in the second session the council turned the Commons towards foreign policy, MPs protested with tears their willingness to do their all for Frederick and Elizabeth; but they indicated as well their confusion as to the crown's intentions, and their lack of interest in the land war of which James talked. But the 1621 foreign policy debates have a significance that goes beyond their exposure of the distance the king stood from those whose views on foreign policy were shaped by religious passions. Those debates revealed divisions at court; but they also revealed divisions elsewhere – divisions that help explain how the nation could divide more deeply in 1642. Not all in the Commons, and still fewer in the Lords, were eager anti-Catholic warriors.

Yet even those who wanted to help the crown prepare for war could and soon did question which war they were being asked to support. Spain had intervened in the Palatinate, but James had made his own reluctance to engage with Spain painfully apparent. Baffled MPs heard councillors accept the case for a war, avoid talking of Spain, and forecast instead that a Palatinate campaign would cost £1 million a year. MPs who remembered Elizabethan privateering successes understandably preferred the argument in the *History of the World* by that old warrior Raleigh that £200 000 per annum would suffice for what later became known as a 'blue water' policy. By interrupting the flow of bullion from America, an oceanic war would make the king of Spain 'swim in his own channel'. Indeed, even in the council there was support for an Anglo-Dutch attack on Spain in the Low Countries and at sea, and not simply on grounds of cost. In their awareness of the divisions as well as the uncertainties at court, the Commons responded eagerly when Sir George Goring, a known client of Buckingham, seemed to give a signal of support for war with Spain. Goring probably sought another parliamentary threat as a bargaining-counter against Spain, but a house that lacked clear guidance was not the place for subtleties. Its anti-Spanish feelings finally released, it called abruptly for preparations for war and, logically enough, an end to the negotiations for a Spanish match for Prince Charles. Infuriated by this apparent challenge to his dearest prerogative, that of dynasty, the closest of all to his body, James reminded the Commons once more that they held their privileges of the mere grace of kings.

That reassertion of the position James had taken in 1604 at last brought constitutional issues to the fore. The king's message provoked the Commons to stop business, and thus to sacrifice bills both they and the king thought essential. Instead they composed a Protestation that consciously echoed the 1604 Apology in its insistence that parliament was 'the ancient and undoubted birthright' of Englishmen. The parallels with 1604 are marked, for in both instances the king was genuinely misinformed of the Commons' aggressiveness. The house had in reality shown considerable self-restraint, over impositions and also in its refusal to become involved in several potential privilege disputes. But self-restraint was one thing, forcible restraint quite another, and the Protestation insisted that without the privilege of free speech there was little future for parliaments. That future seemed all the more in question when James melodramatically ripped the Protestation out of the Commons' journal and, more practically, arrested five MPs after the dissolution.

If James had scant solution for the European crisis, he had none at all for the ills of the economy. As it became clear during 1622 that the coming harvest would be bad the depression intensified. Soaring grain prices eroded domestic demand for cloth and so worsened unemployment – and this when London's broadcloth exports had slumped to about 40 per cent of their 1618 level. The next harvest was even worse, and the crisis became a disaster. Amid reports of scattered rioting in the clothing counties, a Lincolnshire gentleman reported in 1623, 'There are many thousands in these parts who have sold all they have even to their bed-straw, and cannot get work to earn any money.' In the isolated northwest it became a genuine subsistence crisis, with local death-rates doubling. The council pressed JPs to ensure that the markets were supplied with grain for the poor, while it strove to protect clothiers from their creditors, and thus keep them in business. As so often, the concern for community and stability overrode care for private property rights.

The intensity of the depression did, however, encourage a search for longer-term solutions. From the beginning the baffled council had consulted outside opinion – parliament in 1621, merchants, clothiers, JPs. In 1622 these efforts culminated in the establishment of a standing investigatory commission, the forerunner of the long-lived board of trade. Though most of the advice offered was inconsequential, the crisis did prompt the elaboration of a body of thought that later ages labelled 'mercantilist'. Since coin was so vital in the economy, attention naturally focused on a 'balance of treasure', and exchange controls against the outflow of money. But one commentator, Thomas Mun, saw what continuing difficulties were to make many others realise by mid-century, that the problem in a closed, organic world was one of a 'balance of trade', whose remedy lay only in a surplus of exports over imports. Not surprisingly, official action did not end the depression.

The government's energies were anyway distracted by the expanding war in Europe, and its domestic repercussions. The 1621 parliament had turned James more determinedly than ever against military intervention, and he intensified his efforts for a Spanish match for his son Charles. In the summer of 1622 he ordered the judges to relax the penal laws against Catholics. Protestant opinion had long foretold that a Spanish match would lead to this, and worse: as John Pym, the future parliamentary leader, had put it apocalyptically in 1621, 'If the papists once obtain a connivance, they will press for a toleration; from thence to an equality; from an equality to a superiority; from a superiority to an extirpation of all contrary religions.' James's fears that a European crisis would not be easily contained were soon confirmed. The threat to protestantism abroad came at a time when the domestic Calvinist consensus was unravelling in the universities; it therefore provoked quite disproportionate anxiety. In 1622 new instructions to preachers ordered that sermons be confined to the most uncontroversial matters of faith and obedience. The ban on the preaching of militant protestantism when a Spanish queen was in prospect seemed to many to signal imminent changes in religion.

Protestant watchers might have been less alarmed had they realised that their enemies were as fearful of contamination. The fate of the last Spanish queen of England, Catherine of Aragon, gave little encouragement to Madrid, and the devout Philip IV was fiercely opposed to protestant heresy. Prince Charles was left fretting in his frustration, and fancying himself in love with reports of Philip's sister, the Infanta. But, naive and awkward as he was, Charles was also deeply convinced of the efficacy of monarchy, and assumed that his presence in Madrid would cut through all knots. He was encouraged in this by Buckingham, who was eager to second Charles's wishes in order to ensure his own position in the future king's goodwill; furthermore, the not unastute favourite may have calculated that action might at least resolve negotiations that had for so long preoccupied James. In February 1623 the two young men rode off for Madrid, disguised with false beards and with merely a single servant. They left the king distraught and the court in an uproar.

The Spanish journey quickly turned into a comedy of errors. English courtiers flocked to Madrid, though that famine-stricken city could scarcely support its own population. The easy intimacy the adventure had generated between the prince and Buckingham, newly created a duke, shocked the etiquette-ridden Spanish court as much as Buckingham's exploits affronted the resident English ambassador, the Earl of Bristol. When Charles discovered that Spain was not anxious for a marriage he was reduced to climbing walls to catch sight of his beloved and to enlarging his offers of religious concessions, although with little return in offers of Spanish aid over the Palatinate. James, desperate for the safety of his son and his favourite, willingly agreed to underwrite whatever terms emerged from Madrid. But the comedy had a dangerous edge. The lovelorn negotiators had come close to offering toleration for English Catholics, and suspicions at Whitehall and in the country grew. Buckingham's clients repeatedly warned him that summer of the risks he ran, and these promptings reinforced the duke's exasperation with the Spanish. In time even the more obtuse Charles appreciated that Spain was merely temporising, to forestall any English military action.

The failure of the Spanish journey was a climacteric in English politics, and not simply because it rooted the duke forever in Charles's affections. The return of the prodigals without a bride generated the clearest and most widespread expression of public opinion before the Restoration. For a few exhilarating months the prince and duke were popular heroes – to his puzzlement, Charles was not to enjoy the experience again. But for the moment it eased the task of defending Buckingham at court: concessions could be blamed on Spanish duress, while Bristol, who posed the major threat to the official account, could be accused of urging Catholicism on Charles. In a shift of immense significance, the court swung from dreams of marriage to thoughts of war; and Buckingham and Charles, frustrated, resentful, led the charge.

The war party had, however, to reckon with the king. James may have been physically deteriorating with age and illness, but he was still 'rex pacificus' – all the more determinedly since war would require another parliament. The first task facing the prince and the duke was therefore to assure the king that a new parliament would be orderly. They had powerful assets. Charles's ability to promise the future meant that few courtiers and officials were anxious to oppose them. And there were ideological openings to exploit, for among Buckingham's courtly enemies, Pembroke in particular welcomed the prospect of war with Spain. But it was on the Commons that James's impatience had focused; and Sir Robert Phelips, Sir Edwin Sandys and Sir Edward Coke were willing to give assurances that if the king called a parliament and broke off the treaty with Spain, they would ensure that the Commons did not challenge impositions or the issues of parliamentary privilege raised by the angry close of the 1621 parliament. Still protesting, James was persuaded to revert to his policy of 1621, of using parliamentary anger against Spain. He summoned a new parliament for February 1624.

The prospects for war were by no means secure. Charles and Buckingham counted on the excitement of their return, and surging anti-

Catholicism, to overcome members' reluctance to call for what must be major expenditures in a deep depression. They were to find that anti-Catholicism could not be so easily channelled. In London in October 1623 a building that was being used by Roman Catholics for clandestine worship collapsed with major loss of life; to the providentially minded – who were not just the puritans of caricature – this seemed God's judgment on English backsliding. The Catholic threat was an issue in several elections, but when Sir Richard Grosvenor as sheriff of Cheshire harangued the county's voters it was to a domestic danger to religion that he pointed. There lay the disruption that James sought to avert. Heartened by renewed Spanish proposals designed to wean him from the hawks in the new parliament, and justly confident that Madrid did not control events in Vienna and Germany, the king merely asked parliament's advice on what to do about the negotiations. He also made it clear that any war must be in and for the Palatinate – an undertaking which in 1621 the Commons had been warned must cost £1 million per annum. When he demanded that his debts (amounting now to around £1m) be paid first, it became an offer that was easy to refuse. The refusers included the usual members apprehensive of the costs of any war that was not defensive, and far readier to legislate against abuses; but the hawks too had their own priorities.

Charles and Buckingham had to work furiously to save the parliament. In moves that were to create colossal future problems for themselves, they handed out informal assurances that a war would be the one the Commons' strategists favoured – the Elizabethan way, of action at sea and perhaps an Anglo-Dutch diversionary campaign in Spanish Flanders. Once James had been dissuaded from requiring aid with his debts, the Commons offered slightly under £300 000. It was a large sum, enough for an oceanic but scarcely for a land war. The prince and duke distracted their parliamentary allies from enlarging on the potential here for misunderstanding by offering them a sacrifice, Lionel Cranfield, now Lord Treasurer Middlesex. Like most economisers, Middlesex was opposed to the profligacy of war; but he had also tried to tie the king closer by foisting yet another handsome young man on him while the duke was in Spain. Not even James could protect his servant against the consequences. There were murmurings of suspicion in the Commons that Middlesex intended further impositions, but Buckingham's allies were in fact the driving force in the treasurer's impeachment for corruption. And Middlesex had few supporters, since stopping pensions had been central to a retrenchment programme he had conducted with an unbecoming arrogance.

Despite developments that seem in retrospect full of constitutional moment, the 1624 parliament was part of a familiar world. The parliament's major legislative measure, the statute against monopolies, can scarcely be read as constitutional aggression, since the Commons quite deliberately left loopholes for government – for corporations, for inventions, for royal officers – that Charles in the next reign eagerly exploited.

The further development of impeachment in the campaign against Middle-sex, and the requirement of the 1624 subsidy act that expenditures be accounted for to treasurers appointed by parliament, were closely connected to court contests; and if there was an 'opposition' it was in a very real sense Charles and Buckingham. Indeed, the seventy-three statutes of this 'happy parliament' were a record for a single session. Yet the Commons were neither myopic nor submissive, and not all was harmony. MPs did not challenge the king on foreign policy, but that was partly because Buckingham's supporters worked hard to conceal the divergence of the king's preferences from theirs. And while the appropriation of supply to parliamentary treasurers did originate at court, it would scarcely have been needed but for the widespread suspicions of what James wanted the money for. There was nervousness of the future too: the warning given by Sir Benjamin Rudyerd, a prominent client of Pembroke, that 'if this parliament fail, it will be the last of parliaments', voiced a common concern.

The aftermath of the 1624 parliament proved disastrous enough to warrant Rudyerd's fears. The Commons had pointedly and repeatedly shied away from involvement in the morass of Germany, and had granted James a large supply on what they took to be undertakings by Charles and Buckingham. But James, ailing though he was, was still king and still controlled policy; the intense frustrations of the young pair with that fact provide a plausible background for the subsequent rumours that Buckingham poisoned him. No naval war came, nor even a public breach with Spain. James declared his anxiety to avoid such a breach by suppressing performances of Thomas Middleton's hugely successful anti-Spanish play, *A Game at Chess*. By the time of his death James had committed England to an annual expenditure of £720 000, most of it in support of various powers' land forces in central Europe. The resulting incomprehension was to ruin the new king's relations with his early parliaments, for it made central the hugely emotive but usually unspo-ken matter of Charles's honour.

Few kings have come to the throne with their honour more heavily and publicly compromised than Charles. The failure of the Spanish match left him needing a bride of appropriate grandeur and with an appropriate dowry. The logical provider was Roman Catholic and yet anti-Habsburg France, which as an ally would lessen the chances of the religious war James dreaded, and so make him more willing to engage. Thus might Charles and Buckingham redeem their parliamentary credit. But to the surprise of the eager warriors, Louis XIII was reluctant to sell his sister in a military package deal, and insisted on religious concessions as exten-sive as those offered to Spain. Since both James and Charles had in the 1624 parliament committed themselves never to make such concessions to gain a marriage this caused them to hesitate; but their strategic needs soon triumphed. The recusancy laws were suspended once again, and a public chapel, that would mean access for English Catholics, was promised for Charles's future bride, Henrietta Maria.

The French entanglement determined the course of domestic history more than did any other diplomatic episode of the early-modern period. James, Charles and Buckingham made large concessions in the vital areas of religion and honour to obtain a marriage that they assumed would be the basis of a wider alliance. Only slowly did recognition dawn that Cardinal Richelieu, Louis's able chief minister, was happy to see England fighting Spain, but not to join in that cause himself. So all that the French alliance yielded was Louis's agreement to join James in financing a proxy descent on the Palatinate by the German mercenary Count Mansfeld; and even this was lost when a revolt by the Huguenots, the French protestants, caused Richelieu to turn his attention inwards. The luckless force of pressed English infantry that set out under Mansfeld in January 1625 wasted away on the Dutch coast amidst Anglo-French bickering.

Worse followed. As earnest of English good faith Richelieu had demanded naval help to suppress what at first seemed a localised revolt by the Huguenot Duc de Soubise, and James and Buckingham jumped at the chance to show their value as allies. To their horror the revolt spread to involve most of the French protestant communities, and the awful prospect arose of English ships and sailors suppressing their co-religionists. In its anxiety to avoid handing them over, the government even sponsored a mutiny amongst the sailors. James's death in March 1625 left Charles facing political disaster with his marriage. French coolness had driven James, and then drove his young successors, to make repeated concessions in the futile hope of drawing France closer; in so doing they baffled those who had heard what seemed very different undertakings in the 1624 parliament. The growing frustration of Charles and the duke, inexperienced diplomats as they were, with what the duke called the 'shitten mouths' of the French, led eventually to war in the most catastrophic circumstance – a yawning credibility gap.

The new king was ill-suited to repair the damage. Not unadvisedly, Clarendon began his great *History of the Rebellion* with Charles's accession in 1625; so too, from a very different perspective, did the Commons' Grand Remonstrance of 1641. And while it would be foolish to conclude that the Civil War occurred simply because Charles was king, it would be equally foolish to underestimate the part played by his personality. Charles had been brought up very much in the shadow of his glamorous elder brother Henry, and it is tempting to see his diffidence, his awkwardness, his habitual stutter, as consequences, and to trace to them his insistence on the dignity of kingship. That stutter, and his preoccupation with majesty, may explain his reluctance to explain his actions – never one of James's failings. His terse speeches from the throne to his parliaments suggest a vision of rule that entailed conformity, not consensus.

Reluctance to explain was the more unfortunate since Charles badly needed parliamentary help. At his accession he found an empty treasury, and the royal credit almost exhausted. He was immediately forced to mortgage £216 000 in land to the City to restore the credit his father had damaged and to secure a paltry loan of £60 000. If he were merely to make good the commitments in Europe that his father had made, let alone act for himself, he had to call a parliament. The timing of that parliament, which assembled in June 1625, was scarcely opportune. Questions were asked at the polls about the 1624 taxes, and Charles had nothing to show but the tolerance of recusancy required by the marriage, the charade of the loan ships sailing back and forth across the Channel, and the disintegration of Mansfeld's troops. Etiquette demanded the extravagant celebrations feting the arrival of the new queen in London, but since these exactly coincided with Charles's plea to the parliament for aid they did not help to quell scepticism.

Worst of all, James's death was promptly followed by the outbreak of what was to prove one of the worst plagues since the Black Death. By the end of 1625 about 20 per cent of London's population was dead, about the same proportion in Norwich by the plague's end in 1626, and considerably more in Exeter. The epidemic devastated the economy in the summer of 1625, as merchants, magistrates and even ministers fled. And it was politically damaging, since providentialists saw plague as divine judgment for backsliding. The council's cessation of the prosecution of Catholics seemed to threaten the lives of all.

Plague dictated only one timetable for the parliament: a speedy supply and then adjournment to a happier time. But Charles found himself the prisoner of his own diplomacy. He needed to prepare a fleet for use against Spain, since England's worth to France as an ally rested on its navy. But were he to declare war on Spain and thus convince parliament to give money, France would see still less need to commit itself. Keeping the purpose of his fleet a mystery may have been a diplomatic necessity, but in the context of the 1624 misunderstandings and the affair of the loan fleet it was a disaster for domestic confidence. Anyway, few protestants could understand how suspension of proceedings against recusants could accompany war against Spain, since their Elizabethan upbringing had taught them to equate patriotism with anti-Catholicism. While Charles was assuring the Lords, and parliament as a whole, that his marriage would bring no privileges for English Catholics, 'papists' were coming into the open. The Scottish Earl of Kellie reported privately from London in late July: 'You can not believe the alteration that is in the opinion of the whole world touching his majesty.'

The French connection and the plague deflected the first parliament of Charles's reign into misunderstandings that were to shape the new king's attitudes. In his opening speech Charles abruptly and characteristically claimed that parliament was morally bound to support him since it had 'engaged' for war in 1624; but uncomprehending MPs would not go beyond their meagre offer of two subsidies, or about £120 000. Charles then found himself trying to fight a war without support, and felt betrayed – all the more so when the Commons cast a questioning eye on other branches of his revenue. The duty of tonnage and poundage, a branch of the customs, was conventionally granted for a king's life at the start of the reign; but, fearing that the usual statute might justify impositions for life too, several members urged revisions.

The Commons' leaders were scarcely bent on confrontation. Phelips and Coke were ready to greet the new reign with retrospective sanction, in a tonnage and poundage act, for the existing impositions, thus preserving the principle of parliamentary control while leaving the crown the revenue it needed. But since plague was rife, Phelips proposed a one-year grant and the postponement of reform. Pressed by the council, which had no desire to be coerced into meeting parliament on the Commons' timetable, the Lords killed Phelips's proposal, and Charles was thus left without parliamentary authorisation for a revenue he had to have if he were to go to war. Suspicions of impositions, complaints of what the depredations of pirates revealed of Buckingham's tenure as lord admiral, frustration at the evaporation of the good feelings of 1624, all help account for Phelips's nervous reminder that England alone in Europe retained its 'original rights and constitutions'. Indeed, assumptions of harmony were becoming frayed by misunderstanding and mistrust. Sir John Coke, shortly to become secretary of state, warned the Commons that if parliament would not pay for the war 'some new way' must be found. There is no evidence that any of the king's servants were planning constitutional innovation. They were, however, encountering all those frustrations of organising a modern war effort on medieval conventions of financing against which Salisbury had rebelled.

It is in the field of religion that claims of innovation seem plausible. Such claims certainly had more urgent effect. Under James English protestants had been able to assume that the church was united in its basic beliefs and, somewhat less certainly, in its practices. James had carefully protected a small strain of academic dissent, which is usually though not very helpfully known as Arminianism, after the Dutch theologian Arminius; but not until 1624 was there a public assault on Calvinist orthodoxy. It came from Richard Montagu, a minor cleric whom leading court 'Arminians' like Bishops Laud and Neile happily used as a stalking-horse. They saw an opportunity in James's impatience with the strident anti-Catholicism born of the Thirty Years War to wean him from Calvinism. With their encouragement, Montagu's *New Gag for an Old Goose* boisterously challenged the identification of the pope as Antichrist.

The new king went further and faster than the episcopal schemers could have hoped. Montagu's riposte to complaints in the parliament of 1625 was to dedicate his far more provocative *Appello Caesarem* to Charles, who promptly took Montagu into his personal protection. Within months of his accession the deeply ceremonialist and authoritarian king was extending visible support to self-consciously anti-Calvinist clergy. Alarmed, the Earl of Warwick and Viscount Saye and Sele, both leading Calvinists, tried to clarify matters by persuading Buckingham to call a theological debate. Up to this point Buckingham's ecclesiastical and political patronage had spanned the theological spectrum, doubtless as an insurance against every possible eventuality. But, knowing which way the wind from the throne was blowing, at the York House conference in February 1626 he leaned decisively against the Calvinists. It was a sign that intelligent observers did not miss: that very month leading Calvinist clergy guided by John Preston came together with lay allies to form the feoffees for impropriations, a secretive body that sought to rationalise and improve private funding for Calvinist preachers. And for the first time since the middle years of Elizabeth the state of the Church of England became a major and divisive issue.

Scarcely coincidentally, the court as a whole grew more isolated. Whatever his own affections, James had balanced his court as determinedly as he had his foreign policy, even protecting those who were at odds with the favourite. His death removed every obstacle to the duke's sway. Buckingham's most astute move had been to recognise that the awkward prince Charles needed affection and admiration. The charm in which he bathed the prince, particularly on the Spanish journey, had its reward in a devotion even greater than James's: the duke's enemies were now the king's. Not only did Charles's accession send James's old and independent-minded Scottish friends into eclipse, and isolate the hapless Bristol more than ever; it also allowed the duke to move against others sceptical of war. Lord Keeper Williams was dismissed after the 1625 parliament while the Earl of Arundel – a spokesman for the old nobility's resentment of the duke – was put under house arrest early in 1626. Within a year of Charles's accession the only major figure independent of Buckingham left at court was Pembroke, whose commitment to a Spanish war helped him swallow his differences. Such changes at court were bound to have an effect in the country. When Buckingham turned his hegemony over the king's ear into a monopoly politicians, finding access blocked, were driven to employ new tactics. Like many MPs from clothing areas, Sir Thomas Wentworth had little sympathy for a Spanish war that would disrupt Yorkshire's textile trade. Thrust out of his local offices for his pains late in 1625, and finding no redress save by paying court to Buckingham, he broke with convention and made a vindicatory speech at the Yorkshire assizes.

The disturbances emanating from the centre were intensified by the material consequences of an active foreign policy. The council in late 1625 turned to arbitrary means to make good what it had lost by the dissolution of the parliament, and levied in the form of a forced loan the equivalent of the two subsidies. The poor, especially in the coastal counties, probably suffered more than the propertied taxpayers, since the impressed men (for Mansfeld in 1624 and to serve in the 1625 fleet) had to be paid for and billeted locally; repayment only came, slowly, after 1627. And since war plans focused attention on the militia, the council sent out detailed instructions in the summer of 1625 for the regular training and equipping of a 'perfect militia'. Such burdens were not readily understood, for fear of plague made men all over the country shun company and stop trading, and left inhabitants of the clothing areas facing starvation.

Politically more damaging was the fate of this military activity. The fiasco of Mansfeld's expedition was as nothing compared to the disaster that met Charles's forces when they finally sailed against Spain in September 1625. Gentlemen had volunteered in droves, hoping to revive the glories of the 1596 raid on Cadiz, but the adventure was appallingly planned and badly executed. That winter's return to southwest England of the tattered remnant, starving, unclothed and disease-ridden, was an irreparable blow to confidence in the administration. One Dorset minister preached that 'the late repulse' was God's punishment on a land that 'was not governed by justice, but by bribery and extortion'. There were those like the Suffolk lawyer John Winthrop, future governor of the Massachusetts Bay colony, who began in their private meditations to advance apocalyptic interpretations.

The king's decision to call a new parliament for February 1626 might suggest an almost perverse recognition of parliament's centrality in the body politic. But Charles, who imagined a fairly circumscribed role for his parliaments, had very practical hopes in the winter of 1625–6. Once again, foreign affairs held the key. The loan ships had eventually been handed over in a lull in France's civil strife; but to the anguish of Charles's council the revolt flared up again, and the ships were after all put to effective use against protestants. All the resentment against the French that had built up during the marriage negotiations broke out anew, exacerbated by the fact that relations between the king and his new bride were proving less than loving. But Charles could not simply abandon a diplomatic entanglement that had already brought him intense political embarrassment, for he had still to restore his sister to Heidelberg.

With royal patience exhausted, disaster threatening in any new parliament, and Buckingham facing likely destruction, a new foreign policy emerged in late 1625. England was to take its rightful place at the head of the protestant cause. Recusants were persecuted once again, while the council planned a firm alliance with the Dutch, renewed action against Spain, help for the suffering French Huguenots – and action against France. Observers concluded that Charles would go to the new parliament asking for support for a godly war. However little parliament had been able to determine James's foreign policy in 1624, desperation had led Charles to shape his policy to parliamentary tastes.

Soon after the election writs went out, the French pulled the rug from under him. Fearing war on too many fronts, Richelieu established a hasty peace with the Huguenots and left Charles without a policy when the parliament opened. The prospects for this parliament looked bleak. Continuing depression in the textile industry, intensified by the plague and another bad harvest in 1625, was further exacerbated by foreign policy, for exports of new draperies to southern Europe were disrupted by the tensions with Spain and France. The plight of starving neighbours was likely to move parliament-men from the clothing regions more than their concern for the protestant cause in Europe – particularly since Charles had not yet shown much commitment to that cause himself. And neighbours might make their views very apparent: the magistrates of Bury St Edmunds in Suffolk, a hardpressed clothing town, declared during the 1626 elections that 'in general they would give no voice [vote] to any courtier'. Charles had good reason to approve the topic of the opening sermon to parliament: the importance of unity in Jerusalem. But his choice of bishop Laud as preacher must have contributed to the disunity he deplored.

No more than in any other 1620s parliament were the Commons heading into 'opposition'. Even Sir John Eliot, who was soon to take the lead in the attack on Buckingham, recognised the crown's problems as he invoked the interdependence of the whole:

> Cut off the king's revenues, you cut off the principal means of your own safeties, and not only disable him to defend you, but enforce that which you conceive an offence, the extraordinary resort to his subjects for supplies, and the more than ordinary ways of raising them.

Eliot advanced a conservative formula for getting the crown off the people's backs – the resumption of grants of crown lands and pensions. But the chief attraction of that formula lay in its implication for Buckingham, the prime recipient of such grants and the object of far greater animosity than in 1625. The growing number of English ships lost to pirates and Spanish privateers could, like the Cadiz disaster, be laid to the door of a lord admiral whose monopoly of office, extravagance, and diplomatic failings all resented. Back-bench distaste was reinforced by the cries of jealous courtiers, and Pembroke's clients focused on the charge of 'single counsel'; it was one of these who opened the way to impeachment proceedings.

The charge that the duke was the 'grievance of grievances' was vital to those who wished neither to criticise the king's government nor to admit that the body politic might be seriously unwell. But impeachment foundered when Charles in mid-May interposed the king's own judgment against that of the majority of the Commons, and personally cleared the duke of all fault. Until then Pembroke's clients might have been able to lead the house to accept Buckingham's abandonment of a few offices, and a firm Anglo-French alliance; but though they might guide, the aristocratic patrons could not control the Commons. They could neither extract supply from interests damaged by a pointless crisis, nor soothe the ordinary gentleman appalled by the reports of corruption and Catholicism at court, and above all in Buckingham's family. The anger and perplexity over the course of policy since the parliament of 1624 spilled over as the Commons confronted a king who seemed determined to set himself against them. When Eliot likened the duke to Sejanus, the tyrannical favourite of the deeply flawed Roman emperor Tiberius, it did not take much imagination to think of parallels to Tiberius.

The attack on the duke tested all the tactical sophistication of the Commons. With impeachment blocked, the house delayed its vote of supply, hoping to use it as a lever to persuade the king to dismiss the duke. But the £200 000 it had offered in supply was scarcely one-third of what Charles needed for the year, even if hostilities were not to expand to include France. Desperate though the king was, he could recognise the extent of the shortfall, and both councillors and king promptly threatened 'new counsels' and 'other resolutions' of the sort that had led to the disappearance of parliaments in Europe. The survival of this parliament into mid-June owed little to the financial arithmetic.

The king's concerns now centred above all on his honour, and for the first time in years the Lords held the stage. Charles had excluded several of the duke's enemies from the parliament. The Commons had conspicuously not protested when the king disabled Coke, Phelips, Wentworth and a few others by appointing them sheriffs; but the seclusion of the Earls of Arundel and Bristol provoked major storms in the Lords. Bristol, tired of his long house-arrest, complained that he was being victimised by Buckingham because he had information against him; Charles retaliated, in the hope that the Lords would drop the matter, by charging Bristol with treason committed in Madrid. But the Lords' sense that the Buckingham years had besmirched the honour on which aristocracy rested made them at this point even more conscious of privilege than were the Commons. They would not give way even when Charles put Arundel – an ally of Bristol and holder of several proxy votes – under house-arrest. The Bristol affair was the more serious of the two. The charges and counter-charges, centring on who had tried to convert Charles to Catholicism in Madrid, involved the public washing of some very dirty royal linen. Charles insisted that his honour be vindicated, but not surprisingly the Lords were reluctant to proceed with such dangerous business. Only when it became clear that they would not condemn Bristol did Charles dissolve the parliament, though he threw the blame on the Commons as he tried to rebuild bridges to the peers.

Even a parliament generous with supply would probably not have saved Charles's strategy from ruin. The Danish allies his father had acquired in 1624 had collapsed; immeasurably worse, France had made peace with Spain in the spring of 1626, so thwarting Charles of his grand alliance. More gratingly, Cardinal Richelieu maintaining his pressure on the

Huguenot stronghold of La Rochelle, even while pressing Charles to fulfil the terms of the marriage treaty and improve the lot of English Catholics. The marriage itself, to a headstrong and unhappy teenager, was headed downhill. Mutual marital and maritime provocations inexorably took Charles into a war with France in which few English interests were involved and few strategic possibilities appeared.

Charles lacked the money to make a reality of war. While financial strains were common to all belligerent nations in the global environment of endemic liquidity shortage, the English government's borrowing ability was more limited than most. The City of London declined to lend, and Charles was reduced to trying vainly to pawn the crown jewels in Amsterdam. In the absence of funds as well as of a clear objective the fleet Charles assembled in the summer of 1626 wasted away almost as miserably as had Mansfeld's forces. The 'new counsels' that had been threatened in parliament came to seem the only alternative to a humiliating peace.

The conceptual unity of the body politic was beginning to fracture. Preoccupied as he was with the vindication of his honour in the war in which he found himself, Charles was now convinced that parliament-men disloyally located the source of all authority in the wider community, in 'popularity'. He is reliably reported to have enquired how Louis XIII had eliminated the estates-general; and the metropolis certainly abounded in late 1626 with rumours of his hostility to any talk of a parliament. Buckingham for his part had little cause to relish the prospect of a parliament, and good reason to hope for the success of any alternative; and Bishop Laud, Charles's favourite clergyman, sensed that a parliament would mean a challenge to his vision of the church. But most of Charles's councillors still hoped for harmony; and none had sufficient drive to create a new order. By the winter of 1627–8 one councillor, Sir Thomas Edmondes, had been left nervous and hesitant in face of innovatory proposals, 'without either the consent of a parliament, or the hope of gaining the submission and conformity of the people thereunto'. Edmondes's colleagues probably sincerely believed their public defence, that the new measures they adopted were temporary and emergency expedients.

Emergency or not, Charles's attempt in the summer of 1626 to collect as a 'benevolence' the subsidies lost by the dissolution of parliament was ill judged. There was considerable support – in the church hierarchy, in the Lords in 1628, in the country too – for the king's claim to an absolute prerogative empowering him to defend the realm, and requiring the subject to assist. But by summoning all the tax-payers Charles seemed to emphasise that parliament was being by-passed. And that possibility could not seem a matter of detail in the country. On the day after the 1626 dissolution Charles issued a proclamation forbidding public argument about sensitive matters of religious doctrine; he cited domestic tranquillity as justification. Although James had issued not dissimilar orders in 1622, this proclamation was more certainly interpreted as an attempt to restrain the preaching of orthodox Calvinism. It required no great political sophistication for Calvinists to note the timing, and to link their creed to the survival of parliament. That coupling, and its converse – popery and absolutism – proved explosive. But alarm was not limited to godly circles, for the king's appeal to doctrines of necessity looked familiar to those kept informed of continental developments. The market for the courantos – embryonic newsbooks – and broadsides pioneered in the gathering 1620s crisis points to the existence of a political public. The abject failure of the 1626 benevolence indicates that parliament had put down deep roots into that public.

Under the goad of an angry king bent on extracting obedience as much as money, the council became more peremptory. Although the forced loan demanded late in 1626 was, like many of its predecessors, a loan in name only it was less constitutionally provocative than the benevolence had been; but it was novel in its scope and in its systematic execution. Subsidy-payers were summoned to meetings where local commissioners, often reinforced by itinerant privy councillors, pressed them individually to pay. Such a direct and unremitting approach to individual allegiances proved remarkably successful. Although the economy was still in disarray, few dared, or were willing, to withstand the king's name. By the end of 1627 a sum only slightly smaller than the five subsidies sought in the 1626 parliament had been raised, and in a much shorter time than a large subsidy collection normally took. The loan, whose yield is eloquent testimony to what the council could achieve by sustained effort, rescued Charles from immediate bankruptcy.

The crown's greatest asset was a general realisation that the country had to be governed, and that the king alone had the right to govern. That realisation was heightened by the military activity then in train. Local elites co-operated with the deputy lieutenants who since 1624 had worked thanklessly, if not enthusiastically, to levy and billet some 50 000 conscripted soldiers, or about 1 per cent of the total population. The men were often weak or unsuitable, and their arms only too often rusty cast-offs. Yet local self-government produced men and money for an unpopular cause through means which – as the 1628 debates showed – were wide open to legal challenge. Equally remarkably, humbler householders whose lot it was to provide billets acquiesced; the only significant disturbances occurred when Irish or Scots soldiers inflamed local xenophobia.

But the council could not capitalise fully on the readiness of the nation to conform. It could neither translate all its wishes into commands, nor make all its commands felt. Preoccupied with disciplining loan defaulters, it was distracted from the final objective, the military preparations. The expeditionary force Buckingham led in 1627 to aid the Huguenots of La Rochelle found itself supplied with wheat but no means to bake bread, and with scaling ladders too short for the job; troops arriving at rendezvous found neither orders nor officers waiting, and commanders were left for weeks without instructions. The disorganisation reinforced the arguments for political consensus, and in particular for having the parliamentary gentry vote and collect taxes themselves. The council did not have the resources to translate the king's authority into effective personal government.

By the end of 1627 the crown's credit had proved unable to bear the strains of war. In return for the liquidation of debts of some £230 000 owed to Londoners, and the extraction of one further loan, Charles that winter turned over to the City the last major saleable body of crown lands, worth about £350 000. With that sale disappeared the crown's independent reserve of security for loans and its last hedge against crisis at the onset of war; and so, it might be said, disappeared the medieval monarchy. With little land to sell or to pledge for loans, the crown was left exposed to emergencies. Charles certainly turned for aid to the customs farmers, who used their own private credit and the security of their control of the customs to channel loans from merchants to the crown. But – as the next decade was to confirm – even the farmers could not finance a war. In the winter of 1627–8 the farmers seem to have refused to lend unless a parliament was called to grant Charles additional revenue as security.

The council was badly divided that winter. Its morale could scarcely have been helped when the king used £18 000 of his non-existent resources to snap up the breathtaking art collection of the Duke of Mantua as it went on the market. The purchase – however aesthetically brilliant – showed as little regard for strategic realities as the king had done when in 1627 he sent Buckingham to raise the siege of La Rochelle by an ill-planned assault on the outlying Ile de Rhé. The duke's withdrawal with the loss of more than half his forces was the crowning military humiliation.

As the nation grew angry and embittered, Charles waxed scornful of parliaments that had not fulfilled what he saw as the 'engagement' of 1624. Determined to uphold his honour through an effective war-effort, he had billeted troops on the civilian population and gaoled loan-refusers without filing charges. When five of these sued for *habeas corpus* in the so-called Five Knights' Case of 1627, the king saw a chance to obtain a binding precedent legitimising the crown's extra-legal powers of arrest. But though the judges quite properly accepted the narrow argument of Attorney-General Heath that the crown must have emergency powers that it was trusted not to misuse, the technical form of their order was not what Charles wanted. Accordingly, he insisted that Heath surreptitiously amend the record. But the nerves of a majority in the council were less steeled for conflict. They knew that the loan had only been raised in hard-pressed counties along the south coast by offsetting payments against military expenses, such as billeting, already incurred: rather less than the £260 000 of the accountings actually reached the exchequer. And they counted the political costs. The gaoling of seventy-six gentlemen and an earl, the dismissal of four leading peers from local office, and of Chief Justice Crew for refusing to support the loan, boded ill for the further innovations – such as an excise tax – the king favoured. With the position of hard-liners like Bishop Laud and the duke weakened by disaster, the council prevailed on Charles to summon a parliament, to meet in March 1628.

Charles's determination to fight an incomprehensible – and incompetent – war during a depression strained the informal ties and the inarticulate acceptance that were so vital to the functioning of society. The disruption was widespread. In Scotland, whose formal institutions were open to royal manipulation, taxation was extracted annually throughout the 1620s; those levies bred new resentments at absentee and irresponsible rule. In Ireland, the decade ended in a disastrous sense of betrayal as the crown abandoned its offer of major concessions to Roman Catholics – 'the Graces' of 1628 – after it had extracted a large supply as quid pro quo. In England the strains could be seen in the 1628 elections, which saw a growing aversion to courtiers. Nor was the discontent merely localism. The Suffolk clergyman John Rous noted, 'Men be disposed to speak the worst of state businesses', and from Lincolnshire to Cornwall there was ominous popular support for newly released loan refusers. The newsletters of disaster and the verses on scandal and corruption collected by quite minor gentlemen like William Davenport in Cheshire or Ralph Ashton in Yorkshire suggest the excitement, while the manuscript copies of parliamentary speeches indicate where the hopes for reform centred.

If the organic metaphor held, Buckingham's bodily transgressions must jeopardise the entire body politic. The scurrility of the tales about the duke is insufficient to explain his hold on the national imagination. Such stories had implications for readers of the Old Testament and the classics alike, for both taught that politics was about moral actions and that the vice of rulers brought catastrophe. For the providentially minded, evidence of God's impending judgment abounded in disasters at home and abroad. Conventional Calvinists like Coke, Phelips or Wentworth undoubtedly shared the hopes of moderate councillors like Pembroke for some compromise that would bring reform and yet allow them to retain local support and gain favour at court. But the godly were less sanguine as they brooded on 'papist' advances. In Canterbury the local official, and newly elected MP, Thomas Scott stigmatised the 'dukists' who betrayed the land to Antichrist. Equally alert, John Pym saw in the favour shown to Laud, Neile and Montagu confirmation that the enemy was already within the gates. Few went as far as to join John Winthrop and his East Anglian friends in emigrating to New England; yet their very departure shows a novel religious estrangement. Unlike the marginalised Pilgrims on the Mayflower in 1620, Winthrop had been a respectable member of the Jacobean consensus.

The 1628 parliament opened in crisis mood. The king began unapologetically, insisting that though he now turned to the 'ordinary way' of parliaments, he did not need to in an emergency. Such a claim seemed, like the Five Knights' Case, to expose a vagueness in the law's adjudication between power and liberty. And indeed, some MPs were genuinely agitated over the relation of law and war, and over just which condition then applied – the succession of parliaments and regular sittings of the law courts argued peace, while the levies of money and men pointed to war. But Sir John Eliot at least detected not legal imprecision but incipient tyranny: 'Where is law? Where is meum et tuum [property]? It is fallen into the chaos of a higher power.' The first priority was to keep parliament in being, for as Thomas Scott noted in his journal, 'If free parliaments be gone, all is lost.' The attack on Buckingham therefore had to wait. Anyway, Charles – ever determined not to bargain away the crown's powers in return for supply – seized the initiative. Demanding a speedy supply for war, he urged the houses to trust him to govern by the laws for the future, and in return invited them to reconfirm Magna Carta and allied statutes.

By making explicit the issue of trust in the king, so fundamental to the very being of the commonwealth, Charles split his critics. Most important, he rallied to his side the Lords, with their training in service to the king. But as his conduct in the Five Knights' Case became clear, MPs reacted by tying up funding in committee. Even though their offer of five subsidies, or about £280 000, was painfully inadequate to Charles's war needs, his financial desperation gave them their chance. Their goal was to strengthen, rather than merely reconfirm, the law in four key areas where it had been challenged by Charles's use – and claim – of emergency powers: billeting and martial law (used to dispose and control the troops even within England), and forced loans and arbitrary arrest. The aim, the Earl of Warwick's cousin Sir Nathaniel Rich insisted, was to strengthen both commonwealth and king by protecting the subject. The king shocked the Commons by resisting at every step.

Everywhere the king saw the advance of 'popularity' – a term he clearly interpreted as covert republicanism. The most vocal MPs seem to have intended a statutory condemnation of recent practices, but Charles fiercely opposed such a measure both for its retrospective and its prospective force. An angry dissolution seemed likely, with unforeseeable consequences for a country whose king intended to continue at war. Seeking to dispel the tearful panic that beset the house, Sir Edward Coke urged the antiquated procedure of a petition to the king. Such a petition, for matter of right rather than grace and favour, would, if sent from both houses and accepted by the king, be enrolled in the law courts, and would thus bind the judges; it would also avoid the language of compulsion that Charles abhorred. The Lords were the crown's natural allies in matters of governance, and they had favoured a proviso acknowledging the crown's emergency power; but they gave way before the Commons' insistence. Charles was left under enormous pressure, political now as well as financial, to accept the Petition of Right. As so often, his capitulation was graceless: one witness to the performance noted, 'Prince did never speak with less applause.'

The Petition's appeal to an 'inherited . . . freedom' showed its continuity with the abortive Apology of 1604 and with the Protestation of 1621. These too had declared that, no less than the powers of the crown, certain rights were guaranteed by law and integral to the body politic. In its effort to maintain old barriers against abuses rather than erect new ones, the Petition of Right reveals the sheer conservatism, the hostility to innovation, of the critics of royal policy. Yet the Five Knights' Case had bred suspicions that the law, however 'fundamental', might not be able to stand alone in face of power; critics were therefore driven into novel courses. Coke, appealing to misty fundamentals, conceded in debate that the provisions of the Petition were only implicit in existing law. John Selden took the Commons in a different direction, towards a positivist vision of the law: for the Petition appears to insist that there ought to be statutory warrant for every executive action. The implications of that position were that the polity – conceived more broadly than the king alone, although certainly not excluding the king – must preserve itself.

The public response to the passage of the Petition of Right suggests that Selden's legal philosophy was part of a wider shift in political attitudes. The body politic was an organism that went about its business; yet the king-in-parliament, the supreme manifestation of that organism, had done precious little business in the 1620s. Only the parliament of 1624 had produced more than a handful of statutes. Nevertheless, the rejoicing was widespread in 1628: bonfires dotted London's streets, the city of Bristol enshrined six books of the arguments in its records. The two houses of parliament had rooted themselves deeper in public affection not through collaboration with the king in government and legislation, but through checking his government. New understandings of the polity were emerging under the strain of an unpopular war, corruption, and what were taken to be abuses of power.

Despite the rejoicing, passage of the Petition did not calm the Commons. During the winter of 1626–7 the government had patronised sermons on behalf of the loan; the sermons, few though they were, seemed to confirm John Pym's suspicions that the Arminians intended to advance absolutism in order to bring in their forerunner of popery. The 1626 proclamation against Calvinist doctrinal preaching had suggested as much, and indeed in the winter of 1627–8 Laud argued in council against a parliament for fear of a religious storm. The most outspoken loan sermon, by Roger Manwaring (ironically no Arminian himself) had urged the religious duty of paying fiscal tribute to princes as Gods on earth; it thus transformed what most would have accepted as theory, the divine origin of kingship, into practical politics. The practicality of those politics seemed the greater when Charles had the sermon published under the title *Religion and Allegiance*. The Commons moved swiftly to impeach the author, as the godly began to suspect the existence of a domestic fifth-column at the king's right hand. The dawning suspicion that only parliament, and no longer the king, could be trusted to protect religion and liberty was to make civil war possible.

Apprehensions of an apocalyptic conspiracy took firmer shape during the long debates. Members learned that the king had early in 1628 considered introducing an excise tax, thus flouting the Commons' restraint on impositions throughout the decade. Anger flared in early June with the discovery that Charles had tried to raise cavalry in Germany – not all could believe that he intended it for service in France. Some members asserted that cavalry were to enforce the excise, others that they were Buckingham's tools for a coup, 'praetorian bands' in Eliot's phrase, with all that it implied of imperial tyranny. An emotional response was guaranteed when Coke named Buckingham as the 'grievance of grievances': members exploded, 'It is he! It is he!' Charles had hoped for statutory backing for the militia and for his continued collection of tonnage and poundage. Instead, he closed the session by prorogation in order to head off a remonstrance indicting his whole regime along with his favourite.

Although the two houses seemed to hold public opinion, Charles held the vital cards. The Petition of Right had claimed only to declare existing law, and since it did not explicitly condemn the crown's emergency powers the judges readily concluded that those powers remained intact: Charles therefore felt he could accept the Petition. To make manifest his unrepentance he withdrew the agreed text and published a mangled version, with an assertion of his right to collect tonnage and poundage. Merchants who refused payment of that duty were rebuffed by the judges, who held that the wording of the Petition was too general for application to such a case. Worse was to follow when the judges did accept the Petition, and allowed bail to Richard Chambers, a merchant whom the council had gaoled for comparing English government unfavourably with Turkish despotism. Charles retaliated by having Chambers heavily fined and gaoled by the prerogative court of star chamber. The Petition had little effect upon discretionary power, though it did help to give firmer shape to convictions. It was probably at this time that Sir Robert Filmer wrote the bulk of *Patriarcha* (though it was not published until 1680), the most extreme English statement of what may be called absolutism.

If the courts and the merchants could not change Charles's course, direct action could. Buckingham was at Portsmouth in August 1628 preparing for another expedition to La Rochelle when a disgruntled officer took a knife as well as the Petition of Right to him. Charles's personal grief was overwhelming, and the near-universal rejoicing of his subjects did as much as anything to estrange him from them. The immediate effect was the disordering of the military preparations, although these were soon rendered unnecessary anyway by the capitulation to starvation of the Rochellois. Charles had in the spring of 1627 guaranteed the Huguenots' safety, and this new blow to his sense of honour gave him a further argument against reliance on parliament. It could, of course, equally have been taken as an indictment of the rashness of his policy.

The duke was by no means the monster of contemporary imaginings. Most obviously, he used much of his huge income to bail out the king's war effort in 1626–8. Not incapable as a naval administrator, he appreciated the value of small fast frigates in a way that Charles, preoccupied in the 1630s with ponderous hulks that would trumpet the glory of monarchy, did not. But the conjunction of his impulsive rashness with Charles's idée fixe of royal honour brought English foreign policy to disaster in the simultaneous and confused war with both Spain and France, and in the unconcern with the limitations the Commons had sought to make clear in 1621 and 1624. His implementation of that policy was scarcely more creditable. The selection of the politically loyal Viscount Wimbledon to command the 1625 Cadiz raid was catastrophic, and whatever the duke's own bravery his failure to mount an effective rearguard during the withdrawal from the Ile de Rhé in 1627 contributed largely to the slaughter. But he was, after all, the consummate courtier. Dazzling, immensely charming, an eloquent if sometimes incoherent orator, Buckingham was a political pragmatist. Although his hegemony had kept out some able men, like Bishop Williams, and although he had opposed calling a parliament that would threaten him, he was readier than his master to change policy: he was responsible for the promotion of Sir Richard Weston, an opponent of war, to the lord treasurership in the summer of 1628, and he then reconciled himself to the equally non-bellicose Arundel and Wentworth.

Yet even Charles could recognise some political realities. The collapse of the Huguenots removed his major reason for fighting; peace with France duly came in 1629 and with Spain, which was desperate to focus its dwindling resources on The Netherlands, the following year. In both cases peace was very much on the basis of the status quo ante. The gains had been nil, and the material costs of war and diplomacy over the decade more than £2 million. The political cost had been incalculable, and those whose minds were running along apocalyptic paths and who saw Romish conspiracy at every hand were scarcely mollified by the the curtailment of hostilities. But Charles could at least find consolation for the factiousness of his people. With his only friend dead he looked elsewhere for companionship, and there developed one of the great royal love affairs of history, that of the king and queen: Henrietta Maria's first confinement came nine months after Buckingham's death.

The new relationship with his wife brought Charles closer to France, but it scarcely reunited him with his people. Indeed, with the duke's pragmatic hand removed the scales of royal favour tipped unmistakably towards the anti-Calvinists. A royal proclamation after the parliament against preaching on matters of divine grace seemed to the king even-handed, but to outraged Calvinists it barred any response to the anti-Calvinist onrush. In late 1628 Charles promoted Laud – whom James had distrusted – and Montagu and Manwaring. A parliamentary complaint against a clergyman seemed the surest way to give him a bishopric.

Such gestures, coming on top of the hysteria of the previous June, make Charles's decision to meet parliament again in January 1629 seem surprising. He was close to £1.5 million in debt; but the winding-down of hostilities in western Europe, and his willingness to let his major creditor, the financier Philip Burlamachi, slide into bankruptcy, seemed to free him from the most pressing urgency. Nevertheless, he was still committed by the agreements of 1624–5 to support the armies of his uncle the king of Denmark, one of the less successful of the Thirty Years War combatants. Furthermore, the difficulties in the collection of tonnage and poundage underscored the arguments for a parliamentary confirmation; and the Commons' denunciations of Buckingham may have encouraged him to hope that with the duke gone mutual good-will might yet be restored. Accordingly, at the opening of the session he modified his stand of the previous summer, and asserted that he merely collected tonnage and poundage as a matter of necessity rather than right. But this failed to quieten the alarm, for the manner of the printing of the Petition of Right, and the ecclesiastical promotions, seemed to vindicate those who had in the 1628 debates hinted at their distrust of the king.

The Commons certainly strove to vindicate the Petition of Right without confronting the king personally. Eliot and Selden urged that an apparent breach of parliamentary privilege in council proceedings over tonnage and poundage against John Rolle, a merchant who was also an MP, gave them the means to do it. But the house was divided, for Pym, his half-brother Francis Rous, Sir Nathaniel Rich, and a number of others saw apocalyptic significance in the Arminian 'frogs from the bottomless pit'. They rightly feared that opposing the king would break the parliament before they had vindicated their religious cause. But a satisfactory definition of the English church, whether historical, statutory or canonical, eluded them. Since Pym was no radical republican, bent on asserting the Commons' right to define truth, he was unable to show precisely how the Arminians had offended. In the confusion of the godly the initiative returned to those frightened by what they saw as the weaknesses of the Petition of Right.

Eliot's tactics in challenging tonnage and poundage were as unrevolutionary as those of Pym over religion. His position, revealed in his attack on Buckingham in 1626, in 1629, and in his writings in the Tower before his death, was that the body politic was sick. Charles had been misled by evil counsellors, who must be purged. To the anxious conservatives in the Commons the case of Rolle seemed the safest path to this goal – since Rolle's goods had been seized by the customs farmers, who were private contractors, it should be possible to question them and thus to deter any future evil counsellors while avoiding awkward questions of fundamentals. But Charles had no wish to see the erection of a tribunal outside his council to which his officers must answer, and declared that his servants acted on his orders. On this rock of kingly responsibility the Commons stuck, as many were to do again in the 1640s. By the last week in February the house had degenerated into confusion and division, from which Charles rescued it by adjourning for a week, to the second of March.

If the Commons were heading into bankruptcy, the Lords could not redeem them. There may have been little the upper house could do once the Commons determined to focus on Rolle's privilege, though they made no attempt to find a compromise on religion. Instead, with attendance significantly down, the parliamentary diary of the puritan Lord Montague noted 'little done of any note'. After the failure of their brief effort to mediate over the Petition of Right, most peers showed little eagerness to try again.

Charles's eternal inability to recognise that any could honestly differ from him may account for his attempt in the adjournment to reach an understanding over tonnage and poundage. His intention of adjourning parliament again when he assembled the houses on 2 March was not that of someone merely seeking political advantage by a show of conciliation. But many in the Commons had concluded that there was no more to hope for. The low attendance that day reflected an apprehension of the confrontation that duly came when Eliot and his friends, certain that there would be no more parliaments, determined to appeal to the people with three non-negotiable resolutions condemning Arminianism and the payment and collection of tonnage and poundage. However intransigent the gesture, Eliot's fundamental loyalism showed through in his preoccupation with evil counsellors. He identified an implausible, though ideologically essential, substitute for Buckingham when he denounced the new lord treasurer, Weston, 'in whose person all evil is contracted'.

But Weston was an emblem, if not himself a cause. A crypto-Catholic, he seemed to unite in his own person the twin threats of popery and arbitrary rule that had crystallised in alarmed minds. Rous's fear of 'Romish tyranny and Spanish monarchy' was simply a more pointed version of the the Commons' Three Resolutions' charge. But if that was the danger, the Commons were poorly placed to confront it. The emotional climax to the parliament, as Eliot's allies held down the Speaker, Finch, while they read the resolutions, was magnificent theatre, but futile. As they invited a taxpayers' strike, the Three Resolutions claimed a new crime of treason against 'the kingdom and commonwealth'. But though Eliot and his allies might try to drive a wedge between this king and the polity, the future belonged to Charles, who was visibly elated at the dissolution. Reassured by the low attendances in parliament, Charles arrested Eliot and eight others – all but one were to spend long years in gaol, and Eliot to die there – and declared that there would be no more parliaments until the nation understood him better.

The Three Resolutions had implied an identity of Commons and kingdom; the king of course challenged that claim. Parliament as a whole had failed as the venue for affirmation of the body politic, and in Charles's estimation the Commons had been the cause of that failure. In the winter of 1627–8 he had recognised that he could not fight a war without parliamentary supply; but the unwillingness of the Commons in the ensuing parliament to give statutory confirmation either to the militia or to tonnage and poundage convinced him that he could not look to parliaments for sustenance for the kingdom. He might gain supply, if little else, but the Petition of Right showed that the cost could be high. If parliament were no longer useful, there was little point in calling it. The late-medieval convention that the subject would aid the king in wartime and that the king would 'live of his own' in peacetime, had been found doubly wanting. The king must now develop other sources of revenue, and think hard on the wisdom of wars. And if parliament had failed to embody the realm, the king might also give freer expression to his own claims.

6

Renewal and recalcitrance, 1629–1638

Peace, and the benevolent reassertion of the royal will, were Charles's remedy for disarray. Later royalist laments for the 1630s as 'halcyon days' were not mere nostalgia, since peace, amity, concord, were the watchwords of the regime until the later 1630s. Peace itself was not hard to achieve, since the king's continental foes were as eager for it as he, but amity was to be more than a state of mind. In the court masques of which he was so fond Charles trumpeted the affectionate world of which his happy marriage was emblem and seal; and in the lavish family portraits by Anthony van Dyck he commissioned more lasting displays of that claim. This was a very different version of the overlay of body politic and royal body physical from that which James had offered.

If the king could bring peace despite his subjects, he might yet institute order in England (the uniformity of Scotland and Ireland was, even he realised, another matter). The masques offered a clear prescription: thus, *Coelum Britannicum* (the British Heaven) of 1637 held forth Charles's court as the pattern of perfect order, even for Jove's heaven. The guiding spirit of the masque, the great Italianate architect and designer Inigo Jones, maintained a fashionable neo-Platonic position: contemplation of the Ideal would elevate thoughts and ultimately reform actions by provoking spectators to emulation. The masques' exaltation of king and queen thus provided exemplars for the court, and ultimately for the country; a repeated motif had the mere appearance of the king or queen establishing order, offering an intensely hierarchical vision in which the lower members simply took directions from the head. Such a high moral tone might have seemed far-fetched under James, whose delight in 'bawdry and profane abusive wit', in 'fools and bawds, mimics and catamites', the stern puritan (and courtier's daughter) Lucy Hutchinson scorned.

Charles seems to have accepted the poets' case. As the masques proclaimed, decorum, degree, moral improvement might achieve what enforcement could gain only with cost and effort; so the king set about reforming his kingdoms from the court down. Impressed by what he had seen in 1623 of the dignity of Madrid, he issued new orders in 1629 and 1631 minutely regulating the conduct of courtiers, particularly in the areas near the royal presence. He discouraged duelling even more insistently than had his father, pursued marriage alliances for his nobles, frowned humourlessly on sexual escapades, and cultivated the principle of hierarchy in private as well as public. A reinvigorated commission on fees sought to reduce corruption by setting a scale for perquisites. The king abandoned the sale of peerages (resuming it again only in the financial exigency of civil war), and took care to refurbish a nobility Buckingham's sales had tarnished so that it might reflect grandeur back on to the monarchy. Access to the royal presence was strictly limited, while aristocratic display found an outlet carefully orientated towards the king not just in the masque but in the chivalry and ceremony of the Order of the Garter. And hierarchy spread outwards from the court as Charles came close to granting the nobility novel legal privileges. Massive damages awarded by Star Chamber to the Earl of Suffolk in 1632 in a case of undeferential behaviour constituted, it was reported, 'the bravest sentence for poor lords that ever was heard of'. The following year Charles invigorated the nobility further by declaring himself 'willing that all his subjects should find his courts of justice open to all men alike; yet when a man of mean quality shall prosecute against a noble man for an offence of heat or passion', that liberty was not to be allowed.

Such a well-mannered programme offers its own comment on the 'new counsels' the king and some of his councillors had threatened in the aftermath of the 1626 parliament. Indeed, Charles's ability to draw into his service several of the lawyers and leading gentlemen who had at Westminster urged the liberty of the subject suggests his intent to rebuild consensus: Sir Thomas Wentworth was won over in late 1628, and then William Noy, Edward Littleton, Sir Dudley Digges. Such recruitment suggests as well an undercurrent of willingness to trust the king's intentions as the only means to get the country running again and rise in the world.

But there were limits to consensus. The resolution to England's differences, if it came, would not centre in the Renaissance ideal of harmony in discord: consensus must stem from and centre in the head of the body politic. If these terms were not despotic, they were certainly authoritarian. The essence of what has so often been called Charles's 'personal rule' of the 1630s might be found in Wentworth's characteristic contempt, as Lord President of the council in the north and then as Lord Deputy in Ireland, for judges, lawyers and every other 'saucy Magna Carta fellow', even as he exploited loopholes in the law to buttress the king's prerogative. Charles anxiously distanced his rule from the charge of tyranny, and seems to have blocked the publication of Filmer's *Patriarcha*, with its espousal of royal power and authority; he certainly proceeded very publicly in Star Chamber in 1629 against a group of notables for possessing a manuscript on military despotism written in 1614. But though he asserted his commitment to ancient ways, a 1629 proclamation indefinitely prohibited further talk of a parliament; like the harrying of Eliot and his allies, that prohibition indicates the king's inveterate hostility to 'popularity'.

Charles would have wholeheartedly endorsed Wentworth's insistence that subjects 'attend upon [the king's] will, with confidence in his justice, belief in his wisdom, assurance in his parental affections'. It was scarcely unusual for a king and his minister to insist on royal headship of a docile body politic; what was unusual was the way Charles lived out that belief. More certainly than James in his 1604 speech to parliament, Charles believed that the king was the kingdom. Indeed, he had broken with tradition by being crowned in white vestments to symbolise his rebirth at the moment of his coronation. Elizabeth had determinedly used ceremony as a political instrument, but the shows Charles put on were for himself. His devotion to the masque is suggestive, since the masque focused its visual perspective on the king as the prime spectator, within the closed theatre of the court. The only public ceremonial with which he seems to have been genuinely concerned was that of the royal chivalric Order of the Garter, and this was played out in the small town of Windsor, not in London. The ceremonies of the Garter, with their vigils, prayers and processions, declared Charles's almost liturgical sense of his office. The annual rite when he touched sufferers from scrofula, to heal them of 'the king's evil', was the one occasion when he approached his ordinary subjects. He took its religious trappings utterly seriously.

Charles lived out his personal headship of the body politic in more practical ways. Not only did he attend busily to the minutiae of the ship money proceedings, and fuss over Laud's reports on the state of the church; to the consternation of foreign ambassadors, he also broke with convention by insisting that they see him before his ministers. The king, and not some dominant councillor, made policy and appointed officials. Charles's unprompted promotion of Bishop Juxon of London, a secondary figure, to the lord treasurership in 1635 is symptomatic of his determination to control. Although Juxon's predecessor, Weston, Earl of Portland from 1633, was the leading councillor until his death in 1635, his power was checked by Laud and others, with whom he was at odds, and by his own worsening health. Laud certainly was highly influential – after 1634 he served on all the key committees, and gained the appointment of Francis Windebanke as secretary of state in 1632, and the dismissal for religious dissent of Chief Justice Sir Robert Heath in 1634; but Laud's priorities remained ecclesiastical, not secular. Wentworth, serving in the north and Ireland, was removed from the real centre of power until 1639. Charles's closest ally was probably the queen, who was not herself a councillor – and even she could not win him to a French-style moderate church policy. Indeed, the king's tendency to override or ignore his council helps explain the speed of its demoralisation and collapse in 1640. He was

far more adept at creating intimacies with a handful of aesthetes and confidants than at selecting and trusting advisers. Having neither chief minister, nor, after Buckingham's death, favourite, to turn to, Charles ruled
personally as well as reigned.

With parliament gone, court and council assumed undisputed prominence as the only organs that might pass as 'the representative body' of
the kingdom. But Charles's incomprehension that any could honestly differ
from their king circumscribed their roles. Under stress, Charles could be
drawn into what sometimes looks like sheer dishonesty. While he justified
his weasel ways in the negotiations with his enemies in the 1640s as the
only means to deal with rebels against God as well as God's annointed,
no such explanation can be offered for his readiness to blacken Bristol for
the fiasco in Madrid, or (as we shall see) for his treatment of Balmerino
in Scotland in 1633. Mistaking the functions of his councillors, he turned
his councils, and especially that in Scotland, into bodies of yes-men. On
more than one occasion he suppressed the record of English privy council
proceedings in which he had faced dissent, leading Laud to conclude sadly
that Charles was 'more willing not to hear than to hear'. The king's
distrust of men of independent judgment like Wentworth led him to turn
away, in his choice of advisers, from men with solid landed bases in the
country. The death of Pembroke in 1630 removed one of the few front-
rank figures who was also a local magnate. This had a significance beyond
narrowing the range of advice the king might receive, for it also diminished the numbers of those who might tie the court to the country. As Sir
Thomas Lucy, the leading gentleman in Warwickshire lamented in 1633,
Secretary of State Sir John Coke 'is the only councillor left I have had the
honour to be acquainted with'. Few of Lucy's neighbours were better
placed. The increasing introversion of Charles's court may be traced to
his aloofness, and perhaps to his conviction of his domestic bliss; but it
was intensified by authoritarianism.

Authoritarianism and aloofness left Charles dangerously insensitive to
the requirements of patronage. Benevolence and mutual gratification
bound the body politic and ensured its fecundity. But Charles 'knew not
the art to please', Bishop Williams confided. Clarendon was, if anything,
more damning: 'not in his nature very bountiful', the king 'paused too
long in giving, which made those to whom he gave, less sensible of the
benefit'. The report of the Countess of Leicester on her reception at court
suggests psychological as well as ideological constraints: the king had 'an
inclination to show me some kindness, but he could not find the way',
except in an awkward sexual innuendo.

The religious character of council and court heightened their isolation.
Charles was less concerned with private opinion than he was with church
uniformity, and left in place some of Buckingham's Calvinist clients like
Manchester, and Secretary Coke; nevertheless, after Pembroke's death
misgivings about popery in high places grew, as the earl's funeral sermon,

with its remarkable premonition of religious war, made painfully evident. Both Portland and his subordinate at the treasury, Cottington, were rightly suspected as crypto-Catholics; they were in 1632 to have a co-religionist in the new secretary of state, Windebanke. The religion of Laud himself caused widespread unease, while too many gentlemen of the bedchamber were, or were feared to be, papists. Charles's Italianate aesthetic tastes undoubtedly made conversions fashionable, and he was insufficiently concerned about them: to him the purity of his own motives was sufficient guarantee. His indifference to public opinion reached its height when he admitted papal agents (Gregorio Panzani in 1634, George Con in 1636) to court to please his wife and further his diplomacy.

The story ran that Charles was supposed to have been Archbishop of York with his brother Henry as king. True or not, the legend conveys some of Charles's conviction that as Christian king he exercised his care over the Christian commonwealth. Accordingly, the personnel of church and state merged a little: in the later 1630s there were three bishops on the English council (Laud, Juxon, and Archbishop Neile of York), while in the localities senior clergy were added to the commissions of the peace – the Kent commission included eight clergy. In both instances, the totals were the highest since the Reformation. Similarly, Scottish bishops came to dominate the Edinburgh council, and the king encouraged Wentworth's determined exaltation of the Irish church after 1634. Charles's priorities are more fully revealed in the attention he paid to the church in his capitals. It was to Wentworth's campaign for propriety in Dublin cathedral that he gave his fullest backing; it was to the refurbishment and ornamenting of the chapel in Holyrood House in Edinburgh that he turned on his 1633 Scottish visit; and it was above all on the rebuilding of St Paul's cathedral in London that he concentrated his energies of devotion. These were prestige projects of a ritual monarchy as much as they were pious gestures.

Styles of churchmanship, not intricacies of doctrine, were what counted to this king. Like James towards the end of his reign, Charles disliked public controversies over faith; indeed, he even subjected anti-Calvinist as well as Calvinist preachers to restraints (although Calvinists, committed in principle to the primacy of preaching, were of course the primary targets). Order and reverence were central, in church as well as palace. But though he might lament the disputatiousness of clergy of all stripes, his taste for ceremony and reverence was bound to incline him towards clergy of a very partisan character. And for their part, Bishops Laud and Neile recognised that in the king lay all their hope – though they also insisted on the historical continuity of the English church from apostolic times, and the sanctity and independence that continuity conferred on the whole. It is hard to say whether the king's devotion or Archbishop Laud's dependence did more to ensure that James's Hampton Court dictum, 'No bishop, no king', would come true.

Laud may not have been much more of an instinctual theologian than was Charles, but theology held the key to the archbishop's position. Calvinists prized edifying sermons, but Laud even more than Charles looked to the sacraments. For him the altar rather than the pulpit provided the means to salvation – reverence replaced conscientious engagement. His private book of devotions reveals a Lutheran, and very non-Calvinist, sense that in the communion service the believer received Christ's 'blessed body and blood' – as he gratuitously added, 'I quarrel not the words.' All else flowed from that sacramental position. Laud's sacerdotalism, the elevation of the dignity of the priesthood which so offended anti-clericals, made sense if the clergy were mediators at the altar between God and man, rather than merely expounders of God's word. So too his ceremonialism: all to do with the altar must be seemly, and the clergy must wear distinctive vestments. As his opening sermon to parliament in 1626 showed, with its account of the tribes coming up harmoniously to Jerusalem to worship, his concern for religious reverence reinforced, and was reinforced by, a vision of the earthly community. Like Charles, he vehemently believed in the existence of a divinely ordered hierarchy in the universe, on which both church and kingdom should be modelled.

Laud's preoccupations dictate caution when talking of Arminianism. The archbishop was clearly an Arminian in his flat distaste for the 'fatal' doctrines of predestination that would doom some irremediably; and Calvinists everywhere bewailed the doctrinal challenges under his rule to what they saw as the orthodoxy of divine omnipotence. Equally alarming to the godly who saw in sermons the hope of mankind, Laud set limits to preaching. His ideal was one sermon a week from the pulpit, to be delivered not by nonconformist unbeneficed lecturers but by orthodox parochial ministers, who were prepared to observe the full ceremonial of the prayer-book service. The rest of the sabbath should be given over to catechising, or to the legitimate pastimes enjoined in the book of sports of 1633. Accordingly, to the dismay of those who saw Satan's hand in impediments to preaching, Bishop Wren forbade afternoon sermons in his Norwich diocese. But unlike Wren, who in 1636 silenced five of Norwich's most effective preachers for whom the corporation vainly vouched, Laud did not strive to control the doctrine preached. He would on occasion add an Arminian's writings to the list of Calvinist works to be suppressed, since he claimed the continuity of his church with the protestant community defined by Elizabeth and James.

Where Laud's vision differed from that of Elizabeth and James was in his very clear sense of the church, nationally and parochially, as a ritual community. Despite the long-standing protestant indictment of 'idolatry', Laud aimed to restore a scenic apparatus – stained glass, an altar to which worshippers would bow and at which they would kneel, bowing at the name of Jesus. He sought through that 'beauty of holiness' to inculcate sufficient reverence, and through his insistence on a shared parochial

worship to induce sufficient charity, that worshippers might become receptive to the grace of the sacraments. The community might then become
truly Christian. There was certainly ground enough for Laud's complaints.
Reports spoke of dogs fouling unprotected altars and birds flying through
dilapidated churches; his old cathedral, St Paul's in London, had become
a thoroughfare for merchants and gossipers. And some of the preachers
whom Laud's officers silenced had in their very particularised denunciations of the sinners before them set their flock against each other. But if
Laud strove to build community in the parishes he could not do it without
political cost.

Laud's means and his ends alike came under challenge. His programme
was enforced not only through determined visitations of the dioceses
by the two busy archbishops and their officials, but also by some well-
publicised legal actions, especially over St Gregory's, London, in 1633 and
Beckington in Somerset in 1635, and against the much-disgraced Bishop
Williams of Lincoln in 1639, who had sought to defend a less ceremonialist vision in his *Holy Table, Name and Thing* (1636). But coercion had
its limits. The 'beauty of holiness' cost money, and money demanded for
alterations that many churchwardens saw as idolatrous and popish was
not easily gathered. By 1640, only one-quarter of Somerset parishes had
obeyed Laud's injunctions over the communion table. There were more
dangerous objections. Among the puritan clergy, or the most sophisticated
of their lay supporters like John Pym, the doctrinal challenge of Arminianism dominated calculations; but to more ordinary minds ceremony and
symbol constituted the visible challenge. The 1633 book of sports, in
contrast with that of 1617, was enforced with some seriousness. With its
apparent invitation to desecrate the sabbath, the book occasioned the
largest number of suspensions of ministers since the broils of 1604: one
Somerset minister insisted flatly, 'the king did allow of that which God
did forbid'. The lawyer William Prynne's response, the recording in
his *Divine Tragedy* (1636) of the sad fate of sabbath-breakers, helped
lose him the remains of his ears and gain a branding in 1637. For Prynne,
for Nehemiah Wallington in London, there could be no community
with Antichrist.

The reverberations of the book of sports underscore the social dimension of Laud's ritual community. All too often, the 'pomposities' of
assertive and low-born Laudians seemed like an assault on hierarchy
rather than the affirmation of it that Laud claimed. Town corporations
whose elevated pews in municipal churches bishops removed in the name
of 'decency' resented being levelled with the multitude – understandably
enough when, like the Norwich aldermen, they were deliberately jostled
by their new pew-mates. Ceremonialism, support for a festive culture,
assaults on local oligarchies: aspects of Laudianism may have been
'popular' in ways that we rarely consider. Even in the godly redoubt of
Coventry one Calvinist visitor found among the critics of the magistrates

alarming support for Arminian opinions. The local protests in the later 1640s against parliamentary puritanism and in favour of prayer book and ceremonies suggest that if Laud and his royal master had moved with a little more tact and circumspection they would have gained their objectives. As it was, they merely aroused the godly members of the local establishments.

Laud intended a more frontal challenge to those establishments. Part of that challenge was piecemeal. He used the church courts to discipline socially prominent sexual offenders who had always counted on their immunity; to probably even less effect, he harassed lay impropriators of livings to persuade them to pay higher stipends to their ministers, or to divest themselves of the power over clergymen to which he so much objected. But more urgent issues were involved. As early as that 1626 sermon to parliament he had declared his conviction that puritanism was a conspiracy against church and kingdom.

Puritan organisation there certainly was, though it was no foundation for rebellion until Laud made it so. His evidence for the charge of subversion was above all the feoffees for impropriations. Their thirty-odd grants were unimpressive enough; but in their concentration on towns rather than established parochial structures, and in their aim of extending their activities to the purchase of advowsons, or rights of presentation to livings, the feoffees seemed the very institution of 'popularity'. In 1633 Laud had them dissolved. If the York House conference of 1626 had been a milestone, for some that dissolution was the end of the road. John Davenport, one of the clerical feoffees, emigrated to New England, and the correspondence of others among the East Anglian connection of clergy and gentry shows increasing disaffection. Laud meanwhile was certain he had found the tip of the iceberg. Not content with idiosyncracies like setting a spy on the Calvinist Bishop Morton, he also inflicted brutal punishments: the ear-cropping he visited on the pamphleteers Prynne, Burton and Bastwick was the more provocative in paying no respect to their gentle status. Laud thus confirmed the godly in their habit of looking to martyrologies for meaning and purpose; they were soon to repay him for his vehemence.

Despite its provocativeness, Laud's campaign made little headway. His church, however purified, dwelt within the body politic. Nonconformity in worship had to be presented for prosecution, and this required the co-operation of churchwardens, who might themselves be puritans. Accordingly, the hard-line Bishop Wren's campaign in his new diocese of Ely in 1638 failed because he could not find out from the churchwardens who his targets were. Lay patrons could be counted on to protect 'their' ministers; thus, the Earl of Warwick provided a refuge for the radical Hugh Peter, while powerful gentry like Sir Robert Harley in Herefordshire could usually protect their clients. And the church courts, even those of his Canterbury diocese, were clogged with other business that was usually more lucrative for fee-hungry officials.

Nevertheless, Laud's challenge to old-established patterns of worship, and of relations between church and laity, did not lack for determination. Presbyterian dissidents under Elizabeth had had prominent defenders at court in Leicester and even Burghley; Laud's enemies had none to look to at Charles's court. Warwick, Lord Saye, Lord Brooke and John Pym contemplated emigration; even Sir Robert Harley, a royal official, could in 1634 plead with his local clergyman to 'do what you can for us, that we be not driven to leave our native country and friends'. By the late 1630s the local alliances between church and state were coming unravelled. The magistrates of Chester feted Prynne on his way into exile after mutilation in 1637; by 1638 the Sussex magistrates' bench had become a sounding-board for denunciations of Laud's reforms. The Laudian attempt to establish the ritual community of the English church had fractured political community.

Most dangerously of all, the Laudians were operating in a context of the king's and not of their own making. Despite the archbishop's protests, Charles allowed successive papal agents to operate at court, and to make some spectacular converts in the later 1630s. He did little to stop ostentatious displays at the chapels of foreign ambassadors, or even Catholic processions through neighbouring London streets. Laud's bid to change the face of the church gave ominous meaning to such popery in high places. Apocalyptic fears of a popish plot had been evident in the Commons in 1628–9; a decade later they were much more widespread. Foxe's *Acts and Monuments*, with its ideal of the Emperor Constantine, the godly prince, had made the protection of true religion the ruler's chief duty. The growing conviction of the godly that Charles was in default could not help but call his very legitimacy in question.

Whatever the growing divisions in religion, the political community was bound by other ties. Not least, every classically educated member of the elite recognised that there had been other emperors besides the godly Constantine: Augustus, not to mention a long line of English kings, offered powerful models on which loyalty could centre. Indeed, the forces of cohesion tying the localities to the centre were legion: law, custom, history, all reinforced London's gravitational effects.

Arguments that trace roots of the 1640s conflict to the divergence under Charles of the 'two cultures' of court and country must therefore be carefully modulated. Certainly, many of the Titians and del Sartos Charles pursued while building up his art collection were works of Roman Catholic devotion. Equally, Thomas Carew's revelling cavalier poetry contrasted dangerously with the desperate certainty of puritan sermons that God was turning his back on England. But it was of the essence of royal courts at any time to set styles, and Charles was not being necessarily 'popish' in following Italian models, particularly since the latter derived largely from anti-papal Venice rather than from the more advanced Baroque of Rome. Nor was the splendid realism of van Dyck's portraits inherently unEnglish, different though it was from the rigid blacks and whites of so many country 'limners'. Staunch parliamentarians of the future – Warwick, Arthur Goodwin, Lord Wharton's family – could sit for the fashionable van Dyck as eagerly as could the queen; equally, the list of purchasers of Charles's collection after his execution indicates the unwisdom of using culture to mark a political divide, for the regicide Colonel Hutchinson bought many bargains. John Milton could still write, in *Comus* (1634), a non-court masque; and the puritan lawyer William Prynne gained remarkably little public attention when he had his ears mutilated by Star Chamber in 1633 for his virulent attacks in *Histriomastix* on the sinfulness of stage plays and players, including by implication the queen. Plays such as Massinger's *Believe as you List* of 1631, or the lost *Cardinal's Conspiracy* of 1639, critical of courtly values and performed at the popular London theatres, the Red Bull and the Fortune, suggest the continuing vitality of a common culture.

The hold of common political assumptions is no less evident in the crown's social policy. Although Charles declared his hostility to 'popularity', the council responded to distress and disorder in conventional fashion.

The end of the 1620s had brought high food prices, and an industrial depression as grievous as that of 1623. Exactly one-third of the twenty-four known incidents of food riot in Kent between 1558 and 1640 occurred in 1630–1. The origins of the malaise, insofar as they extended beyond atrocious weather and plague, lay in politics. The earlier textile depression had never wholly eased, and renewed crisis in the new draperies now underscored the vulnerability of the economy. Privateers from Dunkirk devastated trade in 1629–30, despite the imminence of peace, while the merchants' protests against tonnage and poundage increased the disruption. By the spring of 1629 there was mass unemployment in Essex, Suffolk and other new drapery regions, and isolated bread riots. The lot of the poor worsened catastrophically when the harvest brought in in 1630 was as bad as that of 1623. As usual, higher food prices eroded domestic demand for cloth, and unemployment soared. And there were more specific causes of unrest. In the southwestern forests, the so-called 'Western Rising' flared intermittently from 1626 to 1632 as poor commoners strove to protect their livelihoods against royal efforts to sell woodlands to speculators for disafforestation.

The crisis elicited the usual ameliorative response from local governors. Parish worthies everywhere did their duty under the Elizabethan poor laws, and by the end of the 1630s parochial poor relief had become virtually universal. Urban magistrates endeavoured to prevent economic ills turning into social conflict by stepping up relief and by regulating food traders – only in the most godly, and hard-hit, towns like Salisbury and Dorchester did such activity extend to institutionalised relief projects centring on a municipal brewery. For its part, the privy council showed its commitment to old ideals of community by joining the poor in blaming high prices on exploitative middlemen.

The council's broader response to the social ills of 1629–31 contrasts suggestively with the prevailing rhetoric of kingship. The two books of orders sent to local magistrates in the winter of 1630–1 were once thought symptomatic of the new determination, paternalism, centralisation of an unfettered king of these years in 'personal rule'. Yet the details of regulation of alehouses, of markets, of vagrants, and the remedies for plague and for unemployment, were in fact generally conventional, and owed much to the Northamptonshire experience of Lord Montague, the brother of a senior councillor, the Earl of Manchester. Nevertheless, a dream of order gave shape to the details: JPs were instructed (as they had often been in the past) to report on their activities to the assize judges, and diligently to hold petty sessions every month to ensure the good governance of the countryside; the assize judges were in their turn to report to the council.

Was this discipline on the model of the 'Thorough' soon to be practised in Ireland? It is a comment on the transition from war to peace that the emphasis on regularity was the work of Viscount Wimbledon, the hapless commander of the 1625 Cadiz voyage, who now sought some way to recommend himself to a king preoccupied with order in his capital and kingdom. A still more eloquent comment on the realities of rule is the failure of most counties to submit regular reports, or indeed any reports at all after 1633. And despite another plague epidemic and more abysmal harvests in the later 1630s, the council showed little concern at such backsliding. The 'books of orders' were no system, but simply an unusually energetic attempt by the head to work with and through the proper local organs of government to reduce recurring ills.

The vital test of the health of the body politic, and of the sustenance it could give the king and his rule lay of course in finance. And by that measure, the auguries were good. The recovery of his financial position from the painful debility of the later 1620s left Charles with little cause for alarm at home.

By 1635–6 the crown's regular incomings and outgoings, the so-called 'ordinary account', were in the black. That the king arrived at this unusual and happy state was due most of all to the customs. Peace and its accompanying expansion of trade, further impositions, and Portland's revision in 1634–5 of the book of customs rates to take account of the increasingly valuable colonial imports, raised the customs revenues from about £300 000 per annum to almost £500 000 per annum during the decade. Total annual income from all sources, including extraordinaries like knighthood fines, rose from just under £750 000 to over £1 million. The larger picture is revealing. Crown revenues almost doubled in real terms, allowing for inflation, between 1603 and 1639; the royal debt, which had stood at £2 million in 1629, was almost halved by Portland's death in

1635, to the rough equivalent of one year's total income. The recovery of royal finances had powerful implications for the political community, and in particular for the future of parliament: had Charles not blundered in Scotland, might parliaments have gone?

The measures of 1626–8 had seemed novel and threatening, even without the talk of 'new counsels' that surrounded them. But with the glaring exception of ship money, the fiscal devices of the 1630s were less provocative. As both Salisbury and Cranfield had found, the obstacles to fundamental reform were considerable; it was no wonder that the stock response of Charles's council to its need for money was to look to the past for inspiration. The financial crisis was not deep enough to persuade them to look elsewhere, the political dangers too obvious, and councillors' own instinctive conservatism too rooted. The tired collection of precedents for benevolences and forced loans that Attorney-General William Noy listed in a 1634 enquiry into how to raise money by the king's 'absolute prerogative' was, in view of the debacle of 1626–8, distinctly unpromising. Portland's exploitation of Henry VIII's statute for compulsory use of the longbow was more likely to scandalise than to alarm.

The king himself had no stomach for the action that would be needed for systematic innovation. Whatever Charles's hostility to talk of parliaments, he appointed as treasurer after Portland's death in 1635 the honest but unimaginative Bishop Juxon, rather than the far more dynamic Wentworth. Accordingly, the later 1630s saw little further reduction in the debt; instead the king limped along by courtesy of the customs farmers. Indeed, his dependence on these was so great that he was unable to extract from them any major increase in rent, despite a recovery in trade during the 1630s. Even before the Scottish crisis broke he was regularly 'anticipating', or spending in advance, over £300 000 per annum of the following year's revenues – a level similar to that in the strife-torn 1620s. Although Charles was by no means as profligate as his father, he had already signalled his mixed priorities when in 1627, amidst war and financial crisis, he acquired the fabulous Mantuan art collection. Much of the increased income of the 1630s was similarly absorbed. The queen's palace at Greenwich, designed by Inigo Jones, cost £133 000; the massive rebuilding of Whitehall that Charles was planning in 1638 would have cost far more. Since he was drawing to the full on the credit of the customs farmers through anticipations, the king had scant margin for emergencies. His great sale of crown lands in 1627–8 had left him little to offer as security to other lenders; and the bankruptcy of Burlamachi in 1633, like the repeated harassing of the City, gave little encouragement to other potential creditors. In 1640 only his servants would lend to him. Charles's finances were not sound enough to give him much safety in the troubled Europe of the 1630s.

The French crown was currently forging a new order centring on the king by creating and selling offices and taxing office holders. Charles's council did nibble at administrative reform; and Wentworth for one saw the attractions of a salaried bureaucracy that was both more efficient and responsive to the king. The commission on fees, sporadically active in 1629–31 and again in 1637–8, might have been a vehicle for reform – the later commission in particular uncovered massive fraud (the household accounting officials alone were cheating the crown out of about 1 per cent of its income throughout the early seventeenth century). But this was not the start of any restructuring; neither did it yield appreciably, for only about £35 000 in fines was levied. As so often, the king had the worst of all worlds. In harassing his officials pointlessly he added to his reputation for ingratitude, and helped ensure that only half the office-holders sitting in the Long Parliament would ultimately side with him.

Time after time the king affronted the cardinal political principle of reciprocity, all the while gaining returns inadequate to warrant the resentment provoked. Perhaps the most glaring example of fiscal antiquarianism, as well as of political short-sightedness, was the campaign to fine landlowners for encroachments on ancient boundaries of royal forests. One forest court, or eyre, extended the limits of Rockingham Forest in Northamptonshire from six to sixty miles, and fined the Earl of Westmorland £19 000, the Earl of Salisbury £20 000. But in so doing it alienated the crown's natural allies, with scant justification in equity if not in the letter of the law. Characteristically, Charles believed that to impose such large fines and then to remit the bulk of them would both affirm his power and display his magnanimity, thus generating gratitude. Instead, it bred only distrust and anger. As always, the king's practical gains were small, probably only about £20 000 for the whole campaign: the rest was skimmed off by courtiers and officials.

One short-term device did yield an appreciable revenue. In 1629–30 the council began to fine landowners worth the now-trifling sum of £40 per annum for ignoring their ancient duty of presenting themselves to be knighted at the king's coronation. Though the council's concern was patently fiscal rather than chivalric, few were willing to withstand a demand that was undoubtedly legal, although obsolete: even Oliver Cromwell paid up, and so did the usually tax-avoiding Londoners, who paid almost half the total. By 1635 almost 10 000 landowners, or probably half the non-knighted gentlemen in the country, had paid over £174 000. But though they seemed to affirm the customary order, knighthood fines were no formula for solvency. The very different analytical categories deployed by the Venetian ambassador were as revealing as his disdain: the fines were 'false mines for obtaining money, because they are good for once only, and states are not maintained by such devices'.

Charles's ministers would probably have agreed with the Venetian verdict, for they knew that their regime was maintained above all by trade, by the revenues from impositions. But while the soaring customs revenues justified the fears voiced in earlier parliaments that the crown might become financially independent, there was a wider significance to the changing trading patterns.

The socio-economic diversification of the 1630s challenged the implications of completeness, of closure, in the organic metaphor. This was the decade of the 'great migration'. Around 70 000 people left England and Wales in the 1630s, close to 2 per cent of the population; most of these crossed the Atlantic to the new colonies of the Caribbean and the 'howling wilderness' of the mainland. What has proved for obvious reasons a defining episode in early American history scarcely registers in many English accounts of the period. The passage of so many people westwards speaks of religious fears, and blighted hopes of a livelihood; but the emigrants did make their marks on England. Those who survived the rigours of the sea-crossing needed supplies, and there quickly developed a piecemeal and unquantifiable trade in manufactured goods with the new settlers, in southwestern Ireland and across the Atlantic.

The growth of the supply trade in a newly opening Atlantic world was not just symbolic. The settlers had to pay for their goods, and furs from New England, tobacco from Virginia and, increasingly, sugar from the Caribbean, varied the mix of English imports and gave new profits to lesser merchants and shopkeepers in London, Bristol, and beyond. Indeed, the 1630s seem to have formed something of a watershed in English, as well as Virginian, economic development. Surging consumer imports speak of new tastes and the ability of new sectors of the population to gratify those tastes. England was close to self-sufficiency in basic foodstuffs, in wool, in leather; yet annual imports into London nevertheless averaged around £3 million (in official valuations) in the 1630s; in James's first decade they had averaged £1.25 million. Imports of raw silk surged, from perhaps 120 000 lbs a year around 1620 to 220 000 lbs by 1640, suggesting something of the consumer market. Its relative importance can be seen in the comparison of the £480 000-worth of London's broadcloth exports in 1632 (not a particularly depressed year) with the £527 000-worth of imports from the Mediterranean and East Indies in 1630, £689 000 in 1634. The crown benefited as much as did merchants and consumers, since the resources available to the customs farmers to tap were increasing, with consequences visible in the revenue figures.

The surging yields of the customs might have had fundamental consequences. The possibility for a powerful new political alliance between the crown and the merchant surely opened with the oceanic trades. Instead, policy towards the corporate world of which the king claimed to be the emblem and warrant remained fixed in a short-term, and usually exploitative, mode. Thus, while in 1634 Charles confirmed the privileges of the Merchant Adventurers, in 1635 he licensed an interloping scheme run by the merchant Sir William Courteen, with the courtier Endymion Porter, to break into the East India Company's trading monopoly to the Indian

Ocean. Still more revealing are his dealings with the City government, the collective voice of the great merchants. In pursuit of minor pickings from the fees of those wishing to trade free of City restrictions, Charles in 1636 dismayed the City fathers by incorporating a new body, the corporation of the suburbs, outside their jurisdiction. Most provocative of all, he hounded the City corporation and the City companies throughout the 1630s, in hope of fines and confiscations over the administration of the great 1627–8 transfer of crown lands, and of the City's estates in the Ulster plantation. Since these were both ventures into which the crown had coerced the City in the first place there were grounds for resentment.

The crown was not systematically looking beyond the landowners to the merchants as foundation for a new absolutism; but nor was it engaged in some neo-feudal reaction. Everywhere, short-term fiscalism triumphed over policy. The policing of degree through the court of wards remained a matter of fiscal exploitation. The encouragement of traditional agricultural employments by means of the 1633 commission to limit enclosure and depopulation in the Midlands quickly degenerated into a scheme to sell licences to enclosing landlords, despite Laud's moralist concerns. The attempt to curb the unrestricted growth of London was similarly undercut, as Charles's ban on new building, and his attempt to bring the spreading suburbs under closer control, metamorphosed into fiscal pursuit of the fines to be raised from new buildings and the fees to be had from tradesmen. Furthermore, the crown's own record as landowner, as a converter of tenures on the Duchy of Cornwall estates, as a speculative encloser and depopulator in the southwestern forests and the fens, was often innovative and disruptive.

Nowhere is the congenital opportunism more apparent than in the 'popish soap' monopoly. The soap patent was granted in 1632 to a syndicate that included some of Portland's Catholic clients who claimed (spuriously) to have discovered a superior means of making soap. It brought in £33 000 to the king; but the gritty stuff the patentees unloaded on the market was as incapable of cleaning clothes as it was of redeeming the government's reputation. Pym calculated in 1640 that the crown received about 10 per cent of the profit on a patent for licensing wine sellers, and a modern estimate is that the crown received about 13 per cent of the proceeds on monopolies overall: courtiers and contractors scooped the rest. The extent to which Charles's administration was besmirched is suggested by the sardonic comment of one Kentishman that the book of sports of 1633 would be a good device for making money. Wentworth's pious observation in 1637 that some projectors ought to be hanged, to take 'the reproach off all [the king's] upright and well meaning ministers', suggests his sense of the threat that corruption presented to the moral ideals through which early-modern rule was always represented.

Charles had insisted in 1629 that a return to the conventional means of expressing the body politic, to the king-in-parliament, would hinge on a restoration of mutual love and understanding. The devices by which his government impinged on the ordinary subject did not augur well for such an outcome.

Mutual love and understanding of course hinged on peace. Only peace would foster the growth of trade, the restoration of royal finances, and ultimately the refurbishment of royal authority. Peace allowed English shipping to capture Dutch markets and also some of the Dutch carrying trade between Spain and northern Europe. Peace brought higher customs revenues. And peace allowed the king to shelve some of the more provocative measures to which he had turned in the stresses of war. But peace, however beneficial, was a state of mind as well as a political condition; and Charles's mind was steadily torn between the grandeur of his crown and the straitness of his resources.

Charles's vision of monarchy was not just domestic, ceremonious and uplifting; it was also strikingly imperial. The heroic stance of Le Sueur's equestrian statue of the king commissioned by Portland in 1630, still more van Dyck's triumphant equestrian portraits of 1633 and 1638, challenge all the affecting portraiture of the royal family. Such representations may seem ironic: after all, one of the most purposive airings of imperial claims came in the masque, *Britannia Triumphans* (1638). The architecture was often superficial in the strict sense, as in the classical west front Jones imposed on the old Gothic cathedral of St Paul's, the classical facades Laud added to St John's College, Oxford, and Wentworth to the King's Manor at York. Charles's art collection was scattered in the whirlwind of the 1640s. Indeed, the only royal works of substance to survive from the 1630s are the queen's house at Greenwich (1633), and Rubens's superb ceiling in the Whitehall banqueting house begun under James. But the imperial palace at Whitehall Charles was planning with Jones in 1638, that might have made London the wonder of Europe, suggests the scale of his aspirations.

Charles aspired to the position in Europe which he felt his due as king of so many kingdoms. He had two prime objectives – to be respected, and to retrieve his own and his country's honour by the restoration of his sister's family to the Palatinate. In pursuit of the first objective, Charles quickly resumed Buckingham's naval building programme, and commissioned researches into England's putative claims to the sovereignty of the seas. These were to bear fruit in John Selden's tendentious work *Mare Clausum* (the Closed Sea) of 1633, in the ship money fleet initiated in 1634, and in the first English great ship of advanced three-deck construction, the deliberately named *Sovereign of the Seas*, launched in 1637. The second objective, the Palatinate, was more problematic. His subjects showed by their hunger for the news retailed in Dutch corantoes, or newsbooks, their preoccupation with the fortunes of European protestantism. But they were no more eager for land engagements than the king now was.

Charles's hopes centred in Spain. Not only might Spain, hardpressed as it was in its endless wars with the Dutch, benefit from English naval protection in the Channel to the extent perhaps of being willing to pay for it. As the senior branch of the Habsburgs, and possessing the American treasure, Spain might also persuade Vienna to restore the Palatinate: here at least Charles agreed with his father. Such hopes, and his distaste for the Dutch as republican rebels and trading rivals, actually led Charles to allow Cottington to negotiate in Madrid in 1631 the dismemberment of The Netherlands. Even when Spain's near-bankruptcy, and its justified scepticism of English capacities, dispelled the king's dreams, he had little enthusiasm for the obvious strategic alternatives. To the dismay of many of his subjects, in 1632 he banned the circulation of corantoes, with their reports of the German conquests of that protestant hero, and French client, Gustav Adolf of Sweden. War with the Habsburgs, even a 'blue-water' war with Spain, would necessitate a parliament, and in 1633 Charles badly 'rattled' Lord Keeper Coventry who was urging such an outcome.

New possibilities seemed to open after Gustav Adolf's death in the disaster of Nordlingen in 1634. France's entry into the war in 1635 meant that an anti-Habsburg alliance need not be a protestant one, with all the attendant risks of religious excitement. After Vienna in 1636 coldly rejected Charles's empty pleas for a restoration of the Palatinate, high-placed courtiers talked of a change in alignments, and Charles's nephew, the young heir to the Palatinate, hurried to London to urge the case. But Charles had forgotten neither his old distrust of France, nor his aversion to a parliament, and gloom mounted in the chambers of court Calvinists like the Earl of Holland and their ally the Queen. The furthest Charles would go was to permit some minor privateering in the far Atlantic by the Providence Island Company, established in 1630 by Warwick, Lord Saye and Sele, Pym, and other puritan investors who had despaired of an effective war. Though Charles's hopes of an active alliance with Spain had gone, he insisted on a benevolent neutrality in Europe. Spanish troops, treasure and supplies were convoyed up the Channel; in 1639, Spanish soldiers were even allowed to march across English soil.

Charles's unwillingness to commit himself may have stemmed from a proper sense of the costs and political dangers of war. If so, his realism did not amount to a coherent policy. Although Charles asserted his naval dignity in the most flamboyant fashion, he gave his newly expanded fleet little to do but try vainly to compel the French and Dutch to recognise his claims to maritime sovereignty. In 1639 Charles was given a golden opportunity both to maintain his posture and to apply pressure to Spain one way or another when Dutch ships attacked a Spanish fleet just off Dover. But he left his fleet to stand by without clear instructions while the Dutch destroyed their enemies in English waters. Such blustering and vacillation earned the contempt of other European rulers while running a real risk of prompting one of them to call the English bluff. Laud and

Wentworth had some grounds for fearing, even before he drove the Scots to rebel, that Charles's activities would provoke a crisis that would necessitate a parliament. And there were signs in the mob assaults on the survivors of the Spanish ships attacked off Dover that a parliament would be critical.

The king's dream of extricating the Palatinate from the European catastrophe forms the context for ship money. But the Palatinate scarcely tells the whole story, for as Maximilian of Bavaria sardonically observed, the English fleet counted for little in central Europe. That fleet, commanded to enforce submission to the English flag on all who passed through the Channel or entered the British seas, was the product of ideology, of the same royal determination to make an issue of superiority and obedience that had generated the forced loan. In both cases, the consequences for governance were overwhelming.

Ship money was one more product of fiscal antiquarianism and the exploitation of legal imprecision. The ports had long been compelled to provide ships, or money in lieu, when required for defence of the realm. In 1634–5 the council extended the convention to the coastal counties as a whole, and in the following years to the entire country, on the grounds that the prosperity of all suffered from pirate raids. With this expansion went an increase in the sums demanded: from c. £80 000 in 1634–5 to almost £200 000 per annum for the rest of the decade save 1638–9, when plague, a disastrous harvest and political crisis persuaded Charles to reduce the levy to c. £70 000. These figures contrast with the total of about £1 million levied by parliamentary subsidy and forced loan over the whole previous, belligerent, decade. The novelty became still more apparent with the increase in the assessed population, which was rated for money now as well as land: in Essex about four times as many householders were burdened with ship money as had paid the 1628 subsidy. For the first time the country was being asked for regular direct payments to its government. And the money came in, to a degree remarkable by seventeenth century European standards: the shortfall on the 1636–7 levy was only 3.5 per cent.

Acquiescence was scarcely the result of innovatory enforcement. True, the post office was reorganised in the mid-1630s, and there were some improvements in the council's book-keeping. And on the assumption that a single officer would be more responsive and responsible than the multiple commissioners who otherwise ran local government, the council made the sheriff, formerly the dogsbody of local peace-keeping, the key to the system. The sheriff's thankless task it was to deal personally with the multitude of constables who made up the lower levels of local government, and who were instructed to allocate the sums due on householders, and distrain the property of the recalcitrant. These were not the traditional proceedings of local government, and the increasing reluctance during the 1630s of householders to serve as constables points to strains.

Most payers conformed, not least because Charles went to considerable lengths to make it clear that this was not arbitrary taxation. It was an emergency rate, to be used (as indeed it was) altogether by the navy. Conformism was often reinforced by particularist considerations, for where there was a genuine threat of piracy, or of enemy raids, tax-payers seem to have accepted the legitimacy of the levy: thus, the vulnerable south-coast counties of Hampshire and Sussex paid right to the end. Furthermore, the strength of the old quid pro quo rule of politics was clear in, for example, the relative success of ship money in Cheshire. There both the county and the city of Chester vied for a hearing from the council on their rating dispute, and each strove to bolster its claims against the other by responding with alacrity to the council's demands. Whatever the climate of suspicion, the practical links between court and country had to be maintained.

Yet there was opposition, and its character is revealing. Much of the early resistance took the form of rating disputes, challenges to the distribution of the burden between areas. A myriad such disputes eventually ground collection to a halt in many counties, for the majority had to be settled by the catastrophically overburdened council: thirty disputes from Essex alone reached Whitehall in 1637. But challenges to the equity of assessments were sometimes camouflage. When in 1637 the king threatened the local power base of the Earl of Warwick, who was the leading dissident in Essex, Warwick promptly switched to challenging the validity of the local rates. Nor did it need noblemen to co-ordinate opposition. The Sheriff of Rutland in early 1637 sensed widespread refusals on 'matter of conscience'; his colleague in Lincolnshire encountered articulate opposition even in areas without resident gentry. Even ordinary householders seem to have been reluctant to concede Charles's claim to an absolute and uncontrollable prerogative when there was no evident emergency.

Ideology as much as foreign policy had occasioned ship money, but events abroad changed the tempo. The near-collapse of his foreign policy in 1636 determined Charles to seek legal reinforcement of his position; to his delight, early in 1637 the judges unanimously upheld the principle of ship money. Telling Wentworth boldly that he was now as far from a parliament as ever, and ignoring the covert reservations of many of the judges, he then allowed a test case to be brought. That test case is famous for the name of the defendant, the rich Buckinghamshire gentleman, John Hampden, who was one of a number of prominent dissidents, mostly associated with the Providence Island Company, eager to bring the matter to a head. Hampden's counsel Oliver St John, who was also legal adviser to the Earls of Warwick and Bedford, argued that the recurrence of ship money payments meant they constituted not an emergency levy but a tax, for which parliament ought to have been summoned. The case had abundant plausibility in the desultory performance of the ship money fleets, reported assiduously in the newsletters, and in the anthems to peace sung by court poets and masquers. Nevertheless, seven of the twelve judges took the legally sound view that the king was the only judge of emergencies, and of the action required.

The judges spoiled their case by provocative asides in the packed courtroom. Judge Berkeley's off-hand remark that the king was 'lex loquens, a living, a speaking, an acting law', was in the circumstances fiery stuff; so was Chief Justice Finch's declaration that 'no acts of parliament make any difference' to the crown's power to raise money for defence of the realm. Finch's views suggested the very extension of the prerogative that the Petition of Right had striven to block, and he caused further alarm by expounding them in the counties in propagandist charges on the assize circuit. *Hampden's Case* had not settled the matter. Observers noted the narrow margin for the king, and one constable in Northamptonshire thought ship money might cause trouble akin to that welling in Scotland.

Time still seemed to be on Charles's side. Although the arguments of the five judges who sided with Hampden gained a wider circulation in the country than did Finch's, the yield of the 1637–8 levy fell eventually only 9 per cent below target; and in the immediate aftermath of defeat Warwick, Lords Saye and Brooke and John Pym were all contemplating emigration to America. But only intense, and unrepeatable, conciliar pressure obtained the 1637–8 yield. And although it was above all the Scottish crisis that persuaded the leading dissidents to remain, the trial itself had not been without effect. In Kent gentlemen debated the constitutional issues with learning and sophistication – although, in an ominous pointer to future developments, both sides found supporters. When in the following year the Scottish crisis divided the council's energies and emboldened the discontented, chastisement of defaulters wound down and non-payment soared. One-third of the much lower demand of 1638–9 could not be collected, and by early 1640 collection had all but collapsed.

England was troublesome enough to a king whose watchwords were unity and order; but his other realms were far more disunified. Charles had been prevented by greater Britain's political intractability from calling on all its resources in the wars of the 1620s. Worse, the religious divisions of Scotland and Ireland affronted the dignity of a powerful monarchy and, Charles and Laud were confident, affronted God too. If he were to be properly a king, take his rightful place in the world and do his duty to God, he must bring order. And such order would be Anglocentric: he had blithely sold titles of honour in Scotland and Ireland in the later 1620s to aspiring Englishmen who lacked any Scottish or Irish lands, with no thought to the offence this might give. Charles, much more than James, was oblivious to the political risks of attempts by the core kingdom of dynastic states to impose religious forms or fiscal demands, or both, on neglected and resentful outliers.

The larger task lay in Ireland. The ravaging of the crown's lands and revenues by war and settler greed had left the Dublin government to run at a substantial deficit throughout James's reign, and it proved incapable of funding new fortifications or providing more than ill-equipped recruits for Charles's French and Spanish wars. Desperate, Charles decided to do a deal with the leaders of the Catholic 'old English' (that is, Anglo–Irish descendants of pre-Elizabethan settlers): in the 'Graces' of 1628 he offered them some security of land tenure and the removal of political and legal disabilities. Happy though he was with the £120 000 the Anglo-Irish agreed to pay, he was happier still when peace with Spain freed him of the pressure to ratify his side of the bargain. Nevertheless, by the end of the decade the crown's position seemed bleak. Not only were the Anglo-Irish angered by the king's breach of faith; they and their Gaelic co-religionists were heartened by the Catholic missionary priests who had begun to arrive in significant numbers during the 1620s. On the other side, 'new English' protestant settlers were outraged by the king's willingness to negotiate with the enemy. And in Ulster the political arithmetic was further complicated by the 8000 presbyterian Scotsmen who had by 1630 settled on lands confiscated after the flight of the earls.

In Ireland more than anywhere else in his dominions Charles sought to make a reality of his rhetoric of kingship and order. At the beginning of 1632 he appointed as lord deputy Wentworth, who had made a name for himself by his forceful government of the north. Wentworth's broad goals were summed up in 'Thorough', the slogan he shared with his great ally Laud: the restoration of the position of crown and church – and, not incidentally, the building of his own – despite all obstacles. There were other similarities between Wentworth and Laud. Both were domineering, both had a total sense of their own rectitude and an equal inability to sympathise with the motives of others; and both believed from the first that danger lay all around.

Wentworth saw himself in an heroic mould, and to some extent his characterisation, if not at first his sense of crisis, was justified. A bold strategist and brilliant manipulator, in his parliamentary attacks on maladministration and the follies of war in the 1620s he had shown himself as well a commanding orator. Wentworth may not have been the tyrant of legend, but he was authoritarian in temperament and practice. Convinced that political harmony in England could only be achieved if passions subsided sufficiently for a loyal and docile people to trust its well-meaning king, he was adamant that desperation for supply should not drive the king into bargaining with a parliament. Ireland's role was to contribute to the English exchequer instead of running at its usual loss; such an outcome would also of course give Wentworth a strong claim to promotion. Peace was the prerequisite, since it would allow Irish trade with the continent, and thus customs dues, to recover. And peace would also allow him to extend to the rest of Ireland the programme of plantation that had so transformed the political map of Ulster, and that was fast transforming the economy of the southern province of Munster.

The novelty of Wentworth's rule lay in the way he struck out against all groups, not just the usual target of the native Irish. The political weakness of all English deputies in Ireland had lain in the ability of their Irish enemies to find backers in the factions at the English court. Not content with extracting Charles's explicit promise of support, Wentworth made sure of this by carefully controlling through his ally Laud the flow of information to the king. Secure of the king's ear, he could play off against each other the two major Irish political groupings, 'old' and 'new English'. Brilliantly manipulating the Irish parliament he summoned in 1634, Wentworth gained a lavish grant of taxation, and power to vet titles to land. He then used his new position with utter self-confidence as he set about the confiscations needed to drive plantation into the western province of Connacht, the key to his strategy of reducing the whole of Ireland to the crown.

Adapting legal process to 'a little violence and extraordinary means', as he blandly put it, Wentworth strove to undo the effects of generations of plunder by English settlers. Through blatant intimidation of juries, he upheld the crown's claims to four-fifths of the land in County Galway. Of the next, equally intimidated, jury in County Clare he wrote, in apparent seriousness, 'in all my whole life did I never see . . . men with so much alacrity divesting themselves of all propriety in their estates'. The new English could not relax as they watched old English join Gaels as victims of English confiscations. Not only were new English lands in the west at risk in Connacht; there was little security anywhere. Indeed, Wentworth had already forced several major new English landowners, including his enemy and the greatest protestant magnate, the Earl of Cork, to disgorge lands they had taken from, and scale back their domineering over, the church. The more hamstrung Laud watched from England in grateful appreciation.

The application of Laudianism had particular dangers in Ireland. Wentworth deemed uniformity urgent less because of any Catholic threat than because of the rooting of presbyterianism in Ulster. But protestantism was a badge of the colonists' identity, and anti-Catholicism a necessary buttress to their superiority. Under its 1615 articles of faith the church of Ireland became more uniformly Calvinist than the church of England under Abbot. But at the Irish convocation of 1634 Wentworth and his Laudian allies recast the Irish church as 'the church of England in Ireland'. Not only did they curb its claims to independence. The articles they pushed through enjoined a more Laudian order than prevailed in England, although enforcement was limited to Dublin cathedral and a few other sites of Laudian infiltration. Nevertheless, the clearer articulation of Ireland's subordination made the Ulster Scots and their mainland compatriots take notice of Wentworth as the man most likely to overturn the protestant cause.

Charles sought a closer integration of Ireland – fiscal, ecclesiastical, economic – into England's hegemony. But traffic could never flow in only one direction. Contacts between the Ulster Scots and those across the narrow channel in Scotland were beyond Wentworth's control, and so were certain connections between Ireland and London that were of the king's making, not his. On grounds of breach of the plantation undertakings, Charles in 1635 fined the City of London £70 000 and confiscated its extensive Londonderry estates, though James had forced the City into the scheme in 1613. Wentworth thereby incurred the dangerous resentments of the City of London, and also of its Ulster tenants whose tenures were jeopardised: these included John Pym's friend Sir John Clotworthy. The estates, valued by some at £18 000 per annum, then became a valuable prize at court, and Wentworth found himself in a heated competition for them. His chief rival was a striking phenomenon of Charles's reign – Randall McDonnell, Earl of Antrim, grandson of the great O'Neill dispossessed in 1607, titular Lord of the Isles as descendant of the Scottish McDonalds, now married to the Duke of Buckingham's widow and allied to the king's cousin, the great Anglo-Scottish courtier the Duke of Hamilton. Such a rival was well placed to agitate against Wentworth's arrogance, and against the appearance he gave of hypocrisy as he expropriated others and enriched himself.

Wentworth's gains were huge. He raised his own income, through office, from some £2000 per annum in 1628 to £23 000 by 1639. But his career did not wholly subvert the ideal of 'Thorough'. New English plunderers like Cork, and like the popish soap monopolists in England, made their fortunes by defrauding the crown, the people, or both; Wentworth consistently made money for the crown as well as himself. During his tenure the crown's revenues in Ireland doubled, and for the first time the Irish treasury began to contribute to the English exchequer. But in the inter-connected world of the three kingdoms, reshaping Ireland into a docile subsidiary of the crown lay beyond even his capacities.

The bold moves that characterised Wentworth's tenure in Ireland found a striking analogue in Scotland. While Wentworth divided and ruled in Ireland, only at the end to unite all factions against himself, Charles demonstrated he could himself unite highly diverse elements, and in so doing create an irresistible opposition in Scotland. Forgetting his father's caution, he drove noblemen resentful at the reduction of their country to the status of a frontier province to make common cause with clerical militants. The combination of aristocratic and clerical protest had torn apart France and The Netherlands in the sixteenth century. It was to prove equally destructive in Scotland.

James had shown tact as well as persistence in rebuilding royal authority and church order in Scotland. He had worked steadily and with some success to rebuild the office, if not the wealth and power, of bishops; and he had temporised his hopes of importing greater ceremonial into the

Scottish church when his Five Articles of Perth of 1617 encountered opposition. Charles showed no such delicacy. One of his gravest errors came at the very start of his reign in an an act of revocation that in 1625 cancelled all grants of crown or church lands made since 1540. Such measures were customary when monarchs who had succeeded to the throne as minors reached maturity; and Charles's aims of firmer funding for church ministers and clearer recognition of the crown's feudal supremacy were unobjectionable enough. But he had succeeded as an adult. While he made little effort to enforce the revocation once he had extracted better provision of teinds, or tithes, the gesture unnerved the new noble families that James had 'erected' (established) on former church lands, and created a broad climate of distrust.

Aristocratic distrust was not allayed by the nature of Charles's government. His concern for the church, and his preference for obedience over advice, led him to place nine loyal and conformist bishops (most of them suspect for their Arminianism) on the council. Noble members of the council soon dissociated themselves from what they came to see as a pointless exercise, leaving the council largely in the hands of bishops and officials, and incapable of withstanding royal pressure. When Scottish visitors to Charles's increasingly formal court in London were ostracised as uncultured boors, the avenues of communication between king and country became dangerously narrow.

It did not take long for the king to create something close to national opposition. Scotland had experienced annual taxation for the king's military posturing of the 1620s, for its complex representative structures of parliaments and conventions allowed the crown considerable influence. That painful record seemed to acquire new meaning in the early 1630s as Charles manipulated and exploited Scotland's economy: customs rates, new coins, a new fisheries company, all benefited favoured Englishmen. But what both broadened and cemented the opposition, and undid the king, was his imperviousness to the ecclesiastical lesson James had learned after 1617: the Scots' conviction that theirs was the purest and most reformed kirk on earth.

Charles was affronted by the dominance in Scotland of ways of worship he was endeavouring to root out in England. Not only did Scottish practices challenge his belief in the divine warrant for the forms Laud was elaborating in England; the presence of presbyterianism in Scotland could only hearten puritan dissidents in England. When in 1633 Charles profited from southern tranquillity to travel northwards for his Scottish coronation he indicated his intent to reduce his northern church to the English pattern. Confirming the affronts he had given in 1625 to legalism, he then forced through the Scottish parliament an affirmation of the king's powers in religion. Suspicions of his trustworthiness solidified when he had Lord Balmerino sentenced to death – although the sentence was not carried out – merely for possessing a petition against his actions.

The new pattern for the kirk was as objectionable as many had feared, and its introduction more incompetent than any could have hoped. Charles in 1636 demanded obedience to a prayer book that he declared was on the way, and thus allowed free play to fear and rumour. The notice given of its introduction in Edinburgh churches in 1637 then allowed the opposition the chance to mobilise. Although Scottish bishops were involved in the prayer book's compilation, its form for communion service was even more Laudian than was the English prayer book's; and its preamble stressed the virtues of religious unity in Charles's kingdoms, rather than the scriptural purity Scottish presbyterians treasured. Imposed by prerogative, and without reference to the general assembly of the kirk or to parliament, the prayer book threatened rule that was arbitrary as well as from London. When Edinburgh burst into rioting in July Charles's Scottish council showed itself less determined than the Bishop of Brechin, who read the prayer book over loaded pistols pointed at his congregation. The council promptly withdrew the book and went into recess for a month while it consulted the king.

The prayer book provided both a focus and symbol for the discontented. Many saw it as flat popery – even the Earl of Montrose, soon to be a devoted royalist, denounced the book as 'the brood of the bowels of the whore of Babel'. That conclusion revived memories of the bloody sixteenth-century troubles over religion, and of what had then been done. In February 1638 almost one-third of the parish clergy and still more of the nobility met in Edinburgh to subscribe a national covenant to defend the kirk. Although the wording of the covenant was loyal, it was manifestly a gesture of defiance. Moreover, its recitation of past covenants of God and nation heightened the Scots' sense that they were God's chosen. That stirring identity, and the prospect of imminent struggle with the popish Antichrist, quickly displaced more familiar loyalties, to the crown or to noble feudatories. Many nobles were to live to regret the return of the kirk militant.

The Covenanters' passion was of course reciprocated. Compromise might have been possible in 1637 had the king withdrawn the prayer book, but he knew only a religious duty to impose uniformity, and an equally religious duty not to admit any derogation of his kingship. He now found how limited had been the gains of the 1630s. He had been lulled into an aggressive stance, at sea, and then in Scotland, by servants reluctant to confront the myth of royal power he displayed so confidently in the masques. By anticipating the revenues of future years they had contrived to assure him that all was well. But reality intruded, and in the summer of 1638 Charles was driven to postpone military action. Even after years of peace he had been unable to build a financial reserve, and long carelessness about royal credit now reaped its reward. Nevertheless, Charles's determination to use force remained, and in June he instructed his cousin the Marquess of Hamilton, the leading Anglo-Scottish magnate, to buy time: 'flatter them with what hopes you please . . . until I be ready to suppress them'.

Charles's confidence in 1637 that a parliament was far away had hinged on his assumption that he could choose his enemies, French or Dutch, and that a war would be at sea. But he had provoked the Scots into a confrontation that was to call on landward resources; land wars were always more expensive, and more unpredictable in their political implications, than were naval. And religious struggles were most unpredictable of all. He was to live and die with the consequences.

G.P.

Although the Scottish crisis was to shake the king's sense of control, others had already acquired a well-developed sense of the vulnerability of the world. The godly who watched the advance of Catholic forces in the Thirty Years War, and of anti-Calvinists at home, knew a storm was coming, and increasingly in the 1630s turned to code to express their convictions in correspondence. More striking is the decision of Laud and Wentworth in 1637 to join them in their secrecy, perhaps out of fear of court rivals, but out of apprehension too of the risks their master's policies were running. The decade had opened in England amid royal insistence on the king's responsibility for his people, and that theme resounded in the crown pleadings in Hampden's Case. But in the excited response to that case, in the anxious market for news of Europe, in the more perilous market for news of Scotland, signs multiplied that ways of thinking about order and authority that had been held in a comfortable fudge were beginning to crystallise out as the king was seen to set himself more firmly on a partisan course. Patriarchalism, divine-right monarchy, the body politic, the ancient constitution, the godly prince, had been thought reinforcing. They might yet be found in conflict.

7

Crisis in three kingdoms,
1638–1642

see prev.
page
w. Marquer

The Scottish crisis demonstrated how great a challenge ideological division might pose to a polity that was systematically imagined in organic terms. It was not only for reasons of honour, and to stop contamination spreading to England, that Charles determined to enforce the Scots to obedience. His belief in the sacral nature of kingship led him to insist repeatedly on the non-negotiability of the entire domain of the sacred. Presbyterians could only be republicans: as he quickly told Hamilton, 'the number of those that are against episcopacy who are not in their hearts against the monarchy, is not so considerable'. No less urgent was the Covenanters' conviction that theirs was the 'best reformed church' in the world, shadowed in scripture, hallowed by providence – and no less incapable of diminution.

The crisis had the unfortunate effect of confirming the stereotypes that fuelled violence. On the one hand the Covenant bore out Laudian claims of the dangers of Calvinism, and rendered plausible the common court argument that Catholics were better subjects than were puritans. On the other, the court's own changing religious complexion came into sharper focus. Religious estrangement of country and court in England had been lessened by the presence of an anti-Spanish, and therefore pro-French, group of protestant courtiers clustered around the queen: the Earl of Northumberland, Holland, the elder Sir Henry Vane. This group fragmented in 1637 when the king turned his back on a French alliance at the very moment that he embroiled himself with France's old ally Scotland. And all the while the papal agents, Panzani and Con, pressed Henrietta Maria to act out the uncomplicated role of 'good Catholic' queen facing rebellious and heretical subjects. The hostile caricature of the court, Catholic and pro-Spanish, steadily took hold of protestant imaginations.

The crisis was not only resistant to compromise; it was also at root British, rather than Scottish first and later English. Its roots lay in *toppling Laudian episcopacy*

Scotland's subordinate status within a composite monarchy, and its resolution required some adjustment of that relationship. The protagonists were determined to hasten such an adjustment. The Covenanters concluded that since the king and his bishops (above all the bishops in England) threatened their godly order, that order must be secured by the toppling of Laudian episcopacy in England. Accordingly, in November 1638 the Scottish General Assembly that Hamilton had unwisely allowed to meet at Glasgow declared that episcopacy was not just inconvenient but unlawful. The significance of the latter verdict for both Charles and the Covenanters was that it was less capable of being politically contained within Scotland. Scots protestants had long recognised the need to make common cause with their English neighbours against a hostile world; the Covenanters hoped now to make the whole empire of Great Britain presbyterian. The king had an equal need to expand the conflict, since his position in Scotland had collapsed so rapidly. His only hope of bringing his northern kingdom back to obedience lay in the resources of his other realms.

From its very outset the widening reach of the Scottish crisis was apparent. Laud suspected, and for good reason, a Scots fifth-column among English puritans; indeed, from perhaps the end of 1637 the Scottish Covenanters had an agent in London. They drafted their propaganda with an eye to the sympathies of eager London readers like Nehemiah Wallington, while Pym's friend Clotworthy, the Ulster planter, was one of several puritans who found their way to Edinburgh. Yet Charles bore his own responsibility for expanding the struggle, and not simply by declaring his intention to use England against Scotland. He also harkened to a transnational private enterprise – the efforts of the anglicised Ulster Gael, Antrim, to lead back the scattered remnants of clan McDonald to the homelands in the Western Isles they had lost to clan Campbell. Antrim's plot, to strike the Covenanters in the rear in Campbell territory, backfired, as Wentworth for one feared it would. It succeeded only in cementing the Covenanting sympathies of the Earl of Argyll, the greatest Scottish nobleman and the head of clan Campbell. But the activities of Scots fifth-columns and Roman Catholic Ulster plotters illuminate the complex dynamics of the three kingdoms that were unloosed by the Scottish prayer book and were to dominate the following decade.

the Antrim Plot

For all his confidence in the royal will, Charles was by no means oblivious to realities. In order to placate English opinion, he reduced the 1638–9 ship money demand. In order to buy time, he instructed Hamilton to make concessions to the Scots. But in England he intended above all to maintain the crown's primacy. Showing just what he had learned from his experiences in the 1620s, he became the first king in over 300 years to try to fight without calling a parliament. Similar priorities were evident in his reluctance to consult his English privy council over the affairs of his other

use (abuse) of parl.

kingdom of Scotland. Northumberland, now Lord Admiral, confided helplessly, 'We are as great strangers to all proceedings as if we lived at Constantinople.' Instead, the king turned to those who told him what he wanted to hear: the queen, Arundel, and Anglicised court Scots like his cousin the Duke of Richmond and Lenox, and Hamilton.

As a measure of what the prerogative could achieve, the levies of 1639 were impressive. A royal army of 20 000 gathered near Newcastle. But the military option had an air of unreality. Money and supplies were lacking, for no surplus had been accumulated in the exchequer, and the credit of the customs farmers was as incapable of supporting a war as it had been in the 1620s. Trained officers too were in short supply. The king pursued honour as much as victory, and turned away from professionals skilled in European methods of war to the likes of Arundel, whom he appointed commander on the grounds of status. In like manner, he issued a neo-feudal summons to English landowners to do their duty. Over a half of the gentry summoned evaded the issue; and while the bulk of the nobility responded, the outcome could not inspire much enthusiasm – even the Earl of Bridgwater, President of the Council of Wales, found half his complement of ten horsemen amongst local drunkards. Equally seriously, horses and cannon proved as deficient as was the supply of decorative plumes. Nor did the infantry yield more comfort. The legal status of the militia, the obvious source of foot soldiers, was open to challenge, so the council hesitated to order it to march, let alone to invade another country. Instead, it allowed the soldiers to send substitutes – untrained and ineffective though these often were. The Earl of Manchester, one of several privy councillors who were to desert their master in the coming storm, took comfort in the belief that the motley force would be 'but a show', and that Charles intended, as in 1626–7, merely to test the obedience of his subjects, Scots now as well as English.

Folly and incompetence ensured that such a test of loyalties would be less than searching. The ill-clothed, ill-armed and ill-led English foot soldiers gave one answer as they headed north smashing church ornaments, the symbol of this 'Bishops' War', and helping enclosure rioters pull down hedges. Charles allowed insufficient time for Wentworth to give another answer with his Irish contingent. The third plank in the royal strategy, an amphibious descent by Hamilton on Scotland's east coast, broke since every potential landing-place was thoroughly hostile. The Covenanters therefore had ample time to concentrate their forces opposite the king's army on the border. And although they were not anxious for battle against their king, they had chosen professional officers from among their countrymen who had rallied home from the German wars. At last Charles recognised reality, and in June 1639 signed the pacification of Berwick. He then proceeded to prepare for the next round.

The king's political position had weakened. He had brought disaffection out in the open by demanding of the assembled nobility in the north a personal oath in support of his war, only to be personally rebuffed by Lords Saye and Brooke. And he had given substance to the old, and potentially all-consuming, phobia of a popish plot by neither banishing Con from court, nor curbing the public activities of Catholics there. Henrietta Maria had tried to raise money from English Catholics to put down the Calvinist Scots; Arundel, commander of the 1639 expedition, rode conspicuously in Con's coach, adorned with the papal insignia. For those persuaded of an international popish threat the worst conclusions came easily – all the more so when Charles that year allowed Spanish troops harassed by Dutch raiders to march across English soil. But there was still room to escape. In the aftermath of Berwick, leading Covenanters, and his sister's protestant supporters at the English court, vainly urged Charles to launch a British force into the European wars. It was his best chance to divert the religious passions and the chivalric yearnings of a protestant aristocracy that was soon to turn against him.

Honour and action appealed as strongly to the king as to any godly nobleman. The Scots must be chastised. And while he had previously kept the forceful Wentworth at a distance, he now saw his viceroy in Ireland as the only man for the hour. Not only had Wentworth long trumpeted his successes; he was preparing for the present crisis, imposing his 'black oath' against the Covenant on resentful Ulster Scots, and adding to his army Catholics happy enough to fight Scottish Calvinists. In October 1639 the Lord Deputy returned to England and promotion to the lord lieutenancy of Ireland and the earldom, of Strafford, he coveted – and to rescue the king. But the Scots had less need for anxiety since they received ample intelligence of developments in England from the English aristocratic opposition: Saye and Brooke both contemplated flight to Scotland, and Saye's son Nathaniel Fiennes seems to have visited. Their hopes that Charles's efforts would disintegrate were reinforced in June 1639 when the City of London, judging Charles's credit wanting, rejected his request for a loan of £100 000. Correspondingly, councillors and officials gave signs of demoralisation. The ordinary functions of government began to be affected: as early as July 1639 Attorney-General Bankes declared his reluctance to issue a proclamation, for 'the times were ill for proclamations'.

Though Strafford deplored the prevailing chaos, and had long urged that kings should never go to their people on the defensive and desperate for money, he concluded that a parliament would have to be called. English dislike of the Scots might be manipulated to draw from parliament the means to rescue the king's war effort; if parliament-men failed in their duty, that fact would justify sterner measures. And others certainly heard the call, for a forced loan levied on courtiers and office-holders yielded £232 000 between December and May, not far short of the £300 000 which had been hoped. That sum was, however, only collected on the understanding that a parliament would be called, which would enable the loan to be repaid; and the loan lacked a contribution from the City of London.

That winter the last court masque, *Salmacida Spolia*, took as its theme Charles as king of an ungrateful people, and beset by wild tribesmen. Whatever that courtier verdict on the Scots, who in Laud's view had brought Charles 'upon his knees to a parliament', the English themselves were proving less than tame. Government was still far from breaking down: JPs continued to serve as efficiently or as inefficiently as ever, and the deputy lieutenants worked hard both in 1639 and 1640 at the thankless task of raising the forces demanded. But England was close to a taxpayers' strike as ship money collapsed during the winter of 1639–40. The council responded to the deterioration, and the frequent local violence against collectors, by heaping blame on the sheriffs, forty of whom had been threatened with Star Chamber proceedings by February 1640. Lord Keeper Finch instructed the judges on their duty 'to break the insolency of the vulgar', but the council had no idea of how this might be done. When informed in March of the sheriff of Northamptonshire's problems, which included a grand jury presentment against ship money, the council could only bury its head in the sand: 'We have had the patience to read your tedious letter,' which it then condemned as a tissue of excuses.

The elections that spring gave large numbers of Englishmen the chance to express themselves after eleven years of silence. They showed themselves far less concerned with the military threat on the northern border, on which Strafford had hoped to focus them, than with domestic grievances, with ship money and papists. Yet there was little evidence of outright alienation from the regime. While towns usually, as in the 1620s, preferred men with local ties, they often did not reject courtiers outright: thus, Laud failed to get his secretary elected at Canterbury, but he was successful in his home town of Reading. As one courtier judged perceptively, the newly elected Commons were neither as good nor as bad as they might have been.

What proved to be the Short Parliament was therefore open to persuasion. But Charles's characteristically terse opening oration on 13 April boded ill for his understanding of the crisis, his sense of the political community, and his appreciation of the rule of quid pro quo. He offered no explanation of the Scottish war, and merely demanded money to help end it. His promise that if the Commons would proceed with supply 'they should have all their just favours' caused 'a great hum' for its challenge to their claim to rights. There could have been no clearer reflection of the different senses of the polity. The keynote platitudes of Lord Keeper Finch, newly promoted after eager ship money service, about respect for the ancient constitution similarly earned 'a general hum', presumably of sarcasm. Probably a majority in the Commons had deduced a pattern of assault on titles to property in all three kingdoms, and the long-serving MP Sir Francis Seymour quickly denounced those who had 'betrayed the king to himself' by telling him 'his prerogative is above all laws'. That tortured construction, advanced by someone who was later to become a leading royalist, betrays an uneasy analysis of the relation of the king's two bodies, the official and the personal.

There was, however, considerable support among the peers, whose followers had filled the king's ranks in the north, and in the Commons too for a deal with the king to get rid of the ship money they feared. The Covenanters had hoped to build a common front with English parliamentary dissidents. But many parliament-men were ready to trade Charles supply, and therefore help in building an army for use against the Scots, in return for affirmation of English liberties. Even though many MPs, especially from the north, reported that their military charges now exceeded ship money, and though the king had done little to inspire trust, Charles was able to find buyers for his high price of twelve subsidies for the abandonment of ship money. One explanation must be the sheer perplexity of members who knew that ship money, as it had been applied, could be the end of parliaments, but were as devoted as Seymour to the principle of a royal frame of government. Another explanation might be found in the ancient distaste for the Scots that Strafford hoped to exploit.

Looking back on the storm through which he had lived, Edward Hyde, Earl of Clarendon, perhaps its greatest historian, thought Charles's abrupt dissolution of parliament on 5 May his gravest error. In a great two-hour speech on 17 April John Pym had worked hard to deflect the Commons from an agreement on ship money, reminding them of the burden of military charges on the north, of the crying need for regular parliaments, of the advance of popery and the excesses of the bishops. But his central contention, the claim of a popish plot, lacked sufficient purchase, and Sir John Culpepper from Kent and Hyde quickly came to the defence of key features of the existing church. But Charles was not content to wait. Report had reached him that Pym, who with his aristocratic friends had for some time been in contact with the Covenanters, was about to petition for a peaceful settlement. Ill disposed as he was to conciliation, and impatient at the lack of speedy supply, Charles was spurred by the imminent embrace of his Scottish and English foes to turn abruptly back to his own counsels.

It is hard not to quarrel with Clarendon's estimate of the significance of the short parliament of the spring of 1640. Not least, it helped the English catch up with the ideological sophistication of their neighbours. The Covenanters had grown accustomed to governing Scotland by committee, first through the 'Tables' that co-ordinated the kirk's revolt, and then in 1639–40 through parliamentary variants; as they did so they adopted a quasi-republican language of 'the state'. Such a transition came more slowly in England, but Pym helped pioneer it. Unlike Seymour, he had a firm sense of the self-regulative capacity of the body politic, and in his 17 April speech he linked the two vocabularies that were to reshape the polity. Harping on the popish threat that served to explain every abuse, he quietly sidelined this dangerous king as he invoked 'the commonwealth' instead of the kingdom – and then signalled his intent by apologising coyly 'for the last slip of my tongue'. The world beyond Westminster was growing more aroused at the same time. One returning Kent member, Sir Thomas Peyton, was sure that parliament had made men think beyond their petty local grievances. They now found their grievances shared; and that realisation could not be confined, for the common people 'received a diffusive knowledge from the dispersed house'.

What filled the consciousnesses of alarmed Londoners was the Laudian remodelling of the church. The king had accorded a new autonomy to the ecclesiastical convocation which met that spring, and insisted that it require all clergy and graduates to swear that the church hierarchy, listed with an ominously vague 'etc.' accorded with the word of God. There were to be no loopholes here for the Covenanters. To those who smelled a popish plot, the oath was confirmation: the pope lay hidden in that 'etcetera'. London apprentices and artisans, already smarting from economic depression born as much of political insecurity as of harvest failure and plague, greeted the dissolution with riots against Laudian targets. Some were close to panic – Nehemiah Wallington and his friends among the London godly armed themselves to face an attack from the royal garrison in the Tower, to be led by the crypto-Catholic Lord Cottington.

Despite such evidence of disaffection, and though his finances were in ruins, Charles sought still to confront the Scots. Northumberland attended council gloomily, convinced that 'in these broken times' no wise man could advise raising a new army, but aware that his views would not be heeded. Strafford, ever the gambler, and trusting to his Irish army, told the king what he wanted to hear: the failure of parliament showed the ancient constitution had broken down amid the exigencies of war. Arguing that Charles was 'loose and absolved from rules of government', he advocated extraordinary measures. Strafford's advice, given at a council meeting on 5 May, was to be remembered against him by other councillors, though it probably revealed more present desperation than arbitrary intent. Anyway, Charles lacked the resources to act on it, and Strafford's not altogether joking suggestion that a few aldermen be hanged in their robes in order to shake money from the Londoners' coffers offered little hope that those resources would be found. Though Spain was equally wracked by domestic and international pressures, the king looked there vainly for repayment in the form of a loan, even military aid, for the naval assistance of the 1630s. Equally rash were his plans to seize merchants' bullion deposited in the Tower, and to debase the coinage by 75 per cent. Merchant outrage forced the abandonment of both these ventures, but the insecurity they engendered only intensified the gathering depression. Financial desperation boded ill for military action.

The nation was if anything less ready for war than it had been the previous year. Many of the English soldiers had abandoned their weapons on their way home, many more had died of disease. And the king's determination to go to war on the heels of an angry dissolution of parliament had only concentrated political disaffection. The aldermen of Exeter who sat with their hats conspicuously and disrespectfully on while support for the enterprise was being urged in the cathedral, played as large a part in the second fiasco in the north as did the council itself, whose repeated changes of plan saw the men and their supplies dwindle. The result was beyond doubt. Almost one-fifth of the men who had arrived in Yorkshire by August were unarmed, and the equipment of many more was unserviceable. Equally alarming were the men themselves. Their new commander, Northumberland, was himself contemptuous as only a northern lord could be of the 'beggarly Scots', but he found the English soldiers 'readier to draw their swords upon their officers than against the Scots'. The troops raised in the 1620s had been disorderly enough, but the disturbances of 1640 were very different. Popular opinion can probably be gauged less from the elections than from the trail of broken and burnt altar-rails left by troops marching north, or from the lynchings of two Catholic officers, perpetrated with revealingly little hindrance from bystanders. The horror shown by the Earl of Bedford at this volatile anti-Catholicism suggests how rapidly the godly cause imagined by conservative gentleman might fracture.

The Covenanters, who had locked up compatriots alarmed by the growing presbyterian militancy, were freer of dissensions. When they entered England in August 1640 under the guise of petitioners, Charles's army disintegrated after token resistance at Newburn on the Tyne. The Scots, who had not expected quite such collapse, found themselves holding the two northernmost counties and Newcastle, the fourth city of the kingdom and the source of London's coal supplies. There was little to stop them, since Strafford's vaunted Irish army was only slowly assembling across the Irish Sea. But they had no intention of proceeding further, since the cause of the Covenant was not military: its makers, hoping for a godly federation in Britain, looked for common cause with the disaffected in an English parliament.

The pressures, political as well as financial, on the king were enormous. The two Bishops' Wars had cost £1 million; and to compound the humiliation, a week after Newburn twelve peers petitioned for a parliament. Despite what he correctly suspected of the twelve peers' ties to the Covenanters, Charles seems still to have put his hopes in the nobility as a whole. They had in the Short Parliament given him some support; might they not now, with the Scots on English soil, recall their traditional role as king's councillors and come to his aid? Accordingly, Charles engineered a feudal revival by summoning a great council of peers to York in September 1640. But though he had so assiduously bolstered their privileges, the nobles had no desire to stand against what they, far better than the king, knew of feeling in the country. The king's opening announcement that he would call a parliament meant less to Bristol and other nobles than his declaration of continuing hostility to the Scots. Seeking to heal the English body politic, they advised the king to accept his defeat, make peace, and turn to a parliament. Charles's council could suggest no better. Laud urged his colleagues that month that they should 'put to the king, that we are at the wall, and that we are in the dark, and have no grounds for a counsel'. As always, Charles wavered between the conciliation that was urged on him and his own taste for confrontation. That month he contemplated intervening in the London municipal elections to secure compliancy: 'let innovate, and spare not, it may be a good example for me, to doe the like, upon occasion hereafter'.

The new realities of politics quickly became clear. The first was distrust of the king. The great council had, at Charles's request, appointed commissioners to negotiate a peace that he hoped would leave him room for further manoeuvring; the Covenanter leadership insisted that he be excluded from the talks. The other realities were British and financial. All the Covenanters wanted of the talks at Ripon in Yorkshire was a truce, with payment of their expenses – the colossal sum of £850 a day – and the postponement of negotiations until an English parliament could meet. They hoped that their friends would then join them in co-ordinating the governance and faith of the two realms, in order to provide security for both. The treaty of Ripon left Charles mortgaged to the parliament it necessitated, and ensured that that parliament would not go the same short way as the last. For the Covenanters in the north constituted the central fact of the first session of the parliament that met on 3 November 1640. The Scots army, and the remaining English troops, had to be paid until such time as a settlement brought disbandment. The soldiers' hungry bellies were the wall behind which parliament sheltered, for only parliament could supply taxes, which in turn provided the vital security for loans for army expenses.

The effect on what had been the king's government was considerable. Most councillors joined the rest of the political nation in assuming that, as soon as a parliament was called, the king would abandon his intransigence and restore harmony. To that end they began freeing political prisoners – Prynne, Burton, Bastwick. The likelihood grew that compromise would become a rout, for some councillors' nerve failed: Laud, for one, avowed his anxiety not to compromise his home-town of Reading by trying to influence its election. Such restraint certainly played a part in the reduction of courtiers and office-holders in the Commons to about 15 per cent of the total, in contrast to the level of over one-third in 1614; but the retreat of the court was much more the consequence of a political awakening.

One courtier defeated at the elections claimed the nation was polarising: 'the opinion is grown general that whoever is not Scottishly must be popishly affected'. There were more contests, in perhaps a third of all constituencies, than ever before, though the contests usually stemmed from gentry rivalries, and the issues were usually local. Nevertheless, the meaner sort could not help but be involved and educated when, as in Worcester-shire, the assembled militia heard one candidate repeatedly denounced as 'fitter to break parliaments than to serve in parliament'. At Marlow in Buckinghamshire, where the simply dressed carrier Toucher Carter urged Bulstrode Whitelocke to stand to vindicate the commons' rights, popular involvement was even more direct. The MPs who assembled on 3 November 1640 for what was to become the Long Parliament spoke to such supporters, for they looked mainly to visible evils – Laudian innovations in local churches, ship money in the neighbourhoods. And their concern to lead England back into its ancient ways and to purge it of corruptions was one with which country sentiment could readily connect.

Backbenchers' concerns were soon given shape, for as one wrote home, 'God be praised, here want not skillful agents.' The famous cohesion of the two houses in the early stages of the Long Parliament stemmed not just from shared grievances but also from management. And since the privy council had all but collapsed, this came from elsewhere, from two very loose connections, each spanning the two houses. These collaborated effectively in the early months of the parliament, but their different emphases were to grow into significant divisions.

The cohesion of the godly network was eventually to gain it unflatter-ing recognition as 'the junto'. In the Lords it included Bedford (Pym's patron, and the mastermind of the twelve peers' petition), Essex, Warwick, Saye, Manchester's heir Viscount Mandeville, and in the Commons men like the great broker Pym, the Earl of Clare's son Denzil Holles, Saye's son Nathaniel Fiennes, and Hampden and St John of the ship money case. A sprawling East Anglian cousinage provided links to religious radicals such as Oliver Cromwell. Understandings forged in the 1630s through country-house gatherings in the Midlands, through planning for Hampden's trial, through meetings of the Providence Island Company, had been bolstered by Providence Island's connections with traders to America among the City's puritans; these proved invaluable in the spring of 1641 when Pym wished to apply pressure to waverers in the Lords. But neither magnate domination nor party discipline should be assumed. Bedford did find borough seats for Pym and St John; but Warwick was reported to have deployed preachers such as Stephen Marshall, as well as his bailiffs, to secure electoral victory for his allies in Essex.

The cohesion of patronage connections became much less apparent as the business of the parliament grew complex and contentious. Bedford's clients, St John and Pym, differed over financial matters, and Bedford himself seems to have differed with Pym over church reform; in the wider grouping Pym and Holles clashed repeatedly. Influence could at best guide, not dominate, and Pym was to find in 1641 that the City's purse could no more be opened at his suggestion than it had been at the king's. The leadership had therefore to tune other strings. A favourite device was the selection of sympathetic clergymen to address the Commons on their ceremonial fast days. Thus, on 17 November 1640 the preachers were Stephen Marshall, Warwick's client and the most influential preacher in the coming revolution, and Bedford's client Cornelius Burges, who later testified that he and Marshall met weekly with the 'junto' leaders. Their theme in the opening fast sermons was the 'Nimrods', tyrants, who had perverted religion and the laws.

The second network was less moved by anti-popish zeal. The most famous of the group sat in the Commons – Edward Hyde, Sir John Culpepper, Lord Falkland, with Sir Francis Seymour until his ennoblement in early 1641. But undoubtedly more influential in 1641 were the peers: long-standing councillors and courtiers like the Earl of Dorset and Charles's kinsman Richmond, as well as Bristol, Southampton, and Seymour's brother Hertford, a signatory to the twelve peers' petition. These are usually known as the 'constitutional royalists' for their condemnation of the measures of the 1630s and their insistence that the king, like the subject, was bound by the rule of law. But their commitment to harmony and the ancient ways of the body politic extended equally to the church. Opposing Laudian innovation, they frowned too on puritan schemes of reformation, and treasured the Book of Common Prayer. They could trace not only their characteristic churchmanship but also their distinctly constitutionalist emphases to their scepticism about the power and reach of popery. Unlike many of 'the junto', they were not driven to see every abuse as a symptom of a far deeper evil. Though not as adept in techniques of management, perhaps they did not need to be. They were almost certainly closer to the centres of both houses on matters constitutional and ecclesiastical.

Parliament-men were subject not just to the promptings of factional leaders but to lobbying, whether by constituents or by clergy – 'the black-coated walkers of Westminiser Hall', as the Kent MP Sir Edward Dering called them in disgust. Most of all they became subject to petitioning. Politics had never stopped at the gate of the court, and nor did it now stop at parliament's doors. The growing importance of petitions of grievances, from seamen, from the godly householders of London, from most of the counties of England and Wales, points to the involvement of a wider public in the political process. It suggests as well the importance politicians attached to being able to represent (or to misrepresent) the sense of a country that the king could no longer be assumed to personate.

Parliament-men also became the subjects of a flood of newsprint; some of them contributed eagerly to that same flood. Censorship had never been total, and the later 1630s had seen growing numbers of illicit imports from The Netherlands and Scotland, as well as from a handful of pirate presses. But the disintegration of censorship in late 1640, and still more 1641, brought a dramatic change in the composition, organisation and activity of the domestic printing industry. Artisan, and increasingly partisan, print-shops multiplied, giving access to men and women, patricians and plebeians. The 1640s saw a battle of books, or rather of ill-printed pamphlets, as much as of bullets: in each of the years 1642, 1643, 1647 and 1648, over a thousand separate works (excluding newspapers) were published on political or religious topics; and while the 1620s had seen the genesis of the English newspaper, the 1640s brought its flowering, with on occasion over ten journals a week appearing. Printed copies of parlia-mentary speeches testified to a political, as well as commercial, desire to gratify the popular appetite for news.

Whatever the novel pressures and partisanship of print, the petitions tell a different story. The overwhelming majority of the political nation in late 1640 sought to recapture an idealised vision of an Elizabethan harmony in church, state and the localities. Versions of that yearning, and certainly its preoccupation with the evil instruments who had frustrated it, were shared by both parliamentary connections, who made it their business in the early months to pursue Strafford, Laudian clergy, monopolists, corrupt officials. Pym was, however, at odds with virtually every petitioner in his attitude to taxation, which he thought essential to a state that was to defend itself. Attitudes to popery also differentiated him from a growing number of petitioners, as county after county became caught up in the crisis and raised its voice in petition. Pym and many of his allies insisted there must be a thorough purge of the enemy and its works within; but for Hyde and Culpepper, for Seymour and Falkland, and those whose petitions they presented, Laudian excrescences were one thing, an onslaught on ancient and accustomed ceremonies was quite another. The true English church they petitioned for was not quite what Pym, still less the radicals Brooke and Cromwell, had in mind, attuned as these were to international currents.

But all could agree that the essential means to any recovery was the survival of parliament. The triennial act of February 1641, mandating a parliament every three years, famously provided formal security, and it was greeted with rejoicing in London and godly Coventry. But in this conservative parliament it appealed less as an attack on the king's prerog-ative than as a means of guaranteeing the pay of the soldiers in the north. Indeed, the status quo in the north was not just the guarantee of parlia-ment but its central concern. Since the privy council was demoralised and disintegrating, with several of its leading members under investigation, and since parliament alone could open purse strings, a huge amount of detailed but vitally important work fell to committees. The securing of loans, the supply and regulation of the troops, all fell under parliamentary commit-tees, which were also involved in the negotiations for peace. And the peace negotiations were of course drawn out by the reluctance of 'the junto' and their godly allies among the Covenanters to see the Scots' army speedily disbanded.

Business as usual it was not, but it was certainly business. Any parliament had to respond to the mundane stresses of provincial life with bills to regulate light-houses or weirs and watermen on the Thames. This parliament also set itself to investigate ecclesiastical abuse, the military burdens on the north, the perversion of the courts of justice, even to fix the rates for landing coal and wood at Westminster. Before the end of 1640 a 'committee for committees' was considering which of the Commons' rapidly multiplying committees ought to be dropped. A tacit transformation was taking place. The more active parliament-men acquired an invaluable administrative training, while those outside became habituated to obeying parliamentary orders. But the conscious conviction of a parliamentary mission to govern was not yet widespread. By January 1641 the Commons occasionally found a quorum of forty difficult to attain. It is little wonder therefore that despite a widespread conviction that Charles's government had threatened the religion and liberty of the subject, the only reform to emerge in the first six months was the Triennial Act. Other reform legislation had to wait until the summer of 1641.

Reform had to compete not only with business, but with political crisis. Within a week of the opening of the session Pym had co-ordinated what was to become an impeachment for treason of Strafford. The lord lieutenant's vulnerability lay less in what he had done to the inhabitants of Ireland – few Englishmen objected to that – than in the threat he posed to the other British kingdoms. The Covenanters were outraged by the 'black oath', forswearing the Covenant, which he had inflicted on the Ulster Scots, and by the Irish army he had vainly assembled against Scotland. And for the anglocentric, the lord lieutenant, with his advocacy of stern measures when back in England, exemplified the meaning of tyranny. But he personified more than that to others: the Catholics in his army in Ireland and his treatment of protestant landowners like Cork and Clotworthy were read against the backdrop of leniency to papists and priests at Whitehall, and the Laudian corruptions of the church. All the plot of popery was there. But though the process of formulating the impeachment charge gave firmer shape to such rumours of conspiracy, and thus served to stiffen the Commons' majority, the parliamentary managers could not feel safe. Preparing the case would take time, and the animus against Strafford might drop amid the minutiae of legal proceedings.

Pym and his friends therefore worked to maintain an atmosphere of excitement. From the first week, reports of popish plotting came in. Constituents in Herefordshire informed Sir Robert Harley that there was to be a two-pronged attack on London from royal forces in the Tower and from Laud's at Lambeth, and that papists in the Welsh Marches were arming. Pym, zealous as ever, exploited such stories to the full. Brilliantly manipulating the vicious potential of the body politic, he flourished the ultimate in popish poison pen letters – what purported to be a bloody plaster from a plague sore, delivered to him on the floor of the house.

The Bishops' Wars, and the stockpiling of arms in the Tower, had heightened fears; and the 'etcetera oath' focused these, seeming to prove that Laud, 'the sty of all pestilential filth' to the godly lawyer and MP Harbottle Grimston, intended to introduce the pope. In December the Commons voted to impeach the archbishop as 'an actor in the great design of the subversion of the laws . . . and of religion'. That vote contrasted markedly with the reluctance of the Short Parliament to accept Pym's claims of conspiracy. Only time would tell how much damage the gathering zeal of anti-popery could do to hopes of settlement, which must depend on trust and compromise.

An equal threat to parliament's survival was immediate division. On 11 December a large throng of Londoners introduced a petition, signed allegedly by 15 000 of their neighbours, against episcopacy in all its 'roots and branches', against the whole structure of power in the church. MPs could agree in denouncing Laudian pomposity and power, but agreement would assuredly end if they were asked to abolish the whole order of bishops; it would end still more acrimoniously if they looked for a replacement. Accordingly, Pym and his allies strove for months to keep religious reform from the floor.

With Laud sent to join Strafford in the Tower, the parliamentary leaders pressed on, seeking not just vengeance but also to make examples for future servants of the crown. Into a frightened exile fled the crypto-Catholic Secretary of State Windebanke and Lord Keeper Finch, a key figure in Hampden's trial. And the courts, where the king had chosen to fight so many of his battles, also felt the rod of the new justice. Charles's determination to exploit the letter of the law in order to erect what many thought a legal tyranny earned its reward in the impeachments begun over the winter of 1640–1 against all but one of the surviving judges of the 1630s. Yet for all the noise, the Commons did not press home their attack, either on Laud or the judges. To have done so would have been to risk fissures among the moderates in both houses.

The sporadic nature of the attacks on the king's 'evil counsellors' also reflects on the interplay between Westminster and Whitehall. By the autumn of 1640 the morale of the council had been shattered as its agenda; but not all councillors fled or fell. Whatever Charles's own views, many of his councillors, particularly those who leaned towards the 'French' rather than the 'Spanish' side, had in the 1620s and even the 1630s dreamed of working with parliament to restore harmony. With the body politic so wracked, it was no wonder that they now sought to re-establish relations with the political nation through collaboration with the Commons' leaders. Their aristocratic constitutionalism suggestively parallels that of the *frondeurs* who were soon to challenge French absolutism. The Scottish disaster had anyway hardly strengthened their faith in Charles's judgment, and his secretiveness had left some resentful. Some perhaps had baser motives: Holland feared an attack on his role in the forest courts, and the Secretary of State, Sir Henry Vane snr, had a family feud with Strafford. But their co-operation, and that of Lord Admiral Northumberland, of Leicester (Strafford's successor as lord lieutenant of Ireland), of Lord Privy Seal Manchester, as well as of the king's legal officers, with the growing parliamentary government is suggestive. All of them were non-Laudians, and orthodox Calvinists; and they knew Charles better than most.

The impossibility of talking at this juncture of a 'government' and an 'opposition' suggests a further reason for parliament's limited legislative achievements in its first six months. Few of the purgative measures eventually passed in the summer of 1641 involved particularly complex drafting, and they proved uncontentious in parliament when they finally emerged. It may therefore be that the leaders of what is often called the 'opposition' may not have wanted to do too much. The constant castigation of the 'evil counsellors' who had misled the king is one side of a coin of which the other is the intense efforts of a group who were soon to be called the 'good lords' to enter office. If they were to become the king's servants they might not want to see the reins of government mangled.

But how might they strengthen their hold on those reins? The fate of the Petition of Right left the parliamentary leaders with few illusions about the strength of statutes. An angry king who had power in his hands and who had harkened to judges preaching the inalienability of the prerogative could always evade statutes. Essex, Bedford, Pym and the rest therefore intended another safeguard. They were scarcely averse to effective government: Pym for one, who had for years been a minor revenue official, merely insisted that it be sound in religion, well-disposed to parliaments, and respectful of the subject's liberty. And they now aimed at the traditional safeguard of aristocratic dissidents: control of the council. As early as December 1640 there were reports of negotiations for office, and predictions that Bedford would gain the lord treasurership, Saye the mastership of the court of wards, and Pym the chancellorship of the exchequer. Since magnates no longer led armed retainers, security would come from control of the purse strings. Not only did 'the good lords' seem able to open the parliamentary purse; they also intended to take over the customs farms, the major source of royal credit.

Charles himself initially had few objections, since he saw office as a means of winning men over. His one constant was his determination to chastise the sinful and rebellious Scots; indeed he was at this time secretly negotiating with the papacy for a loan for a new army. But he was never averse to inconsistency, and co-operation with Bedford's group seemed the best way to money – albeit for purposes of which they would not have approved. Accordingly, early in 1641 Charles made some largely honorific appointments: Bedford, Essex and Saye joined the council, and St John became Solicitor-General. Charles ensured the Catholics at court kept a low profile; and on 16 February he signed a subsidy bill and the triennial bill. But the king had not experienced a conversion to the cause of consensus, and his assent was a long complaint that parliament had 'taken the government all in pieces, and I may say it is almost off the hinges'.

Not content with protesting, Charles insisted that Bedford and Pym show that they could and would do him service by sparing Strafford and gaining him funds. Hyde in his *History* criticised Charles for destroying Bedford's scheme for bridging appointments, perhaps the last hope of reuniting king and country. Yet by demanding delivery in advance Charles was not merely displaying his usual incomprehension of the quid pro quo rule of politics. He felt bound in honour to protect Strafford, his former servant, and not only because he had promised to do so. He would probably have found a rapprochement with his critics repugnant on various grounds, and not least his fury at Pym's attacks on the queen's 'papist' friends. But a deeper problem lay in the king's knowledge of the 'junto's' contacts in 1639–40 with the Covenanters. Since the 'junto' had good reason to suspect he knew, they also knew that any security for a deal would have to be iron-clad if they were not to suffer as traitors.

A deal was also open to practical objections. Should Bedford and Pym prove unable to lead their followers there was little point in turning to them. Pym had never identified with 'country' sentiment in the Commons, and his fiscal enthusiasm left him dangerously exposed: Sir John Hotham saw him as a new Strafford that spring, and likened his schemes for reforming the subsidies to a Turkish despotism. Indeed, in the chaotic environment that was taking shape Pym could no more save Strafford than he could get a speedy fiscal reform, and settlement of tonnage and poundage, through parliament. Outside parliament hatred of the lord lieutenant ran deep, among the Scots, and among their paymasters in the London merchant oligarchy who remembered all too well Strafford's threats against them. Both of these had the clout to advance the complaints of the New English in Ireland that formed the backbone of the impeachment. The high politics of the king and the parliamentary leaders were thus derailed by interventions from outside – from Scotland, from Ireland, and from below. The City's threats to withhold loans unless Strafford died raised the spectre of troops rampaging unpaid, and provided a powerful stimulus, especially to northern MPs like Hotham. In his anxiety to hold on to a settlement and the Scots, and in fine disregard for the Petition of Right, Pym even proposed that the Londoners be compelled to lend.

The Scots did the greater damage to Pym's hopes. Defending themselves against what they saw as the Londoners' slurs on their motives, and seeking to head off the growing signs of ecclesiastical moderation in parliament, the Covenanters on 24 February 1641 called for Strafford's execution and the abolition of episcopacy in England. Scottish intervention in English politics gave a spur to those unnerved by innovation. Hyde and Falkland had already spoken out in defence of an episcopal church in early February, and their disquiet now gained a strong constitutionalist tinge: Strafford's death gained through Scottish pressure would not be worth the price. While the moderates became more conscious of a cause to be defended, the 'junto' knew still that they needed the Scots. The failure of Bedford and Pym to distance themselves from the Covenanters' demands in turn convinced Charles that what he cherished most in public life – his honour as well as his church – was not safe in such hands.

The uneasy sense of a world coming apart undoubtedly determined many to hold out for final judgment on the still-ominous Strafford. As the Earl of Essex put it, 'Stone dead hath no fellow.' Although Cork and Clotworthy pressed Straffords' outrageous acts against protestant settlers in Ireland, the lord lieutenant's fate hinged on notes, surreptitiously obtained, of the English council meeting of 5 May 1640. He had coupled his disregard for 'rules of government' with the observation that the army in Ireland could be used to 'reduce this kingdom'. Whether Scotland or England was intended was unclear, but there were plenty of reports from the leaky court that the outspoken Strafford had threatened England. When the impeachment opened on 22 March 1641, St John and the other managers responded to the difficulty of trying the king's servant by alleging what has been called 'constructive treason': Strafford's individual acts may not have been treasonous, and they may have been done in the king's name, but cumulatively they amounted to a design against the kingdom as well as the king.

Precedents existed for the Commons' approach, but its weaknesses were enough for Strafford. In a magnificent performance that almost warranted St John's characterisation of him as a 'beast of prey' he tore apart the charges, humiliated the Commons' spokesmen, and gained numerous supporters amongst his judges, the Lords. It was a Pyrrhic victory. The majority in the Commons responded by abandoning the uncertainty of legal proceedings and opted instead for the simpler, and more arbitrary, way of a bill of attainder. This would merely declare Strafford guilty.

Strafford's trial underscored Pym's weakness. The abandonment of impeachment slighted the judicial capacities of the Lords, but on their co-operation depended all hopes for accommodation. Much of Pym's prominence stemmed from his ties to Bedford's circle, and with Hampden he vainly opposed the shift. Gaps were widening in the Commons too, as the uneasy and the bored voted with their feet – the momentous final vote of 204:59 on Strafford mustered a bare half of the Commons' members. The division also revealed other strains. The scale of the attacks on the king's government, and the arbitrariness of the destruction of Strafford, appalled some members, as did the publication of the names of the 'Straffordians' in the Commons who had opposed attainder. The breach of parliamentary secrecy, and the mob intimidation it invited, gave clear indication that threats to harmony did not only come from the king. Bristol's son Lord Digby, a stalwart of the early opposition, now swung away from his former friends. By early April one prominent Welsh family, the Wynns of Gwydir, had begun to stockpile arms for 'if the times prove bad', and the growing fear of violence helps explain the support in the Commons for the violent measure of attainder.

The Wynns' fears were well founded. Convinced by April that the Commons would never do anything substantial to aid him against the Scots, and determined not to submit to 'popularity', the resentful Charles tried other courses. Not content with looking for foreign loans that would allow him to break with parliament, he once more dangled 'the Graces' of 1628 before 'Old English' leaders in Ireland. And although his moderate governor of the Tower of London rebuffed his clumsy attempt to reinforce the garrison there, he felt on firm enough ground to inform both houses on 28 April that he would not dismiss Roman Catholics from court nor disband the Irish army unless his finances were restored by parliament. The Venetian agent in England feared civil war. Violence came closer when the king encouraged discontented remnants of the English army in their plans to rescue Strafford from the Tower. News of this scheme broke on 3 May.

The discovery of the army plot was a turning-point. The popish conspiracy surrounding the king seemed more real than ever, and the frightened Commons at last enjoined the covenant of the nation before God of which Pym had long dreamed. The Protestation of 3 May 1641 was an attempt to identify the popish enemy among the non-subscribers; it was also an oath of association to counter a royal coup. Some needed little stirring. On 3 and 4 May mobs surged around the House of Lords, intimidating into absence those peers who had doubts about the plot; as a result, perhaps only nine voted to save Strafford. The crowds then turned on the king, and throughout 8–9 May huge demonstrations massed outside Whitehall calling for Strafford's head. On the 10th a shaken Charles conceded, released by Strafford from his promise that he would protect his servant, and fearing now for the lives of his own family. The lord lieutenant was executed on 12 May. His death allowed some, both in and out of parliament, a sense of security – Nehemiah Wallington exulted with 'the church of God' in the downfall of the tyrant. But Pym and his friends now knew that Charles was prepared to use force; and Charles had seen the tumults in the streets.

The death on 9 May of Bedford, around whom the bridging plans had revolved, was less significant in the collapse of accommodation than the fact that Charles and Pym now genuinely feared for all they held dear. As Secretary Vane concluded gloomily in June, 'We are here still in the labyrinth and cannot get out.' While Charles seemed to sacrifice Strafford in the name of unity, and in his panic underscored this by putting his signature to a crucial act declaring that the parliament could not be dissolved without its own consent, the rumours that he was looking abroad for aid persisted. In a second army plot in June Charles seriously considered using the English army in the north to overawe parliament, although the news was not to break until the autumn; and in July he thought once more of Strafford's Irish soldiers, although this too was unknown to the opposition. More public were his plans for Scotland. He had for some time hoped to exploit the growing resentment of Montrose and others at the influence of Argyll and clan Campbell among the Covenanters, and the growing distaste of proud nobles for presbyterian zealots. In May 1641 Charles announced his intention of going north to settle peace. Like Pym and the Covenanter leaders, he knew the British card was there to be played.

Charles's plan to go north changed the tempo of politics. The prospect of the king's proximity to soldiers occasioned remarkable scenes of anguish in the streets of London. It also gave a spur to the two houses' legislative efforts that summer, and reform measures at last emerged from committee. The disquiet the army plot had aroused is nowhere better seen than in Pym's success on 24 June in gaining passage through both houses of ten propositions calling for a purge of papists from Charles's entourage and the appointment of counsellors in whom parliament could trust. Many peers and parliament-men who were soon to fight for the king were sufficiently alarmed to follow the 'junto's' lead. Suspicions increased further when Charles left London the day after the completion of the very peace treaty with the Scots – which conceded most of their demands for a pure kirk and regular parliaments – whose negotiation was supposed to justify his journey north. The houses declared their distrust by dispatching a committee of four to watch the king and to counter his efforts amongst the Scots.

The heightened crisis brought an increase in parliamentary power. Since the council was moribund, the king's departure from London left the two houses the de facto government: as secretary Vane reported in August, 'The affairs of state are now in his majesty's absence in the parliament.' But the two houses were not now simply the executive. The erroneous labours of Sir Simonds D'Ewes, an indefatigable antiquarian, satisfied them that the houses, as the king's great council, had in the past made good law without the king by issuing ordinances – a term reminiscent of the Lords Ordainers who had long ago usurped the government of Edward II. Reassured, the houses took a series of precautions against popish disorder in the three weeks before the scheduled recess in September, and then established a joint committee to prepare for any military contingencies during the recess. Royal officials duly co-operated with the recess committee as they had with the two houses throughout, and Pym's signature as its secretary to the committee's orders began to acquire him the nick-name 'King Pym'. Those who accorded him the title did not see him ruling over a united nation, for the summer's developments were driven by mistrust.

In the crisis of Strafford's attainder and the army plot, Pym no less than Charles had abandoned thoughts of accommodation. Like many in both houses, he would probably have seized with relief on the medieval solution to ill-advised and untrustworthy kings, an enforced regency, had there been a suitable candidate, for he showed great familiarity with precedents drawn from the periods of Edward III's senility and Henry VI's insanity. Charles's nephew, the young Elector Palatine, successor to the hapless Frederick, hovered no doubt hopefully in the wings, but Charles kept him close.

In the absence of any viable regent, Pym that summer tried to formalise the growing parliamentary control over the administration. He may not have intended a permanent constitutional departure: as they emerged in 1642 his proposals would have altered the balance of power for the likely length of Charles's life. But he did seek to take power away from this untrustworthy king. The essential foundation had been laid on 10 May, when in the effort to provide further political security for loans Charles passed the act declaring that parliament could not be dissolved without its own consent. Parliament thus gained some protection against an abrupt end. The summer months also saw the rushed passage of the great reforming statutes whose progress during the winter and spring had been so slow. Pym was readier now to dismantle a government of which he had given up hope, and allowed country sentiment its head. There were many, in both houses, eager to redress the balance the king had tipped in the 1630s. June and July saw the abolition, without controversy, without even a single division, of ship money, knighthood fines and the extension of the forests. The courts of ecclesiastical high commission and star chamber also went down, the latter widely disliked for its enforcement of Laudianism and its harassment of sheriffs over ship money. Fears of arbitrary rule similarly led parliament to condemn some of the privy council's judicial powers, effectively dooming the provincial councils in the north and in Wales, whose prime function had by this time become judicial. The failure of accommodation had brought a constitutional revolution, that placed large limits on royal power.

But however uncontested the constitutional revolution, its makers were unable to effect it. The collapse of accommodation in the spring of 1641 had had ecclesiastical as well as secular consequences. And if the understandings of parliament's leaders with Charles were fractured by the British dynamic, it was religious turmoil that rent the consensus at Westminster, and in the country too.

Hyde in his *History* castigated Pym and his allies for the encouragement they gave the radicals by failing to advance positive reforms. Yet the initiative was not altogether in Pym's hands. He had recognised from the outset that parliament was far from unanimous on the issue of church reform, and that debates would divide; in sharp contrast to his conduct in 1629, he took little part in the debates on the church in the spring of 1641. He busily heightened feelings against Laudians and popery, but he sought to harness these energies to the pursuit of Strafford, and financial reform.

There were many, both inside and outside Westminster, who were more single-minded. In London in early 1640 there had probably been only about a thousand actual separatists from the national church, and even fewer convinced presbyterians. But the mood changed in the developing crisis. As London's 'root and branch' petition of 11 December was followed in January by petitions from thirteen other counties, the Commons were dragged into the religious fray.

The 'junto' did intend something more than mere destruction. Indeed, this seemed the heaven-sent moment of reformation, yearned for by generations of protestants. Perhaps a majority of parliament-men in the early spring of 1641 hoped to substitute 'primitive' for 'lordly' episcopacy or 'prelacy'. Decentralisation of authority in the church would overthrow the bishops' tyranny while preserving the continuity of their office – which many of those whom Laud had thought 'puritan' still deemed essential. And redistribution of ecclesiastical wealth would strengthen preaching clergy enfeebled by parochial poverty. These schemes now caught up such diverse figures as Archbishop Ussher, the broadly respected Calvinist primate of Ireland who was in close touch with Pym; Laud's enemy Bishop Williams, soon to become Archbishop of York; and puritan clergy like Marshall, Burges and Calybute Downing, who were shortly to forget their moderation. Associated with the various schemes for primitive episcopacy was a bill aimed at excluding the bishops from the upper house – a bill given political point by the Lords' doubts over Strafford's trial.

The programme made rapid headway as its conjunction with Bedford's bridging scheme seemed to promise a broad settlement. But the goodwill of the Commons and probably of most of the articulate clergy was not enough. It was this programme at which the Covenanters took aim in their declaration of 24 February in support of root and branch. Their intervention exposed the distance of Scottish divine-right presbyterianism from the prevailing English commitment to an erastian, or state-imposed, settlement. The damage it did to Pym's coalition was reinforced by the opposition of most of the Lords to any attempt to tamper with members of their house. The peers were probably encouraged by Charles, whose love of church hierarchy coincided with his desire to retain his episcopal supporters in the Lords.

But neither the 'junto' nor the king was in control, since the rush of events had a force of its own. The Laudian collapse encouraged nonconformists to return from exile, to make new beginnings in the provinces as well as in London. In Cheshire one returned New England minister was in January 1641 denouncing all organised forms of worship as 'loathsome unto God'. Reports came in from the counties around London during the spring of sporadic attacks on the prayer book by those newly convinced that set forms and ceremonies were idolatrous. No region could escape altogether, for the fall of Laud at the end of 1640, and the demoralisation of the church courts, had taken most press censorship down. A flood of broadsides, often selling for a few pence, condemned episcopacy as they called for reformation.

The political dangers were obvious. The Commons encouraged petitions as they buttressed their claim to speak for the nation; but as one Kent gentleman warned, 'the monstrous easy receipt of petitions makes authority decline'. The potential for disorder alarmed peers and MPs deeply persuaded of the vulnerability of the whole frame. As the poet-MP Edmund Waller was soon to put it, if the bishops went down, 'the next demand perhaps may be lex agraria [a reference to the Roman republic's abortive land reforms], the like equality in things temporal'. And, of course, the radicals were not the only ones who cared about the church. Laud had so estranged moderate opinion that scarcely any spoke in favour of the current establishment. But the new challenges to church discipline and worship seemed to some just as objectionable. The threat to parliamentary unity was clear in the emotional warning of the Welsh MP Sir Charles Williams that he would flout the dictates of consensus and divide the house on episcopacy even if he could count on only six votes.

The failure in the Lords of the bill excluding bishops from parliament occasioned the introduction into the Commons in June of a bill to abolish episcopacy in all its 'roots and branches'. Some saw in this primarily a tool with which to press the Lords to exclude the bishops. To stern anti-Catholics such as St John and perhaps Pym, it offered the simplest remedy for all the entrenched evils of pride, interest and complacency: theirs was a pragmatic awakening, rather than a principled conviction of the utter unlawfulness of episcopacy. But although most of its parliamentary supporters saw 'root and branch' as merely the most hopeful means to a purer reformation, some members were being swept along in a rising tide of excitement.

The apocalyptic potential inherent in the English Calvinists' adoption of Foxe's *Book of Martyrs* as their history had been inflamed by the growing spectre of a popish plot. It broke out in the upheaval of 1640–1. The sudden shift from persecution to a dawning reformation was one of the most important developments of the seventeenth century, not least in its impact on the obscure East Anglian back-bencher Oliver Cromwell, or on Sir Henry Vane jnr, who had journeyed to New England in the 1630s. They looked forward eagerly, not to primitive episcopacy but to the new freedom for the godly that the reduction of discipline would bring. Historians often talk of 'functional radicalism', a non-ideological response to circumstances, and such a term certainly fits the houses' de facto take-over of government. But the 'root and branch' bill showed something else. To Lord Brooke the Holy Spirit was breaking forth, no longer simply affirming interpretations of scripture but bringing new illumination to the souls of men. As he proclaimed in 1641, 'The light still, will, must, cannot but increase.'

Those who looked to numbers and symmetries had long dreamed of 1656, since Noah's Flood was commonly dated to the 1656th year from the Creation. Scholarly tastes were now inflamed not just by the onset of overturning. A large majority of the sermons delivered to the Long Parliament on fast says were strongly millennial, and millennialianism suffused much of the religious material published in the 1640s. While, in 1641, only a few looked to an imminent apocalypse, many thought that godly rule could at last be established to hasten that event. Preaching to parliament on the eve of that summer's recess, Stephen Marshall was driven by the fall of Laud to see 'hopes and beginnings of a Jubilee and Resurrection'. His belief that this was the 'time of times' was shared by increasing numbers of his parliamentary audience, particularly after the surprisingly peaceful disbandment of the armies in the late summer: even the prosaic Sir Simonds D'Ewes looked to the imminent abolition of atheism, profaneness and blasphemy.

The new awakening was still more evident outside Westminster – if only because those outside had previously been unheard. But while parliamentmen imagined the preservation of distinctions and degree in the orderly, national reformation towards which they strove, others dreamed other dreams. Even that cultural elitist John Milton prophesied that the imminent return of Christ would 'put an end to all earthly tyrannies', and not merely that of bishops, as he looked to the reformation God was working first, as his manner was, with His Englishmen. Thomas Goodwin, preparing to return from exile in The Netherlands to his London pulpit, proclaimed priority of place in God's battles to 'the meaner sort of people'. Such enthusiasm boded ill for the body politic, let alone for hopes of reform.

The 'junto' leaders were trapped between increasingly vociferous radicals on the one hand and increasingly alarmed social and religious conservatives on the other. The first formal measure of religious reform came after nearly a year's sitting, and it was extraordinary. On 8 September, on the eve of the recess, Pym pushed through a thin House of Commons an order for the destruction of relics of Laudianism in the churches. The likeliest explanation for an order that conspicuously failed to enjoin respect for prayer-book worship, and was issued by the lower house alone, is fear as much as zeal. Fear was surely dictated by events in Scotland. The Covenanters were at that moment being courted by the king, and if Pym lost them he lost the game: he desperately needed to redeem himself in their opinion. The Lords retaliated the following day by ordering that services should be conducted as the law provided.

The gulf between the two houses over the September orders on religion showed Charles how far his position was from lost. Dwindling attendances in the Commons during the summer testified to a growing unease, and to weariness with this unprecedentedly long parliament. However uncontentious the passage of the constitutional reforms, the few divisions on other issues revealed a surprisingly close balance of opinion. A royal policy of tact might have isolated Pym and his allies, and not merely from honour-bound conservatives in the Lords. The revered model of Constantine, the godly prince leading godly people, guaranteed the king a deep reserve of loyalty even among the godly; and the *Book of Common Prayer*, and long traditions of worship, possessed abundant appeal. Charles had made some well-timed moves when in late May he appointed various non-court peers to minor offices, and even gave the embittered Saye the lucrative mastership of the Court of Wards. He flourished his public posture of conciliatoriness yet more assertively in the following months, accompanying his assent to the destructive bills with ringing declarations of harmonising intent, and of his readiness to sign whatever his loyal parliament sent him. The boast was safe enough, given the growing tension between the houses.

Although the recess committee had appropriated government to itself, the late summer and autumn of 1641 was an anxious time for Pym. The parliamentary coalition crumbled as apathy and disillusion set in. Fear of the plague and desire to go home had reduced attendances in the Lords to around a dozen by the end of August and to less than seventy in the Commons. Even the sternly radical Sir Arthur Hesilrig went home early. And while divisions opened in parliament, the peace with Scotland brought with it the disbandment of the army that had been Pym's guarantee. The paper security of statutes gave little reassurance, for the army plot had shown Charles's willingness to use force, and that message was dramatically underlined during the visit to Scotland. There, as the king had hoped, he found supporters among those nobles who had been alienated more by royal slights and by threats to land-tenures than by affronts to the kirk's mission. In the so-called 'Incident' of early October he seems to have manipulated the jealousies of some of these for Argyll and for Hamilton too – the king's cousin, the potential regent of Scotland, and now joined in a dynastic alliance to Argyll. But though the attempt to seize the pair was botched, it was damning enough for the king's reputation. Charles compounded the damage by going with hundreds of armed supporters to the Edinburgh parliament to deny the existence of any plot.

The Incident ensured that the second session of the Long Parliament, which opened on 20 October, would resume where the first had ended. Instead of standing isolated in face of growing evidence of royal moderation, Pym and his friends had been given one more reminder of the need to deprive Charles of his power. But while Pym's fears had hardened, so had the rather different apprehensions of others. Growing numbers joined Bristol and Seymour in the Lords and Hampden's counsel Robert Holborne in the Commons in seeing the grievances of the 1630s as mistakes that were being rectified or as the work of evil men who were now gone. Most of them were to show by their support of the church of the prayer book that they were not experiential Calvinists; and, lacking the experiential Calvinist's abiding fear of a popish plot, their minds were not set to fear the worst. On the other hand, in the mounting anti-popish fervour, and Pym's mounting demands, they apprehended a real and present danger.

Charles had played to such doubts by politely assenting to the destructive measures of the summer. In the autumn he moved to reinforce those who should have been his natural allies, and in letters from Scotland urged Southampton, Bristol and other supporters to aggravate the friction between the two houses. Bristol's task was the easier since Charles at last named five new, non-Laudian, bishops, to swell the episcopal bench in the Lords. Such ostentatious abandonment of the Laudian past seemed to make reassuring sense of Charles's failure to defend Laud in the first session. The king was striking at the opposition's weak points: the Lords, and reform of the church. Since the Commons' leaders had to have the co-operation of the Lords if they were to survive, they promptly renewed their campaign against the bishops in the upper house. The peers held firm.

There was an increasingly responsive audience for the royal campaign of moderation. Parliament-men had been able to go home during the recess and talk to neighbours less exposed than Londoners to the constant round of rumours, panics and demonstrations. Many countrymen were perplexed at what they heard. Parliament had sat long but gained little; church reform was still neglected, as were long-standing grievances like the scale of administrative fees and all the local matters so prominent in the letters MPs received from their constituents. The only tangible fruit of parliament's sitting had been taxes, all the more unwelcome in that a new plague epidemic in the summer of 1641 intensified the economic dislocation that political instability always brought. Although the need to pay the armies was obvious, the burdens of 1641 weighed heavier than ship money had done. The six subsidies of the spring were followed by a 'poll tax', to fall on every householder, as Pym the great administrator edged towards tackling the problem of chronic under-assessment. Taxpayers and tax-assessors who had objected to the novel devices of the 1630s soon showed by delays and evasions that being part of a 'country' reaction against the crown did not constitute them followers of Pym. As the disgruntled Yorkshire gentlewoman Margaret Eure was soon to complain, 'I am in such a great rage with parliament as nothing will pacify me, for they promised us all should be well, if my Lord Strafford's head were off, and since then there is nothing better, but I think we shall be undone with taxes.' Puzzlement at events seems to have been greatest in areas remote from London, but closer to home Sir Thomas Barrington wondered at the 'strange tepidity' and 'present spleen' in Essex in the summer of 1641.

The fruits of the Commons' September order against Laudianism, and the implications of ecclesiastical change, became clear during the recess. Church disorders drove the Kent MP Sir Edward Dering to abandon his earlier support for 'root and branch'; the city marshal had to protect the altar of St Paul's cathedral during service, and the sheriff of Herefordshire reported that after a fracas in Leominster church some were laying in muskets to kill puritans. Even the most secular-minded, let alone ceremonialists, now found it easy to see bishops, whatever their faults, as an essential link in the chain of order and continuity. Sir Thomas Aston's *Remonstrance against Presbytery*, one of the most vehement of the new defences of episcopacy, found eager readers far beyond its Cheshire birthplace.

Time was now on Charles's side. With the safeguard of the Scottish army gone the prospects for the 'junto' looked bleak, the act against dissolution notwithstanding. The overwhelming likelihood at this point was that Charles would gain sufficient support to dissolve parliament with its own agreement, rather than that he would break it by force. An alarming sign of Pym's altered standing was the appearance in London that autumn of hostile flysheets and slogans, underscoring the lesson of the Scottish Incident. Fearing isolation, and the mounting danger to his protestant cause no less than to himself, Pym in late October sought some means to rally his supporters, in parliament and country alike. A strongly oppositionist committee, established the previous November to survey the state of the kingdom, was ordered to produce its work, and there emerged the document now known as the Grand Remonstrance. Its sweeping indictment of evil and popish counsellors and of 'arbitrary' rule personalised the crisis, for it traced it back to 1625 and the very beginning of Charles's reign. Even in the enormously intensified crisis of November 1641 the implications of such a charge were to split the Commons down the middle. Pym's decision in October to rake over old wounds and blame them on the king, and to appeal to the widest audience by printing the Remonstrance, testified to his desperation.

Just as the Scots had rescued Charles's English critics in 1638–40, so the Irish reprieved them in 1641. The outbreak of the Irish revolt on 22 October (news reached parliament on 1 November) doomed Charles's hopes of exploiting a return to normality. The revolt had to be suppressed. More money had to be raised, and that put the spotlight firmly on London, which was fast descending into turmoil. Troops had also to be raised, an alarming prospect when the commander-in-chief was a king complicit in two successive army plots and the 'Incident'. Most damaging of all, the revolt gave terrifying substance to the popish threat. The rebels' not entirely empty claim to be acting in the king's name was deeply ironic, in view of their sufferings from royal governors; but it lent credibility and urgency to the opposition's charges that Charles was the tool of a Catholic conspiracy.

The 1641 revolt, one of the defining episodes in Irish history, one of the most decisive in English as well as British history, was a complex affair. Its Ulster origins, and its development, offer paradoxical testimony to the increasing integration of the three kingdoms. Sir Phelim O'Neill, Lord Maguire, and the other Gaelic leaders who planned to seize Ulster, were impressively Anglicised; but like many of their neighbours they had suffered in the competition with more market-orientated recent British settlers. Their growing indebtedness was exacerbated by agricultural depression in the 1630s – thus, by 1641 native Irish held only just over half the land in parts of County Down they had been left with after the Ulster Plantation. Resentments at the loss of land and position came to a head in the political instability following Strafford's return to England.

The Ulster leaders proceeded as British politicians rather than as Gaels excluded from the British polity. Inspired by the Covenanters' example, and profiting from the expertise of Irish officers returned from the European wars, they aimed to capture the seat of government, and then bargain from strength. But when the plot failed in Dublin and O'Neill raised Ulster he quickly found himself outflanked. O'Neill bid for support in the language of loyalty. Fully aware of Charles's hopes of money and men from the Irish Catholic community, he proclaimed his concern to protect the queen from persecution and the king from puritan and parliamentary aggression. To substantiate his claim he even flourished what he (falsely) declared was a royal warrant, with seal attached; and he strove to keep this a quarrel with the English by leaving the Ulster Scots unmolested. But his followers were eager to undo the whole Ulster Plantation and regain their houses and holdings through mass evictions. The political protest against the ways of the New English and their government, in Dublin and London, merged with a tenurial struggle against recent settlers.

The character of the revolt changed further in the winter, with catastrophic effect. The Catholic Old English had held aloof from the rising at first. Though they had little cause to trust the king after Charles in the spring withdrew his second offer to confirm the Graces, they saw themselves as English loyalists; and they were appalled by the violence of the Ulster Gaels. But the vitriolic outpourings in London and Edinburgh soon left them in no doubt of the dismal future British Calvinism intended for Catholic Ireland. The conventional English insistence on Westminster sovereignty, and with it the jurisdiction of English statute over conquered Ireland, promised that should the king and his parliament settle their differences (as the king and his Scottish parliament had managed to do), then protestant zeal would be extended to Ireland with a vengeance. Vengeance was the more certain since, when he heard the news of the revolt, Charles indicated that he would happily forge an alliance with his parliament against Irish rebels. Hoping amidst England's divisions to preserve themselves, the Old English leaders in December 1641 declared their support for a rebellion that thus became broadly Roman Catholic rather than simply Gaelic. It was also becoming more violent, for many Ulster settlers had overcome their shock and were banding together to resist. There ensued a war of mutual atrocity, akin to modern 'ethnic cleansing'.

The Irish revolt seemed to confirm every protestant stereotype. The best estimates suggest that under 4000 protestants died violently, and another 8000 when they were thrust from their homes in winter. But objective analysis was impossible for those in London and Edinburgh, even had full details been available, and the atrocity stories soon told of 200 000 deaths. Undoubtedly, the scale of the suffering was exaggerated by some with a vested interest, since damning all Catholics would open all Ireland to confiscation and settlement. Undoubtedly also, protestants committed their own atrocities, leaving the balance hard to determine even when it is divorced from its Cromwellian aftermath. But however convenient the revolt was for Pym, and however skilfully he used it, there is no reason to doubt his horror, or that of the vast majority of his countrymen. Rumours of, and precautions against, a popish rising spread over fifty miles in a night along the Welsh border; messengers from every direction brought reports of popish disturbances to Leicester. At Brampton Bryan in Herefordshire, Harley's household retreated to the castle roof; in Dorchester watch was kept from the church steeple. The national alarm had tangible consequences in the declining incidence of fiscal obstructionism when a major new tax of £400 000, much of it intended for the reconquest of Ireland, was voted in the spring of 1642.

The revolt had partisan consequences. Charles had bid for Irish support in the spring and summer of 1641 by offering concessions, ordering a halt to the disbandment of Strafford's army, toying with yet another of Antrim's plots. These gestures allowed the Old English leaders, no less than Sir Phelim O'Neill, a sense of legitimacy. In the context of a broad Catholic revolt that unleashed peasant atrocities, their protestations of loyalty, like O'Neill's claim of a royal commission, could not have come at a worse time for Charles. Together, they prompted Richard Baxter, a moderate puritan minister in the West Midlands, to doubt the king's title to rule. And the crisis did what Pym's oratory had failed to do: it persuaded members that they must act to ensure the trustworthiness of the king's advisers. On 5 November, the anniversary of the Catholic Gunpowder Plot of 1605, Pym addressed the problem of the control over the troops that were now needed by proposing his famous 'additional instruction'. Unless evil counsellors were removed, the Commons would be 'forced, by discharge of the trust which we owe to the state, and those whom we represent to resolve upon some way of defending Ireland'. For the Commons to involve themselves in military affairs was no longer remarkable – indeed, councillors had gone straight to parliament with the first news of the revolt. But to declare openly their readiness to proceed without the king, and to justify such a move by an appeal to a responsibility to an impersonal state and to the people was a different matter. The additional instruction passed an angry and divided house by 151 votes to 110.

These weeks saw an upsurge of partisanship, and all too plainly an end to assumptions of harmony in the body politic. In the attempt to browbeat the growing resistance in the Commons and the solid conservative majority in the Lords, the opposition leaders introduced the Grand Remonstrance into the lower house on 8 November. Even though the Irish Revolt had seemed to confirm allegations of monstrous popery, the Remonstrance only passed by the narrow margin of 159:148 after two weeks of angry debate that culminated in the drawing of swords in the house. It was a political watershed. Preoccupied with unity as most MPs were, they were congenitally averse to proceeding to a vote, which by definition recognised the existence of disunity; but after the recess divisions occurred in increasing numbers. A 'royalist' party was being born, signified not just by the drawing of swords, but by the threat of Hyde and others in December to make formal protestations against any vote to publish the Remonstrance to the people.

Nevertheless, fear not aggression drove the Grand Remonstrance, despite all its denunciations, despite its demands for parliamentary approval of the king's ministers and a godly synod to reform the church. It reads as a very defensive document, and not merely in its assertion that Romish agents were subverting English religion and liberties. Its authors clearly feared isolation before the wrath of a vengeful king. Parliamentary attendances were unnervingly low – although the Remonstrance brought one of the half-dozen best-attended divisions of the parliament, over two hundred MPs did not vote. More alarming was opinion in the country, where the dangerous conviction that the lower house was in the grip of a sectarian fever was manifestly gaining hold. At the end of a Remonstrance from which the drafters had struck out criticism of the prayer book comes a revealing series of clauses insisting that parliament did not intend 'to let loose the golden reins of discipline and government in the church'. It was to allay a gathering conservative anger that the opposition leaders recounted their mortal struggle against popery.

The alarm of Pym, Holles and the rest was well founded. Despite the intensity of the recent shock, the lull that came in its wake brought a return to a semblance of normality, which in turn brought a real prospect of a royal triumph. Whatever its concerns about Irish papists, much of the traditional political nation was desperately anxious for stability.

The changing mood was apparent in the enthusiastic reception given Charles on his journey south from Scotland. 'Our wives conceive with joy,' trumpeted York's recorder as he attempted to revive the comforting certainties of the body politic. The king received further encouragement in London's lavish welcome on 25 November. Aldermanic memories of sordid money-grubbing by crown and court in the 1630s had faded in face of other grievances. A City committee reported in October that the privilege of immunity for debt enjoyed by members of both houses and their servants had already cost £1 million, more than ship money. Equally disturbing were the disorders in the metropolis, that the parliamentary opposition seemed to exacerbate with its appeals for support. Uncertainty meant a loss of business – activity in the courts of king's bench and common pleas fell by two-thirds between 1640 and 1642, the business of chancery over 90 per cent over the same period. The mayoral election in September 1641 brought a conservative triumph, and Charles seized his chance. Assuring waverers of his devotion to protestantism and ancient ways he made material concessions to the City, and cast the blame for recent strains on 'the meaner sort of people'.

There followed a noisy campaign of moderation, skilfully crafted by Bristol and by new royal advisers, those quintessential moderates, Hyde, Lord Falkland and Sir John Colpepper. Charles followed his appeal to the City with a conciliatory proclamation on religion on 10 December, that was given plausibility by the autumn's appointment of moderates to bishoprics. Most important of all was his very measured rejection of the Grand Remonstrance on 23 December. He reinforced his denial of its conspiracy thesis with a major new initiative that coupled concessions to those offended by religious ceremonies with injunctions to use the prayer book. That Charles had caught the mood was apparent in a surge of petitions in December in favour of episcopacy: one from Somerset claimed 14 000 signatories. The mood itself was reflected in the grim comment of the sheriff of Herefordshire that his neighbours 'if the times would serve . . . would show as little favour to those that they call puritans as any English or Irish papist would do'.

But Charles's persistent refusal to bargain away powers of the crown seemed to belie his promise of conciliation in the church and in the City. Had he appointed the Earl of Essex, who was widely respected and as experienced in the European wars as anyone else at his disposal, to command in Ireland he might have dispelled the climate of fear in which Pym survived. But, and not for the first time, his rhetoric of moderation accompanied an intent to confront. Seeing only the insubordination of his enemies and the growing numbers of his own supporters, and judging further surrenders both anathema and unnecessary, he let it be known that he would go to Ireland himself. When he dismissed the conciliatory secretary Vane, many concluded that he aimed only to build sufficient support to enable him to regain what he had lost. Yet even in that cause the king seemed to be successful in the weeks after his return from Scotland. The Lords held firm; and in the Commons Pym's hold weakened as the house got down to practical matters, such as bills against piracy and scandalous ministers, and raising money for Ireland.

The reign of king Pym would have been short had he been dependent on his parliamentary resources alone. Early December saw him turn once again to a hunt for scapegoats, with futile bids to exclude Bristol and his son Lord Digby, Charles's new confidants, from the Lords; equally vainly, he renewed the campaign against the bishops. But neither Pym nor parliament were to be left to their own resources. If Scotland and Ireland could disturb the establishment of royal authority in England, so too could ordinary English people. Excited demonstrations thronged around Westminster in these weeks, evidence of popular arousal certainly, evidence too of Pym's failure to deliver the measures against the bishops that the London godly wanted. Their sometimes bloody clashes with discharged army officers showed that the king too had acquired some impetuous, and less reputable, supporters. The mounting passions in the streets and alleys of the metropolis were the key to what was to prove the opposition's preservation, the London revolution of December–January.

London's support for parliament was scarcely inevitable. In September's municipal elections the bulk of the City's elite had distanced itself from Pym, and had found considerable support in so doing. But the drama of the streets eventually allowed other groups to exploit the surviving elements of civic democracy and overwhelm superiors who were closely tied by privilege, interest and ideology to the crown. The triggers were both ideological and material. London's dense parochial structure, its lectureships and constant round of visitors, made available a steady supply of preaching for those willing to walk a little way and take a little disciplinary risk; its theatres (not all of them controlled by the court), ballad-singers, rumour-mongers and underground print distributors made available a constant diet of news and views. When the political elites mixed daily with the porters, watermen and cooks in London's vast service sector, exchanges readily passed beyond the commercial. As the demonstrations against Strafford, and as the news of Charles's departure for Scotland, showed, excitement was catching.

The City of course possessed a highly effective government, running from the wards and guilds up to the court of aldermen and the mayor. But depression and crisis allowed influence to flow through other channels, often running from churches, sometimes from the retail shops of traders to America who specialised in tobacco, sugar and godly zeal. Ordinary freemen, many of them genuinely poor artisans and journeymen, were readier to listen to dissident voices since they had been milked, proportionately, far more than their betters during the 1630s, whether by the patentees in the various new corporations or by City magistrates passing on the burden of ship money to their inferiors. The deepening depression that set in with the Bishops' Wars brought new suffering to artisans and shopkeepers alike. Probate inventories, as well as the papers of Nehemiah Wallington the turner, indicate that they kept most of their resources in stock, in items for trade; and Wallington's persistent cash-flow problems left him chronically dependent on credit. Not surprisingly, he was suffering gravely by late 1641 as political insecurity led merchants to curtail their activities. It would be folly to assume a crudely material-ist explanation of London radicalism. London mobs rabbled the separatist congregation of Praise-God Barebone as well as bishops in December 1641. But dislocation and hardship not infrequently take the zealous closer to fundamentalism, and the Irish Revolt invited fundamentalist interpretations. It certainly gave a sharper edge to Wallington's puritan convictions, making him a ready audience for Pym's appeals; and it surely made his fellows potential supporters for those who would challenge the local hold of the ungodly.

A revolution in municipal politics halted what had been the crucial element in the royal designs, the drift of the City towards the king. Through parochial and ward organisations in the City, through alehouse meetings in the teeming suburbs, through the enthusiastic efforts of Cornelius Burges and other puritan ministers, the radical London MPs Isaac Penington and John Venn were able to orchestrate weighty petitions and demonstrations. But the most important London demonstration came at the hustings. On 21 December 1641, the broad electorate of the freemen in the wards rejected almost half of the common councilmen. The emergence of a radical majority in the common council to challenge the control of the mayor and aldermen had immense implications. In early January the City's militia, well trained and numerous, was put into new hands, giving parliament the prospect of protection. Equally important, was control over the City's money bags. Ireland would only be reconquered – and, as it proved, a civil war fought – with money. Much would hinge on whether the City lent king or parliament the means to raise troops.

Yet the London revolution did not affect the balance at Westminster. It offered protection against a coup, but it could not protect against loss of control over the houses. And as the majority in the Lords blocked further bicameral moves on Ireland and on control over force, Pym and his leading noble allies – Warwick, Saye, Brooke, Mandeville – faced the loss of the momentum they so badly needed. The only legitimacy 'the junto' possessed was that which came from both houses, and had the Lords held firm it would have been lost. Accordingly, in December Pym's supporters in the streets concentrated on barring the bishops and the 'popish lords' from the upper house.

As so often, Charles destroyed his own position by intemperate action. Previous crises had seen him try to combine apparently conflicting courses of action. He had failed equally to give full support or to block the army plot, and the Scottish Incident; so now, though he was overtly following Hyde's constitutionalist advice, he gave his ear to the hot-headed Lord Digby, champion of the discharged officers thronging the court. On 22 December, the day after the London elections, Charles appointed Colonel Lunsford, a harsh professional soldier and convicted felon, to command the Tower of London. He was probably only seeking unthinking protection for himself and family, but his opponents saw Lunsford as a step towards a coup. Five days of fierce demonstrations followed, at Westminster against the bishops and 'popish lords', and around the Tower, as the Londoners braved Lunsford's swordsmen. But although Charles capitulated to the pressure of nervous aldermen and replaced Lunsford, many at Westminster now recognised what they could not have imagined a year before, the possibility of war. On the 30th the Commons, lining up strongly behind Pym, ordered that MPs' servants should bring pistols to defend the house. 'There is now nothing sought for so much as guns,' reported John Dillingham, a newsletter-writer close to St John.

The wonder is that Charles managed to create sufficient bipartisanship to destroy his footing in his capital. Not content with driving London's godly to a frenzy with the appointment of Lunsford, he built on that frenzy to alienate at last the majority of the Lords who remained at Westminster. His error lay in not blocking an attempt by twelve of the bishops to exploit the late-December rioting of which they had been a prime target. The bishops' claim that the houses had been acting under duress, and therefore invalidly, when some of their members had been kept away by violence outraged the other peers who had soldiered on. The ensuing sequestration of the twelve bishops as impeachments were prepared gave the 'junto' the control over both houses they had so long sought. Fearing now that Henrietta Maria, his Catholic queen, would also be impeached, Charles was vulnerable to those who counselled action.

Opening one of the great melodramas of English history, the king on 3 January 1642 sent to the Lords charges for an impeachment of treason against Mandeville and against the famous 'five members' in the Commons, Pym, Hampden, Holles, Hesilrig and William Strode (the last two presumably included for their introduction in the Commons on 7 December of a measure to deprive the king of control over the sword, the ultimate warrant of rule). Had he secured them, he might have overcome. But the peers still nursed their affront of the previous week; instead of ordering arrests the Lords temporised. Facing humiliation, the king took several hundred armed men to Westminster the following day in search of his quarry. But his 'birds' had 'flown', forewarned by friends at court; instead a shaken king confronted a house of Commons silent but for mutterings of 'Privilege, privilege'. Charles's readiness to use force was apparent in his guard of 'papists, ill-affected persons . . . panders and rogues'. While the sexualisation of these enemies to the body politic suggests a continuing commitment to the metaphor, the Houses were sufficiently alarmed to adjourn to the safety of the City. The angry crowds that lined the king's way when he tried to fetch the five members from their refuge convinced him that he had lost London. Fearing mob assaults, on 10 January Charles left Whitehall, never to return until he was brought back in 1648 to face trial and execution.

Thwarted at Westminster, Charles was now coming to contemplate civil war rather than the coup that had seemed a possibility while he was still in his capital. Mid-January saw abortive royal attempts to seize the northern arsenal at Hull left after the Bishops' Wars, and other arms at Kingston-on-Thames and Portsmouth; by the end of the month the queen was preparing to depart for the continent to find aid. But civil war was impossible while the king had no more than 200 men with him. The attempt on the five members had shaken Charles's standing not just in parliament but also in the country. To repair the damage, he turned once more to the gloomy Hyde, who swallowed his own doubts to write descants upon the theme of harmony. In a tone reminiscent of his answer to the Grand Remonstrance, on 20 January the king declared his readiness to co-operate with the houses to secure the safety of the kingdom and of protestantism. In the next three weeks he indicated his willingness to work with the houses over militia appointments, to accept the Grand Remonstrance's proposal that a synod of divines prepare a religious settlement, and to withdraw the charges against the five members.

It might have worked, for the revolutionary implications of the events of December and January seemed less clear than they do now. There could be no better indication of the fluidity of politics than the career of the Earl of Newport, who had actually sided with the Commons over the religious orders of September 1641 but who yet became a royalist. There were many such cases of perplexity, and had Charles allowed himself to be guided by Hyde the eventual outcome would have been very different. Even at this late date, the king's enemies owed much to the continuing fear of papists and Irish that drove the majority in the Lords to endorse the new London militia after the attempt on the five members, and that helped drive them, still more reluctantly, to co-operate in the Commons' plans for the nation's militia as a whole. Charles's conciliatory declaration of 20 January caused many peers to think again. Had he held to such a stand before the attempt on the five members, the Lords would never have been lost.

Many yearned to hold a middle ground of moderation and conciliation. But that ground could be sapped by extremists on either side, especially when one of the extremists was the king. In the Commons, ineffectual moderates like Sir Simonds D'Ewes and Framlingham Gawdy left the chamber in despair when the going grew too rough, while the London mob turned out in force to stiffen those inclined to smile upon Charles's conciliatory messages. Such intimidation thinned the numbers in the Lords from around sixty to some forty by the end of January. Charles's fear lest the prince of Wales be held hostage led him to further efforts at conciliation in early February, when he accepted at last the exclusion of the now impotent bishops from the Lords; but by then the ground was distinctly stonier. The king's hopes of the upper house finally crumbled with the interception in mid-February of a letter from Lord Digby, which showed that some prominent royalists were confident that Charles's concessions were a sham. When, after seeing *Henrietta Maria* set sail later that month, Charles turned northwards towards his northern arsenal instead of back to the vicinity of London it became obvious that he thought less of politics in his capital than of force. The houses in their turn sought to rally support, amidst a barrage of reports of Catholic plotting and Catholic arming. On

5 March the Commons passed their 'declaration of fears and jealousies', tracing the crisis of trust back to Charles's 'popish' preparations against the Scots in 1639–40. On the same day the two houses passed an ordinance regulating the militia that omitted even a nominal role for the king. The language of 'fears and jealousies' gives the very flavour of these months.

It took several more months for the mutual fears to persuade a sufficient number in the country to take sides. In the quest for support the houses were at first far better placed than was Charles. The king began to seek volunteers to help him regain his capital and a government that had not, in practice, been his for well over a year. The houses mobilised the militia, a defensive arm, and claimed to defend England against a 'popish and malignant' enemy that by no means all members yet identified with the king. And the houses were defending a working government. Many officials continued to answer to them as they had done for months; indeed, even Sir Edward Littleton – lord keeper of the great seal, the primary symbol of government – supported the houses' militia ordinance in March 1642, before belatedly joining the king two months later.

The political process had failed to contain the tensions of three kingdoms. The gravest blow to Charles was unquestionably the Irish Revolt, which not only raised the crucial question of control over an army that was to occasion war but also raised passions in parliament's supporters that made civil war possible. But the crisis was not somehow un-English. Domestic strains diminished the prospects for a solution to the mutual mistrust. Amid fears of a self-willed king and popery on the one hand, of mob-rule and the destruction of a cherished church on the other, parliament proved incapable of acting as the mediator, as the embodiment of harmony of king and country. There were too many discordant voices: the 'root-and branch' petitioners who spoke out so inopportunely, the London merchants and rioters who hurried Strafford to his death, the 'country' members who disrupted Pym's financial efforts and thus lessened his usefulness to the king, the London freemen voters in late 1641.

Above all, there was a religious divide. Whatever the incomprehension during the summer of 1641 about the nature of the crisis, alarm at the popish threat surged with the Irish Revolt and the Grand Remonstrance. The totals of Catholic recusants presented in 1641 soared – some 2000 in the hundred of Thirsk in the North Riding of Yorkshire alone. A very different measure of opinion comes from early 1642, when over half the counties of England and Wales petitioned in support of the established church and against the sectarian challenge. The fears the parliamentary leaders had shown in the Grand Remonstrance about the state of public opinion were well founded. It took months for the parties to overcome Englishmen's preoccupation with unity; nevertheless, when they appealed in earnest to the consciences of their countrymen they found a sufficient response to enable them to take the field.

8

Taking sides

The stridency of the cries of the extremists only emphasised the prevalence in mid-1642 of conservative manifestations of community. Those who sought to preserve unity, local and national, far outnumbered the activists and the adventurers. Charles was the more embarrassed, since he was seeking to raise volunteers, while parliament was attempting to hold on to what might pass as government. Only two peers went north with the king to York in March 1642; not until the summer did his entourage grow appreciably. Accommodation remained the watchword, even for many at York. That June the Earl of Lindsey, soon to command the first royalist field army, urged Charles to accept parliament's uncompromising *Nineteen Propositions*, which sought – in the name of the nation and his office – to take government, and a church settlement, away from his person.

Charles's propaganda reflected his dilemma. He intensified his efforts to win Anglicans to his side, repeatedly declaring his injured innocence, his zeal for church and prayer book, and his scorn for the sectarian rabble who were whipped up by a handful of scheming malcontents. The secular side to this case was brilliantly developed by Hyde and his friends, who appealed to the middle, and above all to the peers, whom they cast as the 'screen and bank' between extremes. Falkland and Colpepper, who drafted the king's *Answer* to parliament's *Nineteen Propositions*, argued that government was mixed, neither simply regal nor parliamentary; their magnificent concluding peroration dwelt on the threat to all property-owners posed by popular innovation. But their claim that the treasured English balance was the work of human prudence, appealing though it proved to generations of constitutionalists, clashed with the central royal-ist contention that allegiance to the king was indivisible, natural and divine, that obedience was due to his 'natural person', rather than to his office as parliamentarians claimed. It also clashed with simpler verities, dear to Charles. His battle standard was to proclaim the legend, 'Give

Caesar his due.' Clerical supporters such as the Calvinist bishop Joseph Hall amplified the scripture, contending that the king held power in trust not from the people but from God, that resistance was a sin as well as a crime. The brilliant Dudley Digges was soon to develop a parallel and almost Hobbesian argument for an unchallengeable royal sovereignty.

The two houses were no more single-minded. Charles I was not the first English king to persist in being ill advised, and long before 1642 men had sought to distinguish between the office and the physical body of the king. However confusing to the unsophisticated, the houses' claim throughout the war to be defending 'king and parliament', the crown if not this king, cannot be dismissed as simply specious. It underlay Pym's practical demands, spelt out in the *Nineteen Propositions*, that they retain effective power for twenty years – a period that exceeded the presumed life-expectancy of Charles Stuart. And it fit the facts, since the houses remained in the capital attempting to conduct the government from which Charles had withdrawn. Beside this familiar claim stood the vision of England as a community, that had as powerful a hold on some of parliament's spokesmen as on Falkland and Culpepper – though to very different effect. As the controversy over the militia reverberated in the summer of 1642 the houses steadily elevated their status as the 'representative body of the kingdom' into a claim to possess, in the last resort, supreme authority. Henry Parker, Saye's client, substantiated this new thesis of the sovereign and unchallenged power of parliament in his *Observations upon Some of His Majesties Late Answers and Expresses*, as he argued that since parliament represented 'the whole community in its underived majesty' it must by the law of nature take the steps necessary for self-preservation. It was the mirror image of the king's position in the ship money trial.

The outrage of the king's controversialists tells us something of Parker's impact on legally minded waverers. But if Parker's theory was constructed to marginalise Charles, the need for such marginalisation was developed by others. The providentialist claim that God had put man on earth for a purpose was scarcely original to Calvinists, but they maintained it more strenuously than did most. In face of a king corrupted by popish conspirators, a king clay in the hands of the queen and thus of the pope, many argued that their duty to resist Antichrist transcended all other obligations. In February 1642 the Commons heard Stephen Marshall apply the frightening Old Testament text of the cursing of Meroz to all those who withheld their hands from shedding the blood of the popish enemy. Anti-Catholicism had gained an apocalyptic edge, and Marshall sharpened that edge on each of the sixty occasions he preached his call to arms. After the Irish rebels' flaunting of their royal 'commission', Parker's advocacy of parliamentary self-preservation made sense.

And behind the theories hovered the myths, probably the most important elements in recruitment on either side. Both caricatures, the 'malignant cavalier' and the 'roundhead rebel', testified powerfully to the interweaving of church, body politic and body physical within the early-modern imagination. Building not just on memories of the 1630s court but also on the figure of Lunsford, who had so briefly held the Tower for the king, and on the arrival at Charles's side of his nephew Rupert of the Palatinate, who brought a number of hardened officers fresh from Europe's battlefields with him, parliament's partisans elaborated the figure of the roystering cavalier, the 'goddamme blade', all too often papist as well as rapist. A Shropshire royalist complained bitterly that autumn, 'They beat us more in the impression of fables . . . beloved among common people, than any open force can prevail.' But the royalists deployed their counterpart in the 'Brownist', the disreputable sectarian and separatist who desecrated churches, copulated under the guise of conscience, and challenged his (or her) master. The near-hysteria voiced over threats to hierarchy, gender order and sexual discipline reflects the power, as well as the vulnerability, of political norms. It also speaks to the relative appeal of rational argument.

The argumentative strategies of the principals were revealing enough. The king sought to personalise the issue of loyalty, to focus it on his own person. After the abortive royalist attempts on arms stores at the start of the year the houses sent Sir John Hotham north to defend the Hull magazine; when he proclaimed his duty to parliament and shut the gates on the king himself on 23 April, Charles proclaimed him traitor. The exchange sparked greater excitement in the nation than did the king's more measured condemnation of the militia ordinance the following month. And though Charles bid for the middle ground with his increasingly passionate declarations of devotion to the church of Elizabeth and his father, he appealed to personal loyalties in the commissions of array he issued in June to local notables to secure their counties.

Parliament's hopes of isolating Charles of course hinged on its insistence that the danger was popish. With their own sense of the church of Elizabeth, the leaders had no intention of abandoning the protestant mainstream to the king, and earnestly prepared for the synod of divines that would vindicate Calvinist orthodoxy. That spring's attempt to raise forces for the reconquest of Ireland gave them an invaluable opportunity to highlight the character of the enemy, since it highlighted the issue of guilt: the private 'Adventurers' whose subscriptions would fund the immediate costs were to be repaid from the confiscated lands of the malignant Irish. But the fast-developing legend of the 'malignant', however consensual it might sound to English ears in its Irish extension, could not adequately tar the enemy. Accordingly, parliament's declarations dissected the personal loyalty the king invoked. However counterfactual it sounded, its claim to be defending the king, its claim that the king's friends were in fact his enemies, sought to depersonalise monarchy. Parliament was the custodian of the king's 'official' self, of his and the kingdom's best interests.

Opinion in the country was declared in the petitions for accommodation that poured in to answer the partisans' calls for support. Some voiced perplexity, others fear. In Kent Henry Oxinden wept that he was 'between Scylla and Charybdis', and prayed for the emergence of an unchallenged authority. Alarm increased as disorder threatened: the business of the Whitsun fair at Chard, Somerset, fell by a half, scattered rioting against enclosures warned that peasants might profit from disorder, and religious zealots intimidated one another. One young Levant merchant rejected thoughts of marriage: 'These times . . . bend men's minds rather to singularity where trouble may be contracted.'

Everywhere, the gentry sought an escape in localist retreat. The ruin of Germany during the Thirty Years War only reinforced the natural human preference for peace. Even those whose own loyalties were clear, such as the parliamentarian Fairfaxes in Yorkshire, could recognise how much they had to lose and strove to neutralise their own areas. Sir John Hotham's fear lest 'the necessitous people . . . set up for themselves to the utter ruin of all the nobility and gentry', was widely shared. Militia ordinance and commission of array alike lacked appeal. The extreme case was Staffordshire, where the gentry tried to raise a third force to resist outsiders. The town of Leicester shut its gates, and most ordinary countrymen preferred to follow the plough rather than the drum.

Fortress Staffordshire fell, and all the other neutrality agreements eventually collapsed, for no county was autonomous. Pressures existed both within and without. The conflicting principals acted as magnets to the regions around them, a fact that helps to explain the well-known geographical division into a parliamentarian southeast and a royalist north and west. Parliament easily disarmed 'neuters' in neighbouring Kent and Hertfordshire; the movements of the king likewise undermined many northerners' efforts to stay out of the fray. In some areas, paradoxically, the need to preserve the social order did the work of the belligerents. Thus, anti-Catholic disturbances amongst industrial workers suffering from the deepening depression drove frightened gentry to collaborate with the regionally dominant power, whether parliamentarian in Suffolk or royalist in Staffordshire. Such considerations of prudence – who was most to be feared locally? who was likely to win? – probably determined the alignment of most of the population throughout the war. But zealots could be found everywhere, and as Lucy Hutchinson observed, 'every county . . . had the civil war within itself'. Even in areas like Herefordshire and Worcestershire with few puritans, royalists' violence against their cultural foes, however peaceable, could create partisans. The minister Richard Baxter gave a moving account of the flight of some of his neighbours to parliamentarian garrisons and, willy-nilly, to commitment.

The hesitations of Baxter's godly neighbours remind us that this was not solely a war for religion. At all times motives are mixed, probably in a civil war most of all. Not only were individuals' circumstances complex and uncomfortable; on each side there was more than one cause. Among the royalists a visceral anti-puritanism could generate real militancy, and even the occasional atrocity, as in Prince Rupert's sack of Bolton. Such passions jostled with a general commitment to the honour of serving the king, and with the concern of men like Dorset and Hyde for ancient ways. In the parliamentarian camp the holy war against Antichrist was yoked, increasingly uneasily, with a struggle for parliamentary and legal liberties, for the Petition of Right and against 'arbitrary' rule. Not for nothing did lord keeper Littleton stay at Westminster until May 1642. About a half of the lawyers in the central courts whose loyalties can be identified sided with parliament. Their continuing support, and above all that of John Selden, for parliamentarian regimes suggests how wrong it is to accept the claim of Clarendon's *History* that the constitutionalists joined the king. The war against the king was after all fought in the name of parliament, not of the godly people.

The two parliamentarian causes, godly and civil, might be completely separate. The most radical MP was the thoroughly ungodly Henry Marten, and the equally ungodly lawyer Selden the most cogent constitutionalist. More often, though, the godly and the legalist causes dwelt together in the persons of godly property-owners, just as anti-sectarianism coincided with traditional values in most of those around the king. In such conjunctions lay tragedy. The harsh demands of fighting a war, which increasingly seemed warranted only by religious passions, clashed with devotion to law and liberty; and men baulked at the measures they were driven to set their hands to. Not all were as anguished as Sir Edward Dering, who wandered from side to side, but royalists like Dorset and Seymour, parliamentarians like Holland and Holles, similarly cried out for peace as the war progressed.

The importance of religion cannot be underestimated. Sheer anti-Catholicism drove on many conscientious followers of parliament – as Baxter said, religion 'put the resolution and valour' into parliament's soldiers. The parliamentarian battle standards of 1642, with their slogans 'Antichrist must down' and 'Sacra Scriptura', tell the story. When Sir Robert Harley's Herefordshire stronghold of Brampton Bryan fell to the royalists his tenants cited Marshall's vituperative 'Meroz Cursed' as the reason they took up arms. What could be made of the Grand Remonstrance's thesis of a jesuited conspiracy was revealed in the bloody tract *Anti-Cavalierisme*, published late in 1642 by the radical London minister John Goodwin. Its call for total war against Antichrist, and of course the whoremongers as well as the blasphemers and papists around the king, in the opinion of some made the breach irreparable.

It was a war of religion on both sides. Probably the majority of Catholics stayed neutral, to avoid exciting further hostility, but a disproportionate number did support the king. Almost two-thirds of Lancashire royalist gentry were Catholic, about a half in Suffolk and over a third in

Yorkshire. One-third of the officers of Charles's northern armies were Catholic. The traditionalism of their outlook as well as their hostility to parliament's militant protestantism helps account for their alignment. But despite the prominence of Catholics, and despite the king's instructions to Newcastle in September to take no account of the religion of those he took into his army, royalists claimed to be fighting for the true protestant religion no less than did parliamentarians. The twin constants of Charles's declarations were his devotion to law and to the protestantism of Elizabeth; and he maintained that posture even beyond the grave through the pages of *Eikon Basilike*. Rural husbandmen as well as clergymen suffered persecution in the 1640s for using their fathers' forms of worship enshrined in the prayer book; their loyalties may not have been Laudian, but they can certainly be called Anglican. And their hatred of sectarians often mirrored their enemies' loathing of Catholics. Each saw in the other blasphemous advocacy of rebellion and subversion of the social order, with chaos the inevitable outcome of religious deviance. The violence of the sermons of Goodwin and Hansard Knollys was abundantly matched by those of the royalist John Birkenhead (later famous as a journalist and censor), and by broadsheets blasting roundheaded cobblers who desecrated the prayer book. Many itched for the opportunity to pay off scores.

The socio-economic patterns of alignment have proved harder to discern than the religious. Historians have understandably concentrated on the gentry, yet it is doubtful whether the results have justified the time spent in identifying those who were rising and falling economically. At Westminster each side until the royalists' departure had a broadly similar profile; the parallels held true throughout the war. And while the steady decline in the social composition of the leading parliamentarians may suggest their cause was an inherently radical vehicle for social mobility, on both sides cautious magnates with much to lose were displaced during the course of the war by harder men. Parliament's self-denying ordinance of 1645 can be matched by a piecemeal edging out of royalist notables like Hertford and Newcastle by 1644. Lower down the chain of command, perhaps half of the king's officers during the war came from the blurred area where lesser gentry faded into plebeians, while a disproportionate number were younger sons. The former drayman, and parliamentarian colonel, Thomas Pride, had his match in the former Warwickshire 'cowgelder', and royalist major, Thomas Jennings.

English peacetime society allowed only limited social mobility, and wartime service offered welcome prospects, on both sides. With fewer ties of neighbourhood, and less reason to observe social niceties, the upwardly mobile were notoriously prone to efficiency, and to enthusiasm. There were, to be sure, isolated aristocratic hotheads like Brooke and Digby; and Hertford and Dorset would, equally surely, have reasserted themselves at war's end. But a royalist victory won by such as Jennings, under such a king, might have changed the world almost as dramatically as did the New Model Army's triumph. Dorset at least was not unaware of this. Though he was with the king at York, in June 1642 he warned his friend, the equally unhappy, and parliamentarian, Earl of Salisbury that the radicals on either hand were 'men only either of desperate fames or fortunes' whom their betters must strive to check.

Most peers thought they knew who the real radicals were. Although the nobility provided one half of the colonels of parliament's first field army, about twice as many peers eventually fought for the king as for parliament. Like those ill-fated kings, John, Edward II and Henry VI before him, Charles had not only snubbed many of the nobles but had also been defeated in his wars: the wonder is less that he found so many aristocratic opponents but that he found so many supporters. For that, he might thank the peers' recognition of the force of his *Answer to the Nineteen Propositions*: they were the major beneficiaries of the hierarchy of order of which the crown was pinnacle, symbol and guarantee. But undoubtedly more important was the intense focusing during the sixteenth century of the noble honour code on loyalty and service to the crown. It shaped the outlook not just of the peers but also of that majority of the active greater gentry who sided with the king. According to Newcastle's wife Margaret, honour was central to his calculations; more famous is the case of Sir Edmund Verney, Charles's standard-bearer at Edgehill, whose sympathy for parliament's cause was outweighed by the demands of loyalty. Not for nothing did the Nottingham parliamentary garrison during the war distrust the wealthy colonel Hutchinson, thinking it 'scarce possible for any one to continue a gentleman and firm to a godly interest'.

The cause with which Verney sympathised, and which Hutchinson's men suspected, was the cause extolled by the parliamentarian Earl of Northumberland in 1642: 'laws, liberties and privileges'. That cause was personified by parliament's lord general, Essex, a bluff soldier whose personal frustrations and humiliations (his first wife had been the notorious Frances Howard) expressed themselves in a love of degree as much as of divinity. Most peers, on both sides, were aristocratic constitutionalists, and believed that true monarchy rested on, governed through and was limited by a strong nobility. The nobility's sense of its due place certainly played a crucial part in rallying those who surrounded the king. But on the other side the central parliamentarian claim was that parliament – both houses – was withstanding a misled king. Noble recruits were needed to substantiate that claim. And it was duly borne out by the defection from the king's side of long-serving councillors like Manchester, Pembroke and Holland, who simply did not trust Charles Stuart with power and who had a strong sense of the autonomous role of the nobility. The continuing hold of their moderated vision of the polity helps explain the attractions of successive peace proposals during the war – proposals that on the face of it might be thought to have had little chance with the belligerents.

If most of the active peers supported the king, why in a hierarchical society did they fail to carry the country? The extent of their failure has probably been exaggerated, for a resident nobleman could be remarkably effective. The division of Leicestershire behind the Hastings and the Grey families seems to echo that in the Wars of the Roses two centuries earlier; the Earl of Newcastle's northern whitecoats, and on the parliamentarian side the early loyalty of the men of Essex to the Earl of Warwick, point to the continuing importance of the magnates. But too many of the aristocracy had, like Northumberland, become remote courtiers or rentiers, thereby undermining traditional ties. And many too had been less than conscientious as lords lieutenant in the counties, abdicating their militia responsibilities to gentlemen deputies during the decades of peace; Warwick and Hertford are suggestive exceptions. Lesser men were therefore left freer to decide, or to stay neutral, in this crisis.

Gentlemen might be better placed to give a lead, even without the reverence conjured by a noble banner. The higher incidence of resident gentry in the lowland arable belt of southern and central England probably had some bearing on allegiances: largely royalist in Wiltshire and Berkshire, largely parliamentarian in Suffolk or the Oxfordshire neighbourhood of Lord Saye. In such areas too the boundaries of manor and parish more closely coincided than in the upland and woodland zones: parson and squire might speak with one voice, if they would. But environments, and the discipline they fostered, varied considerably. Sometimes a landlordly grid can be imposed on political landscapes far removed from any arable calm: intense landlord competition in the lead-mining Derbyshire moorlands yielded divided alignments that still seem comprehensible through microstudy. Burgeoning industrial areas could also generate something close to class antagonism when political controls fractured in the midst of a deep depression. The fierceness of the rebuff to the Earl of Derby's attempt to raise Manchester for the king, and to Hertford's efforts in parts of Somerset, led many to ponder the prospects for social subordination in a war. Gentry of all persuasions were horrified at that summer's looting of Catholic manor houses around the East Anglian clothing villages of the Stour valley. Had industrialisation progressed further, noblemen and gentlemen might have been still less willing to risk the social peace in a civil war.

The Stour valley rioting raises the question of popular allegiance. Many contemporaries would have agreed with John Corbet, a Gloucestershire minister and historian, that towns were the heartland of parliamentarianism, though they usually divided urban populations into three main groupings. The oligarchs, tied by privilege and interest to the governing elites of country and county, eager for peace and stability, were usually 'neuters' or inclined towards the king: London's merchant princes in the East India and Levant Companies, Bristol's Merchant Venturers, offer good examples. These often found allies in the urban labourers and poor, among whom puritanism had made few inroads. And in between, the 'middling sort', the professionals, the shopkeepers, the craftsmen, provided parliament's local driving force, its recruits and its agents.

Two major provisos are needed. In every social and regional category, the majority would have preferred to get on with their lives, to be 'neuters', if they could. They simply collaborated with the dominant power when they had to; and townsmen had more incentive than most, since towns were tempting targets and movable wealth was easily plundered. Furthermore, the partisanship that undoubtedly existed tended to follow the religious fault-lines of early-Stuart England, which made at best a crazy-quilt of the map. As Thomas Povey, one of the most astute of all commentators, observed, 'Scarce any city or corporation is so unanimous, but they have division enough to undo themselves.'

It may still make sense to talk of preponderances. The pattern Corbet identified in Gloucester and the thriving towns around has been partly upheld by modern studies of several major cities – London, Bristol, Norwich, Exeter, even Newcastle, skewed though the last was by hatred of the Scots for their occupation in 1640–1 (and again in 1644–7). The prominence of middling townsmen from Coventry, from Gloucester, from Maidstone, from Portsmouth, in running the parliamentarian war effort in, and imposing godly reform on, their counties escaped neither resentful local gentry nor modern historians. And most important of all was London. With its alarms and petitioning, its broadsheets, sermons and almanacs, all peddling sensationalism of one kind or another, it was fast becoming a centre of arousal of a very untraditional kind. London was by no means uniformly parliamentarian, for its inhabitants provided many recruits as well as contributions of plate for the king. Nor was it predictable in other respects, for the housewives and market-women among the activists and petitioners suggested that internalised teachings of masculine dominance might not hold under extreme stress. But its trained bands and its ordinary volunteers proved as vital a resource for parliament as did its administrative machine and its financial contributions.

Beyond the major cities, some regional generalisations seem to hold. There were royalist market towns in arable areas of Somerset and Wiltshire, economically dependent as they were on royalist hinterlands; conversely, the port towns' parliamentarianism may owe something to the pull of London. But the parliamentarianism of textile areas in the west country and Yorkshire cannot easily be attributed to outside forces. The relative infrequency of master–man relations in the cottage-based textile industry may have fostered independent attitudes in a work-force that, as Richard Baxter noted, could read and talk at its work. The metallurgical industries varied. In the parliamentarian Mendip hills of Somerset lead seems largely to have been worked by small independent masters, as was iron in the equally parliamentarian West Midland woodlands; in divided

Derbyshire, on the other hand, magnates vied for control of the lead workings. An argument that seeks to correlate industrial organisation with popular alignment might not be shaken by the royalist recruits drawn from the coal mines of the northeast, since the mines often needed considerable capital and may therefore have generated a more dependent labour force. But such an argument surely runs afoul of the largely royalist small masters of the southwestern tin mines.

The cry 'Liberty and Property' voiced by ordinary Somerset parliamentarians cannot therefore adequately explain the loyalties of artisans and craftsmen. There were other variables. The stannaries (tin mines) of the far southwest had ancient jurisdictional ties to the crown, and there were honorific ties too in Cornwall through the royal duchy; these conferred privilege and status on the tin-workers. But Cornwall's notorious royalism extended beyond the tin mines, and stemmed from a deeper cultural difference, the survival of the Cornish language. Without a vernacular Cornish Bible, non-Anglophones were unlikely to become puritans, and all too likely to see parliament's campaign against ritual and ceremony, and the insistent biblicism of so many of its supporters, as English cultural aggression. Reports of Cornish brutalities against parliamentarian captives, especially in the Lostwithiel disaster of 1644, bear out such a supposition. Similar cultural differences surely explain the royalism of the Welsh. The only strongly Anglophone area of Wales was the parliamentarian enclave of Pembrokeshire, in the south. And on the other side of the border, the fears of the Gloucestershire godly as Welsh royalist forces approached betray racial undertones. The wars of the 1640s were British wars, and the British problem was not limited to Scotland and Ireland.

The Civil War was no social revolution, but it was equally clearly not merely a division within the elite. Popular loyalties counted. The shortage of graduate puritan clergy in the poorer uplands before the war, and the barriers to Calvinist scripturalism in non-Anglophone regions, did much to shape partisanship in Wales, the north and the far southwest – 'dark corners of the land' to the godly. The spread of puritanism through the arable belt, or through the isolated wood/pasture zone of the Welsh marches, was also impeded by social barriers in interdependent customary communities that found ceremonial expression in the prayer book. But zeal was freer to spread in less traditional communities, not just in the obvious urban and industrial areas but also in the mixed economies of the ungentrified woodlands of north Warwickshire, or the rapidly commercialising Vale of Gloucester; and such zeal often (although not always, as Baxter's neighbours should remind us) took parliamentarianism with it. One reason for that is suggested by the reappearance in Essex in 1640, after a lapse since 1629, of parish petitions from godly ministers and the 'better sort of householders' for moral reformation, of the poor in particular. The Essex godly saw parliament as the means to godly rule locally as well as nationally. Such groups, although contracted by disillusionment, formed much of the 'honest party' that remained ready in most counties to do parliament's increasingly unpopular bidding throughout the war. And in 1642 it was such supporters, acting in advance of hesitant gentry, who secured for parliament the Somerset uplands, the West Riding clothing area, the town of Nottingham, the wooded north of Warwickshire; most importantly, eager recruits rallied from the City and its suburbs. However oversimplified the slogans of 'papists', 'puritan rogues', peddled by the popular broadsheets and woodcuts, those slogans had power to move. As Baxter observed, 'The war was begun in our streets before the king and parliament had any armies.'

It is easy to assume that parliament held the trump cards in that war. Ensconced in London, it could tap an unrivalled source of loans and administrative capacity that alone ensured its financial survival. Possessing the port towns, and supported by Northumberland and Warwick with their followings among the officers, it gained the fleet. This proved critical, for the fleet convoyed merchant shipping into parliamentarian ports, thus ensuring a customs revenue, the essential security for the City's loans; it warned European powers into neutrality; and it kept coastal garrisons such as Hull and Lyme supplied, thus tying down royalist forces in long sieges.

Yet in the short term at least Charles possessed enormous assets. His own person provided an unmatched device for raising funds and volunteers. The silver plate of his noble supporters could be quickly turned into cash to pay his troops: magnates like Worcester and Newcastle were reported to have contributed colossal sums by the end of the war. In contrast to the plethora of parliamentary committees he gave his cause an undivided source of command (though his habitual indecisiveness blurred this advantage, particularly once his forceful wife returned to Oxford in 1643). And perhaps most important, he had an experienced officer corps, for perhaps 90 per cent of the English professionals serving abroad joined the king when domestic employment opened up for them. Charles also had easier access to vital supplies of cavalry horses through his princely relatives in The Netherlands, as well as in the royal stud. The consequences were clear in the succession of parliamentarian disasters in the first year of the war. Not surprisingly, the king's strategy centred on a rapid strike on London; only slowly was parliament able to reap the benefit of its greater reserves.

|9|

Civil war, 1642–1646

Not for nothing did both Charles and his foes assume that the enemy would be finally unable to fight, for the military incapacity of both parties encouraged scepticism. English society had been steadily demilitarised in the sixteenth century; indeed, even in frontier Ulster the proportion of protestant settlers with muskets had dropped from 12 per cent in 1619 to 3 per cent by 1630. Charles's failure to shape England to his warfaring needs in the later 1620s and again in 1639–40 might have made his enemies complacent; but they had been no more successful. The second Earl of Essex's inability to raise his estates in 1601 had been a portent, and at the end of the 1630s his son the third earl and others who hoped to check Charles had to rely on the Scots to do it for them. The military revolution that had engulfed continental Europe passed the offshore islands by. Individuals crossed to the continent to fight, but fortifications, the provision of weapons and horse, training, all remained underdeveloped.

Yet the military sophistication of England's continental neighbours itself made them less likely civil battlegrounds. They possessed citadels; the vulnerability of Charles's position at the Tower in 1641, and his surrender of it in 1642, suggests how the absence of royal bastions might level the political field. Equally important, no west European state was as divided in religion as England or Ireland, perhaps even Scotland; none therefore contained the animosities and fears that could drive men to breach ancient custom, and to kill one another, with such gusto. England was also unusual in its structures of government. The survival of parliament, a uniquely national representative institution, was obviously central. Constitutional propriety insisted that king-in-parliament made law, but D'Ewes and other wishful thinkers in the crisis months of late 1641 had been able to reassure the houses, and then a wider audience for the houses' declarations, that the two houses as the great council of the realm could pass ordinances with the force of law. It was not far from there to the argument that the two houses were parliament, the representative of the kingdom, and therefore might legislate. But that claim shaded into another, with far-reaching implications: the community of England, the body politic, could act like any natural body to preserve itself. In 1584, in the bond of association against the assassination of Elizabeth, and again in the Protestation of 1641, important sections of the political community had taken steps towards acting outside parliament without the king.

The nature of the two causes reflected the fast-diverging understandings of the body politic. The nature of the two causes also gave parliament something of an advantage. The king demanded the loyalty and service subjects owed to his person, and honour-bound gentlemen responded to that call by rallying to his standard. They thereby left their neighbour-hoods open to those who wished to stay at home and organise. On the other hand, the two houses, with their insistence in the militia that the nation had to defend itself against malignants, encouraged organisation by and in the local communities. The Earl of Derby, trying to consolidate the northwest for the king, saw many of his allies rush south to join Charles; a similar migration allowed parliament to acquire a secure heart-land in East Anglia, a vitally important source of regular revenues. The royalists could never turn their heartlands in the West Midlands towards Wales into a similar resource, for economy and administrative routine alike were constantly disturbed by raiding from the parliamentarian garri-son in Gloucester. Not for nothing were frustrated cavaliers ready to turn to the sword as a fiscal arm.

The greater royalist propensity for the abuses of power was intensified by the way the two sides made decisions. The royalist council of war was generally subordinate to the wishes of the king, whose enjoyment of soldiering and impatience of civilian complaint led him to side increas-ingly with his commanders. The wartime council became therefore steadily more ill-suited to mediating local disputes than the overburdened pre-war council had been. We know more about developments at Westminster, since the defeated royalists burnt their papers. And at Westminster, a clear chain of command was even less evident. Just under 200 still sat in the Commons, around thirty in the Lords; and all of them were early-Stuart parliament-men impressed with the dignity of their office and their insti-tutions. The establishment in July 1642 of a joint committee, the Commit-tee of Safety, to co-ordinate brought little relief, for this was handicapped not only by its size (eighty, drawn from both houses) but also by the reluc-tance of the two houses to surrender ultimate authority. Consequently, the houses themselves, the committee and Lord General Essex all vied for control over strategy.

Nevertheless, there were benefits to the way a legislature drew on its traditions of corporate decision-making to transform itself into a full-time executive. Though the slow and creaking emergence of its war-machine left parliament vulnerable, its ramshackle committee system saved it from the worst excesses. Military commanders on both sides always struggled to consolidate their grip on local resources; but the parliamentary committees that checked and balanced each other, and the survival at Westminster of at least some MPs from most areas, helped limit the reach of the sword. Charles in contrast was dangerously ready to allow his officers a free hand. They were the more ready to take that hand since their paramount ethos of service to the king's person seems to have imposed fewer restraints on them than did the parliamentarians' emerging ideal of service to the country. The distinction proved central, since while the soldiers could extract money readily enough, only civilian co-operation allowed a viable political cause to survive.

Moves towards greater efficiency came slowly and reluctantly. After all, each side believed that the other would collapse in face of the drawn sword, and each insisted that it was fighting not to innovate but to conserve. Accordingly, each side strove to use what was to hand. Although king as well as parliament raised a mobile field army for strategic victory, each turned as well to local gentry leading forces to consolidate the counties, and to magnates to secure the regions. Indeed, until the end of the war parliament had as many men in local garrisons and local forces as in its field armies. The king's main field force, under Lindsey and then his replacement the Scottish professional Patrick Ruthven, Lord Forth, was matched by the parliamentarian army under Essex; the royalist regional magnates included Hertford in the west, Newcastle in the north and Worcester in south Wales; their parliamentarian equivalents included Brooke in the West Midlands, Lord Willoughby in Lincolnshire, and Sir William Brereton in the northwest. Volunteers filled all the garrisons and mobile forces; not until late 1643 did parliament, followed by the king, dare breach legalist values by openly introducing impressment. And both parliament and the king asserted their respect for law by claiming to support these volunteers on a voluntary basis, on what purported to be 'loans' – in parliament's case, raised through 'propositions' to the country in the summer of 1642 for repayment on 'the public faith'.

But in the localities as well as at the centre the war brought change. The unwieldiness and unreliability of the old work-horses, the JPs, needed little discovery, and both sides cobbled together their alternatives. Charles distrusted a militia establishment that had won him so little glory in his wars, so in a typical exercise in innovatory medievalism, he appointed his leading supporters in the counties commissioners of array, to levy and arm locally. Like most such antiquarian exercises, this proved a political and administrative mistake. Not only could their enemies misrepresent the unfamiliar Latin commissions as warrants for tyranny. The commissioners' responsibilities and authority were dangerously unclear, leaving them vulnerable to any proud colonel with good connections at Oxford.

The two houses' turn to the deputy lieutenants appointed under the militia ordinance was less startling, but it did begin a dramatic concentration of power in these county committees. Presuming their loyalty, and knowing they commanded forces, parliament thrust upon them the duty of raising money, first upon the propositions of 1642 and then with the new fiscal ordinances of 1643. There was no appeal from them save to the houses themselves, since parliament expressly put their actions outside the jurisdiction of the courts. Royalist commanders in the localities soon established petty dictatorships; but the parliamentarian county committees, especially when run by petty tyrants like Sir Michael Livesey in Kent, were no attractive alternative. Indeed, only the jurisdictional competition in the regions and at Westminister prevented the county committees, with their expanding civil and military functions, appearing from the outset the monsters that they were to seem by the end of the war.

The two camps mirrored each other politically as well as organisationally. The parliamentarians' divisions are notorious, but the cavaliers' pursuit of honour and loyalty gave their disputes a bitter personal edge; from this arose their delight in the duel, and such damaging if dramatic gestures as Falkland's suicide at Newbury in 1643, or Newcastle's self-exile after Marston Moor in 1644. But not all was personal. Divisions centred, in Charles's court at Oxford as well as at Westminster, on the way to fight and win the war. When Charles in late 1642 appointed his nephew, the homeless prince Rupert of the Palatinate, to a senior command he invited feuds, for the dashing and charismatic Rupert had a prickliness and arrogance that could shade into brutality; but he also signalled his determination to destroy rebellion. He was seconded in this determination by the queen, by Rupert's bitter enemy Lord Digby who succeeded Falkland as secretary of state, and by the young men who hoped to ride to fortune on a victory. Over the course of 1643–4 Rupert and hardened soldiers like Sir Richard Grenville and Lord Byron steadily displaced the regional magnates like Hertford and Newcastle; and in the hothouse intrigues of Oxford their counsels and those of Digby were preferred to those of the moderate politicians such as Hyde, Southampton and Falkland, who thought a settlement based on some middle ground the only hope of permanency. The anguish of those who saw so much to lose is exemplified by the royalist Earl of Sunderland, who was contemplating exile should the king win the war even as he went to his death with Falkland at Newbury.

Parliament delayed its great military reorganisation until the winter of 1644–5, but this does not mean that its internal rifts were any less urgent than the royalists'. Whatever the propaganda claims, few at Westminster or in the army command could conceal from themselves that they were fighting Charles as much as, or perhaps more than, his evil counsellors. The question of trust was central, and to fight and win might entail enforcing terms on a resentful king. As war became a reality, those implications grew more unnerving; meanwhile, emphases that had in 1641 seemed variously moderation or hotheadedness became cemented. Of those remaining at Westminster by the end of 1642, over a half were quintessential back-benchers, often localist, infrequent speakers, but puritan in a non-doctrinaire sense. What have been called the 'peace party', the 'war party' and the 'middle group' sought to sway these by appeals to interests of religion, region, and social cohesion. In the Commons the competing groups comprised perhaps thirty members each, loose clusters associated for limited political ends, and crucially dependent on a handful of allies in the Lords.

The strength of the peace party lay in loyalism. Many were the lords and gentlemen who bewailed the need to fight their king, and who hoped against hope that a defensive war, or a stalemate, would persuade Charles to compromise. They were driven too by social conservatism – Denzil Holles, who quickly lost his early militancy, expressed a common fear that 'servants should ride on horses' when they saw what rebellion could achieve. As such men watched others' attitudes, and the likely peace terms, stiffen with the bloodshed, they grew steadily more fearful. While setbacks increased the fervour of the more apocalyptic, they intensified the peace party's gloom. When Essex's army managed a shaky draw in the first major engagement of the war, at Edgehill in Warwickshire on 23 October 1642, Northumberland and Holland led a successful peace party push for negotiations; to widespread alarm, they pulled in their wake Essex himself, once he had raced the royal army back to London. Such a drama of despair was to be replayed repeatedly.

The war party mirrored the views of royalist extremists like Digby in their determination to destroy the enemy's power to do ill. Their most vociferous members included Henry Marten, the younger Vane and Hesilrig, who gained extra fire from the 'northern men', those parliamentarian MPs whose estates lay under the control of the king's northern armies and who were eager for their speedy reclamation. Yet war-party radicalism did not only lie in the depth of distrust for the king, or the location of estates. Vane and Hesilrig were moved also by an urgent godly zeal (though of very different kinds, as events would prove). But Marten was as irreligious as any, so his radicalism clearly arose elsewhere. Indeed, a sense of the capacity of the community underlay much radical parliamentarianism. Marten was unusual at the beginning of the war in resting a veiled republicanism on the claims of the community; but as parliament's uneasy winter of 1642 gave way to an even grimmer summer, others joined him. As they watched the 'peace lords', Holles, nervous lawyer-MPs like Bulstrode Whitelocke, edge closer to Oxford, London militants struck out in new directions. The abortive 'general rising' of the summer of 1643 was their work: a plan for an independent military force to be raised and controlled by the radicals. Their clerical spokesmen, in particular Jeremiah Burroughs, even hinted at popular sovereignty as they used the claim that any political community must protect itself to oppose a sell-out peace by parliament. But whatever the implications of factional division, its occasion, at least until 1645, was not religion or the constitution but the question of how much Charles could be trusted, and whether to talk or to fight.

The distance between the extremes explains the middle. Pym was as distrustful of Charles as was Marten, and as fiercely anti-Catholic as Hesilrig; but, like his ally St John, he had been shaped as well by his long connections with noblemen. It was that unusual combination that fitted him to be 'the director of the whole machine', as one observer called him. The middle group, unlike the war party, included several important peers, notably Warwick and Saye. Backed by the prudent John Hampden, and carrying that supremely pragmatic militant Oliver Cromwell along much of the time, Pym urgently pursued security in *de facto* control over government and the sword. Equally urgently, he headed off radical gestures from his allies that might provoke more of the 'peace lords' to defect to Oxford and thus split the cause. Accordingly, in the seasonal flux that brought politicking in the winter and military preparations in the spring and summer, the middle group worked with the peace party to keep negotiations open and yet joined Vane and Hesilrig in strengthening parliament's war effort. The measure of Pym's success lies in the fact that the two wings of the uneasy parliamentarian alliance did not fly apart in 1643 as he worked to pass the excise and impressment – extensions of government that sat uneasily with the heritage of 1628. His skills were to be more sorely taxed by the return of the Scots that he had laboured so hard to secure.

The parliamentarians' discomfort almost brought disaster in the early months. Prince Rupert did not share the belief of Essex and the 'peace lords' that during negotiations fighting should cease. On 12 November he attacked Brentford on the outskirts of London. Fearing a sack, the London-trained bands rallied with Essex's forces to suburban Turnham Green and there outnumbered and out-faced the royalists; they thus foiled Charles's dash for London, and with it his hopes of a speedy end to the war. Characteristically, Pym ran with both war and peace parties during the crisis, and managed to salvage far more than the simple stalemate of Turnham Green. While expressing support for the lords who pushed for peace talks he exploited another response to the shambles at Edgehill and beyond, one typified by John Goodwin, whose *Anti-Cavalierisme* (1642) found apocalyptic meaning in the bloodshed. As Rupert and Charles between them heightened the zeal of the London godly, Pym at last persuaded the two houses to embrace the fiscal coercion that they had sought to stave off through loans, voluntary contributions, or diversion of the supplies raised for Ireland. The readiness of the citizens, whether militants or mere frightened property-owners, to be taxed in their own defence allowed the houses to introduce the principle of compulsory weekly assessments on London.

Cold feet were not the only impediment to war; equally damaging was the prevailing localism. Each county looked for help from elsewhere and rarely thought to yield any return, since each threat to a neighbour too often seemed to demand that local defences be strengthened. Thus, when parliament finally passed national fiscal measures in the spring of 1643 most county committees determinedly and improperly held on to the money they collected: it has been estimated that only 2 per cent of the money collected before March 1645 in Cheshire (which was admittedly contested, and distant from either centre) ever left the county. But after Edgehill and Brentford the need for defence could not be denied.

Both royalists and parliamentarians quickly recognised the strategic nonsense of administrative boundaries, and in late 1642 leaders of many counties 'associated' with neighbours for common defence. Such moves gained ready approval at both Oxford and Westminster, though approval was not the same as planning. Anticipating only a single campaign, both Charles and parliament allowed anomalies to multiply. The parliamentarian Eastern Association, centred on East Anglia, was geographically rational, but the East Midlands Association stretched from Derbyshire to Buckinghamshire; by mid-1643 Shropshire was listed in five parliamentarian associations, and provided an invitation to evasion and disputes. In their confusion, neither parliament nor king gave their associations much financial or organisational substance. Nor did they specify the relations between the new associations, the colonels of earlier regional volunteer forces, and the respective generals. Long feuds reverberated in the localities and at Westminster between association commanders, such as the Earls of Denbigh and Manchester (formerly Viscount Mandeville), and regional colonels, such as Sir William Brereton and Lord Willoughby, who vied with them for rank and resources. Such feuds were paralleled at Oxford. Charles failed utterly to reconcile the interminable and vicious quarrels of Digby and Rupert among his advisers, or the disputes among his field officers, such as that in 1643 between Rupert and Lord Wilmot.

The ramshackle associations did little to alter the strategic balance. 1643 opened with the royalists maintaining the initiative that liquid assets and professional experience had given them in 1642. Although parliament over the winter consolidated its hold on most of East Anglia, on the southeast and on Somerset, elsewhere gloom prevailed. The royalists advanced in the southwest, the north, the West Midlands, and raided the surrounding counties from Oxford. Royalist risings were every day expected from the surly 'neuters' of Norfolk and Kent, while Londoners resented their own disproportionate burdens in the economic dislocation brought by war.

The spring of 1643, so painful for those at Westminster and their supporters, was a watershed for the country. Despite the mutual fulminations of king and parliament, neutrality and a yearning for accommodation had been a perfectly logical response for those whose hearts were not stirred by visceral appeals to loyalty or to Zion. Did not both sides protest a similar devotion to law and the Elizabethan church? But the failure of new negotiations at Oxford that spring, in face of the understandable refusal of the victorious Charles to make further concessions, showed that whatever the rhetoric the two sides were far apart. There was now no escaping the conclusion that civil war had to be fought out – or, at the individual level, that painful choices would be needed. As Philip Hunton noted in *Treatise of Monarchie* (1643), the most impressive of all the works of counsel, the individual faced with two legitimate but contending authorities had only his conscience to guide him.

While the last flickers of neutrality pacts in Cheshire and elsewhere died out, polarisation accelerated in the capital. The transformation of the City into a parliamentarian bastion, politically as well as in terms of its earthworks, grew slowly from the Brentford crisis, which allowed the militants to disable the king's wealthy supporters. And in parliament the discomfiture of the peace party at the Oxford failure was intensified that May when Pym wove the ample record of contacts between unhappy moderates in both camps into the story of 'Waller's Plot' (named after one of the MPs in the peace delegation to Oxford) to betray the City.

By tarring advocacy of peace as worse than defeatism, Pym was able to elaborate the measures needed to continue the fighting. His genius was never clearer than in the way he repeatedly exploited crises to refurbish the tottering parliamentary machine. Thus, in the spring of 1643 he worked with Lord General Essex to avert collapse by shifting the fiscal burden from parliament's friends. War often overcomes constitutional scruples, and the ordinance for 'the fifth and twentieth part' imposed a massive forced loan on those who had not lent voluntarily on the 'contributions'. Another ordinance provided for the sequestration, or confiscation for the duration, of the property of 'delinquents'. Most important of all, compulsory assessments were extended from London to all the parliamentarian territory. And instead of relying on out-dated valuations as did the old subsidy, the assessment (modelled, ironically, on ship money) required a specified sum from each county. To their misfortune, the royalists never systematised a tax as effectively as did the committees at Westminster.

But the yield of the spring's fiscal measures took time to gather, and Essex's army was paralysed for lack of supplies. After taking Reading on the road to Oxford in April, it bogged down in the rain and mud of the Thames valley. By mid-summer the lord general, unable to risk another engagement, had seen his 13 000 men dwindle, through typhus and desertion, to a mutinous 5500. Harried by royalist raids, perhaps his greatest loss was the death in June of Colonel John Hampden, his increasingly effective aide and an invaluable link to the Commons' leaders. There were few consolations elsewhere. Despite early successes in Yorkshire by Lord Fairfax and his son Sir Thomas, most of the northeast had by June 1643 fallen to the Earl of Newcastle. In the east, where even localist county committees could see the danger from Newcastle's forces, the cavalry of the Eastern Association was able to sweep its region; but despite the promptings of its commander, the inexperienced but charismatic Cromwell, it was reluctant to cross the Association's frontier. Meanwhile the war in the Midlands turned into a grim and formless struggle for the countless minor garrisons that sought to secure an area and its resources. In the west the news was bleaker still. Sir William Waller had been the most successful of parliament's early regional commanders, and was lionised in the City for his gains in the south and southwest, while Essex was lampooned. But success depended on logistics as well as on skill, and Waller could not consolidate his hold. Royalist victories in July at Lansdown in Somerset and Roundway Down in Wiltshire secured virtually all the southwest for the king. The greatest blow came later that month when prince Rupert stormed Bristol. The second port of the kingdom, Bristol gave Charles access to supplies from the continent and from Ireland, and to customs revenue.

The gloomy summer shook parliament's morale. The western disasters coincided with anti-war revolt in Kent and rumblings in Norfolk, and most ominously of all, with a growing peace movement in London. Seeking scapegoats, the war party blamed Essex's inactivity, and almost drove him to resignation. But Pym, who desperately needed the lord general for the social respectability he brought, for his standing with the Lords, and not least for his huge popularity with the soldiers, as so often gained from apparently imminent defeat. By strengthening Waller he headed off the militant backers of the 'general rising', and reassured the frightened City oligarchy; at the same time he conciliated Essex by winning for him a vitally needed impressment ordinance to swell his forces. All this had to be paid for, and that July Pym gained his most lasting triumph over the peace party and its supporters. Despite all the constitutionalist hostility voiced in 1628 to an excise, or sales tax, the houses now agreed to a levy on such widely consumed items as beer and tobacco.

Administrative reform did less to change the character of the war than did the other great work of Pym and his war-party ally Vane that summer. To the outrage of many, and not just royalists, the houses once more turned to the Scots to compensate for military weakness. The Covenanters, it should be said, were no more reluctant in 1643 than they had been in 1639–40 to do others' work as well as their own. Many had wished to intervene to stiffen the English godly as soon as the fighting began, in hopes of the closer association of the kingdoms in common security and religion. They had been dissuaded by the English parliament's belief in the rosier days of 1642 that it could stand alone, and by their own divisions; but by mid-1643 both conditions had changed. The Covenanters' discovery in June of another 'Antrim Plot' to use Irish Catholics against the west coast of Scotland effectively sealed the Anglo-Scottish alliance. Lowland Covenanters as well as Campbells dreaded the prospect of a union of

Catholic clans in the Highlands and Ireland. Newcastle's 'popish' army across the border only concentrated their fears.

The chief obstacle to an Anglo-Scottish alliance was the very religious fervour that made it possible. The Covenanters' cause was largely ecclesiastical. But while the English parliamentarian leaders had endeared themselves to the Scots by proclaiming their purity and zeal, they were painfully aware of the religious divisions in their own ranks. Indeed, the ardent Vane, who played a brilliant hand, had more sympathy for sectarians in the proliferating London conventicles than he did for clerical disciplinarians in Edinburgh. Accordingly, the houses sought a purely civil league, though in a godly disguise. On 12 June 1643 parliament established the Westminster assembly of divines. 120 carefully picked, wholly Calvinist English ministers, with thirty lay assessors from both houses and eight Scottish commissioners, were to advise parliament on reform of the church. Pym hoped with this to meet various urgent needs: to satisfy Covenanter zeal, to give substance at last to parliament's familiar protestations of godly goals, to gain final vindication against the Arminians, and not least to provide a stable core for an English church that might check the growing ferment in London.

The compromise failed to bring ecclesiastical peace to the parliamentarian camp. The Scots shared the alarm of English conservatives at the spread of heterodoxy, and resented the smallness of the representation they were given in the Assembly, and the dominance of parliament. For their part, even the most desperate and partisan of English parliamentmen baulked at the rampant clericalism of the high presbyterian Covenanters. Long-standing anti-Scottish sentiment merged with widespread scepticism for the 'iure divino', divine-right, claims of any church. Even Sir Simonds D'Ewes, whose hostility to episcopacy as well as to London's growing disorder might have made him a natural supporter of Scottish discipline, denounced the 'tyrannical power' implicit in it. Although the summer's disasters had made the need for allies undeniable, it took Vane's obfuscation of divine right claims to ease the Solemn League and Covenant through the two houses in early September.

The peace party was outraged by the broadening of a war that had previously been cast as defensive. The Scottish alliance publicly committed parliament to the extirpation of episcopacy, and implied a presbyterian alternative. A war for religion was a frightening prospect for those who knew anything of Germany; and the presence of the Scots must disrupt any future peace talks, since their sole demand, presbyterianism, was not one that Charles deemed negotiable. Not surprisingly, the Solemn League and Covenant brought renewed calls for a peace, to pre-empt the calamities that must ensue. Led by family tradition to despise the Scots, Northumberland made moves to defect.

The Scottish alliance thus in the short term brought further polarisation to Westminster, and in the longer term it brought everything the peace party had feared. Capitalising on the widespread recognition that capitulation could be the only outcome of negotiations at such a troubled time, Pym deftly blocked the new peace initiative. In their despair, and probably too in fear of a traitor's death should the royalists win their expected victory, several peace party leaders abandoned the struggle. The Earls of Holland, Bedford and Clare left for Oxford, while in the Commons Denzil Holles and several others lapsed into demoralised inactivity. But Pym did not seek to dismember the parliamentarian coalition. That August he reassured conservatives at Westminister by obtaining the expulsion and imprisonment of Henry Marten for his outspoken republicanism. He thus gained on every hand. The war party lost its most troublesome figure, the peace party was again tainted with treachery and permanently weakened in the Lords where its main strength had lain.

The greatest weakness of the peace party was not Pym's finesse but the premise that the king might compromise. To widespread royalist despair, Charles frowned on the defecting peers, who were in his eyes traitors; he thereby discouraged others from following. Still more damagingly, in September he retaliated against parliament's Scottish alliance by approving the 'Cessation', a cease-fire with the Irish rebels who were now organised in the Catholic Confederation of Kilkenny. He claimed to seek recruits only from the English troops tied down there, remnants of Strafford's old army and reinforcements sent over early in 1642. Rumour soon obliterated the distinction. After the horrors of the winter of 1641–2 there was a world of difference between dealings with presbyterian Scots and with Catholic Irish. Charles's undoubted military gain from the new recruits, especially in securing the Welsh borders, was therefore offset by political loss. For some unhappy royalists, like Dering, who now defected, the 'Cessation' underscored the prominence of Catholics at Oxford and in the king's armies; and Northumberland returned with new zeal to parliament. More than ever, the war became the religious war the peace party feared, and brutalities and intransigence increased.

Charles's eagerness for recruits from Ireland stemmed from his recognition that if he were to win the war he must do it fast, before the Scots tipped the balance. His hopes centred on a junction of the northern and western armies with his own at Oxford. Since Turnham Green had taught new respect for the City's militia, the combined forces would blockade London, thus provoking an uprising in the hard-pressed and restive capital. The plan was plausible enough, for the citizens' distress would have exploded had Newcastle driven south to link up with rebellious anti-parliamentarians in Norfolk, or had Charles struck at the Eastern Association. But the enduring strategic reality of this war was the consolidation of inadequately fortified territory. Sieges could be as crucial as rapid movements and set-piece battles, and the threat posed by garrisons to supply-lines determined the grand campaign of 1643. Two of the three royalist forces turned aside to protect their rear, Newcastle to confront the Fairfaxes' refuge at Hull, Charles to the godly enclave of Gloucester.

The reprieve allowed both Manchester, commanding the Eastern Association, and Essex to build up their forces. Indeed, Charles's diversion enabled Essex to win an unusual moment of glory in the late summer of 1643. The London trained bands were sufficiently stirred by the crisis and the popish threat to the Midlands to leave their homes, and with these the lord general briskly relieved Gloucester at the end of the August. He then caught the king at Newbury in Berkshire on 20 September. It was Edgehill all over again, with Charles once more racing for London; this time Essex out-generalled him. Gloucester was preserved, impeding Charles's access to his recruiting-grounds in south Wales, and London was safe. The war must now be prolonged, straining further the pockets of the king's supporters, while the parliamentarians were able to exploit the undisturbed southeast and East Anglia.

As rapid victory eluded him, Charles turned to harder men and solutions. He signalled his concern for military efficiency by a wave of ennoblements in late 1643: of Byron and Henry Hastings from the Midlands, of Sir Ralph Hopton, Hertford's deputy in the southwest, of the artillery commander Wilmot. What efficiency could mean for traditional relations is suggested by Worcester's outburst against the archetypal professional, Ruthven, 'here today and God knows where tomorrow, and therefore needed not care for the love of the people'. *Noblesse oblige* was a wasting asset in war.

Yet Charles still had political hopes. Not content with importing fresh troops from Ireland, he seems to have intended to dissolve parliament unilaterally. Appalled at such a breach of the non-dissolution act of 1641, Hyde sought in political action of a different kind the breakthrough that had eluded the soldiers. The king's prerogative of summoning parliament remained untouched by the 1641 legislation, and Hyde successfully argued that a summons to Oxford could exploit the anger provoked by parliament's insatiable demands and by the Solemn League and Covenant. Not only unhappy neutrals but even some peace party waverers might be won. The prospects became brighter when Pym died of cancer on 8 December. The stately funeral testified to the magnitude of parliament's loss in its supreme organiser and political tactician. As important, Pym, like those other casualties of 1643, Hampden and Lord Brooke, had been able to work with both radicals and conservatives. That quality was to be sorely needed as the strains of a spreading war polarised opinion still further.

The opportunity was lost to Charles, who had shown by the 'Cessation', and the treatment of the defecting peace lords, that he pursued only victory. In January 1644 the Oxford 'parliament' mustered perhaps three times as many peers as did Westminster (though many were wartime creations), and just over half as many of the MPs elected in 1640. It was a respectable showing. But parliamentary legalism was out of place at Oxford, for the king was more than ever impatient with 'country' complaints. Although the 'parliament' began by trying to call to account corrupt royalist officers and officials, Charles soon brought it back to the business of tamely approving his demands for supply and condemning the parliamentarians. It therefore held little attraction for those weary of Westminster or hopeful of a negotiated peace; nor did it divert the attention of moderate royalists from the soldiers and roysterers, feuds and corruption, at Oxford. By the end of 1644 one visitor could comment on the 'cyphers of the other Lords and Commons, few and poor', he found there.

Pym's death therefore embarrassed Westminster less than might have been expected. Instead of having to watch further desertions, his successors were able to profit from the renewed unity brought by Charles's Irish policy. Most importantly, they could devote themselves to integrating into the alliance the 20 000-strong army of the Covenanters that in January 1644 re-entered the northern counties. By their mere presence the Scots dramatically altered the strategic balance. Though they were soon to be ridiculed for their ten-month siege of Newcastle, they drew the Earl of Newcastle's army away from the parliamentarian heartlands to the south. In so doing, they forever barred the king's three-pronged threat to London.

The Scots extracted a price for their services. Their greatest goal, presbyterianism, was lost to them in the interminable text-mining of the Westminster assembly of divines, and in parliament's own evasiveness; but they found it easier to reshape the parliamentarian machine. The needs of their cold and hungry army provided a welcome opening for those who hoped to displace the peace lords and the now less than militant Denzil Holles who had been appointed to the Committee of Safety in the very different days of 1642. The non-aligned majority in the Commons could not ignore the disorganisation that had contributed to the disasters of 1643, nor the back-biting and recriminations of the various commanders during the winter's lull in campaigning. Regional factors too provided powerful incentives. Even conservative MPs from the north or west whose estates were threatened by royalists might be ready to diminish the power of the equally conservative, but lacklustre, Essex in the Thames valley. Accordingly, the new leaders of the middle group, Saye in the Lords and St John in the Commons, in alliance with the more militant Vane, swept aside the old Committee of Safety in the spring of 1644. They replaced it with the Committee of Both Kingdoms, whose appeal lay both in its joint Anglo-Scottish composition and its greater executive powers.

Restructuring brought some efficiency, but neither consensus nor victories. The ever-more sensitive Essex rightly saw criticism of himself in the strengthening of the regional forces under Manchester and Waller upon which the Committee promptly embarked. As he swung closer to unhappy peers who felt slighted by their loss of power to the new committee, tensions between the two houses mounted. Nor were these offset by military gains. Even when strengthened, Manchester's Eastern Association and Waller's South-Eastern Association forces were still hamstrung by regionalism. The Scots could not be persuaded to march southwards; and instead of advancing north against Prince Rupert, who was busily mopping up the parliamentarians in the Midlands, Essex spent the spring of 1644 politicking for peace. The half-hearted advance on Oxford Essex adventured with Waller in late May soon petered out in squabbling. Charles's advisers now saw a chance of beating his enemies piecemeal when Essex headed into the west. Catching up with Waller, the king's forces bested him in a hard-fought encounter at Cropredy Bridge in Oxfordshire on 29 June, and then slowly moved off in pursuit of the lord general.

The fortunes of war still ran against parliament. The difference in the armies did not lie in the infantry, where parliament's officers and men had by now acquired experience to match that of the royalists: the performance of the London trained bands at Newbury was fully as impressive as that of Hopton's Cornishmen at Lansdown. Rather, the difference lay in the cavalry, the critical arm in so many engagements. The royalists had at first had a very marked advantage in the horsemanship and military experience abroad of many of the gentlemen who flocked to the king's standard. But training and discipline, where there were good officers, had by 1644 gone some way to make up parliament's deficiencies, particularly since the royalist cavalry also had its handicaps. Blooded on the hunting-field, and too often interested in plunder, Prince Rupert's horsemen were unstoppable in more ways than one. Even when the parliamentarian horse far out-numbered the royalists, as at Naseby in 1645, they found it difficult to stand up to Rupert; but despite his charisma, Rupert found it as difficult to rally his men after their first charge. Cromwell, an equally inspired commander, taught the cavalry of the Eastern Association the value of a 'pretty round trot', and the importance of shunning plunder until commanded. His 'Ironside' troopers would reform for an often decisive second charge.

The Eastern Association had another solution to the problem of morale: money. Throughout the first half of 1643 the officers of the Eastern Association army had protested vainly to a divided parliament that they could only fight if the various county committees were forced to look beyond their local priorities to the needs of the association. It took the advance of Newcastle's army into Lincolnshire in 1643 to secure frantic ordinances in July and August of that year giving Manchester and the association committee extensive powers over all forces and resources in the region. The rapid emergence over the next six months of the army of the Eastern Association points to the limits of localism. Only division and uncertainty at the centre allowed localism to flourish; and in the case of the Eastern Association, the houses eventually willed effectiveness. That judgment was reinforced as the results of Pym's fiscal reforms slowly trickled through to the 'marching armies' (garrisons tended to live off their neighbourhoods) in the course of 1644.

Money was not the only source of morale. Both Manchester and his cavalry commander Cromwell were godly men who treasured soldiers who could pray; they also agreed, at least up to the summer of 1644, in wanting to win the war. Accordingly, if not enough gentlemen were willing to lead, they would promote others: 'better plain men than none', Cromwell held. The contrast with other armies was of course not absolute, for efficiency was valued everywhere. But more than most generals, Cromwell could contemplate with equanimity the political consequences of promoting men from the ranks, since he shared the religious radical-ism of many a 'plain russet-coated captain that knows what he fights for and loves what he knows'. Not surprisingly, Holles and the alarmed Lords sought throughout the spring of 1644 to subject Manchester's command to that of Essex.

Despite Cropredy Bridge, Charles faced a significant military challenge by the summer of 1644. The worth of the parliamentarian foot had been shown at Newbury and of its horse on the borders of the Eastern Associ-ation. Royalist hopes of major reinforcement from Ireland had been dashed when Sir Thomas Fairfax's Yorkshire forces destroyed the biggest 'Irish' contingent in January 1644 at Nantwich in Cheshire. Worse, at the end of April a Scottish detachment joined the Fairfaxes in bottling up Newcastle at York. Faced with the imminent loss of his northern army and capital, Charles dispatched a relieving force north under Rupert. The prince rapidly did all that was expected of him by drawing off the besiegers in a brilliant manoeuvre and relieving York; but he was not one to avoid a fight. The parliamentarian forces, now joined by Manchester and Cromwell, numbered 28 000; even with the addition of Newcastle's tired and resentful troops Rupert had only about 18 000. On 3 July at Marston Moor the royalist army was destroyed in the biggest battle of the war. At first it looked as though it would go the other way until the Ironsides reformed after their first charge and broke in on the royalist centre, annihilating Newcastle's superb 'Whitecoat' infantry. York surren-dered a fortnight later and the earl left in despair for the continent.

Marston Moor was a turning-point, if perhaps less militarily, even polit-ically, than ideologically. Although Charles had lost the north, his forces were to win other victories. But to the puritan, God spoke through dispen-sations in this world. While the Scots tried to claim the victory for the kirk, Cromwell was equally emphatic. To his fervent mind, 'it had all the evidences of an absolute victory obtained by the Lord's blessing upon the godly party principally'. That conviction, gathering strength in printed broadsides and around the campfires, was to inspire zealous Londoners as well as the Ironsides.

Religious animosities became increasingly important within the parlia-mentarian coalition in 1644 – so much so that they blunted the military edge gained at Marston Moor. The sudden collapse of controls on the exposition of the gospel had given the laity an unprecedented freedom to speak out. London was the place that mattered above all, since the press could be relied on to report outrages, and there Calvinist orthodoxy began to crumble as unschooled lay beliefs gained an airing.

The primacy of the scriptures, with all their learned apparatus of interpretation, was challenged as layfolk claimed personal illumination. With that challenge came a questioning of all claims of clerical privilege, and even of the principle of an established church with its support in compulsory tithes. Some had been led by the upheaval to believe a new age, the age of the spirit, was dawning. Equally unnerving to the orthodox were the reports of doubts about the fundamental tenets of Calvinism, even of Christianity. Popular rejection of predestination we might think unsurprising; but in the 1640s it seemed to shade into scepticism about the more arcane points of Christian belief, particularly the nature of the Trinity and the existence of hell. Alarmed conservatives had more practical grounds for concern too. As London radicals 'gathered' churches across parish boundaries they undermined not only ecclesiastical order but also civil administration, and parochial poor relief.

The extent of dissolution was certainly exaggerated then, and has been since. Parliament's anxiety to leave the issue of the church open for negotiation with the king meant that in law, if not in practice, an episcopal order survived until October 1646. Even the face of worship often changed little. The overwhelming majority of puritans remained loyal to the idea of a national church, and in the 1640s only a tiny minority in London and a few of the other big towns deserted their parish churches in favour of separatist gatherings. Nor was there much enthusiasm for the antiritualist *Directory of Worship* parliament finally published in January 1645. Most parishes, especially in the countryside, seem to have made do with modifications of the old prayer book, especially once Charles in November condemned the *Directory* and commanded that the prayer book be used. And everywhere parishioners and ministers clung to the celebration of Christmas and Easter, despite parliament's ordinances of 1644 and 1647 against 'superstitious' observance of Christmas and other festivals.

But the decline of discipline and the turmoil of war did bring some fragmentation. Essex's MPs were exercised by the inability of even godly ministers in that county in 1643 to collect tithes. Purges by both sides, and the flight of many ministers from violence, emptied pulpits; and in the ensuing vacuum sectarianism and crude irreligion often seemed indistinguishable. Alehouse cynics who mocked those fighting a holy war were matched by well-publicised sectarian outrages – iconoclastic saints urinating in Canterbury Cathedral, the usual horrified rumours of sexual immorality in secret gathered church meetings. The growing fears of puritan gentry and clergy were channelled against Milton's *Doctrine and Discipline of Divorce* of August 1643. Learnedly championing in the name of Christian liberty the right of divorce – for men – where affection was lacking, Milton denounced the 'tyranny' of the arranged marriage, and aggressively disjoined the body physical and the body politic. Sheer 'blasphemy' was bringing disintegration in its wake.

Church settlement was no more inviting a target for parliament than it had been in 1641. Save for the belated establishment of the Westminister Assembly of Divines, the houses limited themselves to ordinances for the destruction of images and sporadic purges of clergy deemed 'scandalous'. But they would not let others take the lead, and carefully confined the Westminister Assembly to its advisory role. Having defeated Laud they had no intention of allowing another set of assertive clerics to claim independence. But many of the godly took the disasters of 1643 as proof of God's judgment on a nation that had sinned by not pursuing reformation. They must therefore hasten the work of the Lord.

The way of the Lord did not stretch clear ahead. There were some who agreed with the Scots. As early as 1641 several London ministers, including Edmund Calamy, had seen in the strict discipline of the presbyterians the means to establish godly rule, to build the godly nation. The Scots' entry into the war heartened these; but independently of Scottish pressure, most of the sixty or so regular attenders in the Westminster assembly had by 1644 swung towards presbyterianism as they learned that separatists in London were rejecting hierarchical structures and any but voluntary discipline. It was to break the new chains of disciplinarian Calvinism, in England as well as Massachusetts, that the congregationalist Roger Williams in 1644 published his clarion for freedom of conscience, *The Bloudy Tenent of Persecution*. Williams's insistent likening of constraint to rape suggests the continuing hold of the body politic metaphor even in the New England wilderness.

The presbyterians' bugbears were various, but it was in 1644 that these seemed to come out into the open. It was then that seven particular (or Calvinist) Baptist churches in London associated, and published a confession of faith. They seemed the very fount of excess: in their exotic central practice of baptising adult believers into their church, in their insistence on a personal experience of faith, in their challenge to the very principle of a corporate national church, and of course in their provocations (an Eastern Association troop baptised a horse in urine). The 'Dippers' were eagerly vilified, above all for the watery orgies their enemies fantasised for them.

More insidious, and therefore ultimately more dangerous, to presbyterian eyes were the Independents (modern congregationalists), so-called from their demand for congregational independence of any superior discipline. The Independents joined the Baptists in reacting against the legalism so characteristic of Calvinism after Perkins. Drawing from the emerging belief of 1641 that the Holy Spirit was at work in the world, they maintained that truth was to be found in the spirit as much as in institutions and formal creeds. But to the outrage of their opponents, the Independents seemed to straddle the crucial fence. The hallmarks of the voluntarist congregation separated from the parochial church structure appeared in their central tenets: God might yet grant further illumination, so liberty for tender protestant consciences was essential; and full membership of the church and access to the sacraments was to be restricted to those in whom the work of grace was apparent, to 'visible saints' who covenanted together to walk in the ways of the Lord. But most Independents were at most semi-separatists. Still committed to the old puritan ideal of godly rule, of national regeneration, they urged a national church as a discipline for the ungodly.

A national frame that provided the satisfaction of spiritual exclusiveness – here was the dream that attracted to Independency godly but undogmatic gentlemen like Nathaniel Fiennes or his father Lord Saye, or Oliver Cromwell. To the disgust of those who sought to pin them down, Independent pastors ranged from Thomas Goodwin and the immensely learned Philip Nye, ordained ministers of the church of England, to the London leather-seller Praise-God Barebone; and beyond Barebone there was Katherine Chidley, ready to wrangle with her pastor and publish her own defences of the congregational way. Under pressure, the handful of Independents in the Westminister Assembly in February 1644 broke the London clergy's self-imposed ban on public controversy by publishing their powerful, if somewhat evasive, *Apologeticall Narration*. The offence this gave to conservative neighbours was compounded by developments in the important parish of St Stephen's, Coleman Street, where John Goodwin had duly succeeded as minister, only to swing to Independency. By early 1644 he had gathered a church in St Stephen's from all over London and was soon refusing the sacraments to any but these select 'saints', thus effectively 'unchurching' the bulk of the parishioners from their own parish church. The danger of Independency seemed clear to those who had eyes to see it.

Their urgent vision of a presbyterian British Jerusalem made the Scots the most alert to Baptist challenge and Independent subversion. The Scots' commissioners fumed at the delaying tactics of the 'apologeticall narrators' whenever the Westminster Assembly discussed discipline: to their inflamed eyes, sectarianism seemed likely not just to pervert England but even to contaminate Scotland if not speedily crushed. To their bafflement, a divided English parliament would not do their work for them. It took the Covenanters a year to appreciate that the eagerness of their 'dear friends' Vane and St John for their entry into the war did not amount to support for presbyterianism. Nevertheless, by the spring of 1644 the Scottish commissioners had concluded that only the swords of their soldiers would put an end to the disregard for their, and God's, wishes. The outcome of battle came to seem almost as important in the struggle within the parliamentarian coalition as in the war against the king.

That any victories should be Scottish was all the more important in view of developments in the armies. The availability of rich livings in vacant parishes created a chronic shortage of regimental chaplains, and opened the soldiers to whomever would exercise his talents among them – be he a returned New England clergyman like Hugh Peter, whose zeal triumphed over the discomforts of camp life, or be he a layman. Those professional rivals Essex and Waller both strove to restrain officers and soldiers who thought they could preach. Manchester and Cromwell went another way as they strove to build a godly and efficient army in the Eastern Association. By early 1644 that force – and particularly Cromwell's cavalry – had begun to acquire a reputation for Independency and sectarianism. Any victory it won might embarrass its allies.

Conservatives were hamstrung by parliament's divisions. But in the localities, away from the London spotlight, they found it easier to respond. Through the winter of 1643–4 Colonel Edward King, Manchester's subordinate in Lincolnshire, persecuted and imprisoned Independents and other sectaries; at a higher level, Manchester's Scottish major-general, Crawford, commanding the infantry, purged Independent officers, to the fury of Cromwell, who like Manchester had hoped to achieve a union of the godly. Cromwell's triumph at the victory on Marston Moor of the 'godly party' was directed at the unyielding presbyterianism of Crawford and of the Scots in the north. And after Marston Moor Cromwell replied to Crawford in kind, promoting Independents and purging presbyterian officers who threatened those who believed as he did.

The Eastern Association army, parliament's most successful, was reduced to paralysis in August and September. Manchester failed to reconcile his subordinates, and the Committee of Both Kingdoms was scarcely more successful. But Manchester's efforts at mediation did not last long, for the Marston Moor campaign had been a watershed for him as well as Cromwell. For all the undogmatic godliness which had made that 'sweet, meek man' the darling of the war party, Manchester remained a proper-tied nobleman who thought twice when insubordination threatened. The conflicts within his own command, and the hostility between Cromwell and the Scots, now led him to conclude that victory might be followed by something even worse than the tyranny of king and bishops, and that a negotiated peace was the only hope. Manchester's swing to the peace party had immediate military consequences – he even threatened to execute Lieutenant-Colonel John Lilburne for seizing a royalist garrison on his own initiative. There was little doubting the 'continued averseness to all action', of which Cromwell came to complain bitterly, as the Committee of Both Kingdoms deluged Manchester with unheeded orders to march westwards to rescue the lord general.

The late summer of 1644 was disastrous for the parliamentarian high command. Essex was the first to fall. He had ignored the orders of the Committee of Both Kingdoms and set off into the southwest to pursue the glamour that had so long eluded him by relieving besieged Lyme in Dorset, a major obstacle in the path of the triumphant western royalists. Only success could have justified his disregard for orders, and this eluded him. He relieved Lyme, but he then allowed himself to be bottled up by a surprisingly decisive Charles, and by surprisingly hostile countrymen, in the Cornish peninsula. His cavalry broke through the encirclement, but he himself only managed to escape in a small boat. The surrender of his infantry and artillery at Lostwithiel on 2 September offset the moral, if not the strategic, effects of Marston Moor.

The war party was unable to revel for long in Essex's discomfiture. None of the available parliamentarian forces could on its own block the return eastwards of the victorious royal army, so Manchester was detailed to command a joint force. Co-operation was unlikely amidst such friction. When Manchester and the king finally met, on 27 October in the second battle of Newbury, the parliamentarians could only gain an inglorious draw. Further humiliation followed when on 9 November Charles returned unchallenged, and in full view of the combined parliamentarian army, to retrieve the artillery he had left in the neighbouring Donnington Castle. No parliamentarian general in the southern theatre survived the autumn of 1644 unscathed. Essex was tarnished by Lostwithiel, and Manchester and Waller, and Cromwell too, by Newbury. The Scots alone and at last had achieved something when Newcastle fell on 22 October; but their success came too late to save them from the scorn of the war party.

Waller and Cromwell moved quickly to salvage their reputations by blaming Manchester for Newbury, but in late November the earl counter-attacked. Manchester painted an alarmingly detailed picture of Cromwell as a dangerous subversive who purged presbyterians and despised the nobility and the Scots. He attributed his subordinate's backwardness at Newbury to reluctance to see any but an Independent army win a victory, in hopes of extracting toleration from parliament. The charge of ideological motivation was as explosive as the accusations were plausible – Cromwell's delay in moving westwards remains baffling, though his cavalry probably were, as he claimed, exhausted. Cromwell countered by stressing the doubts Manchester had expressed before Donnington: 'If we fight a hundred times and beat him ninety-nine times, he will be king still ... But if he beat us but once, or the last time, we shall be hanged.'

It was Cromwell whose career was most at risk. The Lords jumped at the chance to destroy the most radical of the generals, and pressed the Commons for a hearing. The Scots joined the fray, and in early December made the unnerving suggestion to peace party leaders that Cromwell be impeached as an 'incendiary'. It was the first sign of the great political shift of 1645, when the disillusioned Scots turned against their old war party allies. More immediately, it gave Essex hope that he might emerge unscathed from the graveyard of reputations.

Political crisis, not innate radicalism, thus occasioned the Self-Denying Ordinance, the Long Parliament's most famous break with the past. The groundwork was laid by Cromwell, the pragmatist, who was never more decisive than in face of disaster. In a dramatic posture of self-sacrifice, on 9 December he told the Commons that he like others had erred, and called on all commanders to submit themselves to the public good, lest the already war-weary people 'enforce you to a dishonourable peace'. It was a bid to extricate something from the morass by taking others down with him; and many were surprised by the widespread support it attracted in parliament and press. What became the Self-Denying Ordinance looked like a war-party ploy, prepared by Cromwell, moved by the intransigent Zouch Tate, warmly seconded by Vane. Why should others have fallen for it, when Manchester might have succeeded in eliminating Cromwell?

Self-denial had the merit of appealing to all. Unpartisan MPs were as capable as the war party of recognising that Charles intended to fight to a finish, and that it would therefore be folly to leave the architects of Lostwithiel and Newbury in command. The Commons' army committee had already been considering reducing the bloated officer corps of the three southern armies, and Cromwell's suggestion of a clean sweep at the top opened a path to a more rational military structure. Furthermore, if self-denial was a war-party ploy it succeeded because the war party had stolen the peace party's clothes. The political nation was unaware of the realities of life in a full-time, war-time parliament, where lawyer-MPs were unable to practise and landowners were cut off from their estates. The peace party had protested that but for the lucrative military or civilian posts of so many members of both houses the war would long have been over. Cromwell's plea for self-sacrifice might help appease the weary cynicism in the country. And perhaps most important, that plea, upon which Tate built his proposal that members of both houses should lay down all their offices, drew not only on the language of the peace party but also of mainstream puritanism. In the manifest failures of this godly cause lay God's judgment on self-seeking. Cromwell therefore secured an almost religious hearing.

The Self-Denying Ordinance is inseparably associated with the formation of the New Model Army. In that conjunction many have since seen a radical new departure, and the seeds of victory. Yet remodelling did not immediately invigorate the troops. It brought no change in the rates of pay, which for foot soldiers remained no better than day labourers', and certainly more irregular. Disease was rife, and desertions averaged around 2000 a month for the two months before and after the climactic battle of Naseby; in early June 1645, the month of Naseby, several New Model foot regiments were under strength and several more mutinous. This was not the proud army of later years. It was not an entirely new army either, for it had been formed by merging existing understrength forces. Nor was it a national army, since some regional forces, particularly those of the northern association, and of the western association commanded by Edward Massey from Gloucester, continued to operate more or less independently.

The New Model Army's mixed origin left its unity in doubt, and many royalists relished the prospect of engaging with the 'new noddle'. In hopes of limiting the upheaval, parliament-men recognised that existing regiments must be kept together. The formation of the New Model Army therefore saw less of a purge of the officers, and more pragmatic horse-trading, than used to be believed. On the whole the foot regiments kept their old officers, as did the horse. And whatever new political fire the New Model Army possessed did not rise from its commanders. The new lord general, Sir Thomas Fairfax, former cavalry commander of the northern army, was no sectarian radical though he was more open-minded in his puritanism than many. He was also the most effective, and respectable, general available who did not sit in parliament. Much the same could be said of his major-general, 'honest' Philip Skippon, who had been Essex's infantry commander.

But the New Model Army did break with the past. The rapidity and scale of Fairfax's marches in 1645 testify to the benefits of freeing an army from a regional base. Several godly and energetic plebeians, like Thomas Pride, leavened the New Model's officers. And partisanship shaped its construction from the moment that self-denial was applied to the Earl of Essex by a majority of one in the Commons. Often bitter debates on the officer list left Scottish officers from the Eastern Association among a number of significant, and surely deliberate, omissions.

The response of the peers underscored the political meaning of remodelling. To them the Self-Denying Ordinance seemed the most grievous in a long line of slights. True, they still possessed their institutional role as one of the two houses, and in men like the dignified Essex, 'old subtlety' Saye, or Northumberland, a close ally now of Saye and St John, they included politicians of the first rank. But their self-confidence was sapped by the pressures of war. Distaste for unpleasant decisions, and for the increasingly prominent radicals who took such decisions willingly, had so shrunk their numbers that twenty was by early 1645 a respectable attendance in the upper house. For men who had so much to lose disengagement became a tempting course, all the more so since the Commons repeatedly relied on their control over money matters to shoulder opposition aside. By 1644 Lord Willoughby, witness to continuing pressure by City and Commons, 'thought it a crime to be a nobleman'. The peers' one consolation had been the military prominence of many of their number; self-denial would remove this. If its aim was self-sacrifice, then peers would rank disproportionately among the victims. Not surprisingly, they dug in their heels.

But the pressures of war overcame even aristocratic pride. The inexorable failure during these months of the latest peace negotiations, the treaty (so-called) of Uxbridge, convinced enough of the peers that necessity must be confronted. That failure also gave them and their faint-hearted allies in the Commons a sufficient political shock to force them into line.

The politicking that came with each winter's lull in campaigning had given the Scots their chance to try to convince Charles of the virtues of presbyteries. Cynical war party members were willing to allow their former allies their heads, since Charles's loathing for the kirk was well known. Furthermore, the hardest of military men could see the need for gestures about peace when popular discontent with the war continued to grow, not least in London. Parliament's inability to estimate the costs of war, and its greater inability to ensure that all taxes came to the centre, left it as dependent as ever on the City for loans; and there the old conservative elite had regained some of the power it had lost in the London revolution of 1641–2. Should the Scots be thwarted over peace negotiations, they might be expected to apply dangerous pressure through the control over London's coal trade that the capture of Newcastle had brought them.

Similar considerations applied at Oxford. As Charles countenanced self-help by the soldiers the royalist cause became a harder affair. Not all new men were tyrants, and the greatest of them, Rupert, who ruled Wales and its borders, could use his rank to obtain deference as deftly as Manchester in the Eastern Association. Nevertheless, while the parliamentarians reserved their worst brutality for Charles's 'Irish' recruits, the contempt for domestic disloyalty shown by honour-driven royalist commanders like Byron and Sir Michael Woodhouse gave rise to some ugly incidents. When the Oxford parliament assembled for its second winter session in 1644–5 Charles heard a wave of protests, and of demands for peace talks. He himself felt only disdain for negotiations, and in a letter to his wife in the spring of 1645 denounced critics in the 'mongrel parliament', as he revealingly termed the loyal Oxford parliament he had created. But he had reason to go through the motions.

The Scots nevertheless lived in hope that winter. Their new friends in the peace party were in many respects more congenial than Vane and Hesilrig, since the Scots saw themselves, and presbyterianism, as allies of monarchy and supporters of order; and the new alliance certainly improved the chances for presbyterianism. The houses responded to Scottish promptings by at last sending the attainted Archbishop Laud to the scaffold on 8 January 1645. While that symbolic blow against episcopacy and the popish plot was unlikely to persuade Charles, parliament appeared ready to present him with presbyterian terms. Although the Commons had set their face against the iure divino church of the Scots, most MPs sought discipline and hierarchy more eagerly than ever. In January 1645 they resolved in principle that the future government of the church would be presbyterian; and both houses passed without a division the Westminster assembly's directory of worship, a directory that was far simpler than the old prayer book but still provided a structured form of worship. Neither separatists nor episcopalians would find any place in this sun.

Support for presbyterianism did not, however, entail agreement with the Scots that that was what the war was about. At Westminster the trust-worthiness of Charles was the issue, as it had always been. The peace terms finally sent to the talks at Uxbridge in January and February 1645 therefore amounted to a demand that Charles surrender his powers indef-initely, see dozens of his supporters excluded from pardon – and accept presbyterianism. Charles saw little reason to agree.

Like the most anti-papist parliamentarian, the king would have no truck with ungodly enemies, whom God would surely overthrow – as He had so recently done at Lostwithiel and Newbury. And the parliamentarians were in disarray, not only over the Self-Denying Ordinance but also over the Uxbridge terms: in the manoeuvrings, two of the peace party leaders, Holles and Whitelocke, had engaged in almost treasonable dealings with the king. But Charles's calculus was not confined to Westminster and the English map, for his was more than ever a British war. He planned to bring further troops from Ireland to England, and Ireland was already tipping the balance in Scotland. There, the old Antrim dream of shipping Ulster Gaels across to hit the Campbells in the rear had finally come to fruition. In September 1644 Alasdair McColla McDonald led the Highland charge that brought the Earl of Montrose the first of his remarkable victo-ries over the Covenanters. Together, they might yet undo the results of Marston Moor in the northern theatre.

Parliament's response to such rebuffs was uncompromising. McColla's elan provoked the houses' order of October 1644 that any Irishman taken in arms in England was to be summarily executed. And the commission issued to Fairfax as new lord general omitted the pious declaration that parliament and its armies were fighting to preserve the person of the king. If the houses could imagine the body politic without Charles Stuart to head it, then the Lords could accept military reorganisation. In April, still protesting, they did so. But the ironic result of the winter's efforts, to which so many had agreed in the hope of removing Cromwell, was that Cromwell was left in place. It is possible that this was the war-party ploy of legend; but the Lords' obstructionism certainly helped. The usual rhythm of war was politics in winter, fighting in summer, but the Lords haggled over the list of officers so long that by the time the New Model Army was on the point of meeting the king in battle there was still no lieutenant-general of the horse. Fairfax's urgent request that he be allowed to keep Cromwell, as the best available commander, extracted a grudging three-month commission.

Fortunately for the parliamentarians, they were not alone in their disar-ray. Feuding amongst Charles's western commanders brought to nothing the king's hopes of consolidating that region to balance the loss of the north; and the tetchy Rupert was once more bitterly at odds with the erratic Digby, Charles's main adviser. Rather than resolve the squabbles, as parliament had spent the winter doing, Charles turned his gaze north in the spring of 1645. Chester, vital as the entry-port for reinforcements from Ireland, was under siege; beyond, McColla and Montrose had slaughtered Argyll's Campbell clansmen at Inverlochy in February. Two tempting courses lay open to Charles. He could relieve Chester en route to join Montrose, and regain the north; or he could destroy the fledgling 'new noddle' by catching Fairfax's weary men on their way back towards Oxford from their first, ill-planned foray into the west. There was much to be said for either plan, so Charles opted for both – leaving each of the divided royalist forces smaller than those under Fairfax.

The campaign that culminated at Naseby in Leicestershire on 14 June is an object lesson in divided counsels. Westminster's divisions almost allowed the king to escape. The chance of trapping him in the north between the New Model and the Covenanters had little appeal for the politicians. The peace party thought more of the defence of the parliamentarian heartland, while many in the war party dreamed of Oxford, now stripped of most of its defenders. But when Rupert, the royalist commander-in-chief, sacked Leicester, on the edge of the undefended Eastern Association, all awoke to the dangers of leaving the main royal army unattended to. That the indecisive Charles fought at all when Fairfax's forces badly outnumbered his own must be attributed to the insistence of Digby, who was anxious to spite the more careful Rupert.

Rupert almost won at Naseby, a fact that owes something to the composition of the New Model Army as well as to its weariness. The cavalry wing that broke was of mixed origin, while that which held was purely Eastern Association, suggesting how risky remodelling had been. Rupert's own cavalry once more proved unstoppable; but Cromwell kept his under tight control and brought it round decisively on to the royalist infantry in the centre, destroying Charles's major field army and the remains of his reputation. The king's captured correspondence, published by parliament as *The King's Cabinet Opened*, revealed his contempt for negotiations and attempts to gain aid from the Catholic Irish and the pope, even as it displayed his private uxoriousness. Meanwhile Cromwell and others grew more confident that the hand of God was with them.

The political coup for the war party was as great as the military victory, and both were sorely needed. Despite the failure of the Uxbridge treaty the war party's standing in the mire at Westminster had weakened. Messy disclosures about dealings with Oxford tarnished both war and peace parties during the summer, and though the ensuing attempts on both sides to use treason charges against political opponents detached a frightened Whitelocke from his peace party friends, they also underlined just how explosive would be the making of the final peace. Indeed, the appalling political problem of a likely military victory over an intransigent king reduced the remnants of Pym's old middle group to what has been called little more than a state of mind. But there was no question of the growing pressure outside parliament for peace.

In the country most of the passions of 1642 had been drowned in suffering. The civil war may have begun amateurishly, but by 1643 there were probably 110 000 men in arms, some 10 per cent of the adult male population – a proportion not to be reached again until the French Revolutionary Wars. Although such concentrations brought contracts for clothing, food and equipment, they could devastate economy and society. One-fifth of Gloucester was demolished to strengthen its defences in 1643, two-thirds of Taunton destroyed in the 1645 siege, and Birmingham, Bolton and Leicester brutally sacked. But though areas like East Anglia, Cornwall, mid-Wales, rarely heard the tramp of the marching armies, all had to pay.

The official burdens were bad enough. The parliamentary weekly assessment, paralleled in the more orderly royalist areas by the 'contributions' to Oxford, was the equivalent of an income tax of 10 per cent or more, or almost one old parliamentary subsidy every two weeks. Most counties paid more in assessments every month than they had paid in ship money every year. The opposing capitals saw little enough of this money, but the soldiers ensured that it was collected. After the chaos of the early months of the war counties on both sides made it common practice to make groups of parishes responsible for the support of small detachments. Not surprisingly, yields in both parliamentarian and royalist counties approached 100 per cent. And while it was not until the partial restoration of order after 1645 that the excise had much impact outside London, other rates fell heavily. In some parliamentarian counties the money 'loaned' by householders in 1642–5 on the propositions – a loan in name only, with grave consequences for 'the public faith' – equalled the return on the assessments.

Localised conflict meant far heavier burdens, imposed less officially. The failure of Oxford and Westminster to draw money away from the counties meant that unpaid soldiers lived at free quarter, billeted on householders who were given promissory notes (which were only occasionally redeemed) in return for room and board. Estimates are problematic, but the parliamentary accounts committee in contested Buckinghamshire suggested that free quarter cost more than all forms of taxation. Most regions suffered, for the bulk of the men served not in the main field armies but scattered in local forces and petty garrisons. Since far more men were fighting for a living than for a cause, unofficial costs were probably heavier still. One Cheshire gentleman was pillaged three times by each side. It was during this war that the word 'plunder' entered the English language.

War also had indirect consequences. London's coal-less winter of 1643–4, when the king held Newcastle, was only the most dramatic of the shortages inflicted by the fighting. Big merchants were reluctant to commit their capital, and inland traders suffered from marauding troops of either side. Rents fell as farmers whose horses or cattle were seized, or whose corn was trampled, were unable to pay, or abandoned their holdings. By 1646 it was generally agreed that rents were at one-third of their pre-war levels; in contested areas like the Thames valley often nothing was collected. The business of the central courts similarly declined during the war, by perhaps 50–75 per cent of the already attenuated 1642 level. This decline flowed partly from the insecurities of war. Much of the country was lost to parliament, parties and witnesses were reluctant to travel, and in 1643 parliament refused to allow the judges to go on their assize circuits. But political uncertainties intensified the difficulties, for in 1644 Charles set up competing central courts at Oxford. The clogged judicature of the House of Lords in these years speaks to the desperation of litigants, and so perhaps does the growing animus against lawyers.

Injustices multiplied without redress. The Warwickshire quarter sessions failed to meet for three years, and although the county committee did much of the work, considerable day-to-day business was left undone. By the end of the war, local officials such as constables and churchwardens had not been replaced in many parts of Yorkshire, and rates for road repair or the upkeep of the poor had not been collected; in Dorchester the workhouse for poor children closed from 1643 to 1646. The human consequences of such social dislocation are hard to grasp, but they may be apparent in the unprecedented activities of the 'witch-finder general', Matthew Hopkins, in East Anglia in 1645.

Local administration certainly continued to function. Towns tried to pretend that it was business as usual, although many of their old powers were eroded. Most were steadily subordinated to the county governments, while those that were garrisoned found petty dictators in their governors. In parliamentarian counties the county committees were invariably disliked for their novelty and the arbitrariness of their methods. Abandoning jury presentments, the committees sequestered royalists' estates, with no appeal other than to the central parliamentary committee for sequestrations; they had summary power to fine and imprison for non-compliance, and they also set the rates for fiscal levies. Often too the committees intervened in ecclesiastical affairs by removing 'scandalous' ministers. As one disgusted Essex clergyman, Richard Drake of Radwinter, complained in 1645, 'This is the glorious "liberty of the subject" they used to set forth.' The royalist counties followed a similar path away from the ideals of 1628.

Most historians who have studied the committees have commented favourably on their industry and general probity, but those who suffered at their hands were unlikely to agree. The inclusion amongst the committees' functions of the sequestration of the estates of royalist 'delinquents' had alienated many local notables, who often withdrew out of unwillingness to act against men to whom they might be related; and in areas that had been royalist there was naturally a cleaner sweep of the old governors. The committees co-opted new men, who carried no prestige in their names and who were perforce more reliant on the troops and on the backing of the centre. Sometimes the new men were the humble townsmen caricatured in Sir John Oglander's sneers at the pedlar, baker, apothecary and farmers on the Isle of Wight Committee; more often they came from lesser gentry, professionals and merchants, in the larger pool of which men radical enough, or hardened enough, could be found. Furthermore, the complexity of wartime government bred a strange new species, the petty official. The agent of the county committee or of the excise commissioners probably saw his position as a step on the social ladder at least as often as he saw it as service to a cause, and behaved accordingly. Every revolution throws up its own bureaucracy.

And every revolution generates its own backlash. This was manifested variously, most obviously in the localism and footdragging that deprived the armies of supplies and hampered their movements. It even contaminated the previously energetic committee of the Eastern Association: facing the submergence of its army in the New Model in the spring of 1645 it petulantly declared, 'The safety of the kingdom . . . was not our work.' But hostility to war sometimes took a more active form. Protests were at first piecemeal, with sporadic vigilante attacks on straggling troopers; but there were localised revolts in Kent in 1643 and 1645, and soon trouble came more widely. Charles's efforts to build a new army after Marston Moor imposed further strains on the Welsh borders, and local garrisons whose supplies were diverted increasingly turned to living off the land. In some of the poorer, less 'gentrified' uplands of Herefordshire and Worcestershire village 'clubmen' banded together in the winter of 1644–5 in futile attempts to resist the marauding soldiers.

Not all resistance was merely the work of exhausted neutrals, for many opponents of military abuse still saw themselves as part of an active national cause. That winter, angry gentry in several counties along the Welsh borders came together in short-lived 'associations', seeking to curb the violence of the royalist soldiery by taking on themselves the business of tax collection and supply for the king. Had similar indigenous royalist organisation emerged in 1642, the king's party might not have fallen victim so soon to military abuse. More strikingly, some of the countrymen who associated in Dorset and Wiltshire in May 1645 to halt plunder and preserve the peace were outraged by parliament's recent prohibition of the prayer book, so much a part of the fabric of life. As Fairfax marched west after Naseby he was confronted by huge and threatening demonstrations. In Somerset, on the other hand, countrymen aided Fairfax in his pursuit of the last royalist field army under lord Goring after

Naseby. The distribution of Fairfax's clubmen supporters in the upland wood/pasture zone that had rallied for parliament in 1642 suggests that the patterns of popular alignment discernible then still held, though modified by intense suffering.

Local alignments may have been critical in 1642, but by 1645 they could not halt veteran forces, and above all the New Model, which after Naseby seemed to sweep all before it. Some of its success was probably owed to more regular pay, but some was owed to zeal, in the cavalry in particular. When Fairfax at last caught up with Goring on 10 July near Langport in Somerset, the outnumbered royalists had taken up a commanding position on a hill approached only by a lane wide enough for four horsemen abreast. To the godly officers around Fairfax there could be only one explanation for a victory here. As he watched the royalists break, the sectarian major Thomas Harrison 'with a loud voice [broke] forth into the praises of God with fluent expressions, as if he had been in a rapture'. And Cromwell, always elated by battle, concluded in awe, 'To see this, is it not to see the face of God?' Two months later the parliamentarian control over the southwest was confirmed when, with too few troops to man the walls and a quarter of the population dead of plague, Rupert surrendered Bristol. The city had been the king's last claim to credibility in Europe. Too often slow to show gratitude for past service, Charles never forgave his nephew for the shattering defeat.

At this point the God of battles seemed to be speaking unambiguously everywhere but in Scotland, where Montrose's motley army was repeatedly humiliating the Covenanters. The greatest victory of the charismatic ex-Covenanter and his clansmen allies came at Kilsyth in August 1645, and it left them master of both Edinburgh and Glasgow. If developments in the other Stuart kingdoms had brought Charles to his knees in 1638–41, those kingdoms might yet prop him up again: indeed, they must do so, for God had enjoined monarchy. Since the spring of 1645 Charles had been seeking an accord with the Confederation of Kilkenny, which now controlled most of Ireland. His aim was no longer to gain access to any residual 'English' forces in Ireland but to the Confederation's own troops, though these seemed to many of his British subjects the servants of Antichrist. He sought an accord the more urgently since the papacy seemed about to give full and formal recognition to the Confederation, a move that would undercut his claims over his western kingdom. On 25 August agreement was reached by the Roman Catholic Earl of Glamorgan, Worcester's son. In return for 10 000 Confederation troops, to be used anywhere in Britain, toleration of Catholicism was to be fully established in Ireland.

Charles's pan-British umbrella collapsed as soon as it had seemed to open. In Scotland the ancestral hostilities across the Highland line made the position of Montrose and his Highlanders unstable at best once they reached the Lowlands; it worsened when, instead of consolidating,

Montrose obeyed the king's command to move south towards the border. Unable to convert McColla's followers to the king's British strategy, or to keep them together as they moved further from the hills, he was routed at Philiphaugh on 13 September by Covenanting forces hotly returned from England. The ensuing slaughter of captives and camp-followers was warmly approved by both Scottish and English Calvinists as the just judgment of God on a campaign that had been scarred by tribal atrocities on both sides. The end came in early November with the arrival at Kilkenny of a papal envoy, Cardinal Rinuccini, with demands that even Charles found impossible – not just for toleration but for a Roman Catholic government in Ireland under the king. Although Charles disavowed Glamorgan and briefly arrested him, the capture of some of the treaty correspondence further tainted the reputation of a king shown ready to use Irish Catholics against his protestant subjects.

The king's last hope, of a dash to a popular reception in a war-weary London, crumbled in the spring of 1646. Facing instead the sordid likelihood of capture by an angry army and an equally angry majority in parliament, he turned to the Scots. Encouraged by his more flexible wife and by Scotland's 'auld ally', the French government, Charles saw hope in the Scots' greater willingness to let him retain his civil powers, and hope too in the Anglo-Scottish tensions that had grown with the alliance of the two kingdoms. But no more than in the 1630s could he comprehend the convictions of the Covenanters. He expected that when faced with their God-given king it would be they who would make religious concessions. He was genuinely surprised at the taunts to which he was subject when in April, having slipped out of besieged Oxford, he surrendered himself to the Scottish army besieging Newark.

The Scots' position was awkward. Possessing the person of the king they possessed the prime bargaining card in any settlement, and with it the chance to avenge themselves on their contemptuous English allies. Even an agreement that at Westminster seemed a sell-out would probably hold, given the general longing for peace. But success depended on speed, for suspicions of Scottish intentions were bound to grow, and with them the risk of a new war. Withdrawing to the greater safety of Newcastle, the Covenanters deluged Charles with godly sermons in hope of his conversion. Although in his later English captivity Charles was to show a surprising personal unconcern for the English prayer book, he never wavered in his hatred of the Covenant.

Thwarted, the Scots that summer gave the second bite of the cherry of peace to their former allies. Even though the houses were dominated now by the peace party, the terms sent from Westminster in July grated on Scottish nerves. The newly enacted parliamentary form of presbyterianism was scarcely the covenanted kirk, and there was a further blow in the British component of the propositions sent to Newcastle. The explicit subordination of Ireland to the parliament and kingdom of England was far from the joint defence and security for which the Scots had hoped when they entered England in 1640 and again in 1644. Yet the blow to Charles's pride was worse. In the harsh climate created by his Irish undertakings even peace party attitudes had hardened. The Newcastle propositions promised to extend indefinitely the parliamentary control over the militia and government from the twenty years demanded at Uxbridge the previous year.

Recognition of defeat was no more capable than covenanting sermons of persuading the king. Confident that his English subjects loved the parliament and presbyterianism as little as he did, and that his enemies would fall out anyway, Charles played for time. Frustrated by such disingenuousness, and not daring to take him back to Edinburgh where he would become a rallying-point for the anti-Covenanter sentiment evident after Montrose's victory at Kilsyth, the Covenanters in August 1646 opened negotiations for the transfer of the king to parliament. They were assured by their few friends at Westminster that a safe and moderate, even if not a more presbyterian, peace could be extracted from the goodwill that would well up once Charles was safely in England.

All members of the parliamentarian coalition had assumed that Charles would at last come to terms. To the peace party that point had seemed likely to be when stalemate had been reached, and to the war party, when the king had been beaten. Few had appreciated that in no circumstances would Charles concede. The Scots found others to take Charles from them, but his new gaolers might not be so lucky. That August, Dr Robert Baillie, one of the Scottish commissioners in London, predicted gloomily that 'that mad man . . . will [take] down with him all his posterity, and monarchy'.

|10|

Reaction and revolution, 1646–1649

The ending of the fighting solved nothing. Settlement would have been hard to achieve in the best of circumstances, since new religious divisions had opened and old ones hardened, while assumptions of community and body politic had been challenged in the fighting. But these were not the best of circumstances, dominated as they were by the central fact of an intransigent king whom few of his opponents could bring themselves to trust. There were many more now who would have understood Pym's interest in regencies under amenable princes of the royal blood.

Peace was to prove more inflammatory than war for other reasons. Settlement required the disbandment of the Scottish and English armies; but disbandment required money. Such was the desire for peace and an end to burdens that the City, if presented with a viable plan, would nevertheless probably have tightened its belt further and lent the money until the tax yields could recover. But neither the City nor the parliamentary leaders had freedom of action. The instability of their world was not just the work of the king. In February 1646 the presbyterian Thomas Edwards published the first part of *Gangraena*, his massive survey of unorthodoxy and dissidence in London. However inflated his rhetoric, the fascinating detail he provided of developments in shops, houses and taverns has the ring of truth; and the story he told of a radical awakening was as momentous as his inflamed language of the gangrenous body was revealing. The reactions of the parliamentary leaders to royal malevolence might by now be almost predictable. But what many of them perceived as a gathering threat from below might stampede them.

The forces driving such a stampede were material as well as ideological. The already constricted wartime economy was convulsed by post-war harvests almost as disastrous as those of the 1590s. At its later 1640s level of £120 000 a month parliament's monthly assessment was the equivalent of at least eighteen pre-war parliamentary subsidies every year; and the novel excise had, like most sales taxes, an inequitable impact on poor consumers. Moreover, the proud hopes that the reorganisation of the spring of 1645 would enable the New Model Army to pay its way had taken a mere six months to prove vain. Thereafter the new army took free quarter like all the other forces, and added one more broken promise to a long list.

The burden of the soldiers was intensified by their own discontent. By the end of the war the pay due to all parliament's armies was almost £3 million in arrears, a sum that needs to be compared with the pre-war royal revenues of around £1 million per annum. Although the New Model was pacified throughout 1646 with intermittent funds, the soldiers in the scattered regional forces fared much worse. Between 1645 and the spring of 1647 about half the English counties reported incidents of military disorder or mutiny. In the country discontent flared as both rents and rain fell, food prices rose, depression deepened and a devastating plague outbreak came on the heels of the assorted diseases spread by the ragged armies. Clubmen grew active again, especially in the southwest, and found leaders among local gentry infuriated by the continuing arbitrariness of the county committees.

The post-war outcry was too loud for the houses to ignore. The old peace party of Essex, Holles and their ally Sir Philip Stapleton seized on it eagerly to advance their campaign for a return to normality. But it proved a mixed blessing even for them, since it risked carrying them faster than was politic. That risk grew when, with peace to be pursued rather than the distasteful necessities of war, conservative absentees from both houses drifted back, reinforced by new MPs elected to seats vacated by death or purge. The Commons' aim in thus 'recruiting' the house was to prepare parliament for the negotiations that must come, since royalists were certain to challenge its claims to be representative of England. But there were partisan implications to the 235 'recruiter' MPs, almost half the total membership, elected in 1645–6. Although the elections were, as in the past, primarily local in their concerns they reflected prevailing political realities. Recruiters elected in 1646 tended to be far less militant than those of late 1645, particularly since in 1646 elections were held in pacified, but still largely royalist, counties like Cornwall. The peace party was accordingly reinforced.

The assumption that the king's surrender ought swiftly to lessen the nation's burdens held strongly in the countryside; but if it ever existed at Westminster, it soon crumbled. The parliamentary majority knew the New Model must remain on foot – a vengeful Charles might leave Newcastle at the head of a Scottish army, regroup the defeated cavaliers and impose a presbyterian settlement that would give him the sword. But the Scots' failure to convert the king had for the moment made them easy, if expensive, to deal with. Over the bitter protests of those who felt that the Covenanters had hardly earned their keep, the houses agreed in September 1646 to pay them £400 000 towards the support promised in 1643. Hobbes and Clarendon were not alone in thinking this blood-money for the king. When in February 1647 the Covenanters handed Charles over to their paymasters and went home, it was with Newcastle housewives' cries of 'Judases!' ringing in their ears. Parliament made its preoccupation with the Scots brutally clear when it then promptly voted a drastic reduction in its armies. The wartime total of over 40 000 men would be cut to a standing force of 6400 cavalry and a few minor garrisons; a larger contingent was to be dispatched for the reconquest of Ireland.

Sending the soldiers home was the core of Holles's strategy. Disbandment would pacify country resentment, neutralise men suspected of dangerous radicalism, deprive the parliamentary intransigents of their military allies, and thus permit a less uncompromising stance towards the king. There seemed to lie the road to a lasting peace, based on something like the status quo of 1641. And though Holles was himself by preference probably a moderate episcopalian, he was ready to insure the whole by the abolition of episcopacy. Not only would the lands and wealth of the bishops and cathedrals help to pay off both English and Scottish troops and reconquer Ireland; abolition would strengthen the Covenanters' respect for his credentials. With the Scots duly reassured, Holles moved swiftly to pay them off. Removal of the hated Scots in turn consolidated his support at Westminster, and enabled him turn the committee at Derby House that had been created to oversee the reconquest of Ireland into a more powerful executive body than the lapsed committee of both kingdoms. He then prepared for the disbandment of the English forces whose rationale for existence seemed ended.

However realistic Holles's appreciation of sentiment in the country and in parliament, his was hardly a consensus programme. The old war-party minority feared that disbandment would allow a vengeful king to appeal to a weary nation, and suspected Holles of intending a sell-out. They fought bitterly if fruitlessly against his proposals, dividing the house on the disbandment of each petty garrison. During the war politicians had sought to preserve at least a semblance of unity, but in late 1646 divisions were called as often as in the tumultuous days of late 1641. The struggle for a settlement saw the collapse of the parliamentarian coalition.

Understanding post-war politics is obstructed by our modern hankering for parties. Most seventeenth-century minds thought instead of personalities. 'The Juntoes', the favourite generality for the few dozen contending speakers, signalled the human components. Sometimes, and revealingly, groups were identified in physical terms ('the fiery', 'the luke-warm'), or regional ('the northern men'); but rarely in ideological. While it might be accurate to refer to the Essex–Holles–Stapleton clique on the one hand and the Saye–Northumberland–Vane–St John–Hesilrig–Cromwell group on the other, it would hardly be elegant. Historians have therefore adopted the only generalised contemporary taxonomy on offer for this period when the old labels, 'war' and 'peace' party, are no longer viable. That taxonomy originated with the Scots, who assumed that politics centred on religion, and identified enemies and friends accordingly. Since the threat of sectarianism had driven them into the arms of the peace party they associated the war party with their other bugbears, the Independent divines of the Westminster Assembly; and they assumed that the peace party members were presbyterians like themselves.

Few English politicians used religious labels to explain politics in 1647, still fewer in 1646. Parliament's faltering steps in late 1645 towards the establishment of a presbyterian church had been relatively uncontentious, though preparations for a political settlement in the winter of 1646–7 proved highly divisive. While Holles did see presbyterianism as the only remaining path to order, some of his allies longed for a limited episcopacy; and almost all of them, on the English side of the border, were far more concerned to settle with the king than to establish any specific form of church government. On the other hand, Hesilrig and Zouch Tate, hardliners whom the Scots classed as 'Independent' for their politics, were in fact rigorous religious presbyterians. And in the winter of 1646–7 the discontents of the New Model Army, which the Scots identified as an Independent army at least partly because their enemies had always preferred it to their own, were overwhelmingly material rather than ideological.

Yet the Scots had a point. Many of the old war party were indeed religious Independents, and there were none around Holles. Independents, and Baptists too, were to be found among the New Model cavalry and in its officer corps: it was not for nothing that Cromwell had concluded his letter announcing the victory at Naseby with a plea for liberty of conscience. And since the Scots, who were central actors in the political drama, were moved by religious zeal, all who reacted with or against them were, indirectly at least, also moved. So the presbyterian Hesilrig opposed the Scots for the zeal with which they would sacrifice everything but presbyterianism to the king. The 'presbyterian party' is therefore a useful shorthand for the political allies of the Scots, mostly from the old peace party, and scarcely doctrinaire church-warriors. Equally, the 'Independent party' makes some sense as a term of convenience for the bulk of the former war party and middle group: with very few exceptions not republicans, but deeply distrustful of Charles and of Scottish efforts to settle on a religious platform.

Whatever the complications of analysis, Holles's strategy found justification in the speed with which MPs swung behind the efforts to reduce the armies. The February 1647 vote on disbandment was followed by a Commons' resolution on 8 March to rescind exemptions from the Self-Denying Ordinance and to reduce the officer list. These steps were eagerly represented as necessary economy measures and a return to legal propriety. They were read as partisan moves against Cromwell, who was still an MP, and other officers, like Harrison, or Commissary-General Ireton, Cromwell's son-in-law, who had been elected as recruiters.

Partisan readings came easily. Holles's motives seemed to lie plain to view in the decision to begin disbandment not with the disorderly provincial forces, but with the disciplined, and militarily distinguished, New Model. Petitioners in East Anglia did not vent only material complaints that spring when they feared being 'eaten up, enslaved, and destroyed' by the army; and William Strode MP boasted back in Somerset, 'We will destroy them all . . . Sir Thomas Fairfax will be deceived, for part of his army will join with us, and besides the Scots are very honest men and will come to assist us.' Some of the presbyterian party militants already contemplated using force against the New Model. Not surprisingly, disquiet grew in the army as well as amongst the parliamentary Independents.

The soldiers' unease drew heavily from the material prospects facing them. The pay of the cavalry in particular was over a year in arrears, and the service in Ireland held out as compensation held little appeal. Furthermore, a taxpayers' strike as sweeping as that of 1639–40 was developing. The City of London was 72 per cent in arrears on its monthly assessments from June to September 1646, and parliament itself gave an alarming signal when in its eagerness to gratify the country it allowed the assessment to lapse for the following six months. The excise was no more fruitful: anti-excise riots in London and Norwich in the winter and spring gave violent point to what can be deduced from the army's failure to receive any excise money between November 1646 and June 1649. If left to the goodwill of a country that had had enough of payments, the soldiers faced a bleak future.

There were more emotive issues than pay. The return of peace allowed judges, JPs, and juries to resume some of their normal duties, and to pay off civilian scores against the military. Reports abounded early in 1647 of soldiers being hanged for the horses or supplies they had seized for war service. Men who had fought and bled, and seen their friends die, to stop a common, and some believed an Antichristian, foe, now reacted angrily as they were rewarded with persecution. In mid-March the soldiers, aided by equally disgruntled officers, prepared to petition Lord General Fairfax about their grievances.

This was not yet a revolutionary army. The many moderate or presbyterian officers first appointed to the New Model were still in their posts; and, like all generals, more radical commanders such as Cromwell and Ireton favoured discipline. Of course, no army fitted the hierarchical model, if only because common troopers wore swords, the badge of gentility; all armies offered 'new' men opportunities to rise, and all armies, whether in royal, parliamentary, Scottish or Spanish service, periodically mutinied over their material grievances. But in March 1647 the New Model was silent on the score of religion and liberty. Perhaps half of the New Model's soldiers were conscripts or royalist turncoats. In his short service as an army chaplain in 1645 Richard Baxter worried about the army's irreligion; but he did express concern too about other developments. Amongst the more prosperous and literate cavalry troopers were many 'saints', godly volunteers impatient of the discipline on which parliament seemed bent, and made confident of the justice of their cause, and God's blessing on it, by victory. Fiery regimental chaplains like John Saltmarsh and above all Hugh Peter had played some part in this awakening; but in the dangerous inactivity of peace soldiers and junior officers needed (or, in the largely unprovided army, were given) little clerical encouragement. Plebeian lay preachers, conversions to the sectarian exclusiveness of Baptism: these probably alarmed conservatives less than the spreading conviction that a new age was dawning as Antichrist went down. The antinomianism (the sense of transcendence over the formal demands of the moral law) latent in radical protestantism was fast coming to the surface. The soldiers who believed themselves above all scriptural ordinances appalled Baxter the most.

Whether the army would in the early spring of 1647 have acquiesced in a presbyterian settlement that made provision for its needs is impossible to determine. One of the most militant regiments later testified that payment of a mere four months' of its arrears, instead of the six weeks' cash offered, would have persuaded it to disband. Spread throughout the New Model that would have required about £200 000, by no means beyond the lending powers of a City of London that feared and resented the soldiers. Parliament's demurral at such a prospect certainly deserves sympathy – the taxpayers' strike, the cries from quarter sessions, indeed, the localised reappearance of clubmen in the west, made renewed civil war seem a real possibility should new burdens be imposed. But Holles inflamed the crisis unnecessarily, and by challenging the army gave it a political cause. Here, Essex's death in late 1646 proved crucial, for the earl's concern for his fellow soldiers might have restrained Holles's gut conservatism. Instead, driven by the dire fantasies of City oligarchs and county petitioners that radicals in London and the army were about to make common political cause, Holles over-reacted. On 30 March the Commons published a 'declaration of dislike': the soldier petitioners to Fairfax were 'enemies of the state and disturbers of the public peace'. In the following weeks both houses galloped intemperately towards disbandment.

The radicalisation of soldiers who had expected the thanks of a grateful nation and met instead public denunciation, and the declaration's slur on the very 'honour' of the army, was not long in coming. Facing the bleak alternative of penurious disbandment or equally penurious and undoubtedly dangerous service in Ireland, at the end of April cavalry regiments quartered in East Anglia led the way by electing 'agitators' to act for them. The 'agitprop' connotations of the word were far in the future; furthermore, the election of representatives was a common tactic of discontented soldiers throughout Europe. But while the concerns voiced by both agitators and junior officers throughout most of May remained heavily professional, disquiet over the broader political purposes of Holles's presbyterian majority was and is obvious.

The context of army unrest was by no means merely material and professional. Since the conservative backlash was driven not just by resentments at the burdens of war but also by clerical disciplinarians like Edwards and Ephraim Pagitt – whose *Heresiography* went through four editions in 1646–7 – we should not be surprised that several of the agitators were Baptists. Those activist saints found it easy to make a case. The houses' determined remodelling of the London militia looked like a plot to create a counter-force and then sell out to the king and clergy. At the end of April agitators complained of 'tyrants' amongst the Derby House clique. Their suspicions seemed confirmed when, in predictable reaction, the frightened parliamentary leaders rushed to dismember the army. On 31 May, the day before disbandment was to begin, two regiments mutinied, refusing to disband until justice had been done on men who not only planned a new war but who had also slurred the army's honour in the declaration of dislike. Although the desperate houses quickly voted virtually all the army's material demands, it was too late.

The character of the army changed dramatically in the days around 1 June. Most momentously, the troops gained a secular ideology to buttress the certainty of many that they were God's agents. Convinced that their opponents in parliament were selfishly working to divide the army and gain an insecure agreement with Charles, the soldiers concluded that they alone stood for the public interest, and God's interest too. The unity and altruism of the army therefore became a fundamental tenet, shaping the actions of radical subalterns by checking their intransigence, just as it often had the reverse effect on the more famous career of Cromwell. But the agitators' new demand for a purge of a corrupted parliament was not the only obstacle facing Holles. The army's composition changed with the departure of almost a quarter of the New Model's officers, some for service in Ireland, some in disgust. Their replacements included some who were not only more radical but also socially less elevated. The casualties of war had brought promotions for many eager volunteers on both sides, but in 1647 the proportion of gentry amongst the New Model's field officers fell from five-sixths to two-thirds. The colonelcy for Thomas Pride was one consequence of Holles's intemperance.

The army's political emergence proceeded apace. The increasingly self-confident agitators seem to have aimed to put a new guard on Charles to avert any conjunction between him, the Scots and parliament against the New Model. Cornet Joyce, a subaltern deputed to lead a body of cavalry to Charles's quarters at Holdenby House in Northamptonshire, exceeded his instructions in fear of a counter-attack; on 3 June he seized the king and transferred him from parliamentary to army custody. Fairfax and Cromwell then acquiesced, for they saw God's providence in the actions of others, as they had in face of the mutinies of 31 May, and as they were to do again. Both dreaded disorder in the army; and Cromwell, the more politically sophisticated of the pair, must have seen the advantages in possession of the king.

The final stage in the army's arousal came in the following days. At a general rendezvous on 5 June the regiments espoused the *Solemn Engagement* of the army, drafted by the cool hand of the lawyer and general Henry Ireton, who was to prove the army's finest politician. Modelled as it was on the Scots' National Covenant and on the Protestation of 1641, the *Engagement* affirmed the unity of the soldiery, declaring that the army would not disband until its honour was vindicated and justice done; it also sought to maintain that unity by calling for a general council of the army, containing both officers and agitators. For the first time the army claimed responsibility for the rights of 'freeborn Englishmen'. It was a short step from there to the army's famous *Representation* of 14 June. With his ringing assertion that the soldiers were no 'mere mercenary army' – a gibe here at the Scots – but had been raised to secure 'the people's just rights and liberties', Ireton outlined a political programme. In unpartisan fashion, the *Representation* sought an end to self-interest, by a purge not just of corrupt MPs (the Derby House clique) but also of the widely unpopular county committees, and by audits of all financial accounts. More ominously, it also sought an end to tyranny over body and conscience, through parliaments of fixed duration and toleration for tender consciences.

The greatest threat to the consciences of the saints came from the City, which formed the heartland of English presbyterianism. The London clergy, packed into close proximity, were more used than most to arguing and acting together. Their long familiarity with the Scottish commissioners had exposed them to the Covenanters' argument that when backed by the civil power presbyterian discipline was the means not just to stamp out sin, but to national reformation. Furthermore, in London, the integrity of the parishes, with their highly developed systems of poor relief, was crucial for reasons of social and political as well as moral order. London merchants and clergy therefore deluged parliament between 1645 and 1647 with demands that the vacuum left by the collapse of episcopacy and its courts be filled, and that the challenge of the sects be crushed.

Presbyterianism was also partisan, and the City establishment urged Holles on. City loans would finance disbandment and the reconquest of Ireland, and the powerful City militia, newly remodelled, would offer a conservative counter to Fairfax's ill-supplied forces. And as the resentful New Model Army moved slowly closer, the increasingly royalist City mob turned out repeatedly in June and July 1647 to stiffen the faint-hearted in parliament. Whatever the opinions of the populace had been in 1641, disillusionment had hardened in the long wartime depression. Bitterness at the ecclesiastical anarchy, when compounded with the consequences of parliament's appalling credit record, helped generate that prominent feature of the next century and a half, the 'church and king' mob.

The City was ill-placed to head a counter-revolution. Though its leaders constituted a party of order, they were instigating mob violence and preparing for renewed civil war. Furthermore, they knew that disbandment of the New Model would bring the speedy restoration of Charles, with little hope for the repayment of war loans the City had made to parliament. In later June and again in July the City fathers' resolve weakened. Simultaneously, the trained bands began to disintegrate as Fairfax and Cromwell gradually and reluctantly moved the army closer to London. The nerve of the less intransigent in both houses broke too, for there were few attractions in the rioters around and even inside parliament's doors.

The New Model was, in contrast, reassuringly disciplined. Its political demands were by no means outrageous – Cromwell the country gentleman never sounded more conservative than when in July he angrily told agitator-saints bent on a coup, 'Have what you will have, that you have by force I look upon it as nothing.' And in the king the army held the key to a settlement. Its posture of moderation was boosted when fifty-eight MPs (not all of them Independents), several peers and the Speakers of both houses fled the rioters, to be escorted to Fairfax down one and a half miles of lined soldiers shouting for a free parliament. This was no revolution. The soldiers who on 6 August entered the City without resistance could claim that they were not imposing the army's will but indeed merely restoring freedom to parliament. Holles fled, with the rest of the 'eleven members' whose impeachment the soldiers had demanded.

But despite London's theatre of submission to the now-purged parliament, the generals knew they could not wait. Even while the City was organising, negotiations had been under way between Charles and the army's political leaders, Cromwell and Ireton (Fairfax, their superior, while a superb inspirer of his men, was no politician). These negotiations had been brokered by the king's old and disaffected servants Northumberland and Saye. The motley group's demands were drafted by Ireton and Fairfax's brilliant young colonel, John Lambert, in close consultation with the peers and their parliamentary allies. They were presented to the king on 2 August as the Heads of Proposals.

The Heads would have allowed Charles to retain the royal legislative veto, deprived him of his control over the militia for a mere ten years, and permitted the survival of a non-coercive episcopacy. But this was no closet sharing of power, for the 'grandees' were sensitive to the complexity of the new environment. They sought to reduce one source of friction through a confederal link between England and Scotland, in the joint 'keepers of the peace' at which the Covenanters had aimed in 1640 – though they aimed too to subordinate Ireland finally to the English parliament. And since they now recognised the threat that could come from

Westminster, the grandees coupled restraints on tyranny over conscience with provisions for biennial parliaments of limited duration. It was a remarkably sophisticated programme, that offered England its best chance of settlement. And during the negotiations, Charles repeatedly declared his honest intent.

But though the Heads of Proposals asked the king to surrender fewer of his powers than had parliament's Newcastle Propositions, he was no more likely to agree. According to Sir John Berkeley, one of his attendants, Charles could not trust Cromwell and Ireton, since they asked for nothing for themselves: obedience, gratitude, place and profit were the only respectable political motives. Anyway, those with whom he dealt were rebels against God's annointed. They asked him to surrender his God-given sword for ten years, when he had declared he could not even for a day; and to exclude from pardon too five of his followers (the Newcastle propositions had stipulated fifty-seven) when his conscience still bore the scars of Strafford's death. No wonder he continued to look for a change in his fortunes. There was ground for hope that the French or perhaps the Dutch would intervene; but far more likely, his enemies past and present would fall to blows.

The 'grandees' recognised as well as Charles the fragility of their present position. The Scots might return yet again, the country was still in turmoil, and their own rear was insecure. The provision in the Heads of Proposals for electoral redistribution in accordance with the incidence of taxation certainly reflects Ireton's tidy mind. It was also a concession to others' demands for more fundamental reform. When parliament, in the name of the people, set itself against 'tyranny' it had raised expectations, only to dash these amid the suffering and burdens of war. It thus invited the radical questioning of its credentials that had begun in the dismal summer of 1643.

The combination of growing hardship and excitement, and London's intensifying controversy over religious toleration, brought into being the Levellers – the first recognisably popular movement in politics. The origins of the Levellers lay in radical protestantism. The Baptists, Independents and other sects who congregated in the City's teeming alleys had watched in fear as magistrates and ministers pressed parliament to erect a sterner ecclesiastical discipline. The sects overcame their inherent centrifugal tendencies to campaign for toleration of the godly, insisting on their earthly freedom in order to develop their overriding responsibility to God. But when they saw their own petitions burnt, and activists imprisoned, by the developing presbyterian majority in parliament, they came to question the very nature of political authority. The sects' petitions for reform of parliament and City alike, and their commitment to voluntarist organisation in their churches, were to prove crucial to the Leveller cause. And in that cause the religious impulse remained central. Leveller pamphlets and petitions resound with the characteristic sectarian assertion that the spirit transcends the letter of the law. Yet this was, as John Milton more famously insisted, no warrant for licence. Levellers coupled their demands for liberty of conscience and an end to compulsory tithes with an insistence on 'equity', moderation and equal dealings towards all.

That ethic of responsibility rooted an individualism of the spirit in a familiar corporate outlook. As much as their flair for publicity, it helped the Levellers reach beyond the sects to turn out tens of thousands in demonstrations. They spoke for the many who had thought parliament in 1642 promised a new order, only to find it deliver high taxes, abuses of power, and economic depression. As the Levellers condemned the threats posed by self-interest and the privilege of power to community and the brotherhood of men they voiced the anger of artisans suffering while the contractors and monopoly companies made fat profits; and they voiced the bitterness too of countless Londoners who in their early enthusiasm had lent to parliament on 'the public faith', only to lose interest and principal alike as the public treasury dwindled. Although Leveller petitions in 1646–7 attacked the mercantile monopolies rather than the craft restrictions of the guilds, and thus spoke for master craftsmen and shopkeepers rather than employees, their rhetoric was of a different order. The Levellers' attacks on exploitation were all-encompassing, and exposed a nerve that looks remarkably like class hostility. As their enemies feared, the dislocation and suffering brought by war had shaken the ties of deference. Nothing symbolised this more clearly than the prominence of women like Katherine Chidley and Lilburne's wife Elizabeth in their demonstrations and petitioning.

Nevertheless, the Levellers little deserved the name their enemies foisted on them, with its overtones of enclosure riot. Of their leaders, John Lilburne certainly, and Richard Overton probably, were of gentry stock; William Walwyn was a prosperous merchant and the grandson of a bishop. The secular causes of law reform, electoral reform, the abolition of monopolies, were all the concerns of those who had something, who might vote or go to law. While agrarian discontent was to well up in 1649, the London leaders showed little concern with it, or indeed with the subordination of the women who urged their cause so passionately. They were men of their time and place rather than visionary thinkers.

The genius of the movement was the egocentric Lilburne, who dramatised in vivid prose for all the commons of England his imprisonment by successive parliamentary authorities for challenging the new church discipline. Like the Old Testament prophets, he was suffering in God's name for His people. His autobiography became a political cause. Appealing, like so many of his contemporaries, to the warrant of the Holy Spirit, Lilburne demanded 'equity' in the application of the laws since all were equal before God. But his pamphlet salvoes drew not just on the Bible but also on Magna Carta and Sir Edward Coke. Citing to embarrassing effect the houses' declarations, he asked how parliament had come to oppress the people. He gained a sympathetic audience among soldiers with their own experience of victimisation. It was surely by this route that in 1647 the Lilburnian rhetoric of 'free-born Englishmen' found its way into the army's declarations.

Lilburne's allies were more thoughtful. Overton and Walwyn poured scorn on the unrepresentativeness of England's constitution, on the inequities of laws exacting the death penalty for a range of offences against property and those condemning debtors to gaol, and on the costs of its legal procedures. Their demands ranged from the stock call for the disestablishment of the church and the abolition of tithes to the decentralisation of the legal system and election to all local offices. There is a parallel with the conservative clubmen, who manifested an equal distaste for arbitrary power and an equal concern for the rights of individual and community. The rise of a forceful state (though its critics experienced this as the self-interest of the new breed of committeemen) was breeding a fierce reaction across the political spectrum.

The more rationalist Overton and Walwyn went far beyond the respect for the common law shown by Lilburne as well as by the clubmen. By 1647 Overton was voicing what was to become a pregnant theme, the sovereignty of the people as a bar to the sovereignty of parliament; that sovereignty necessarily entailed a more democratic franchise. Elaborating the common Leveller claim that the laws were the product of the 'Norman yoke' of William the Conqueror and his tyrannical lords, Overton saw them as 'unworthy a free people'. More insistently even than Overton, Walwyn appealed to reason rather than English history as the measure for English governance, and chided Lilburne for his faith in that 'mess of pottage', Magna Carta. Together, they argued resonantly the capacity of the polity to preserve and improve itself as it saw fit.

In their readiness to transcend the letter of the law the Leveller leaders drew from a well that was to nourish far more radical groups too. The fracturing of political authority had encouraged many saints to conclude that the law was being superseded by the spirit. In that lay the warrant for the freedom of the godly. Antinomianism was to prove a powerful stimulus to thinking about liberty. It was less conducive to the tense work of settlement, since it lent itself to suspicions that the more cautious were double-dealing.

Suspicions grew since the march on London had brought few gains, either for the London Levellers or for the soldiers. Although Fairfax now collaborated with parliament in reducing the army, pay was still held up, indemnity for wartime offences had not been voted, the presbyterian party in parliament had not collapsed, there had been only minor changes in the City's government, and Lilburne was still in jail. More alarmingly for some, the gathered churches began to fall away in the autumn, as they saw in the grandees' victory the promise of the liberty of conscience they had always set higher than the Levellers' political reforms. With the main army now quartered in and around London it was easy for Leveller activists to make contact with dissatisfied army agitators, and in October 1647 there appeared the first direct challenge to the high command, *The Case of the Army Truly Stated*.

For all its meanderings, *The Case's* attempt to weave the grievances of the soldiers into a wider cause had a dangerous plausibility. The generals' backsliding from the undertakings of *The Engagement* smacked of self-seeking, its authors intimated. Disbandment with few safeguards was in prospect, leaving the king free to take revenge and thwart the people of the liberties which, *The Case* insisted, the army had intended all along. Remarkably, the generals, who were anxious to hold the army together during the negotiations with the king, responded not with outrage but by laying the matter before the general council of the army. The council, which included officers, old agitators from the regiments, some London Levellers as well as several new and more militant agitators, began its meetings in the parish church at Putney, on London's outskirts, on 28 October. The Putney debates are one of the most revealing and famous encounters in English history.

The debates centred on the Levellers' newly drafted *Agreement of the People*, their attempt to provide a constitution for England that would bar a new, and representative, parliament from acting in certain reserved fields. Skilfully shifting the argument from *The Case*, with its potentially explosive allegations, to the *Agreement*, Cromwell and Ireton, who spoke for the high command, played on the disagreements and uncertainties of those present. But in evading a frontal challenge to their good faith, the generals made possible a remarkable debate on democracy. The Levellers and their sympathisers argued variously for a wide franchise; Colonel Rainsborough went as far as to speak for 'the poorest he that lives', urging that men (significantly he had no word for women) were only bound by their own consent. In reply, Ireton contested the antinomian individualism of the Leveller case, defending a constitution rooted in history, in laws and in agreements. The vote, he insisted, should be vested in property-owners, those with a 'fixed interest in the kingdom'. The franchise was in fact a peripheral issue to the Levellers, a means to godly reform in a variety of fields – the proposal of successive Agreements that political rights be granted only to signatories smacks more of the covenants of gathered churches, that sought to create a godly whole, than of democracy and individual rights. The debates abound in poignant and revealing moments. Commissary Cowling was outraged to learn that the war had not been fought to better the lot of ordinary soldiers. Cromwell, torn between the property-owner's conviction that Leveller antinomianism 'must end in anarchy' and the godly hope that all present could learn the mind of the Lord, was plunged in ambivalence.

The Leveller challenge put an abrupt end to the negotiations with the king. The generals had neither won Putney's debate on the franchise nor answered *The Case*. When they sought to put their forces in a posture of preparedness they faced a minor mutiny at Corkbush Field in Hertford-shire from soldiers declaring for the Agreement and 'England's Freedom, Soldiers' Rights'. Although Cromwell decisively re-established order, Charles used the crisis to justify his escape from Hampton Court on 11 November. Thanks in part to the pens of Clarendon and the poet Andrew Marvell, this has become an episode in the legend of Cromwell the Machiavellian. It certainly brought Charles nearer to the block; but Cromwell was no republican, and had worked steadily that autumn for further negotiations. That Charles headed to new captivity in the Isle of Wight, where Cromwell's cousin, Robert Hammond, was governor, was more the result of misplaced hopes of aid, from both Hammond and nearby France, than of Cromwellian guile.

Charles's plans centred on his enemies falling out. As unable as most of his contemporaries to imagine that a settlement could be made without him, he expected to sell his support to, and then exploit, the highest bidder. The differences between Holles and the City on the one hand and the army on the other, and the improved terms offered him in the Heads of Proposals, only seemed to bear out his strategy. On 24 December he therefore rejected, with biting sarcasm, parliament's latest proposals, which were only marginally less harsh than those offered at Newcastle. His boldness stemmed from confidence that the Scots were at last about to stand by their king.

The Scottish nobility, angered almost as much by the militant clerical-ism of the kirk as by events in England, harkened readily to Hamilton's plans to redeem national pride by restoring Charles to a semblance of his own. On 26 December a delegation of largely Hamiltonian Scots secretly concluded the Engagement with Charles, by which they agreed to help him impose a settlement on his kingdoms. Presbyterianism would be estab-lished for a mere three years in England, barring the royal household, and an assembly of divines, of whose support Charles was probably justly confident, would then give final shape to the church. More important to the nobles, offices and power were to be shared between English and Scots. The royalist–Scottish alliance that Charles had vainly sought in 1641 was finally sealed by means of a true British programme.

An intransigent king joined with interfering Scotsmen could only stiffen English resolves. On 3 January 1648 a revealingly broad coalition in the Commons voted that no further addresses be made to Charles. The king had succeeded in persuading some of his subjects of the virtues of kingless-ness: exasperation might be far from republicanism, but about thirty radical MPs had brought themselves to imagine an alternative to a settle-ment with Charles Stuart. Among these were some who had earlier insisted on negotiations. While Ireton declared that Charles had broken his contract with the people, Cromwell was inscrutable, as he so often was when on the verge of great events. He declared his continued support for monarchy, 'unless necessity enforce an alteration'. If Cromwell was waiting for a sign from God, there were those at his back who were convinced that God was pouring out His wrath on the English for their temporising.

Others saw a quite different meaning in disaster, and yearned only for a return to normality. Famine persisted as the rains fell, and the depression showed no sign of lifting. The anxious Essex clergyman Ralph Josselin noted early in 1648, it was 'a sad, dear time for poor people ... money almost out of the country'. But the discontents that welled up in 1648 were not simply material. The absence of either reform or settlement in the many months since the end of hostilities cast a tawdry light on the broken promises of 1642. No civil war could foster those liberties, especially to due legal process, minimal taxation and unhampered local government by men of local influence, for which many gentlemen had taken up arms. Though peace in 1646 had partly reinvigorated the purged commissions of the peace, the hated county committees retained their punitive powers; and the army still sat in their quarters. That so many of the revolts of 1648 occurred in formerly parliamentarian counties reflects a growing conviction that the cause was not worth the cost.

More alarming to many was the plight of the church. Anglicanism retained its vitality, most visibly in the forcible restorations by parishioners of ejected royalist or Anglican clergymen against which parliament fulminated vainly in August 1647. Its vitality was also clear in the widespread reports of continued use of the prayer book and neglect of the Assembly's *Directory of Worship*. There was some evidence of fragmentation – as early as 1646 the Essex grand jury received complaints from Great Burstead parish of antinomian outrages. But as yet the sects were localised, generally confined to the larger towns and to the army. More widespread were the signs of a dereliction that contrasted bleakly with the hopes of 1641. Not only had the church courts fallen with the bishops; so had the means of ordaining new clergy, though war and purge had created many gaps. About one-third of the parish livings in the new presbyterian province of London were vacant in 1648, and deficiencies aplenty appeared elsewhere.

Parliament had of course tried to fill the ecclesiastical void, and in 1645–6 the houses laid the foundations of a presbyterian church. But they signally failed to build a clerical disciplinary structure. The majority in both houses had as little love for sectarianism as did the presbyterian majority in the Westminster Assembly, and they had in 1644 remained singularly unmoved by Milton's *Areopagitica*, with its ringing cry that truth could only be advanced by free discussion. But a widespread erastian conviction of the supremacy of the secular power, of which John Selden was the most devastating advocate, was reinforced by a gut anti-clericalism that disposed them against the strict presbyterianism urged by Covenanters and London clergy. The moderate Sir John Holland probably spoke for many when he confessed that he would as readily 'live under the tyranny of the Turk as the tyranny of the clergy'. Such feelings were encouraged by endless clerical bickering, that demonstrated to most that there was no scriptural blueprint for a national church and thus no grounds for clerical *iure divino* claims.

The houses therefore reserved to themselves ultimate control of the church order they established. The components came as the end of war neared and London's disarray increased. In August 1645 parliament promulgated the assembly's directory of worship; in the following months it ordained a hierarchical disciplinary structure of classes and presbyteries. The essence of the scheme was the 'presbytration' of the old parish churches. Each parish was to elect lay elders, to assist the minister in disciplining the congregation; they were also to help elect representatives to the next level in the disciplinary hierarchy, the classes, which covered parts of counties. Above the classes were to be ranked county and national assemblies. All were to be subordinate to parliament. As the redoubtable Scottish commissioner Dr Baillie concluded in disgust, it was but a 'lame erastian presbytery' – as the houses wanted.

Despite its neatness the scheme was flawed. Not least, many gathered congregations had even by its inception formed outside the parish churches and thus outside the presbyterian system. A graver problem lay in presbyterianism's lack of appeal. In London and in southeast Lancashire, isolated as the latter was in a sea of anti-puritanism, many ministers and lay notables went promptly to work. But, all told, only eight of the forty English counties made any real effort to implement the scheme; even in London, only three-quarters of the scheduled classes appear to have operated, and often limply at that. Even discipline-hungry clergy might refuse to associate with lay elders for whom they could see no more scriptural warrant than they could for parliament's new ecclesiastical supremacy. One minister offered a London living in 1648 stipulated that before he accepted, 'you which be elders shall wholly lay down your offices'. For their part, many laymen shunned an office that required them to scrutinise their neighbours' conduct and therefore guaranteed them unpopularity. Conversely, as one 1649 pamphlet observed, few parishioners would ever 'submit to come before the lay elders'.

With presbyterian discipline still-born, and the episcopal church dead, parish ministers were left struggling alone to reform their congregations. Many baulked. Exclusion from the communion service, the major sacrament, was the chief instrument for the correction of sinners that ministers possessed, and many were unnerved when they found neither episcopal courts nor presbyteries to shelter behind. Too frightened to try to chastise his parishioners alone, Ralph Joselin ceased offering communion altogether at Earl's Colne in Essex in the later 1640s. To the dismay of the large numbers of the laity who treasured the sacrament, he was not alone. The widespread alternative to cessation appeared to be the abandonment of any attempt at discipline, and the offering of communion to all, including sinners. It was no wonder that the value, let alone the prospect, of godly rule seemed open to question, or that so many hankered for the old ways.

Appropriately enough, the first sparks of renewed civil war flew over a religious festival. In a bloody fracas in the streets at Christmas 1647, Canterbury townsmen challenged parliament's 1644 ordinance against the celebration of Christmas. Later, and still more divisively, they extended that challenge into an assault in the courts on the whole structure of parliamentarian rule in their county. Bloodier, if short-lived, affrays followed in London and Norwich in April. By the end of the month it was clear that a nationwide upheaval was under way.

Ironically, the houses were themselves partly to blame. Recognising their isolation, the political Independent leaders had solicited support in the country for the 'vote of no addresses'. As the self-declared 'honest party' used packed grand juries to vent its case, outraged gentry and clergy in county after county swung back into the political activity they had abandoned after the army's triumph of the previous summer. A spate of petitions in the spring of 1648 called for a treaty with the king, for disbandment, for an end to the whole system of rule by committee. These were given dangerous support when in Pembrokeshire Colonel Poyer, commanding a garrison that faced an unrewarded disbandment, threw in his lot with the petitioners. More ominously still, the Engagers were raising troops in Scotland to vindicate their king.

The imminence of further bloodletting galvanised the army. Believing that divine providence had determined the outcome of the first war, Fairfax's officers saw the king now sacrilegiously intent on challenging God's will and once more defiling the land. Abasing themselves for their 'politic' dealings, they searched the grimmer books of scripture in an emotional three-day prayer meeting at Windsor at the end of April. And as they identified Charles apocalyptically as 'that man of blood' foretold in prophecy, they vowed vengeance. But despite the vote of no addresses, the officers could not count on parliament. Emboldened by the enthusiastic petitions, a resurgent conservative majority in the Commons of almost two to one abandoned the vote of no addresses and passed a stern blasphemy ordinance, directed primarily against the Baptists. In June the 'eleven members' excluded in 1647 resumed their seats. But while the two houses eagerly resumed their course of a year earlier, they were not yet ready to surrender to the king – especially to a king imposed by the Scots.

In the first civil war the political nation had split down the middle. In 1648 the division was more lopsided. In many towns, and some rural areas, a radicalised minority was eager to advance the 'honest' cause, and rallied to the new militias with which the county committees sought to overawe troublemakers. Some of these recruits could be very radical and very determined indeed: those arrayed in Berkshire by Henry Marten, the MP most sympathetic to the Levellers, were notorious. But outside the army, most of the passion in the Second Civil War was to be found in a revolt of the provinces against a hated centre. Old cavaliers were active, in Cornwall, in Wales, in Yorkshire and the far north; closer to London the weathervane Earl of Holland joined royalists in a futile bid to raise the Thames Valley. But in the main the royalists were demoralised by defeat and by sequestration. More typical protesters in 1648 were the rebellious sections of the Kent and Essex trained bands, or of the fleet, whose enthusiasm for the godly cause had largely evaporated. This did not necessarily breed a wholehearted royalism – the south Wales forces, and the fleet, defected from parliament at least in part because of their resentments at the remodelling parliament and Fairfax had set in train in late 1647. But as the impressive petitions from counties around London showed, many former parliamentarians were desperate to persuade moderates at Westminster of the need to return to old ways while they still could.

In Kent, persuasion ended in violence. The bulk of the county's gentry in May backed a petition to parliament against the county committee machine of the quarrelsome and hated Sir Anthony Weldon – a gesture that was not inherently disloyal. But while they may not have seen why their other demand, that parliament negotiate with the king, should have occasioned violence, they were seeking to impose their own will on the minority who had taken a very different reading of the king and of events. When the county committee's forces strove to block the petition by force some seven thousand took up arms. Nevertheless, the 'rebels' remained in essence petitioners. Their leaders strove to distance themselves from opportunist cavaliers, and aimed to coerce by demonstration rather than by violence (as of course had been the case with many in 1642). It was contingents led by ex-royalists who finally fought it out with Fairfax in the streets of Maidstone.

The Kent rebellion illustrates the weakness of localism as a political force. The rebels compounded their hostility to the centre with a fatal deference to it. They were acting for Kent, and were unwilling either to push their protest to extremes or to co-operate with other malcontents. Their attitude appears to have been common. In neighbouring Surrey, and in Dorset, the county leaders gathered strident petitions, and then stood back to watch their effect; and the return of the old sea-dog, Warwick, to command the fleet calmed much of the storm there, and ultimately all but ten ships returned to their allegiance. Indeed, not even the bloodshed in Essex provides much of an exception. There, the pre-war, puritan elite had survived largely intact, and the local focus of gentry resentment was much less significant. The county leaders were therefore less willing than those in Kent to risk unleashing welling popular discontent in an unprecedentedly rainy famine summer. Their restraint allowed royalists to take the lead; these gave a hard edge to a revolt that endured a long and bitter siege in Colchester.

The rebels' lack of co-ordination permitted the government's forces to pick them off piecemeal. London, wary anyway after the 1647 crisis, and Norwich were quelled before Kent rose; the troubles in Kent were collapsing when rebellion flared in Essex; and the upheaval there was contained, and Colchester safely besieged, when the Scots at last entered England. The isolation of the Scots was probably not accidental, for many English rebels hoped to achieve a treaty with the king before the hated Scots could bring their own views to bear. Furthermore, many northern royalists so despised them as 'judases' for 'selling' the king in the winter of 1646–7 that they refused to collaborate.

The Scots had troubles enough. The collapse of the alliance of kirk and nobility deprived the insufficiently godly Engagers of clergy willing to preach a holy war. Delayed by recruitment problems and by bitter political squabbles, the Engager army did not cross the border until July, and it was then hampered by appalling weather as it straggled south into Lancashire. Hamilton's indecisiveness compounded his followers' woes, for it allowed Colonel Lambert's small Yorkshire force to delay him until Cromwell came up, fresh from quashing the south Wales revolt. In a brilliant running fight, from 17–19 August, Cromwell destroyed the much larger Scottish army around Preston. With the fall of Colchester to Fairfax ten days later the Second Civil War was virtually over.

The fighting confirmed the army's mood of the April prayer-meeting at Windsor. If the war itself was blasphemous, the troop cuts begun in late 1647 had made it unnecessarily costly in soldiers' blood. Even the normally courteous Fairfax had two of the Colchester royalists summarily shot, and Cromwell was transformed. Seeing 'nothing but the hand of God' at Preston, he now concluded that justice must be done upon those who had questioned God's 'outward dispensations' of 1642–6. Almost as great a crime in Cromwell's English eyes, those blasphemers had sought 'to vassalize us to a foreign nation' by bringing in the Scots. But should justice extend to the king, as some of the godly in the army and scattered through the provinces, demanded? Ireton and the other officers were in December willing to listen to the prophetess Elizabeth Poole harangue them on their duty to their father the king; Cromwell gave stronger signs of uncertainty. Although there was military reason for him to turn aside in the north to reduce the great royalist stronghold at Pontefract, he was prone in political crises to seek guidance from providence. 'Waiting on the Lord', he now left the nation's destiny in the capable and relentless hands of his son-in-law, Ireton.

The problems facing Ireton were awesome. Amongst the least was that of shepherding Fairfax in a direction to which the latter was temperamentally averse. He showed still greater dexterity in placating on the one hand his allies in parliament and on the other the Levellers. The soldiers' inchoate militancy had hardened in the turmoils of 1648, but fortunately for Ireton the Levellers showed considerable concern for the common cause. When in August the Commons disingenuously released Lilburne from one of his many imprisonments, 'freeborn John' assured Cromwell of his goodwill. Lilburne, like other potential dissidents, was ready to credit Ireton's known commitment to reform, and Fairfax's renown for godly piety. During the crucial winter months radical energies were contained in long debates at Whitehall. As they wrestled passionately with the key question of the extent of religious toleration, a committee of officers, London Independent clergy and Levellers gave little attention to the nature of the state. Whatever the Levellers' views after the ensuing revolution, few participants would have questioned the emphasis at the time.

Ireton was far less concerned with Leveller influence in the army than with parliament's rush to settlement. Even during the fighting the houses had been preparing for fresh talks with Charles, and on 15 September their commissioners arrived at Newport on the Isle of Wight. Lord Saye, a political Independent who had eagerly supported the vote of no addresses, now joined the presbyterian Manchester in clamouring for an agreement; however awful Saye now found the prospect of regicide, he shared the aversion of the younger Vane for the growing prospect of army rule. The Newport negotiations dragged in face of Charles's habitual evasiveness, as he sought still to set his enemies at odds. He confided to friends that this would be but a 'mock-treaty', to buy time; and it was perhaps for this reason that he appeared willing to concede control of the militia for twenty years. The sticking-point was his refusal to surrender episcopacy for more than three years. The Anglican martyr's crown he thus gained would have seemed unlikely earlier in the 1640s, but his hatred of presbyterianism had grown inveterate. Parliament would nevertheless have come to a settlement. The majority in the two houses had scarcely concluded that Charles could now be trusted, but they saw even greater danger in their own allies.

Parliament was not, however, to be left to itself. On 20 November the army presented to the Commons its Remonstrance, in which Ireton argued forcefully that the people were the origin of all power, the king had repeatedly broken his contract with the community, and God had repeatedly witnessed against him. In the name of the safety of the people, the supreme law, justice must be done against 'the capital and grand author of our troubles'. Then followed proposals for electoral reform which suggest that the debates at Whitehall were not simply a ploy to preoccupy the radicals. But Ireton stopped short of offering a constitutional programme, for he had to carry not only Fairfax but also Cromwell along with him; and Cromwell was likely to regard any formed scheme as 'fleshly reasoning', a sinful assertion of human will and a slighting of God's providences. While the judgments of the Second Civil War had convinced him that a stern hand must be used against the ungodly, those judgments did not yet point more clearly. Cromwell's way was to wait for a sign from his God – a posture that the unsympathetic understandably saw as mere opportunism.

Accordingly, though he made no move to dissuade Ireton, he only arrived in London after his son-in-law had initiated the revolution.

The army's revolution was precipitated by the Commons' vote on 5 December, by a margin of 129:83, that Charles's answers at Newport were grounds to continue negotiating. That vote heralded the return of Charles to London – upon which, the officers concluded, all attempts to impose conditions would surely collapse. Next day Colonel Pride's musketeers blocked the stairs into parliament. Ireton had wanted to dissolve an assembly that he saw as hardened in corruption and to hold new elections on a reformed franchise. He was dissuaded by radical MPs like Edmund Ludlow and Thomas Scot, who for once had a more realistic sense of public opinion. Furthermore, although now committed republicans, they recoiled both from the breach with the past that a dissolution would bring, and from the prospect of the soldiers in power. Ireton's own readiness to appeal to history against the Levellers at Putney in 1647 may have made him that much easier to persuade.

In submitting to those desperate for shreds of continuity Ireton took the incipient revolution the first of its many steps backward. Colonel Pride therefore conducted a purge and not a dissolution, as he excluded about 110 MPs; around 160 more, including some radicals like the younger Vane (who had eventually denounced the Newport treaty), withdrew in protest. By the middle of January 1649 the Commons had difficulty in reaching a quorum of forty. But Cromwell, who took the initiative after his arrival on 7 December, intended neither that the revolution should become uncontrolled nor that it should degenerate into farce. He immediately set about persuading seceders to return, though this further tempered godly fire with constitutionalist scruples.

Cromwell's conservative leanings are evident too in his last effort, in late December, to persuade Charles to surrender all his powers. It is often assumed that 'Pride's purge' led inevitably to the republic, but to Cromwell and a number of others in the Commons a drastic purge to avert a sell-out did not mean regicide. But when Charles rebuffed him, he dared go no further. Scarcely a doctrinaire republican himself, he feared lest his radical subordinates should seek a more thorough-going revolution. He therefore bent with opinion in the army in order to contain it. 'Providence and necessity' now gave a definite answer to the question he had pondered the previous January: the king must go to preserve the nation. He was confirmed in this judgment by the vengeful cries of Hugh Peter from the Whitehall pulpit.

The high court of justice that the leaders of the Commons and the army appointed had the unprecedented task of bringing a king to his death in the open. As Scot at least was to proclaim proudly in very different times a decade later, these godly men did not intend a closet murder. Nor did they intend a revolutionary tribunal, despite the claim of the *Remonstrance*, and of the charge itself, that sovereignty lay in the people. As best they could, the managers tried to bring the common law rather than revolutionary justice to bear, and they shaped the indictment to claim that the king had broken the law in remarkably conventional ways. But the form of the high court ventured further, combining as it did echoes of ordinary criminal proceedings and of parliament. And in the high court's composition too the managers made a claim to nationhood. It was only partly to substitute for the refusal of the judges and the Lords to co-operate that the managers named to the court a cross-section of the godly cause, in parliament, army, London and the country. With few exceptions the handful of peers and greater gentry nominated refused to serve. But even had Fairfax, the younger Vane, or Hesilrig joined the solitary peer, the millenarian lord Grey of Groby, in the court, it would have made little difference to public attitudes.

Charles of course refused to recognise the court's authority, maintaining as he had always done that his trust came from God rather than the people. His bearing at the hugely theatrical trial, and then in the cold on the scaffold on 30 January 1649, was undoubtedly the most dignified of his career, and for once his stammer left him. He did far more for the cause of kingship than he had ever achieved during his life, and the cult of Charles the Martyr was not wholly generated by the pious meditations of *Eikon Basilike*, ghost-written by the royalist cleric John Gauden. The huge groan that rose from the crowd when the axe fell challenged the radicals' claims that power originated in the people. To the appalled watchers, and to the eager purchasers of the thirty-six editions of *Eikon Basilike* that appeared in the next year, the headsman had struck at a divine order.

The widespread fears, and the fainter hopes, that regicide betokened a total overturning were unfounded. To some of the zealots Charles's execution heralded the millennium; to rather more, he died because he had blasphemed against providence and marked himself as a man of blood. For Cromwell, even for the more thoughtful Ireton, and certainly for most of their allies in the Commons, there were prudential as well as providential reasons. Charles died because, as the Scots had found earlier, it was impossible to come to an agreement with him; and, in a monarchical state, settlement was impossible without him. Nevertheless, the momentous events of 1648–9 were not simply reflex gestures. Long familiarity with non-hierarchical forms of action and organisation, and sophisticated wartime arguments that the body politic could and must preserve itself, had made it possible to imagine and then effect a transformation of the polity.

11

The English Commonwealth, 1649–1653

In a society bound by custom, the killing of the king could not but have special meaning. Almanacs and astrologers gained new heights of popularity as they promised to tell what this was. For the overwhelming majority of the political nation it seemed to threaten social disintegration, and a flood of black-edged broadsheets played to fears by foretelling the end of civility, perhaps of civilisation itself. Many even of the godly had joined the voluble William Prynne, that victim of Laud as well as Colonel Pride, in his steady drift into disillusionment, from hopes of a new dawn at the start of the decade to grim outrage by the end.

Equally important is the counterpoint, the growing determination of some of the radicals. One component of this was a belief in the passing of all the privilege and acquiescence entailed in the figure of the body politic. At the end of January a newspaper sympathetic to the army heralded the progress since Elizabeth: 'Then were men rather guided by the tradition of their Fathers, than by acting principles in reason and knowledge: But to the contrary in these our days, the meanest sort of people are not only able to write, &c., but to argue and discourse on matters of highest concernment.' Lending urgency to the belief that a republic was the field of action was the conviction of some that the age of the spirit, in which Antichrist would fall, was at hand. Even Cromwell, who had not been driven onwards by prophetic hopes, soon looked back to January 1649 as a time when God had manifested His purposes. Colonel Harrison went further, greeting 'the day, God's own day, wherein he is coming forth in glory in the world'.

1648–9 brought the only revolution in English history. Revolution was signalled by the refusal of a half of the judges of the great common law courts to serve the new order. Monarchy was abolished, and the house of Lords with it, and power concentrated in a purged single chamber that was (in 1659) to be derided as 'the Rump' – a name that has stuck. Radicals could delight in symbol, in the end of the legal privilege that had allowed the nobility to face trial only before their peers: during the republic several were to be tried in the ordinary courts of law. Precious few noblemen were active at the centre or in the localities during the Commonwealth, and the disgusted Saye even retired to his island fastness of Lundy. Indeed, there was a revolution in personnel, for 1648–9 brought a massive displacement of the traditional governors from office. Where local governors had been closely identified with political presbyterianism the regime felt driven to purge. In Herefordshire, dominated by the presbyterian Harley family, about 40 per cent of the membership of the county's various committees changed in 1649. Equally sweeping were the changes in south Wales, where the rebellions of 1648 had revealed the moderation, or blatant royalism, of many of the gentry. The consequence was the hegemony for the next decade of a tiny Baptist clique around Philip Jones. Still more obviously, London had to be purged, and in the carefully controlled City elections of 21 December 1648 two-thirds of the common councillors departed.

There was change too in ideas of the polity. Most of the regime's supporters made a virtue of imprecision when they went beyond arguments of necessity and providence. The characteristic Independent position, advanced repeatedly by Cromwell, and by the great Independent divine John Owen in the 1650s, was that God had left mankind free, and obliged, to erect the government that best conduced to godliness and virtue. But two lines of defence rang more confidently. One led to the millennium, and Admiral Robert Blake in 1651 proclaimed in the city square at Cadiz the imminent end of all earthly monarchies. The other was quite different, and derived from the arguments about the natural rights of the community that had emerged around the time of the 'general rising' of 1643. Some partisans began to improvise an impersonal language of 'the state', to which all owed service; and they buttressed that with new arguments of 'public interest', which attached naturally enough to the republic's formal title of 'the Commonwealth'. In so doing, they developed an economic as well as a moral frame to substitute for the old language of the body.

Yet at the Rump's beginning its apologists sounded notes of awkwardness. In his *Right and Might Well Met* (1649), the Independent minister John Goodwin argued what might have been a good republican case: since power originated in the people, their consent was essential to government and they might change their rulers as they thought fit. Faced with the obvious lack of consent, he lamely retorted that necessity justified the army's actions. John Milton too retreated from the cause of godly nation and people into what were to become his characteristic politics of the few. In *The Tenure of Kings and Magistrates* and *Eikonoklastes* (1649), he denounced the self-enslaved presbyterian royalists of the Second Civil War, and the 'besotted' people as a whole who had been taken in by *Eikon Basilike*. Against these he proclaimed the rights of the virtuous who had not surrendered their moral autonomy. Such men retained their God-given right to change their rulers when they chose, to preserve the liberty they alone possessed. Little wonder that most justifications of the Rump by local magistrates and ministers merely counselled acceptance of St Paul's injunction to obey 'the powers that be'.

The Rumpers themselves were no less pragmatic, for they acted first and only later justified themselves. John Evelyn was not just venting royalist slander when he observed at first merely 'unkingship'. Charles died on 30 January, but monarchy was only abolished on 17 March, 'unnecessary, burdensome and dangerous to the liberty, safety and public interest of the people'; only in May did the Rumpers accede to Henry Marten's urgings and declare England 'a commonwealth and free state', with monarchy implicitly damned as unfreedom. The demise of the House of Lords was similarly undoctrinaire. Voted down on 6 February, it was abolished, 'useless and dangerous', on 19 March – its 'uselessness' apparent in the shrinkage of attendances to a mere half-dozen after the Purge, its dangers in the refusal of almost all the peers to abandon the monarchy that had given them their honours and privileges. There was a supreme irony in the way the Rump's most revolutionary statement, declaring 1649 'the first year of freedom by God's blessing restored', came in a legal context – the new great seal that Marten persuaded his colleagues to affix to the most lawyerly of the republic's documents. Such ironies and hesitations give the measure of the Rump, and help explain how it gained the acquiescence of the political nation.

Acquiescence came from other sources too, for one of the most remarkable features about the execution of Charles I is that none in England then tried to proclaim his son Charles II. In centuries of theory and practice the moment the king was dead the king lived, for his next heir succeeded immediately. In Scotland Argyll proclaimed Charles Stuart the moment the death of Charles Stuart was known. But in England none went beyond derision, whether from fear and demoralisation, from providentialism, or, perhaps, from acceptance of the capacity of the polity represented in what was left of parliament to go on in this new way. The hold of monarchy on those who groaned as the axe fell was certainly deep and emotional; but it did not galvanise them.

Those in power were not reassured. They saw dangers on every hand: resentful Scots to the north, the festering sore of Ireland, and an outraged continent that was soon to applaud as royalist exiles assassinated English ambassadors to The Netherlands and to Spain. An empty treasury groaned under the burden of dishonoured wartime debts; and, of course, purge had brought the old problem of low attendances at Westminster to embarrassing proportions. This was not the time for a reforming crusade that might further estrange conservatives from the old parliamentarian coalition. Accordingly, in the spring of 1649 Cromwell's efforts to persuade MPs who had withdrawn in protest to return to Westminster appear to have gained the co-operation of harder men such as Ludlow, Scot and Colonel Harrison (who had been elected as a recruiter MP). The revolutionaries themselves thus ensured the frustration of reformers' hopes as they willingly admitted mere conformists. These were, after all, gentlemen. When so much seemed at risk they deliberately turned to fellow-gentlemen rather than the assorted radicals who urged them in other directions.

Such conservative choices, taken at the very outset of revolution, reinforced Ireton's earlier decision to purge rather than to dissolve, and exposed what was to prove the Rump's fatal dilemma. Although the sword was the Rumpers' only preservative, the soldiers to whom they were beholden signified not just radical alternatives that were distasteful enough but also military interference. And if there was one thing parliament-men had acquired during the long decade of parliamentary rule in the 1640s it was a sense of the importance of parliament. 'Pride's purge' offended that sense. Throughout its life therefore the Rump tried to distance itself from its creator, asserting its dignity and autonomy in all the ceremonials of office, and seeking the support of the conservative gentlemen against whom the Purge had been directed. Perhaps the Rump's most emblematic moment came in the spring of 1649, when it conspicuously failed to elect Ireton to its new executive, the council of state. Thereafter, army pressure for reform bred an equal and opposite reaction.

The history of the Rump must therefore be written around the problem of survival. The most immediate threat was domestic, since there seemed every danger that radicals might turn the revolution in on itself. On the one hand, the grievances of the soldiery still rankled, and the Levellers were still eager to profit. On the other, the apparent downfall of earthly powers early in 1649 unleashed excited expectations of a new order, and a new age.

The problem of radical penetration of the army seemed the more urgent. Substantive political gains from the soldiers' intervention in politics were, as usual, few, while radical suspicions of the grandees had gathered strength. After the Whitehall discussions in late 1648 the officers around Ireton had drafted their own 'Agreement' as a riposte to another Leveller Agreement, but when they failed to press this on parliament resentments came to a head. For all his impressive arguments for electoral reform, separation of powers and freedom for godly consciences, it seemed that Ireton was merely 'the cunningest of Machiavellians'. Lilburne, Walwyn and Overton responded to his new hypocrisy with a devastating series of pamphlets in the spring of 1649. *England's New Chains Discovered* lambasted the alliance of army and Rump for an unprecedented consolidation of powers that jeopardised every principle for which the war had been fought, while *The Hunting of the Foxes* denounced Cromwell's now notorious ability to speak as both saint and gentleman: 'You shall scarce speak to Cromwell about any thing, but he will lay his hands on his breast, elevate his eyes, and call God to record, he will weep, howl and repent, even while he doth smite you under the first rib.' The Rump, frightened, arrested the authors; Cromwell, his enemies reported, warned the council of state, 'If you do not break them, they will break you.'

But the Levellers' constituency was disintegrating. The saints gathered in the London churches and amongst the officers were wary of the two heretics, Walwyn and Overton, and embarrassed too at disruptive Leveller tactics. It became steadily easier for a godly commander like the regicide Sir Hardress Waller to dismiss them all as 'unclean spirits'. More importantly, the soldiers' material grievances were being met. The army's reappearance in London in December 1648 had prompted the City to pay in its arrears on the assessment, while Ireton quickly persuaded the fledgling Rump to increase the soldiers' pay and to secure their arrears through the sale of crown lands – only time was to reveal the damage pay raises did to the regime's precarious finances. Disturbances in the spring of 1649 amongst the soldiers were thus easily quelled. A swift onslaught by Fairfax and Cromwell against mutineers at Burford in Oxfordshire on 14 May, and a handful of executions, effectively ended the Leveller threat. Occasional murmurings in the army were to greet officers' speculation in lands sold to redeem the soldiers' debentures for their back-pay; but once arrears began to be paid off the army never again seemed likely to rise. Furthermore, the elaborately staged and carefully reported executions of Charles and leading royalists like Hamilton and Holland satisfied some of the resentful passions of the troops. Political symbol thus helped avert further disorder, even as the Rump moved quickly to blame its bad press, and the atmosphere of gloom, on the malevolence of the presbyterian clergy.

Denunciations of the clergy found an eager audience beyond the soldiers, for the collapse of political institutions had led some to conclude that the age of the law, and not merely the age of churches, had ended. To the Digger, or proto-communist, Gerrard Winstanley, 'the old world' was 'running up like parchment in the fire'. What more natural than that the spirit should fill the void?

It is important not to attribute too great a coherence to radical thought. Many were the unlettered men and women who grew convinced in these turbulent and iconoclastic times that God had granted them some personal illumination, or even union with the godhead, empowering them to denounce existing authorities. John Robins, who claimed to be God the Father and his wife the expectant mother of the new Christ, may not have been typical, but the strain of crude popular enthusiasm, blasphemy, and often sheer cynical irreligion, cannot be ignored.

But there was a common denominator in attitudes to the after-life. The early Christian church had defused the apocalypse by asserting an undying church on earth and an immortal soul: Christ's kingdom upon earth was thus both now and, in practice, never. That device crumbled as belief in an imminent end to time heightened with upheaval and with the approach of 1656, and of its alternative, 1666, the year of the Beast. Perhaps encouraged by fashionable neo-Platonism and by the materialism of the early scientists, as well as by the millennialist climate, Milton, Overton, Walwyn, Winstanley and many less famous names held that the soul perished with the body, to be revived at the approaching Armageddon. Mortalism, 'soul sleeping', challenged the claims of all established churches to be the visible church, since if the saints died, the church could only be the congregations of which they were members for their time on earth. The conservative opponents of mortalism readily misidentified it with materialist atheism, and assumed that mortalists denied the existence of an after-life. Such a denial was appalling enough as a religious heresy. But as Hobbes recognised in *Leviathan* (1651), belief in divine rewards and punishments hereafter was the ultimate prop of states with inadequate coercive powers. Mortalism thus seemed to guarantee the end of all order. A soul that perished might be of one substance with the body, which would imply that the flesh was good in the same way as was the soul. Freedom of the spirit might, and did, then become freedom for the flesh.

The body politic seemed to be in its death throes, and not surprisingly Freud rather than Marx might better interpret the ways of the most radical of the revolution's sons and daughters. The prevalence of a sometimes flamboyant antinomianism in the revolution suggests a reaction against the insistent authoritarianism of a patriarchal Calvinist society. The Ranters are the most notorious. Their existence as a group has been questioned, for an exuberant handful were exaggerated in conservative nightmares and counter-propaganda. Yet that handful, and the nightmares, are revealing of the stresses developing by the end of the 1640s. Laurence Clarkson, self-styled 'captain of the Rant', took antinomianism to its extreme when he asserted that to the pure in spirit all things are pure, that sin 'hath its conception only in the imagination'; and Abiezer Coppe's remarkable advocacy of swearing not only asserted his own spiritual freedom but also challenged those consciences overburdened by the puritan stress on sin. Equally novel was the way Ranters and other enthusiasts revelled in those seventeenth-century narcotics, alcohol and tobacco, in hopes of releasing the spirit within the flesh. But the Ranter phobia cannot be explained merely by imagining the eruption of 1960s flower children into high Victorian society. The orthodox held that property and government had been instituted to restrain the consequences of sin. If there were no more sin, if God had 'light and dark sides', in the words of Joseph Bauthumley, then what would follow, especially in such a time of hunger and anger? Coppe provided an answer in his 1649 pamphlet, *A Fiery Flying Roll*, in which he coupled an extravagant hymn to the unity of spirit and flesh, to 'my majesty within me', with a tirade against 'the great ones of the earth'.

The Calvinists' insistence on the essential otherness and distance of God, and their harsh disjuncture of the corrupt material world – the flesh –

from the spirit, bred further challenges. On 1 April 1649, a small group of poor men and women followed in the footsteps of countless squatters on waste land by digging up the common at St George's Hill in what is now suburban Surrey. The leadership of Gerrard Winstanley, a bankrupt cloth merchant, transformed these 'Diggers'. Winstanley was scarcely alone in these years, that saw the journeyings of George Fox and first appearance of the Quakers, in arguing that the spirit was within all men; but, like some neo-Platonists before him, he saw God in the material world too. The way to save mankind was therefore through harmony with the world – he even advocated scientific lectures instead of church services on Sundays. No more than the Levellers was the antinomian Winstanley an individualist in any modern sense. Locked in argument with prevailing orthodoxy, he took the younger brother – the perennial victim of primo-geniture – as his metaphor for the poor. Believing that selfishness had corrupted man, he aimed at true community, and salvation, through the end of private property. St George's Hill was to be the beginning. But as the Digger colony failed in face of local harassment and harsh weather, Winstanley retreated from his millennial hopes. In his communistic utopia, *The Law of Freedom* (1652), he showed an almost Calvinist sense of man's propensity to sin and of the importance of government.

Winstanley was not the only radical to grow pessimistic when the world was not turned upside down. A political revolution occurred amidst enormous suffering, but instead of joining one of the handful of Digger communities the poor everywhere did little more than try to keep alive. Nor did they resort en masse to other forms of self-help. On 25 November 1649 Ralph Josselin in Essex noted 'wonderful hard' conditions, when 'many gentlemen's houses were set upon and pilfered', but the social record generally suggests how unfounded were the fears of the gentry. There was one significant strike in the 1650s, by Newcastle keelmen. Assumptions that the 'industrious sort' were the powerhouse of radical-ism clash with the hostility of London craftsmen and artisans to compe-tition in these years from projects to employ the poor, or of urban craftsmen everywhere to attempts to help disbanded soldiers by relaxing corporate restrictions. Still more revealing, in view of widespread troubles in the sixteenth century and in 1607, was the agrarian quiet. After some scattered enclosure riots in the turmoil of the early 1640s, agrarian protest during the revolution was confined to the old flash-points of the fens and the southwestern forests. Economic and cultural polarisation in the villages had done its work in segmenting, and thus neutralising, the local commu-nities. Realising how much they had to lose, yeomen who might have given a political lead raised the poor rate to feed the hungry.

With the army pacified by summer 1649 the Rump could turn its atten-tion to the threat posed by the young Charles Stuart. Although the Scots had signalled aggressive intent by proclaiming him the new king of Great

Britain rather than of Scotland alone, Scotland was an independent protestant state. Ireland, another centre now of pro-Stuart revulsion at the English parliament, was quite another case.

Despite the 1641 massacre, Ireland had remained a low priority in England. Parliament had been content to leave a small Scottish contingent and local forces to conduct holding operations, while the king had looked there only for aid. But those who now sought to combine vengeance with the elimination of a political threat had other arguments to spur them on. The Adventurers of 1642 (many of them well-placed MPs) had to be repaid, while confiscated Irish lands could reduce the soldiers' arrears. There was opposition. As early as 1646 the millenarian Hugh Peter, suspecting that the Irish problem was one of ignorance as much as ill-will, had urged the army to 'teach peasants to understand liberty'; and many soldiers were as reluctant to venture into the bogs of Ireland as they had been then. Ungodly republicans like Marten, unconcerned with Antichrist, could apply arguments of national liberty to the Irish as well as the English; and some ardent tolerationists in the army's council of officers were willing to apply their principles broadly. But Rumpers must have felt, like Holles before them, that an army deployed in Ireland would cause less trouble at home.

As so often, Ireland contrived to frustrate English expectations, and destroy reputations. Hopes for financial returns soon evaporated, for reconquest cost around £3.5 million. But those who had urged it might not have quibbled at the price (particularly since £2 million of it was levied in and on Ireland), for the Rumpers and their army allies believed that their own survival and the godly cause alike hinged on it. Cromwell intended the spectacular expedition that set out in July 1649 to impress hostile audiences on both sides of the Irish Sea. The gathering Scottish threat put a premium on speed, so immediately after landing Cromwell stormed Drogheda, to the north of Dublin, and put its garrison, with many civilians, to the sword for refusing to surrender. The slaughter at Drogheda forms the basis for a legend of Cromwellian atrocity that gained strength from a second, unplanned, massacre at Wexford, where he lost control of enraged soldiers. The strenuousness of his justifications to parliament betrays his awareness that it was not a pretty moment in his career. Prince Rupert's sack of Bolton in 1644 had been brutal enough, and the local wars in both Scotland and Ireland during the 1640s had been worse. Furthermore, Drogheda accorded with the laws of war, whose reasoning Hiroshima has made familiar: harshness now will save time and avert future bloodshed. But Cromwell's excited appeals to the 'marvellous great mercy', the 'righteous judgment of God', and his willingness to gloss over Wexford by appeals to divine providence, go beyond military calculation. The blood guilt of 1641 was being avenged; and since Drogheda had only fallen to the Confederacy in 1649, not 1641, Cromwell was willing to damn the whole Irish nation.

The harshness of English objectives became clearer that winter. The contempt Cromwell expressed to the Irish Catholic clergy at Clonmacnoise for the mass as a tissue of clerical self-seeking indicated the limits to his tolerance. His insistence on English legal title to Irish land put him close to all those protestant settlers who sought to magnify Irish guilt in order to maximise the amount of land to be seized. He had moved far from those of his officers who the previous spring had expressed reservations. Official attitudes changed little when Cromwell returned to England in the spring of 1650, leaving Ireton to mop up. Indeed, they probably hardened when the war became less a matter of sieges and more of anti-guerrilla operations. As the commander of the new Wexford garrison reported:

> In searching the woods and bogs, we found great store of corn, which we burnt, also all the houses and cabins we could find: in all which we found great plenty of corn. We continued burning and destroying for four days: in which time we wanted no provision for horse or man, finding housing enough to lie in; though we burnt our quarters every morning, and continued burning all day.

The restraints on military violence against civilians, generally observed in England, did not apply in Ireland

Successes in Ireland, trumpeted throughout the press, relieved the worst pressures on the regime and allowed most Rumpers to hope for a return to normality. Yet victory also encouraged the army to speak up for reform, in what was to become a characteristic cycle. The council of officers had every reason to raise its voice in the autumn of 1649, for continuing rains had ruined another harvest, and all around could be heard the tramping feet of the hungry. Fairfax even seems to have expressed sympathy for the Diggers. Although few officers contemplated major social change, they were soon discussing law and tithe reform. But the Rumpers, busily tightening censorship of the newsbooks, recoiled in alarm from reform at a time of radical upsurge. September brought the last Leveller mutiny in the army; in October, to the Rump's dismay, a London grand jury tumultuously acquitted the outspoken Lilburne of treason. The strength of discontent in the capital was made even clearer in December when Lilburne and Colonel Pride were elected to the common council by groups pressing for more democracy in London's politics.

The Rumpers were caught in a vice. Anxious to dissuade other regimes from supporting Charles Stuart, anxious too to vindicate the English patriotism and nascent republicanism that were central to their cause, they sought to establish their credentials as a government. The lure of ceremonial and form therefore drew them powerfully, though the officers saw there only pride and obfuscation. Although the Rump responded to army promptings by debating reforms, it always found the sheer doing of business more urgent. Fear of the king rather than commitment to further change had brought together this heterogeneous body, and there was still much to be afraid of.

Fear drove the Rumpers into courses that seemed designed to placate the conservative gentry, not the army. The radicals were dangerous enough, so the Rump promptly blocked Lilburne's election. More alarming was the sullenness of the country as rains and rents continued to fall and prices soared. In December 1649 the Rump sought to propitiate its enemies by reducing the assessment from £90 000 a month, which was altogether inadequate to support an army of 47 000, to £60 000 after three months, thus plunging the commonwealth deeper into financial crisis. Financial desperation also drove it to remove the main prop of the county committees, the object of near-universal hostility. By taking into its own hands control over sequestered royalist estates and over the 'composition' fines for their release, it deprived the committees of their main revenue, the only prospect of support for their underpaid, and sometimes militant, troops.

Yet the Rump had something positive to offer the godly of conventional leanings. The censorship it reimposed in 1649 looks merely defensive, directed as it was against royalists, Levellers, Ranters, and those Socinians who denied the divinity of Christ. But elements of the godly programme that had been lost in 1641 began to appear. In June 1649 the Rump voted to use £20 000 from the sale of bishops' lands to 'augment' inadequate clerical stipends, and coupled this with the establishment of a commission to rationalise the unwieldy parochial map of England and Wales. Although in August the Rumpers failed by the remarkable margin of the Speaker's casting vote to reinforce the national presbyterian church, in the following spring an act for the observance of the sabbath was followed by others against adultery, fornication, swearing and blasphemy. These measures were hastened by dismay at the Ranters, but they accorded with long-standing puritan concerns, in parliament and the localities. But however strong the concern, local courts and juries flinched at the fierce penalties – there are only four known death sentences for adultery, and perhaps twenty prosecutions under the blasphemy act.

Old puritans in the Restoration wilderness were to pay tribute to the Rump's programme, but the political presbyterian gentry who might have been its natural constituency were not impressed. Continuing discontent led the frightened Rumpers in January 1650 to extend a new loyalty test, the Engagement, to all adult males, barring non-subscribers from office, and from legal proceedings. The undertaking required, a mere declaration of obedience to the current government, was minimal, and the legal sanctions were not widely enforced; but the Engagement was a major political mistake. To demand explicit recognition as the warrant for full citizenship was to concentrate attention on the propriety of allegiance to usurpers, and on the breach of other oaths – most notably the Solemn League and Covenant, with its undertaking to defend the king. Fairfax fell 'melancholy mad' over it, and the diaries of presbyterian clergy tell of anguished attempts to square providences with past obligations.

If nothing else, the Engagement encouraged systematic thinking about the grounds of government. The Rump's apologists urged conservatives to think beyond the old organic and scriptural pieties, and several argued the novel thesis of the irrelevance of moral considerations to government. Building on the bleak Calvinist view of human depravity, Pym's half-brother Francis Rous, the turncoat Marchamont Nedham, and Anthony Asham (whom royalists were soon to assassinate in Spain) saw in protection the over-riding purpose, and therefore in the sword the inescapable reality, of government. The case is more familiar from the two master-pieces of the period, Andrew Marvell's 'Horatian Ode' (1650) and Thomas Hobbes's *Leviathan* (1651). With its brilliantly enigmatic vision of Cromwell, and of the erect sword that inscribed the moment's poten-tial, Marvell's poem is the very emblem of the tensions of the Rump. Hobbes provided the Euclidean geometrician's analysis. His demonstra-tion of the essential egotism of all mankind left protection the universal need; and this, Hobbes the old royalist left unspoken, the Rump as the sitting tenant could provide.

The Rump could in general secure the acquiescence for which its defend-ers called. Where possible it tried to avoid driving further wedges into the political nation. In Chester at least the Engagement seems never to have been tendered, and it was not until July 1651 that the corporation of Coventry was purged. Many local officials were equally willing to live and let live: thus, almost 40 per cent of the members of Barnstaple corpora-tion in 1642 were still serving in 1650. But there were ominous signs of strain. In Exeter and Southampton a quorum for corporation meetings proved hard to find. While few JPs had been active in Devon even before Pride's Purge, thereafter order collapsed in some places, especially in the moorlands, and reports of a rise in crime elsewhere probably owed something to the reluctance of many JPs to act, as well as to the stricken economy. The overburdening of the few active 'pack horses', as the Cornish Rumper John Moyle called them, as much as the desire to remove enemies exposed by the Engagement, made a more widespread purge unavoidable by late 1650. In the extreme cases of Bedfordshire and Cheshire over one-third of the JPs were removed, to expose the failure of the moderate courses of 1649–50. Driven to bring yet more new men, and army officers, into local government, the Rump further increased gentry resentment.

The winter of 1649–50 was therefore a bleak time for those in power. The council of officers wondered if God had turned away His face, and Vane grew convinced that 'the whole kingdom would rise and cut their throats upon the first good occasion'. The Rump's vulnerability grew patent when in the early months of 1650 the young Charles Stuart, his hopes in Ireland dashed, swallowed his pride and moved towards the

Scottish Covenanters his father had thought so hostile to monarchy. Faced now with the threat of a royalist-presbyterian alliance, and with the disaffection of English presbyterians dangerously apparent, the Rump determined on a pre-emptive strike across the border. The abandonment of the defensive posture that had since 1642 underlain the parliamentarian case drove Fairfax to resign his command in protest in June 1650.

Fortunately for the Rump, the Scots were no less disunited. Hamilton's defeat in 1648 had brought vicious proscription. The exclusion from Scottish political life of the Engagers (those who had 'engaged with' Charles I) created an enduring fissure between the nobility and the clericalists. The government of the kirk party with which the young Charles II reluctantly came to terms was therefore isolated, its support largely confined to the fervently presbyterian southwest, and with Argyll its only major noble ally. It was a marriage of desperation for both sides, since the kirk had few illusions about the roystering Charles Stuart. Nevertheless, in June 1650 the Covenanters set about raising a godly host, and dismaying their generals by purging supporters of the Engagers.

Cromwell, who succeeded Fairfax as lord general, and who was in the eyes of some Rumpers their sole prop, must have seen little to hope for. As so often, he preserved his rear by conciliating the radicals – Lilburne, Ludlow, ex-cornet Joyce; but June was late in the campaigning season to be heading north, and he lacked men, money and supplies. The army's fervently millenarian declaration from Musselburgh on its way into Scotland, that it had taken Jesus to be its king, can as easily be read as a gesture of desperation as of confidence. David Leslie, Cromwell's old ally and rival for the credit of Marston Moor, had built an immensely strong defensive line between Berwick and Edinburgh, and Cromwell spent weeks in appalling weather trying to draw the Scots out to fight. By the end of August disease and privation had destroyed about a third of the English force, and supplies were dwindling. Sensing victory, but pressed on too by the dissensions in his own camp, Leslie left his fortifications and pinned the English down around the small port of Dunbar. There Cromwell, grimly conscious of the consequences of defeat, determined to risk everything by attacking the much larger enemy force, and in the dark morning of 3 September his main force followed Lambert's charge. Caught by surprise, the Covenanters were routed. It was Cromwell's most remarkable victory. Won over an army that itself militantly claimed to be God's chosen instrument, it only heightened the sense of election the general shared with his officers.

Dunbar did not end the threat from Scotland, but it changed its complexion. Charles Stuart now turned to the moderate wing of the kirk and to the remnants of the old Engagers. But if the pure army of the Covenant had fallen before the New Model, that of the king fared little better. Although Cromwell's long illness in the spring of 1651 gave Leslie time to consolidate, the summer saw the New Model cut the Scottish lines of communication. Overruling Leslie, who wanted to fight on friendly ground and exploit Cromwell's supply problems, Charles determined to march south and bid for English support.

Nervous Rumpers steeled themselves for disaster as they imagined a Stuart in arms back on English soil. Victory at Dunbar had convinced some beyond the army of new possibilities, and elicited from Marchamont Nedham some remarkable essays in the government's newspaper *Mercurius Politicus*. These developed a positive case for a republic shaped after republican Rome, in which the active citizen would find liberty as well as a dynamic national purpose. But such ardent classical republicanism had as yet limited appeal; the London newsbook *The Man in the Moon* circulated royalist lampoons of the Rumpers' sexual appetites and physical corruption, and left no doubt of the appeal of old metaphors. To counter these, and, no doubt, to reassure the army of their steadfastness, the Rumpers in December 1650 sent copies of the record of the king's trial for inclusion in the records of every county, and set aside 30 January 1651 as a day of thanksgiving for victory. The nation was unpersuaded: 1651 saw demoralisingly sparse attendances of the Somerset gentry at the local assizes, and all over the country assize courts rang with defensive sermons by reliable clergy on the necessity of magistracy. The almanacs whose popularity so perplexed and angered godly Rumpers did not need the stars to guide them in their predictions of a great crisis in the summer. The wounds opened by the Engagement among English presbyterians were still fresh.

Cromwell's decision to let Charles march south into England reflected a good sense of political as well as military realities. Unpopular as the Rump was, few presbyterians were willing to risk ruin, least of all for a king heading yet another invasion of the hated Scots. Fairfax gave his support for this defensive war, while the judicious execution of a London presbyterian minister, Christopher Love, for plotting deterred (though it also outraged) his colleagues; with royalists cowed by defeat and sequestration, only about 2000 Englishmen joined Charles. Indeed, the Scottish invasion generated considerable support for the regime. The godly flocked to rousing sermons in London, and to the county militias the Rump raised that summer. Cromwell therefore had a heavy numerical superiority when he caught up with the Scots at Worcester on 3 September 1651, the anniversary of Dunbar. However unsurprising the victory, to Cromwell it was God's 'crowning mercy'.

The Commonwealth was safe. Irish, Scots, presbyterians, royalists, all were defeated, and Charles Stuart barely escaped from an oak tree outside Worcester into exile. Physical security made it easier for the Rump to appeal to the nation for acceptance. Lawyers who had distanced themselves began to co-operate, while the Independent Lord Wharton, who had broken with Cromwell at Pride's Purge, in 1651 declared himself 'now satisfied'. Amongst the royalists too there were changes of heart.

That year John Evelyn followed the self-exiled Thomas Hobbes home to England, 'there being now so little appearance of any change for the better'. But among the Commonwealth's supporters there were new stirrings. England's triumph over its neighbours bred a heightened millennialism, and Peter Sterry, Cromwell's favourite preacher, foresaw Christ coming out of a united protestant north to free Europe. Cromwell gave such sentiments a different turn when in the elation after Dunbar he urged parliament to stand out for God's people, 'for they are the chariots and horsemen of Israel . . . relieve the oppressed, hear the groans of poor prisoners . . . be pleased to reform the abuses of all professions; and if there be any one that makes many poor to make a few rich, that suits not a commonwealth'.

Physical security brought the question of reform to the centre of politics. Victory as usual persuaded the army to speak out and, by freeing it from campaign, allowed it to do so. Pamphlets from the army's friends left no doubt that the creation of a republic had not satisfied the appetite for reform. But what reforming energy the Rump possessed was steadily diverted. The Rump was an executive as well as a legislature, and all its members were seduced by the pleasures of administration, and by institutional pride. Many of the more zealous amongst the Rumpers and their supporters came to rank the preservation of the republic as an end in itself. Such 'commonwealthsmen' as Hesilrig, a temperamental oligarch, or the provincial lawyer John Bradshaw, who had presided at the king's trial and over the Commonwealth's first council of state, were loath to consider the Rump as merely the path to better things intended by the army. The prospects for reform dimmed further as republicans who drew their inspiration primarily from classical sources redirected their energies. Henry Marten in particular had shown a genuine concern for the poor; but, as military victories flowed in, he, and Thomas Chalenor and Henry Nevile, cast themselves as English patriots. Entranced with the prospect of building what Milton was to call 'another Rome in the west', they sank their considerable energies into external relations and the building of a protestant republican empire.

Reform met other obstacles. It cost money, and the debts left by the civil wars – even without the burdens added later – were a millstone, forcing one parliamentarian government after another into a breathless and crippling sale of assets. First came the episcopal lands after 1646, and then under the Rump the crown lands, the lands of the deans and chapters (the senior cathedral clergy), and finally in 1651–2 the estates of 780 assorted unrepentant royalists. But since the political risks involved ensured that the estates sold at a discount, the financial gains were smaller than the political losses. So hard-pressed was parliament from 1646–52 that it used the land sales to entice unrepaid creditors to 'double', or lend as much again, with repayment to come from the confiscated estates. Those unable to lend more had little hope save to sell their notes at an alarming discount of 50–70 per cent, to widespread public and army resentment – resentment that swelled as the Rump failed to reform the laws against poor debtors. The bigger lenders, who could double, equally resented the rough treatment they received when in 1649 the Rump threatened to repudiate its debts unless creditors lent again for the Irish campaign. The scandalous mistreatment of the state's creditors meant that soon there was nobody left to lend to it; the worsening relations with the army after 1651 only made a bad risk worse. Rumper administration was much more efficient than that of the early Stuarts, but its solutions to the enduring problem of how to provide long-term funding were no better. Its political options were thus as severely constricted.

The gap between aspiration and achievement was greatest where the aims were highest. Although mopping-up operations continued, the Commonwealth after 1651 found itself to its manifest surprise what no previous regime had been: undisputed master of the British islands. As the Rumpers felt their way towards a policy, they came to realise they had in their grasp those British problems that had so perplexed their predecessors. The cynic might note that it was at the expense of Welsh royalists after the 1648 troubles, and of Scots and Irish rebels after 1650, that the Rump pioneered the imperial practice of transporting prisoners to distant colonies. But English aspirations for Britain were not merely crudely coercive.

Ireland seemed in some respects the more straightforward. Endemic rebellion, religious difference and assumptions of constitutional subordination inclined the English to visceral solutions to the Irish problem. Yet some leading Rumpers could still look beyond vengeance. When in 1650 John Cook, the state's solicitor at the king's trial, went to Ireland as provincial chief justice in Munster, he did so determined to use equity against the inequities and rigours of the English common law, the handmaid of the conqueror as well as of the lordly establishment. More signally, in the spring of 1651 Henry Marten helped draft a surprisingly unvindictive settlement for Ireland.

The return of the officers from bloody campaigning brought the debate back to its first principles, and in 1652–3 the so-called 'Cromwellian settlement' emerged. The long list of proscriptions, and the determination to clear Catholics from productive lands and confine them to the stony west, marked the army as the most recent, and thorough, of a long line of English conquerors. Hopes of a new beginning fell victim to the hunger for land and pay. And hopes for protestant evangelism were lost to financial crisis and the interminable bickering between the existing protestant settlers and the triumphant new arrivals, particularly the Baptists, eventually the Quakers.

The sheer novelty of dealing with Scotland, a protestant state with no clear constitutional relationship to England, drove the Rump towards its greatest innovation. Early hopes that the Scots might keep their Stuart king to themselves gave place in 1652 to the Tender of Union. The Rump, and the Cromwellians who later put union into effect, intended complete incorporation, under English law, in contrast to the loosely federal objectives of the Scottish Covenanters. Old certainties of the superiority of English institutions had been strengthened by experience on campaign. The officers and their allies lost few opportunities to publish their contempt for the Scottish lords and clergy who held their countrymen in bondage. Far more clearly than in Ireland, where policy was inextricably mixed with expropriation, the export of English ways would bring freedom. But, as in Ireland, reforms cost money. To challenge the feudal superiority of the Scottish nobility, and the influence of the presbyterian kirk, would require more intensive policing than a cash-strapped English regime could afford. Even in 1653 English commanders in Scotland were courting local support, and in so doing losing what little chance they had of reshaping Scottish society.

The Rump's story is everywhere one of narrowing options amidst financial stringency and political crisis. Perhaps its most important English chapter relates to church reform, since it was here that aspirations were most urgent. Despite the promptings of radicals, the Rump intended a national church. The one great concession to army pressure came after Dunbar in the (wrongly so-called) toleration act of September 1650, that repealed the statutory requirement that all attend parish churches every Sunday. But in an unmistakable sign of its priorities, the Rump gave far more publicity to its blasphemy act.

The Rumpers had two major ecclesiastical objectives. Like Laud, they wished to improve the financial position of the ministry, and they also sought to make preaching more available. But they found the Word harder to deploy than the sword: not least, there was little agreement on solutions. On the one hand, Baptists urged an end to the national church, and the replacement of tithes with voluntary contributions to ministers. On the other, presbyterians (who included Hesilrig) sought to retain, and even strengthen the tithe system. Meanwhile, Independents, whose numbers included at least 130 Independent parish ministers, as well as many virtual separatists, inclined towards the abolition of tithes but favoured some form of compulsory support. But any national measure would have been prohibitively costly, all the more so in view of the devastation caused by war.

The Rump's solutions were therefore piecemeal. It had intended a general augmenting of ministers' stipends, but chronic indebtedness meant that redemption of the 'public faith' claimed most of the church lands sold off between 1646 and 1650. By 1650 seventy-three augmentations had been awarded to Essex clergy and 129 to Lancashire, but around half of these had evaporated by 1653. The 'root and branchers' of 1641 would certainly have approved of the use of Lichfield Cathedral to employ the poor – but not of the transformation of St Paul's Cathedral into a barracks and St Asaph's into a wine shop.

The refurbishment of the national church was also to be measured by its efficiency. The Commonwealth's survey instituted in 1649 was soon receiving petitions, proposals and reports for putting everyone within three miles of a parish church. Even today the detail looks impressive. But the alteration of parish boundaries raised huge problems of property rights, in pews, to tithes, to appointments, to charitable endowments. Colchester and a few other towns on their own initiative amalgamated ill-supplied parishes; but late in the 1650s Cromwell's council was still wrestling with the petty disputes that blocked the survey's recommendations.

Frustrations arose too from the schemes that aimed to propagate the gospel into the 'dark corners of the land'. The godly concern about the backward, Catholic and politically suspect north and Wales was at last given focus by local pressure groups allied to powerful parliamentarians. Urged on by Colonel Harrison and Philip Jones, the south Wales boss, and the charismatic Welsh millenarian preachers Vavasour Powell and Morgan Llwd, early in 1650 the Rump established twin commissions for propagation in the north and in Wales. It set up similar bodies for Ireland and New England, although these inevitably were more ephemeral. Both the northern and the Welsh commissioners ejected assorted 'scandalous' clergy, and nearly 300 went in Wales; but replacements, and particularly Welsh-speaking replacements, proved hard to find. There the commissioners had to rely on some ninety itinerant preachers, scandalising conservatives in England who claimed that the preachers were as bookless as they were rootless. The drive for propagation led to the publication of several evangelical works in Welsh, as well as some for American Indians. But as always, good intentions were thwarted by financial stringency: only a third of perhaps sixty new schools founded in Wales between 1650 and 1653 survived to 1660.

Social reform was even less substantial, though there were ideas aplenty. The intellectual ferment was carried closest to power by the whirlwind figure of Hugh Peter. A favourite of Cromwell since their New Model days, Peter preached often at Whitehall. He saw glimmerings of the millennium in social improvement, and his social conscience was as broad as that of many of his radical contemporaries. His fertile mind ranged from the usual radical schemes for abolishing imprisonment for debt and for establishing state hospitals and cheap local courts to the advocacy of a national bank; and in his call for guaranteed agricultural prices he was unusual in thinking hard about farmers. But the most prolific generator of proposals was Samuel Hartlib, a Baltic immigrant and brilliant publicist. Coupling Francis Bacon's programme for the advancement of mankind through technology with millennial dreams of protestant enlightenment, Hartlib circulated to anybody he thought might be interested, or helpful, plans for reform in all walks of life: agriculture, medicine, education, commerce, all could be improved in order to reduce human misery and reform men and women. The Rump remained unmoved, though one of Hartlib's followers, Henry Robinson, did in 1650 come close to converting the post office into an 'office of addresses', to serve as a glorified patent office and scientific labour exchange.

The cries of the saints from the depths of the worst economic depression in a generation left gentlemen Rumpers cool to sweeping reform schemes. Nor was there much reformism in the localities. In Yorkshire the JPs countered the dearth in time-honoured fashion, harrying both traders in grain and the hapless squatters on wasteland; in Norwich, despite political changes in the corporation, there were no new initiatives. Most revealingly of all, bills against deer poaching, and measures for fen drainage that would worsen the lot of many commoners, fared better in this parliament of property-owners than did reform of the poor laws. Colonel Robert Bennet, a Cornish Baptist supporter of the Rump, thought it 'a sad omen . . . in these days of pretended reformation' that property should be set higher than compassion.

A similar tale of foot-dragging can be told of law and electoral reform. Prejudices against the lawyers had sharpened in the 1640s. All litigants had suffered as the war dislocated the courts. The poor had probably suffered most from the overthrow of the accessible provincial councils and courts of York and Ludlow, Lancaster and Durham, as well as the hugely popular Court of Requests, the central equity court for the poor. Levellers' advocacy of a radical decentralisation of the courts seemed to make sense. So did their attack on a 'Norman yoke' whose legal complexities and French tongue enriched lawyers and condemned poor men to death for minor property offences. Millenarians' calls for the simplicity of the Mosaic code spoke to similar dislocation and resentment.

The Rumpers on the other hand were property-owners, a fifth of them lawyers and most of the rest gentry. But though these might not themselves abhor the antiquated structure and expensive and (to laymen) unpredictable procedures of the courts, they could feel the political heat. In the aftermath of Worcester they established a law reform commission under the impressive chairmanship of Matthew Hale, who was later to become an eminent judge. Hale and his colleagues quickly addressed irrationalities in the imprisonment of debtors; but the lawyers grew nervous when the commission moved to consider another radical demand, decentralisation of the courts and local registers of title to land. The Rump agreed to fill one of the worst gaps left by the collapse of the ecclesiastical courts by at last establishing a procedure for probate of wills. For the rest, it would only concede symbol, not substance: in 1651 parliament replaced archaic law French with English as the language, and archaic court hand with 'ordinary, usual and legible hand' as the script, of the courts. In February 1653 the Rump failed to proceed with the Hale commission's summary report.

Creeping paralysis similarly beset the Rump's progress towards electoral reform. Members could not forget their peculiar status, evident in the

Purge itself. Nor, when attendances peaked at two hundred or so, could they ignore the paucity of their numbers, and the complaints of unrepresented constituencies. But they not unnaturally treasured their own seats, and had few illusions about their support in the country. And they did not relish cutting the state adrift from the last of its constitutional moorings. Only the seasonal nudges of the army drove them into action. The sweeping proposals advanced by Ireton in the 'Officers' Agreement' remained anathema, but after Dunbar Vane drew up a clever compromise that would have left the Rumpers undisturbed in their seats and 'recruited' new members for the vacant, but reapportioned, constituencies. The army, which fully reciprocated the Rump's resentments, saw Vane's scheme as a disguise for self-interest. After Worcester, tensions grew. Although the Rump at last agreed to a dissolution, albeit at the distant date of November 1654, it moved offensively slowly to give substance to its own electoral proposals.

The Commonwealth's claims to lasting historical significance have probably centred less on political revolution than on socio-economic transformation. Assessment of these requires a distinction between intended and unintended consequences.

A case for the progressiveness of the regime might be made on the land. The displacement of the nobility from government, the end of feudalism implicit in the abolition of the Court of Wards in 1646, the regime's forcible sales of crown, church and delinquent royalists' lands, all seem to point to a new order. The 1650s undoubtedly saw the intensification of commercial landownership, but (outside Scotland and Ireland) this was the result of economic crisis rather than deliberate policy. Detailed studies show no revolution in land ownership, and no influx of new and aggressive blood, for the vast majority of royalists had regained their estates through loans or mortgages even by the end of the 1650s. Nevertheless, the forced sales may have encouraged new practices, for the high sale prices ensured that, in order to recoup in a time of high taxes, purchasers had to rationalise. Paternalist traditions, already strained by abandonment of farms and accumulating rent arrears, were further weakened by growing competition between landlords and tenants who were each seeking to compensate themselves after a decade of disruption.

More cogent claims for the Commonwealth as a socio-economic watershed centre on the two Navigation Acts of 1650–1. The first of these, with its concern for trade statistics and the stimulation of manufactures, was powerfully shaped by the Hartlib circle. In its sweeping preference for 'a more free and open trade, than that of companies and societies', it expressed a scepticism shared with the Levellers about organisation through privilege. And in its hopeful if unenforceable gesture towards the subordination of the colonies to England's interest it gave an imperialist tinge to the expansionist economic agenda it announced. A more limited, if more precise, and more anti-Dutch, focus, characterised the 1651 Act. This sought both to replace the Dutch as the entrepot, or middlemen, of Europe, and to displace Dutch shippers: colonial as well as European goods must be carried directly to England, Ireland, or other colonies in English ships or ships of the colony, or country, of origin. The 1651 Act aimed not just at the surging re-export trade, but above all to boost shipping.

The Acts taken together established a national framework for trade. This was not quite the protectionist system that is sometimes assumed (integration of the colonial economies in the English interest emerged more clearly at the Restoration), but it was very different from the traditional, corporate approach to regulation by way of chartered companies. And although the Acts were by no means the programme of a radical merchant clique fast taking over a revolutionary government, they do reflect the developing readiness to think in terms of a 'public interest'.

The crisis that seemed to call for action was undeniable, for the European peace concluded in 1648 had exposed English shipping to superior Dutch vessels and organisation. By 1651 there were fifty Dutch ships to every one English in the Baltic trade, and the Dutch were edging English carriers out of the colonial ports too. They took with them European rather than English manufactures, and returned the colonial products, with their re-export profits, to Dutch rather than English ports. The threat was broad: to manufacturing, to shipping and ship-building (after agriculture, the largest employer of men) and to national security, since seamen and even ships were conscripted for wartime service as needed.

The first reaction of the Rump and its advisers was not to exclude but to copy the Dutch and their low-cost ways. The London interests that had remained most closely tied to the Rumpers were on the whole those with least stake in the early-Stuart trading order – colonial merchants, inter-lopers, inland traders. The structure of regulation had less appeal for these, and still less for the cosmopolitan group around Hartlib, than most. Their first preference seems to have been for free ports that could act as re-export centres on the model of low-duty Amsterdam. In an allied move, in 1651 the Rump reduced the legal maximum rate of interest from 8 per cent to 6 per cent. But admiration for the Dutch economy was tempered with resentment at growing competition from a people demonised in the press as prosaic, plebeian and predatory, and at all the injuries incurred over the decades in the east and in the fishing grounds. The jealous outcome was the Navigation Acts. But as long as English freight charges remained high, Dutch ships would carry the cargoes. It was therefore the bellicose aftermath rather than the Navigation Acts themselves that changed England's fortunes.

Admiration for the Dutch reinforced a very different strain within the Rump. The old dream of a union of protestants against the popish

Antichrist, strengthened by memories of the Elizabethan quasi-protectorate over the Dutch and by envious recognition of what Dutch economic strength had achieved against Spain, was fed by the victories in Scotland and Ireland. That dream gained partisan meaning when the death in 1650 of Prince William of Orange, a steadfast Stuart ally, offered the chance of alliance between anti-Orangist republicans in Amsterdam and anti-Stuart republicans in London. On such a platform protestant millennialists like Harrison and Vane and jingoistic classical republicans like Thomas Chaloner and Algernon Sidney could combine. From 1650 to early 1652 Rumpers sought to persuade the Dutch to submerge themselves, and their economy, in union with England. The Dutch were unimpressed.

The mutual slights entailed in the failure of union, reinforced by growing commercial resentments and a determination to make the world safe for republicans, took England into war with the Dutch in mid-1652. The Rump could ill afford a war, for despite substantial troop cuts since Worcester, the army still cost over £1.3 million per annum. But in one crucial respect the republic was well-prepared. The wartime naval expansion had been accelerated after 1648, when the defection of part of the fleet to Prince Rupert had increased the threat from privateers. After an unnerving beginning, Admiral Blake's navy, and Vane's naval administration, gradually gained the edge in the 'narrow seas', where the momentous innovation of line-ahead attacks on the enemy line was reinforced by prevailing westerly winds that favoured England. By the war's end in 1654 the ratio of Dutch to English losses was over four to one, and the prizes at last allowed English ship-owners to compete more effectively.

The war was not all gain. The scale of the military establishment meant that the Rump ran constantly at a deficit, and it dared not raise the assessment, its major tax, any further. Sporadic riots in 1652–3 showed that the excise was still more resented. The war was therefore fought in an even more hand-to-mouth fashion than most early modern wars as the republic drifted closer towards bankruptcy. Even in 1652 the excise was mortgaged, 'anticipated', for four years into the future. But there were political consequences too. Just as the army could be fired by its victories, so could the Rump. Naval and commercial successes, and organisational efficiency, fostered an unrepentant pride in what 'commonwealthsmen' from the godly Hesilrig and Scot to Sidney saw as the rule of the virtuous. Increasingly convinced of their own legitimacy, the Rumpers set on a collision course with the soldiers.

A growing religious reaction fuelled the confrontation. Partly as a result of the discharged soldier-preachers who returned to civilian life, it was in the early 1650s rather than in the 1640s that the sectarian challenge extended beyond the towns into the countryside. Thomas Hall, minister of King's Norton in Warwickshire, had prided himself on the unity of his parish, but early in 1651 he lamented the first signs of heresy in his flock, and denounced Baptist missionaries from nearby towns. Similarly, in the spring of 1652 the ministers in a combination lecture in rural Somerset agreed to pool their talents against a sectarian onslaught. What the clergy found alarming was not just plebeian enthusiasts like John Bunyan, or the first Quakers, but also the learned biblical exegesis of the Socinian John Biddle, who dared to question the divinity of Christ. The last year or so of the Rump therefore brought a new spate of county petitions in favour of the established ministry, order, and protestant truth.

The Rump responded by setting itself more firmly against the radicals. That old faithful of mainstream puritanism, Stephen Marshall, again became a favourite preacher to parliament; meanwhile, the Independent divines Owen and Nye attracted considerable support as they tried to establish 'fundamentals' of doctrine against Biddle and the sects. Milton the heretic showed his disquiet in his twin sonnets on Cromwell (anxious) and Vane (adulatory). The crowning blow for the saints came early in 1653 when the Rump discontinued the Welsh commission for propagation.

Nowhere that winter did the Rump appear an agent of reform. The dashing of the Hale commission for law reform underlined what could be learned from the worsening legislative record. Only one-third as many public bills were passed in 1652 as in 1649. The pressure of business on a weary legislature that was also a wartime executive explains much. But radicals noticed only what they took to be Rumpers's self-interest – a self-interest that conflicted with the heart of the cause, the cardinal principle of self-denial.

The worst charges of self-interest were surely unfounded. They are offset by Lucy Hutchinson's lament for the Ireton, the soul of self-denial, who died in 1651; and they are offset too by the emerging ideology of 'public interest', and of service to an impersonal state. There were moves towards a salaried administration, the sale of offices declined, and the taking of fees incurred disapproval. What we know of administration speaks well of the godly consciences of the Independents and Baptists who provided so many of the servants of the new and growing state. Nevertheless, offices still tended to be seen as private property, and MPs certainly accumulated them. Where the Rump did err was in its concentration of executive, legislative and judicial power. The harassment of Lilburne in 1652 for a feud with Hesilrig smacked of tyranny, and when the interests of God's people were jeopardised by the tired Rumpers' long weekends, Cromwell could but scent gross worldliness. His angry tirade when he eventually expelled the Rump had some plausibility.

Many of the saints were less restrained in their denunciations. The growing conviction in the months of frustration after Worcester that the men and institutions they had trusted were corrupt drove some to ask fundamental questions about the nature of authority. The excitement born of the British as well as the Dutch wars, of constant political upheaval and enduring economic dislocation, led millenarians in various gathered churches to put a firmer interpretation upon prophecy. Charles's execution in 1649 seemed the end of the fourth, and last, earthly monarchy foretold in scripture; the fifth monarchy, that of Christ and his saints, was beginning. Artisans and craftsmen in the inchoate and unprogrammatic Fifth Monarchist groups listened eagerly as the Londoners Christopher Feake and John Simpson, the Welshman Vavasour Powell, and their great patron colonel Harrison, preached that the time for the politicians was past and that the hour of the saints had come. The Fifth Monarchists probably numbered less than 10 000, but they had vital supporters, like Harrison, in the army.

The army was not the monolith it had been in 1647. The soldiers were now more obviously professionals than partisans, their sense of injured pride had diminished, and their quarters were more scattered across the country. Yet opinion in the army had hardened in other respects, for ideological sophistication was growing. While probably no more of the soldiers were saints than in 1647, their Musselburgh declaration of 1650 for King Jesus, which cast the whole struggle of the 1640s in apocalyptic terms, boded ill for a parliament whose reformism had died. Furthermore, Nedham's editorials of 1650–1 in *Mercurius Politicus* had helped disseminate Machiavelli's argument that a vigorous people in arms was the mainstay of a free republic. That contention had considerable appeal to an army whose central political tenet remained its 1647 denial that it was a 'mere mercenary army'. Even the godly Lilburne was coming in the early 1650s to appreciate classical historians' analyses of the dialectic of freedom, corruption and tyranny, and the application of such a dialectic to the Rump. The officers still found 'freedom' difficult to define – Edmund Ludlow, an officer and Rumper, later claimed vaguely that the soldiers had fought 'that the nation might be governed by its own consent'. They demanded free elections, yet no matter how careful the electoral provisions no new representative would be any friendlier to the army and its goals than was the Rump. Both Rumpers and officers were trapped by their principles. The chief end for the former was the survival of parliamentary sovereignty, for the latter by the winter of 1652–3 it was getting rid of the Rump. There was recurrent talk of a coup.

The key to the conflict lay in Cromwell. Rumper and general, he personified the tension that had always characterised the parliamentarian cause, between the moderate constitutionalism of the gentry and radical puritanism. Tithes were to him both a perplexing anomaly and a matter of property rights. Most MPs had to wrestle only with the disillusionment of politics – a great argument for the Dutch war was, in Vane's eyes, the opportunity it gave God to break 'the great silence in heaven' after Worcester. But Cromwell's prolonged experience of the battlefield had kept his millenarian enthusiasm alive. He could share the impatience of officers and gathered churches with the Rump's pomp and ceremonial as it flaunted its success in governing the state, though its reforming energy, and moral credit with the saints, was exhausted. But his own priorities were as they had been in 1647, a settlement along traditional lines and reform. He was still the man of the old middle group, the friend of St John; and in the aftermath of Worcester he had talked of a settlement with 'somewhat of monarchical power in it'. It was probably his growing desire for an executive with the power to reform, as well as his weariness of the bickering between Rump and army, that led in November 1652 to his outburst, 'What if a man should take upon him to be king?'

The exact cause of Cromwell's expulsion of the Rump will never be known, since he seems to have destroyed the evidence. In the winter of 1652–3 he strove as he had in 1647 to avoid the use of force. Moderating between the officers and MPs, he even persuaded the Rump to bring forward the date for its dissolution to November 1653. Though he recognised that fresh elections would be a disaster, he remained adamant that the Rump must go, if only to preserve the all-important unity of the army. He seems to have hoped that the Rumpers would entrust power to a small body of godly reformers until the world became safe for elections. But in April 1653 he discovered how violently the Rumpers opposed the army. His plan would have allowed the officers an indefinitely extended role in politics, and this the Rumpers could not tolerate. The Rump does not seem to have tried to perpetuate itself by reviving Vane's plan for recruiter elections, as the army later claimed. Rather, it hurried a bill for a November dissolution and fresh elections that would leave a committee of former Rumpers the judge of those elected. The officers saw this as a recipe for continuing affronts from the civilians. After weeks of withdrawal from politics for his customary 'waiting on the Lord', Cromwell angrily called in the troops on 20 April.

As so often, Cromwell acted first and then tried to work out the implications later. He later testified that the move into the constitutional unknown made his hair stand on end. The nation seems to have been less unnerved by the demise of such a long parliament. Uncertainty about the future was clearly outweighed by relief at the fall of the Rump with all its committeemen: as Cromwell himself noted, 'there was not so much as the barking of a dog' in protest. One Independent minister reported that all was quiet, 'and could we but be eased of taxes, we should not much mind who ruled over us'. Quarter sessions continued to meet, and – apart from some uncertainty in the management of levies for the Dutch war – the country continued to function, although all legitimate authority had gone. A major worry for the officers had been the expiry in June of the current act for the monthly assessment. The readiness of taxpayers to defer to what became thereafter merely an arbitrary demand illuminates both the power of the sword and the acceptance of the claims of the state.

Nevertheless, the army needed a long-term solution, for Cromwell as lord general was left the only power in the land. The council of officers, dominated by Independents and Baptists, had given little thought to the future, and was, like Cromwell, more interested in godliness than in constitutions. But some amongst them felt capable of filling the void. The secular-minded Lambert advocated a small executive council, to govern until the time was ripe for a new parliament; Harrison urged an assembly of saints, modelled on the Old Testament sanhedrin, to fit the land for the imminent coming of Christ. Although few officers were Fifth Monarchists, Harrison could appeal to the broad millenarian hopes of many. Not least of these was Cromwell, who repeatedly declared his belief that the kingdom of Christ would be realised spiritually, in the hearts of men, and not physically on earth: the way to it was through liberty of conscience and the elimination of evils. Characteristically, he achieved an unlikely compromise. An assembly, nominated primarily by the officers, was by its reforms to win the people over to godliness, thus preparing the way for a new, and godly, parliament. In the meantime the officers appointed a new and army-dominated council of state.

Through May and June the interim government struggled with the problems of security. The demands of the Dutch war were compounded by the beginnings of an almost nationalist revolt in Scotland, causing trouble as far south as the Borders; reports came of armed bands in Yorkshire as economic crisis continued. In this tense atmosphere the council of officers, drawing on its knowledge of local conditions, rather than on any sectarian 'slate', prepared nominations to the new assembly. Cromwell must have breathed a sigh of relief when he handed over power.

The nominated assembly was eventually, and famously, satirised as 'the Barebone's Parliament', after one of its members, the London leather-seller and radical Independent, Praise-God Barebone. The first 'British' assembly, containing (hand-picked) members for Scotland and Ireland, the Barebone's (as we may, reluctantly, call it) contained few regular officers, since Cromwell was eager to take the army out of politics. Nor was it generally disreputable – over one-third of the members might have warranted election to any ordinary parliament, and nearly two-thirds had been JPs for more than three years. Indeed, some hardly fit the zealous profile: thus, Sir Anthony Ashley Cooper, future Earl of Shaftesbury and patron of John Locke, already inscrutable in his religion, had probably attracted Cromwell's notice as a reformer on the Hale commission. But the assembly did contain many more minor gentry than had other parliaments, with perhaps a dozen Fifth Monarchists (often allies of Harrison and Powell from north Wales) in a total of 144 members. Their impact was magnified by their energy, and by the way that just as in the army command they acted as an activist leaven in a more largely millenarian lump.

Cromwell typifies that broader millenarianism. In his opening speech on 4 July he enthusiastically declared that 'this may be the door to usher in things that God hath promised and prophesied of'. But while Harrison was certain that the time had come to break down earthly powers,

Cromwell warned, 'These things are dark.' He looked towards a time when all the nation were God's people, but he made clear that the new sovereign authority was only to sit for a limited time, and was to prepare for a return to parliaments. This was not to be the constituent assembly, reshaping England, to which it has sometimes been likened. Any reshaping was to be moral, not constitutional.

The early proceedings suggested that the polarisation of the Rump was past. The act of self-aggrandisement by which the assembly promptly declared itself a parliament was opposed both by Fifth Monarchists and by moderates who saw this as no true parliament. The new council of state the parliament elected in July was also reassuringly bipartisan, balancing a handful of Fifth Monarchists with moderates and officers. Indeed, considerable bipartisan reform work went on until the end. Nor was there a radical take-over: the house's November poll for the council of state produced a more moderate body than had the July vote. Most impressive, however, was the conscientiousness of members; in its five months' existence the Barebone's passed over thirty acts and had other major bills in preparation. And much of the content of these was eminently worthy. There were bills continuing Rumper efforts to unite the commonwealths of England, Scotland and Ireland, to settle Ireland, to revise the excise and to limit both confusion and corruption by uniting the many separate treasuries into one.

But godly reform was the reason for the assembly's existence, and by such reform it was and is judged. Members had been given a good start in the field of law reform by the Hale commission, and they drew on its work as they gave piecemeal relief to suffering debtors and to creditors. The civil marriage act, one of the few substantive measures, was a belated and plausible attempt to repair damage done by the destruction of the church courts. But though few doubted the need for some matrimonial jurisdiction, the requirement that marriages must be performed by a JP rather than the parish minister was unpopular, and patchily observed. Confusion ensued, about which the North Riding JPs complained, while the grand juries of Essex and Lancashire presented misregistration of marriages as a grievance to the commonwealth.

Even the notorious August vote to abolish the court of Chancery forthwith was less peremptory than it seems, coming as it did amidst other moves to reduce lawyers' fees and foibles. Chancery was vulnerable as an equity court, a court of conscience, when some radicals felt the consciences of lawyers should give way to the consciences of saints. But there seems to have been surprisingly little opposition to the vote for abolition. Chancery had long been criticised as the most arbitrary, clogged and expensive of all courts – there were said to be 23 000 cases pending in 1653. In the country even Anthony Nicoll, one of the conservative 'eleven members' of 1647, could view its demise with equanimity, provided it was replaced with another equity court.

For all its careful work, the Barebone's also manifested the dangers of pressure-group politics. Progress with reform was of course assured by the barring of conservatives, but it accelerated as wealthier, and perhaps more moderate, members withdrew to the country to escape the City's heat and bustle. Few were left determined enough to counter the fire of the zealous. And the fire was fed from outside. The prospect of change had brought a new Leveller flurry, and demands were heard in the streets and in the press not for Hale's proposals but that the laws be reduced to 'the bigness of a pocket book' in the interests of cheapness and justice. Likewise, the Fifth-Monarchists' pulpits resounded with calls for the Mosaic code, the only positive laws given by God. Vavasour Powell caught the spirit of both groups when he declared, 'Laws should stream down like a river freely, . . . impartially as the saints please [sic], and . . . should run as rivers do, close to the doors.' Rather than the rationalisation that many sought, a wholesale onslaught on the body of law seemed at hand. Alarm grew, among moderates at Westminster and beyond. A Cheshire gentleman concluded gloomily that a sale of land would be difficult because of his father's 'uncertainty of what alterations may now be in the law'.

Religious reform was as dangerous. On one extreme stood the conservative gentry who owned tithes and advowsons and saw them as legal property to be touched only at great peril. On the other stood the increasingly clamorous sects, who rejected all compulsion, whether in worship or in payment. In the middle, as during the Rump, were the many who recognised the abuses of the tithe system but feared the disintegrative effects of complete voluntarism. It was the strength of the last group that brought a vote in November for the introduction of a bill outlawing patronage in church livings, and persuaded 56 members to join in the crucial vote of 10 December against a conservative defence of tithes. Moderates could vote with radicals for goals that the reformers of 1641 would have recognised. But some in these times had rejected the aspirations of 1641, and the sects and the Fifth Monarchists petitioned the house against a national church and the universities too as a relic of the old popish Antichristian captivity. The threats to the ministry were long to shape clerical and conservative attitudes. In 1653 Ralph Josselin resolved to stop buying books, such was his fear for the future.

Cromwell had more immediate grounds for concern. The old civilian hostility to the army resurfaced, in a remarkable new guise. The well-organised radical caucus in the house, which was now as alert as Lilburne to the different faces of tyranny, blocked the renewal of the excise and attacked the monthly assessment, the army's chief support. When sailors were rioting for lack of pay this led Cromwell, who had studiously left the new sovereign power undisturbed, to complain that he was 'more troubled with the fool than before [during the Rump] with the knave'. Indeed, the executive capacity of the council of state was sadly deficient, and a war was being fought. Furthermore, while some Fifth Monarchists embraced war with the Dutch devotees of Mammon as the best place to begin breaking down earthly powers, many moderates thought that recent naval successes should allow a speedy and favourable peace. For his part, Cromwell still hoped for a protestant alliance, and grew steadily more impatient with the council, and with the haste of parliament's reforms.

The rejoicing among the lawyers and clergy at the eventual demise of the Barebone's parliament suggests something of the alarm it had caused. After the event, John Thurloe, secretary to the council, sent a horrified report to England's solitary ambassador abroad of the magnitude of the threat that had been posed. It was not just the December vote on tithes; the radicals' bellicosity would have ruined trade, while arbitrary rule threatened conscience, liberties and estates, and risked driving the soldiers to dangerous distraction. The propertied had other reasons to worry. There had been huge demonstrations in London in the autumn to celebrate Lilburne's acquittal on yet another capital charge. Equally ominous were the changes in local government. At some point between mid-1652 and late 1653, and probably in the Barebone's period, massive changes occurred in many county commissions of the peace. Over two-thirds of the Surrey names were deleted, over a half in five more counties, and while some of the newcomers were probably mere anti-Rumpers rather than fiery radicals, it was certainly in late 1653 that yeomen and shopkeepers first appeared on the Cumberland commission. In order to stop the rot, forty or more moderates in the house, who included the aged Speaker Francis Rous, Sir Charles Wolseley and other future Cromwellians, staged a parliamentary coup. Exploiting the absence of radicals at a prayer meeting, they trooped off to Whitehall on 12 December to return their power to the lord general.

This time the army leaders were more prepared. Lambert had in late November urged Cromwell to take the crown, in hope of the reform mixed with stability they both craved. But Cromwell flinched once again from using force, and from the crown too – as he was soon to claim frequently enough for plausibility, he did not seek self-exaltation. More important, he had never taken a political initiative unless necessity enforced it. It was only when providence, or rather the moderates who had doubtless been schooled by Lambert, thrust power into his hands that he took it. He did so the more willingly for being able to console himself later with the thought that Barebone's would have brought 'the confusion of all things'. Those sentiments were a far cry from his zeal in July for the cause of 'the people of God'; but unlike Harrison, Cromwell always coupled the interests of 'men as men and Christians as Christians', and protested that 'He sings sweetly that sings a song of reconciliation between these two interests.' Like countless other parliamentarian gentlemen before him, he was to come to recognise the difficulty of harmonising them.

|12|

Oliver Protector, 1653–1658

To republicans of various stripes the events of 1653 were the great betrayal. 'Commonwealthsmen' such as Vane, Hesilrig, Ludlow, Scot, never forgave Cromwell for the expulsion of the Rump, while godly enthusiasts of the Barebone's lamented the turn to earthly concerns. Others welcomed the inauguration of the protectorate, and early in 1654 the Marquess of Worcester was exchanging pleasantries and tokens with the new lord protector. He would not have been surprised had he heard the protector remark to his first parliament that year, 'A nobleman, a gentlemen, a yeoman, that is a good interest of the nation and a great one.' Yet the protector presented his rule not as reaction but as a golden mean between monarchy and commonwealth, between licence and tyranny. In December 1653 Lambert dusted off the scheme he had urged in the spring and presented it as the Instrument of Government, England's first written constitution. The mixed forms of government it offered were not to be the lowest common denominator but a serious attempt to apply the lessons of recent experience to English practices.

The single-person executive (the lord protector), restrained by a parliament and a council, that replaced the Commonwealth's sovereign single-chamber parliament was akin to Pym's goal of 1641. Pym would most surely have approved of the insistence that in stipulated areas the protector was to act only with the consent of his council. These restrictions may have been more than paper, for Cromwell complained to his second parliament in 1657 that he had been hemmed in as 'a child in swaddling clouts'. Equally close to the hopes of 1641 was the insistence that there should be no legislation nor taxation without the consent of parliament, and that control over the militia was to be shared with parliament. But it was on the work with Ireton in 1647, and the labours of the winter of 1648–9, that Lambert drew for the Instrument's electoral reforms and for its weakening of the ruler's legislative veto.

The constitution-makers had learned under the Commonwealth that threats to liberty did not only originate at court. Parliament too had a potential for tyranny, and of course for obstructionism. Accordingly, the novel theme of the separation of powers is implicit in the Instrument, and indeed explicit in some of the early defences of the protectorate. While the *Nineteen Propositions* and the Heads of Proposals had sought above all to limit the executive, the Instrument provided government with considerable freedom of action. The protector could issue ordinances with the force of law until the first meeting of parliament, scheduled for 3 September 1654 (a striking concession to protectoral superstition, for that was the anniversary of Dunbar and Worcester); he could raise certain funds indefinitely for the support of the army and navy independently of parliament; and parliament was to have only limited control over the council. Appropriately, the main defence of the Instrument, Nedham's *True State of the Case of the Commonwealth*, showed a trace of weariness with parliaments as it deployed the fashionable republican argument of public interest.

But governments are judged not just by their forms but by their conduct, and the company they keep. Here the protectorate seems more than ever an exercise in ambiguity. Though Cromwell did not take the crown, his official signature to documents, 'Oliver P.' departed only slightly from the regal form 'Charles R.' He also reclaimed some of the dispersed treasures of the late king that had escaped the Rump's self-aggrandisement. In his celebratory poem, 'The First Anniversary', Andrew Marvell deftly caught the undefinable when he concluded, 'Abroad a king he seems, and something more,/At home a subject on the equal floor.' For in stark contrast to the flattering portraits of Charles I, Cromwell's famous instructions were that he be painted 'warts and all'. The installation of the protector, with Lambert bearing the sword of state and Oliver himself clothed in plain black, carefully combined pomp and circumstance with the military and the godly. This was no monarch embodying the body politic; but neither was it the active citizenry embodied of republican visions.

The flavour of Oliver's rule can best be caught from those around him. The departing republicans were replaced at the centre by a small group of officers less millenarian than Harrison, and by civilians like Wolseley and Ashley Cooper who had had no connection at all with the revolution of 1648–9. And Pym's old ally Oliver St John was at the protector's elbow throughout. A regular court appeared, though the gentlemen of the protector's chamber were army officers rather than the Stuarts' Anglo-Scottish lords. Those courtly officers symbolise aptly the protector's continuing efforts to sheathe the sword. But sheathing the sword was not the same as laying it down, and the continuities with the immediate past are as evident as the departures. In the localities, the protector left in place the remaining garrisons that so troubled the gentry and clergy, and the many army officers who served as JPs. And while he seemed to don the trappings of monarchy, handed out knighthoods, and included more civilians than serving officers on his council, the other figure at his side for much of his rule was the brilliant, witty – but still soldierly – John Lambert.

The Instrument's weaknesses are obvious in retrospect. There was no provision for amendment, nor for the adjudication of disputes. Its provisions for liberty of conscience and for the independence of the government ignored the very different concerns of most parliament-men since 1642. Nevertheless, the Instrument did wrestle with the central problems of an over-mighty prince and an over-mighty parliament. Given mutual tolerance and adequate funding, it might have worked.

The government's immediate problem was that of transition. None could be sure of the willingness of the nation to obey, and there was a war on, with the Dutch. As the first of many half-baked royalist and Leveller assassination plots troubled the protector's peace, the council lost no time in preparing a new treason ordinance, and in reincarcerating Lilburne. But Oliver had a large asset in the reaction against the Barebone's. Fifth-Monarchists denounced him as 'the dissemblingest perjured villain in the world', but the silence in the army that greeted Harrison's dismissal showed that discipline was far stronger than millenarian fervour where it really mattered. The protector made an elaborately staged entry into the City in February, and eagerly broadcast the deference he was displayed. But a more typical response may have been Matthew Hale's when he accepted a judgeship, thinking it 'absolutely necessary to have justice and property kept up at all times'. Anyway, taxes kept coming in. As always, authority, and the sword, prevailed when chaos was the alternative.

Cromwell hoped for more than acquiescence. True to his old 'middle group' credentials, he sought 'healing and settling', as he was to tell his first parliament. Accordingly, the council purged some of Harrison's radical allies from the Welsh commissions of the peace, and smiled as a few political 'presbyterians', such as Sir George Booth in Cheshire, crept back into local office. Fewer of the moderate, unpartisan country gentry responded than Oliver must have hoped, and the commissions of Devon, Cumberland and Buckinghamshire remained virtually unchanged. But there were some gains, and by 1655 the average income of the Worcestershire JPs was almost twice what it had been in 1652. Gentry life slowly regained a semblance of normality, and Buckinghamshire hunting parties included formerly royalist Verneys as well as Oliver's son Richard and his son-in-law John Claypole. But Cromwell's aim was never simply to conciliate the gentry.

Political stability was to be within a godly commonwealth. The two main defences of the protectorate in 1654, *The True State of the Case of the Commonwealth* and Milton's *Second Defence of the English People*, laid great stress on public and personal virtue; and Cromwell himself, who had never been committed to formal programmes, repeatedly urged rule by good men. The appointment to the bench of Matthew Hale, the finest lawyer, and one of the most tolerant minds, of his generation, gave some substance to his claims.

But the protector's hopes went beyond good men. Oliver confessed his bafflement at the rickety structure of England's laws. He brought in as his legal adviser the most far-sighted legal reformer of his day, William Sheppard, a country lawyer and author of *England's Balme* (1656); and intermittently in 1654 he urged the profession to reform itself. But his council was no readier than the Rump to confront the legal profession's hostility to decentralisation. The one step towards improving access to law in distant areas was, ironically, the restoration in 1654 of the ancient palatine, or semi-independent, jurisdiction of Lancaster. Not for nothing had Thurloe, soon to be secretary of state, confided in January that henceforth the people would be 'governed by the good old laws'. Ignoring army pressure, the council entrusted reform of chancery and the common law courts to senior lawyers. So the measures for simplifying procedure and reducing frauds and fees in chancery that the ordinance of August 1654 introduced were thoroughly moderate; indeed, they seem to have been moderate enough to have some effect with the foot-dragging lawyers. Still less far-reaching were the internal orders the common law judges introduced that December to regulate their courts. The level of reform consonant with 'healing and settling' was proving low indeed.

Merchants as well as lawyers could find reassurance in a government that, like its royal predecessors, reacted to petitions instead of initiating. Many of the protector's more radical supporters in army and country assumed that ideals of self-denial and commonwealth precluded privilege and corporate restrictions; but Oliver was not averse to the forms of monopoly permitted by the 1624 statute. Not content with upholding the Leeds merchant oligarchs in their long struggle with the clothworkers, Oliver reinforced merchant oligarchy in his only new urban incorporation, at Swansea in 1655. His council bowed again before local interests when in 1657 it brought framework-knitting (a new craft omitted from the Elizabethan regulatory statutes) under corporate control. Under the Rump the trade of the East India Company had been open to interlopers, but in 1657 the council restored the old mutual dependency of government and company, with loans being the return on grants of privileges, when it granted the company a new charter. Neither revolution nor Navigation Act had liberated England's economy.

Social reform was was even further from realisation. Ever ready to respond solicitously to individual approaches, the protector had little to offer the poor as a whole. His hard-pressed government made no move to reduce the number of items subject to the excise, a levy that like most sales taxes fell heavily on the poor. The social issues on which the army had campaigned in 1647, such as pensions for soldiers' widows and orphans, remained as dependent as ever on local initiatives at quarter sessions. Only indirectly, through the sizeable military contracts the government handed out, and through its success in keeping nearly 3 per cent of the male labour force under arms, thus raising wage rates for the rest, did it benefit those for whom the agitators had claimed the war had been fought.

It was in its religious policy that the protectorate held closest to the army's ideals of 1647. The soldiers had declared that their intentions were to maintain unity and to secure freedom for tender consciences – not to establish Independency. The protector's lamentations for the disunity he saw all around, and his simultaneous complaints at those who sought to 'press their finger upon their brethren's conscience', were thus entirely in keeping. Cromwell's record has been celebrated as one of protestant ecumenicism at its finest; and at the time one Baptist wrote feelingly, 'this alone is worth all the blood and treasure that hath been spent'. But the protector aimed as little at toleration in the modern sense as had the soldier-saints in 1647.

The Instrument guaranteed freedom to all save papists, prelatists (or episcopalians), deniers of Christ and disturbers of the peace. In practice toleration was certainly wider than that, and despite the abolition of the prayer book and occasional bursts of repression in political crises, Anglicans on the whole worshipped unmolested. Visitors to London seem to have had little difficulty in obtaining Anglican sacraments, and these were probably readily available in many parts of the countryside. Similarly, whatever the government's political anti-Catholicism, individual English Catholics fared better than they had under kings greedy for money from recusancy fines. But the liberty for which Oliver strove was emphatically a liberty for godly protestants. He contemplated with equanimity the punishment of such a denier of the divinity of Christ as Biddle the Socinian, or the Ranters whom he regarded as 'diabolical'. It was not simply the conservative gentleman in him that sympathised with those who cried out against excesses. Like most of his contemporaries, he saw antitrinitarianism and antinomianism as heresies, not simply errors and disorders, and as invitations to God to punish the land.

Accordingly, Oliver strove to reunite the godly. He was too much the Independent to pursue a confession of faith or formulary of practices. Instead, he sought a broad frame for a national church that could avert scandal and win over dissidents. He might have been successful. The ageing of the surviving bishops meant that, unless renewed, the episcopal leadership of the old church of England must die out in the next decade. And there was much to build with. The parochial order still more or less functioned, especially in the countryside, and probably half the nation's pulpits were occupied in the 1650s by those who had filled them in 1642 – less than a third of the clergy were purged under the various parliamentarian regimes (in Herefordshire, only thirty-three parishes were affected, out of more than 200). Cromwell turned to the 'fundamentals' proposed in 1652 by the anxious Independents, Owen and Nye, as he set about adding to this old puritan remnant: a centralised test of basic requirements would provide a national frame to bolster orthodoxy. A March 1654 ordinance therefore set up a commission of 'triers' in London to examine those seeking appointment as 'public ministers' in parish livings. While critics complained that the triers sometimes sought evidence of the spiritual arousal dear to the saints rather than of pastoral suffi-ciency, the episcopal examinations of old had often been haphazard enough. And Cromwell was careful to balance Independent and Baptist triers with presbyterians in his bid to build a broad, and doctrinally ortho-dox, church.

Internal discipline would be provided locally. A second ordinance, in August 1654, established county commissions of 'ejectors', composed like the triers of both laity and clergy. These were to purge ministers and schoolmasters guilty of moral, political or gross pastoral failings. At least 150 ministers were ejected, close to 2 per cent of the parochial total. Although the council (unlike Restoration authorities) made some attempt to provide for the families of victims, ejectors were generally reluctant to proceed against the livings of ministers without statutory warrant. It was the old story of the obstruction of reform by property rights. Neverthe-less, Cromwell attached considerable importance to the triers and ejectors, and boasted, 'There hath not been such a service to England since the Christian religion was perfect in England.' Richard Baxter, looking back after the Restoration, was tempted to agree.

Among the regime's supporters some had hoped that conquered Ireland might be made a blueprint for reform in England. But perhaps even more here than at home pragmatism and financial constraints blocked the reformers' aspirations.

The novelty of the so-called 'Cromwellian settlement' did not lie in its outline. The protector merely implemented the plans of the Rump, which in turn had adopted the gist of the schemes of the Adventurers of 1642 and their adaptors in 1647: Catholic miscreants should pay for their own punishment. Rather, novelty lay in the sweeping scale.

Debts dictated policy. Beyond the huge costs of reconquest, and the £300 000 debt to the Adventurers, the pay of 35 000 soldiers was in arrears. But not even massive expropriation of Irish Catholic landowners could bring financial stability and protestant hegemony. As the remark-able land survey carried out by William Petty proceeded, it became clear that the land available could never satisfy all the demands on it. Nor could physical security be achieved through the establishment of a loyal protes-tant yeomanry. The brutal intention of clearing the ground for others by expropriating the Irish 'according to their respective demerits', as the act of settlement put it, soon foundered.

Protestant settlers proved no easier to attract than they had been for James's Ulster plantation. The easing of economic conditions in England, and delays in the settlement of claims, ensured that only about 7500 of the 35 000 soldiers entitled finally settled in the country. The rest, weary and disillusioned, sold out to officers, speculators and pre-war New English. But the purchasers still needed labour, and connived at the presence of Catholic labourers and even tenant farmers; similarly, town corporations winked at Catholic townsmen who illegally stayed on. For the landless Irish poor, who formed about three-quarters of the total population, the Cromwellian settlement probably made little practical difference to the hardships they already suffered.

Nevertheless, the effects of the settlement should not be minimised. The enforced migration of some 40 000 Catholic landowners and their families in the winter of 1654–5 is a story of horror. There was not enough land in Connacht, and many of the dispossessed took to brigandage, becoming 'tories' in the language of the time. They thus prolonged the brutalities inflicted by one side or other on the survivors. Others emigrated, whether voluntarily or forcibly as England developed the practice of penal trans-portation. More far-reaching were the social consequences of the settle-ment, which laid the grounds for the later 'protestant ascendancy'. Catholics held some 60 per cent of the land in Ireland in 1641, but just over 20 per cent in 1660. The exclusion of Catholics from urban trades and offices left little chance of a Catholic middle class forming, and in consequence religion became more than ever an index of nationalism.

There were few positive achievements to balance the equation. The protectorate's near-bankruptcy thwarted dreams of new schools and church buildings. Protestant evangelism was dissipated in internecine friction amongst the diverse churches and interest groups, military and settler, especially during the 1653–5 rule of Cromwell's godly and ineffec-tual son-in-law, Charles Fleetwood. When Fleetwood was succeeded by Cromwell's more determined, but conservative, son Henry, English policy focused increasingly on Strafford's old goals of financial self-sufficiency and commercial expansion. That outcome was both symbolised and sealed by the prominence at court of the Earl of Cork's son, Lord Broghill.

Scotland too disappointed reformers. Although no such sweeping overhaul was intended in protestant Scotland as in Ireland, there were similarities. Ironically, the republic pursued some measure of uniformity even more aggressively than had Charles I. Not only did the protectorate, following the Rump's plans, abolish the Scottish and Irish parliaments and allot each subordinate 'commonwealth' thirty seats in the British parlia-ment at Westminster. It also sought to extend English law into Scotland. Overthrowing Scottish feudalism would both free the common people and bring down the magnates who had led the Scottish invasions of 1648 and 1651. Indeed, the republic went far beyond the old royal policy of attack-ing the hereditary jurisdictions of the nobility, and English officials and officers favoured tenants and creditors in actions against Scottish nobles. Idealism and prudence similarly merged in the government's efforts to curb the overmighty kirk: weakening a political enemy might also foster the spread of Independency. The results were explosive. As English policy became clear, recruits flocked in 1653–5 to the royalist rebels Glencairn and Middleton in the Highlands. The resentful kirk stood aside as debt-ridden Scottish magnates, threatened with ruin by the government's stand, took arms.

Rebellion put a brake on reform. That very professional commander and turncoat, George Monck, sent to Scotland in 1654, was both pragmatic in his politics and skilled in scorched-earth tactics after serving in the old royal army in Ireland. Reformist goals were not altogether sacrificed to pacification. The mid-1650s were crucial in the establishment in Scotland of JPs, who encroached not only on aristocratic justice but also on the powers of ministers in kirk sessions. But the priority of political stability and fiscal restraint was signalled by the arrival in 1655 of another former royalist, to head the civil administration. Lord Broghill did more than propitiate politique elements among the clergy and nobility. He secured considerable local co-operation for a programme of improvement. The forcible suppression of aristocratic brutality, and the curbing of heritable jurisdictions, brought better justice and order; and economic recovery came with freer trade in peacetime.

But despite all the moderation of Henry Cromwell and Broghill, imperialism proved a wasting asset. Expenditures exceeded revenues in Ireland by around £100 000 per annum, and in Scotland by at least £130 000 per annum, thus further dashing hopes of reform – in England as well as elsewhere.

The growing financial crisis dictated a policy of retrenchment. But the protector's motto read, 'Peace is sought in war,' and Marvell had spoken prophetically when in 'An Horatian Ode' he declared that 'restless Cromwell' could not rest content in 'the inglorious arts of peace'. Conscious of England's prophetic mission, and haunted too by the legend of Elizabethan glories, Cromwell told his council in the summer of 1654, 'God has not brought us hither where we are but to consider the work that we may do in the world as well as at home.' Fleetwood, his son-in-law, concurred, telling Thurloe in July, 'The work begun will not end in these three nations.' Doing that work was to make England the most respected military power in Europe in the 1650s; but the resentments at the taxes Cromwell's foreign policy required only increased his problems at home.

Such an ambiguous outcome reflects the protector's ambivalent policies. One legend is of Oliver the imperialist in 1654 sending troops to aid England's American colonists against the Dutch in New Amsterdam and Blake to the Mediterranean to suppress pirates. The other legend is of

Oliver the besotted trading England's interest for the chimera of a protestant crusade. Yet the protector was also the political realist – Blake's expedition after all helped foil a French attempt to conquer Naples.

Paradoxically, much of the controversy centres on the peace the protector made abroad. He settled with the Dutch in the Treaty of Westminster of April 1654 not simply because he was unhappy to be fighting fellow-protestants. He was aware that English naval victories in the narrow seas had not been matched in the Mediterranean or the east; he was conscious too of the burden of a wartime navy of 20 000 men, and of England's isolation in Europe. Immediate partisan politics similarly dictated peace. To secure the survival of his regime, he needed to ensure the survival of the Dutch republicans in Amsterdam. Accordingly, and in return for their agreement to block the pro-Stuart house of Orange, he refrained from exploiting England's local naval advantage. The 'commonwealthsmen' who had helped establish that advantage never forgave him for it; ignoring English failures further afield, they broadened the charge of betrayal even as they sharpened the economic claims in their developing ideology of republicanism. Yet the eventual shape of Cromwell's relations with the Dutch shows considerable sophistication. With peace Cromwell brought an end to Dutch aid to royalist exiles, and he strove to balance Dutch strengths by extracting concessions from Portugal in the East Indies and Sweden in the Baltic. This was not quite the myopic pursuit of a protestant alliance against 'the old enemy' in Rome and Madrid that the commonwealthsmen alleged.

A similarly mixed verdict must pass on the protector's relations with the other great protestant power, and potential ally, Sweden. The object of fascination among the godly since Gustav Adolf's great victories in the early 1630s, Sweden had also responded warmly to the republic in 1652. Friendship with Sweden was not only a matter of protestant tradition, it was also strategically plausible, for it would balance the Dutch alliance with Denmark in the Baltic, from whence came naval supplies. Yet Cromwell in the mid-1650s sought more than that: hoping for another protestant hero in the energetic Charles X of Sweden, he dreamed of a pan-protestant alliance that might yet permit a march on Habsburg Vienna. He did not recognise soon enough that Charles X aimed only at a regional hegemony.

Assessment of the protector's relations with the Catholic powers is more complex. Political stability and reform at home would have been best served by peace, for neither France nor Spain, exhausted as both were, constituted a threat. French support for Charles Stuart was certainly awkward, but it might have been resolved with fewer costs than those Oliver brought on himself. But – 'against the rule of politics', as the eager Fleetwood conceded – he dreamed still of dislodging the pope, of bringing godly liberty to Europe, at the least of aiding the suffering Huguenots around Bordeaux. And as always there were sharper considerations. Just

as the Long Parliament had been unable to pay off the army in 1647, so
Oliver in 1654 was unable to pay off the fleet used against the Dutch: it
might be cheaper in the short run to keep ships and men in active service.
Accordingly, despite his instinctual dislike of Spain, despite his detestation
of the persecution of protestants in the French dependency of Savoy, and
despite too his preference for a protestant alliance, Oliver allowed himself
to be courted throughout 1654 by the two great Catholic powers. At the
end of the year he opted for an assault on Spain's West Indian colonies,
and drifted slowly towards friendship with France.

The arguments for turning against Spain were revealing. The protector's
declaration recited the 'black legend' at length: Madrid had allowed no
freedom of worship to England's merchants, nor security to England's
colonies; and 'the ancient glory of the English nation' demanded vindication. Madrid also had an empire from which a rich trade in slaves, sugar
and tobacco was hoped, where protestantism might be advanced, and
from which treasure might still be seized. And as in the case of the Dutch
peace there was a strong political argument. Royalists sheltered by a
Spanish enemy would be less dangerous, for ideological reasons above all,
than royalists in French ports. The motives of the Providence Island circle
as well as of the pragmatist could readily be reconciled by one who
believed his country God's chosen nation.

Oliver's foreign policy is remarkable for its use of force to advance
commerce, if not godliness. In the Mediterranean Blake's 1654 voyage
helped to secure English traders against Barbary corsairs; in 1656–7 Blake
succeeded in keeping his fleet on station in the Mediterranean through the
winter, a remarkable feat that established British power near the vital sea
lanes around Gibraltar. Dutch and French colonists on the North American mainland, and ultimately the Spanish in the Caribbean, all experienced
British aggression. Yet as in the British Isles, imperialism had its costs, and
reservations expressed by the hard-headed Lambert in the summer of 1654
were to be borne out. The 'western design' in the Caribbean took England
in 1655 into a conflict with Spain that was to prove both economically
and politically disastrous.

Everywhere financial and political realities drove the protector to temper
the desirable with the possible and the necessary. In 1654 the annual deficit
was running at about £300 000, and the accumulated debt stood at about
£1.5 million, or just below one year's total revenue – manageable enough,
had long-term credit been available. But the scandal of the 'public faith'
left Oliver's borrowings even more hand-to-mouth than the Stuarts' had
been. Much hinged on the parliament that the Instrument of Government
required Oliver to meet on the auspicious date of 3 September 1654.

How that parliament would behave was unclear. For one thing, it was
to be elected on a new franchise. True to Ireton's proposals of 1647–9,
the Instrument redistributed the 400 English seats for the new single
chamber assembly in accordance with the tax burden – not, as the

Levellers would have had it, with population. While the Instrument eliminated many rotten boroughs and enfranchised the new industrial towns
of Leeds, Manchester and Halifax, it awarded most seats to the counties.
There were anomalies, and London, long the butt of provincial jealousy
and also perhaps of the army's political suspicions, was markedly under-
represented; but on the whole representation was fairer than it was to be
again until the later nineteenth century. It seems clear that by replacing
the trifling forty-shilling freehold franchise in the counties with a requirement of £200 in either real or personal property the Instrument narrowed
the electorate, despite the arguments about democracy in 1647. Nevertheless, there was a basic consistency. The army had in 1647 denounced
corruption and the pursuit of private interest; impoverished cottagers and
rotten boroughs, alike the targets of the Instrument, were vulnerable to
just such corruption. But sadly for the protector, idealism proved politically counter-productive. Although the military in Scotland and Ireland
controlled the elections there, the small boroughs included the few English
constituencies where government interest could have been deployed. In the
counties too, independent property-owning voters might oppose the army
and the social ramifications of religious reform. Lambert's Instrument had
strengthened the backwoods.

The 1654 elections revealed much of political attitudes. Apathy is
suggested by a generally low turn-out, though local partisanship generated
some angry disputes, as in Leeds. The threat to the clerical profession brought
a fierce clerical backlash. A total of 20 per cent of the Essex voters were
reported to have been clergy, clergy canvassed in Wiltshire, and deluged the
new parliament with calls for support. Vainly ranged against them in Oxfordshire and Wiltshire were local alliances of saints and commonwealthsmen
striving to reverse the catastrophes of 1653. With royalists excluded from the
polls, most MPs were moderate puritan gentlemen, of the sort who had
eagerly supported the 'presbyterian' drive for settlement in 1647–8. They
might applaud Cromwell's opening appeal for 'healing and settling'; their
attitude to the sects and the soldiers was another matter.

The protector's unease was clear. He desperately needed this parliament.
It was not only ambitious 'kinglings' like Ashley Cooper (who was shortly
to resign from the council in disgust) who saw in it the chance for the
permanent settlement that would put an end to the more obvious features
of military rule. Cromwell the country gentleman shared such aspirations.
Oliver's short-term purposes also demanded a settlement, since the Instrument sanctioned the rule of protector and council no longer than this
parliament. Accordingly, before the opening the council cut the monthly
assessment from £120 000 to £90 000, a major sacrifice for a regime near
bankruptcy. Lest this move fail to buy 'country' support, the council also
rushed through a flurry of ordinances, some reforming, some administrative, while it still could. It also excluded a handful of manifest royalists
who had gained election.

The government's apprehensions were well founded. Its hopes of speedy ratification of the Instrument were blocked by a few obdurate common-wealthsmen and by many more country gentlemen, all eager to do more than put a polite stamp on a constitution so obviously drawn by the sword. The protector had not reckoned with the concern for parliamen-tary sovereignty that had lain so close to the heart of the parliamentarian cause, and was outraged when he had to send troops to Westminster on 12 September. He justified himself as so often by appealing to history and to the record of God's providences. Desperate for legitimacy, he pointed too to the support of the City and 'the good people'. He then insisted that MPs take a 'recognition' to accept 'the government, as it is settled in one single person, and a parliament'. About a hundred intransigents withdrew in protest – country gentlemen outraged by one more display of military power joining commonwealthsmen like Hesilrig and Scot in a dramatic if futile gesture. Yet pressure on what Oliver now declared 'fundamentals' – liberty of conscience, the status of the army, the position of the protec-tor – did not end with the withdrawals. Although the truncated parlia-ment was ready to accept the rule of single person and parliament, it clearly hoped to make the protector responsible to parliament.

The story of this parliament can, however, be told in terms of concili-ation as well as conflict. If MPs tried to shift the tax-burden from land to the customs and excise, and to reduce the army from 54 000 to the 30 000 the Instrument envisaged as a permanent force beyond the present emergency, they at least accepted the principle of regular taxation and the existence of the army. And eventually members accepted the compromise proposal of the homely, if formidable, orator, the presbyterian ex-colonel John Birch, that for the present the assessment be merely reduced to £60 000 a month. Equally, while Cromwell baulked at parliament's attempt to enumerate heresies, he was willing enough to suppress 'prodi-gious blasphemies', like Biddle's. But there were grounds for concern. The fierce clerical campaign against the sects indicated a danger to the Baptists, whom Oliver held dear. Non-communication was rife: parliament had by mid-November received little guidance in fiscal matters, 'in regard much of it still rested in the breast of the Lord Protector, who had given no answer'. For his part, the protector felt forever slighted. More importantly, he reacted fiercely when civilian criticisms seemed to merge with army discontents.

Carpings in parliament at the protector's authority had both liberated and provoked stirrings outside. That autumn Fifth-Monarchists infuriated by Oliver's quest for earthly rather than heavenly warrant cried out to the soldiers against 'the father of lies', Oliver Protector. Oliver's protectoral dignity offended commonwealthsmen too, and in October a group of officers prepared to denounce the retreat from the Engagement of 1647: only 'constant successive parliaments, freely chosen by the people' would save England from corruption. The following of 'the three colonels' was as small as their trust in the voters was misplaced, and Oliver dismissed them without incident. But that winter discontent spread, amongst the officers in both Scotland and Ireland, and in the major garrison at Hull. There were signs too of links between Leveller and royalist terrorists. Over Christmas Oliver reinforced the strong points in London, and waited impatiently for the expiry of the five months – lunar, in his disingenuous calendar – fixed by the Instrument as the span of a triennial parliament.

When he angrily dissolved parliament on 22 January 1655 Oliver characterised the army as in effect a separate estate in the nation, its position warranted by the protection it gave the godly. As one opponent of parliamentary control rightly feared, 'such parliaments might hereafter be chosen as would betray the glorious cause of the people of God'. The protector sought to quell such misgivings among the saints and the soldiers in personal interviews after the dissolution, though he needed a long prayer meeting to settle his own unease. He craved a parliamentary settlement that would secure the liberty of 'men as men', but he had also fought for liberty for the Christian conscience. Only the army, and the rule of the good, could guarantee the latter. But to cynics, it appeared that the rule of 'the good party' might be woefully self-serving.

The spring of 1655 brought the crisis of Oliver's protectorate. Among the least of Oliver's worries was the conspiracy that had troubled him over Christmas. Most royalists were cowed into submission, and the hotheads too divided to co-ordinate effectively. Their ill-planned rising fizzled limply on 8 March, when a handful of cavaliers in the north and Midlands slunk away from each other, 'strangely frightened with their own shadows'. Only in the southwest did serious trouble occur, when perhaps 200 royalists, led by the former colonel John Penruddock, seized the assize judges in Salisbury; but finding little support they fled westwards, into the arms of watchful troops.

The constitutional predicament was more alarming. The Instrument had provided for rule by the executive until the first parliament. That parliament's refusal of the necessary endorsement cast doubt on the protector's powers to legislate by ordinance, even to raise taxes. The Norfolk assessment commissioners debated uncomfortably in March whether to act, since the protector had not dared 'meddle with the legislative power himself, but put it upon us, and we must by action establish it a law, and so may be sued, and may prove a ship-money cause'. In the end they conformed, but the parallels with the 1630s were indeed close, not least in that few relished confrontation. Although outright opposition came only from radicals, from Barebone and a few purged commonwealthsmen, constitutionalist scruples were widespread.

The judges found themselves uncomfortably exposed. Like the nation at large they had adapted themselves swiftly to the various changes of 1653, doubtless encouraged by Oliver's alleged observation that if the men of the red robe would not enforce the law his men in red coats would.

The judges' professional bias in favour of political stability inclined them to support Oliver just as earlier judges had supported Charles, and they had not flinched when the protector, like his various predecessors in government, ignored the niceties of *habeas corpus*. But parliament's failure to ratify the Instrument now forced them to confront issues they would clearly rather have overlooked.

In court after court the protectorate came under attack. Penruddock's legal challenge at his trial troubled the government far more than his rebellion had done; still more disturbing was the concurrent case of George Cony, a merchant and religious radical, who had refused to pay customs duties. In May Cony's counsel, all prominent conservatives, disputed the entire Instrument; although they were promptly imprisoned, their arguments swayed the bench. Oliver's removal of Chief Justice Rolle and two others, and his exasperation at the use of 'magna farta' by pettifogging constitutionalists, shows how far government was becoming business as usual. Further embarrassments in Chancery increased the protector's impatience. Bulstrode Whitelocke and Sir Thomas Widdrington, two of the three commissioners of the great seal, rejected the 1654 Chancery reforms, alleging their inconvenience; but the usually pliant Whitelocke's objections were constitutional as much as they were professional.

Constitutional crisis extended beyond the courts, where the council quickly found replacements for the five scrupling judges. Confusion in the north Midlands suggests a temporary breakdown of legal process. Constitutional crisis also encouraged London presbyterians to exploit the apparent lapse of the Instrument by mounting a new attack in the courts on Baptists and on Biddle, alleging that the swingeing 1648 blasphemy ordinance was still in force. Oliver had to forestall further moves against the Baptists by reluctantly sending Biddle, whom he abhorred, into exile beyond the reach of the common law. Coming after the frustrations in parliament the debacles emphasised his failure to obtain much more than the barest acquiescence from the political nation.

Divisions at court grew, as the military interest and the new 'courtiers' and 'civilians' urged coercion or conciliation. And characteristically, Cromwell responded to the turmoil in contradictory ways. Showing the flexibility that was his political strength he moved to appease the gentry. Cutting the assessment to the £60 000-per-month level that Birch had urged in parliament, he then made a virtue of necessity by reducing the soldiers' pay, and their numbers to 40 000. The desperately needed savings totalled about £300 000 per annum, though they did not make good the loss on the assessment. But despite the fiscal concessions, Oliver's solution to the constitutional dilemma was partisan. Convinced by the failure of 'healing and settling' that the nation at large remained unregenerate, the protector swung sharply against civilian counsels.

The major-generals to whom the protector now entrusted rule in the provinces were to shape the legend of the Cromwellian years as the triumph of blue-nosed puritanism. But for all their work at moral reform, security remained a prime concern. While the enforced troop cuts had left the council uneasy in face of the latent discontent uncovered by Secretary Thurloe's efficient intelligence work, the local response to the royalist risings suggested a solution. 3000 of the 'honest interest' were reported to have turned out in Somerset, 400 in the old parliamentarian fortress of Gloucester; in Leeds and in Maidstone, wartime alliances were rediscovered. The council therefore turned to this godly remnant to give life to its search for a new militia that would, like the militia of old, be cheap, local, and yet politically reliable. Local volunteers were to be strengthened by the inclusion of a powerful leaven of regular army officers among the county militia commissioners. All would come under the direction of a major-general heading each of the eleven districts into which the country was divided.

Partisanship underlay the funding as well as the rationale of the new forces. To the applause of many of the zealous, whose morale was heightened by the denial of traditional community, the major-generals were to 'decimate' royalists who had not demonstrated their change of heart. Those with a landed income of over £100 per annum, or with over £1500 in goods, would be fined at 10 per cent. In justification the council cited the royalists' intransigence that made protection necessary: better that they rather than the innocent should pay. For, Oliver maintained, the cavaliers were separating themselves from the nation, intermarrying as a caste. 'That generation of men', argued Thurloe, must be dealt with 'as the Irish are.'

Despite the fears of a massacre such language aroused, decimation was not entirely the instrument of tyranny it seemed. It was indeed a fundamentally arbitrary executive procedure, since the lapse of the protector's power to issue ordinances left it based only on the council's instructions to those concerned. Yet the readiness of royalists to produce their estate papers before decimation suggests a measure of consent that Hobbes's sovereign would have appreciated. Decimation's flavour seems caught in the plea of Major-General Berry, responsible for Wales and the Marches, that the protector 'let us alone awhile with my lord Coventry'. But Oliver was reluctant to do this: still the man of the old middle group, he could see the dangers in alienating those otherwise quiet.

Cromwell's congenital ambivalence is nowhere clearer than in the way he held back subordinates he had empowered as extraordinary agents. His often sympathetic response to aggrieved royalists dismayed major-generals who saw their revenues from decimation, and thus the readiness of their militias, decline. The yield dwindled too in face of Oliver's refusal to heed his subordinates' pleas that he lower the relatively high income threshhold required for decimation. The major-generals spent most of their first six months in office on decimation work, yet they had to reduce the militia by one-fifth the following summer, and many could not muster their remaining men for fear of meeting demands for pay, which was often a year in arrears. Decimation may have demoralised the royalists, but the zealous were perturbed by the implications of the protector's moderation. As Major-General Whalley in the Midlands lamented, 'It makes the country think, that great men have most friends, as formerly.'

The significance of the major-generals was, however, not merely partisan and fiscal. As Oliver in council in the autumn of 1655 shaped the instrument that providence, and the careful Lambert, had put into his hands, his thoughts ran higher. In successive calls for days of humiliation in 1654–5 the protector had preached jeremiads upon the sinfulness of the nation. His prophetic zeal was heightened by the approach of what was widely thought to be the climacteric year. Throughout Europe, Christians expected great things of a time so close to 1656, and to the apocalyptic 666. Such expectations led the council into intensive discussion late in 1655 on the readmission of the Jews to England. The way to the millennium might be prepared.

Accordingly, the instructions to the major-generals turned increasingly to godly rule. Local studies have indicated the general conscientiousness of local administrators in the 1650s. Poor-rate expenditures rose as far afield as Yorkshire and Essex, though food prices were falling fast; quarter sessions from Warwickshire to Kent dealt with the poor more urgently than in the 1630s, by means of almshouses for the infirm as well as by outrelief and the fierce punishment of both parents of bastards. Yet social regulation was far from godly evangelism, and there was widespread evasiveness when the council called for lists of Catholics in 1655 as it prepared for war with Spain. In his second parliament Oliver was to denounce the JPs as 'owls', loath to be scorned by their neighbours for exerting themselves.

The major-generals were to spread zeal throughout the land. In county after county the arrival of a major-general coincided with quarter sessions' orders against alehouses. Charles Worsley, the most energetic of them all, saw to the suppression of 215 alehouses in a single hundred (or subdivision) of Lancashire, and almost 200 in the city of Chester. But Worsley found aid locally for, isolated amongst religious conservatives, the godly of the northwest were more self-conscious than most and Worsley was able to turn to them for information. Where local puritans were less aggressive, major-generals depended on their own efforts. Worsley literally worked himself to death, but the godly William Goffe, Cromwell's least successful appointment, wrung his hands ineffectually in Hampshire and Sussex.

It is tempting to see the rule of the major-generals as the high point of early-modern centralisation. There was a central register of information, albeit a patchy one, on royalists; and Cromwell's brother-in-law Desborough took the astonishing total of over 5000 bonds for good behaviour from suspects from all walks of life in the southwest. But Cromwell had turned for enforcement not to institutional reform and centralised procedures but to godly men. His anger at the brief vacation from Wales taken by the hugely burdened Berry is symptomatic, both of his hopes and of his failure. Any 'system' in the major-generals' rule extended no further than the paper of their instructions. Each of the major-generals had his own emphases, and these often look fairly conventional, and local in their roots. Boteler harried vagabonds in the south Midlands, and Whalley carefully policed the market regulations and strove to enforce the antiquated enclosure laws. Robert Lilburne in the northeast backed local demands for local courts and the short-lived third university at Durham, while Whalley presented himself locally as a spokesman to the protector for local concerns. The major-generals were, appropriately enough, denounced in the ensuing parliament as 'cantonisers' for dividing up the country, rather than as centralisers.

The problems of the towns, far more than of the counties, drove the major-generals into arbitrary acts. As previous monarchs had found, the jurisdictional autonomy of towns gave central government far less control than it possessed over the appointive JPs in the counties. There were occasional outbursts of urban zeal, as at Bristol where magistrates, influenced by the radical garrison, stopped the water conduits on the sabbath; but on the whole conservatives had crept back in municipal elections since the Engagement. The major-generals soon complained that urban magistrates were 'all asleep'. A characteristically blunt proclamation in September 1655, of no legal validity, extended the Rump's expiring statute against royalist participation in municipal politics, and added a new demand that magistrates be godly. On that flimsy basis the major-generals systematically purged town corporations, pressing their victims to resign 'by an usurped, illegal, pretended power', as the outraged town clerk of Lincoln noted. The impact of such tactics, which extended to surrounding the town hall of Hythe in Kent with troops, was remarkable. Desborough drove nine to resign from Tewkesbury corporation, five from Tiverton, two from Bristol, four from Gloucester, and probably more.

Oliver's decision in the summer of 1656 to swing from repressing the nation to seeking its aid in a new parliament may seem quixotic. But though he had never lost hope of a settlement, he had found, as Charles had found before him, that the expedients born of financial desperation and military adventurism created their own dynamic.

Lambert's misgivings of 1654 about the costs and consequences of a 'western design' against Spain's empire had been borne out. When Spain retaliated against English shipping in 1655 the protector was drawn into a European war. In retrospect, from the humiliations of the 1660s and '70s, his efforts dazzled: Europe had courted his alliance, and Admiral Blake swept the seas of pirate and foe alike. At the time it seemed different. Few Englishmen understood the problems of amphibious warfare, least of all in the tropics, and Oliver trusted too much to God's aid to give his usual care to the preparations. Instead, he reassured the commanders of the expedition to the Caribbean, 'The Lord himself hath a controversy with your enemies; even with that Romish Babylon.' He sought a substitute for the lost Providence Island colony of his old middle group friends, a base for attacks on Spain's treasure fleets as well as its empire. But when in the spring of 1655, ill led, ill supplied, ravaged by disease, the raw recruits reached their destination of Hispaniola even the weak Spanish presence proved too much for them. Oliver drew little consolation from the capture of Jamaica, which was eventually to prove far more valuable, and concluded that God was chastising a sinful nation and its magistrate.

Hispaniola was a turning-point, for it challenged Cromwell's conviction that God was with him. As some of those on the expedition reminded him, to set booty as a prime objective sat ill with self-denial. When in September 1656 Captain Stayner finally captured some of the Spanish treasure fleet, the thanksgiving sermon to parliament chastising those 'who are too apt to say, that God never owned you since you undertook this business', suggests the damage that had been done to morale.

God's scourging was soon made apparent. The government sought to arouse patriotic fervour, but unlike the Dutch Spain had little shipping, beyond the elusive plate fleet, to attack. English merchants, on the other hand, were as vulnerable as ever to Dunkirk privateers. By mid-1656 the council was deluged with protests about losses. Equally damaging politically was the discontent in the new draperies regions that depended on trade with Spain. Funding was in shorter supply than ever, with scant prospect of loans from London, since the City's long suspicions of government credit were heightened in 1656 by the levy of a virtual forced loan of £50 000 on the East India Company. In desperation, the protector in July resorted to the intensely provocative step of ordering the payment in advance of the monthly assessment for the following December–June, in effect doubling the rate for late 1656. The political nation once again acquiesced to an arbitrary demand. Still, there seemed neither to the council nor to major-generals anxious to pay their militias any alternative to a parliament.

Oliver, shaken, was not enthusiastic. The signs are that he had to be persuaded to call his second parliament, that he would have preferred to tighten decimation, and that he only issued the writs after the major-generals assured him that they could contain disaffection. Most of them faced the elections confidently: they had, as Whalley exulted, struck 'an awe . . . into the spirits of wicked men'. Their optimism may not have been altogether unfounded, for the perennial eagerness of constituencies to secure friends at court ensured the election of an unprecedented total of over forty officers. These helped constitute an official and 'courtier' group that comprised a respectable third of the attenuated house. Yet the government at the centre did little to influence the polls. The major-generals dared not muster their unpaid militias, and the council mounted no propaganda campaign, though the emergency of 1655 had brought tighter censorship and the suppression of all but the two government newspapers. The protector himself made no appeal for the return of the well affected.

Others were less abashed. Sir Henry Vane wove a nostalgic appeal to the usefully vague 'good old cause' as he strove in *A Healing Question* to unite estranged commonwealthsmen with godly providentialists dismayed by the failure at Hispaniola, even perhaps to persuade an uneasy protector out of his arbitrary and imperial tendencies. More ambitious was James Harrington's *Oceana*, with its coherent classical–republican vision of a people (rather than professionals) in arms. Harrington's argument was to shape both British and American republicanism. The basis of political power lay in property; the king had been defeated because the nobility no longer held the balance of property; and the only path to freedom and to political stability alike was to vest political power not in a 'single person' but in the people, who now held the preponderance of property. *Oceana* was as compelling as it was massive. But although Harrington's arguments and Vane's were to prove influential in 1659, they were damp squibs in 1656.

Popular sentiment was made clear in the violence offered to radicals at the Middlesex and Westminster polls. Even under the Instrument, elections left 'free' by the government would declare nothing else. The rule of the 'swordsmen and decimators' had united the gentry, whether presbyterian, neuter or crypto-royalist, against military high-handedness and the suppression of horse-racing, cock-fighting and the sociability that symbolised community. As Henry Verney complained in Buckinghamshire, 'All sports put down, and the gentry not permitted to meet.' The consequences were clear in 'presbyterian' triumphs, in the failure of Major-General Kelsey to gain one of the eleven Kent seats, and in the bottom place secured by the collaborationist magnate Sir Thomas Barnardiston in Suffolk.

The outcry at the hustings against 'soldiers and courtiers' aroused fears of a new rising, and hopes of counter-measures. As Major-General Kelsey protested, 'The interest of God's people is to be preferred before a thousand parliaments.' But the new parliament-men took care not to provoke such a response, and for three months avoided any attack on the major-generals. They had learned the lesson of 1654, that confrontation would only intensify military rule. Anyway, the sitting MPs were consciously conformist, for the council had disingenuously, indeed, outrageously, exploited the Instrument's insistence on MPs of 'integrity' to exclude a hundred or so political opponents at the start. Commonwealthsmen such as the inseparable duo of Hesilrig and Scot, presbyterians like Birch, as well as known royalists had gone, taking with them another fifty who withdrew in protest.

Remarkably, those remaining quickly went to work. Quietly passing over the massive breach of privileges, they declared their goodwill by repudiating Stuart claims to the throne, and worked away at all the mundane bills, for law courts at York, for draining lands in Hampshire, against 'undecent' dress, that had been so long neglected. Thurloe's complacency in late October, at the absence of any 'contradictory spirit to anything', seemed well justified. Most MPs evidently hoped to persuade the protector to 'civilianise' himself, and the protector played to this by putting on a full-dress ceremonial the following month when some bills passed into law. The impression of a house pursuing 'business as usual' in the manner of some of its 1620s predecessors is strengthened by its attitude to the Spanish war. While it rallied willingly enough to the protestant banner, all the more so after Stayner's exploits, it preferred to fight an anti-Catholic war not by voting taxes but by passing anti-Catholic measures, to the embarrassment of the more tolerant Oliver. Members preferred 'jogging on' after their own affairs, as an increasingly anxious Thurloe noted.

The incoherence of the parliament in late 1656 reflects Oliver's own uncertainties, as well as the growing competition at court between the 'military men' and 'civilian' counsellors appalled by decimation. Once committed to a parliament the protector had wined and dined MPs, but had given no lead beyond desiring that his government be upheld, toleration accepted, and a 'reformation of manners' instituted. His providentialist posture of 'waiting on the Lord' was as ill suited to giving a lead through the minutiae of politics – as opposed to the crises – as it had always been. But there were deeper problems. A financial establishment would only come if MPs were assured of the kind of government they were establishing. This Oliver could not, or would not, tell them. Consideration of the revenue was anyway derailed in December by the case of the ex-soldier, James Nayler. This brought into relief still more brutally than had the successive attempts to punish Biddle the Socinian the limits to the concern for freedom for tender consciences sought by the godly. It underlined too the constitutional problems of the protectorate.

James Nayler was as charismatic a leader of the early Quakers as his famous ally, George Fox. But he lacked Fox's sense of the practical, and erred catastrophically when he allowed enthusiastic followers to re-enact Christ's entry into Jerusalem as he rode into the deeply divided city of Bristol on an ass in October 1656. His gesture symbolised the Quaker teaching that Christ was within all human beings, that in the spiritual sense Christ had come again. But undiscriminating gentlemen and magistrates, and indeed, many army officers and ordinary people too, saw in Nayler and all Quakers only grotesque blasphemy, the most disturbing manifestation yet of the sectarian spirit.

The Quakers flourished in the millenarian context of spiritual arousal that had given rise to so many groups in the previous decade. Independents, and still more the presbyterians, stressed the primacy of the scriptures in order to hedge in the antinomian implications in a fallen world

of any appeal to a spiritual freedom in which in principle they too
believed. But more than most sects, the defiantly unpredestinarian Quakers
had moved outside the Calvinist consensus. Believing as fully as those
called Ranters in an 'inner light' that supplemented, or even in some cases
superseded, scripture, the Quakers (so-called from their ecstatic habit of
'quaking' before a God of whom they claimed immediate knowledge) felt
commanded to transcend convention. While they emphatically did not
reject the moral teachings of the Old Testament, their emphasis on 'Christ
within' led them towards a belief in freedom from sin that their enemies
took to be Ranter. Those early Quakers who went 'naked for a sign',
rejecting all formalities and claiming parity with the Old Testament
prophets to whom God had also spoken, seemed simply outrageous. Like
Ranters, and some Baptists, they often testified to the immediacy of their
God by disrupting the mediated rituals of the 'priests' in the 'steeple-
houses', as they called the parish churches, and by challenging them to
hugely attended public debates. Mainstream protestantism had never been
more directly challenged.

The Quakers also challenged the underpinnings of a society based upon
deference. Eager to bring down pride in men who were all equal before
God, they refused 'hat-honour', the doffing of hats before those in authority. Refusing to take God's name in vain, they shunned oaths, on which
all legal proceedings hinged. Doubly distressing to a male-dominated
society were the disproportionate number of women who responded to
the Quaker teaching of Christ within men and women alike, and who
hinted at the instability of gender divisions in a revolution. Moreover, the
Quakers were not the pious, respectable pacifists of later years. 'Friends'
were instructed to go 'as one man' to the 1656 Yorkshire election; many
soldiers turned Quaker, as did radicals of various hues – John Lilburne
certainly, Gerrard Winstanley probably. In Leeds, and still more importantly in Bristol, Quakerism in these years was associated with challenges
to the magisterial oligarchy. The vituperative Quaker denunciations of
unjust magistrates, and their millennialist rhetoric of God's impending
judgment on 'the great ones of the earth' could not be ignored. Although
there were Quakers in all walks of life, they seemed to threaten a rising
of the dispossessed.

More than any other group, the Quakers made a reality of the sectarian challenge. The dynamism of Fox and Nayler, the organising genius of
Fox's patron and eventual wife Margaret Fell, and the heroism of the the
men and women who joined them, took Quakerism into all the counties,
to the army in Scotland and Ireland, and overseas, to Massachusetts, to
Istanbul. And their numbers soared, from nothing to perhaps 50 000 in
the 1650s. Their successes, particularly in the north, suggest the neglect
of large parts of the country by the established church, and the unpopularity of Calvinism; but the clergy thought not of their own failings but
of the challenges to their beliefs, to their authority and to their position.

With lay impropriators they might face refusals of tithe, which could, many feared, be a prelude to the refusal of rents. The response was immediate and almost pathological. JPs whipped Quaker missionaries as vagrants, mobs beat them, while clergymen turned from anxious debates with Quaker challengers long enough to howl in anguish as their world seemed to turn upside down. London pulpits rang during the ensuing parliament with clarions to the defence of the established ministry.

Quakers touched a nerve not just because of what they did but also because of what they reflected of the failures of what has so often been called 'the puritan revolution'. Despite the best intentions in 1641, and under the Rump, little had been done to strengthen the church in the parishes materially. In 1655 there were only two settled ministers in the sixty parishes of Anglesey, in 1656 one in the five parishes in Leicester. And within the parishes, ministers' morale had often weakened as the collapse of the church courts and the failure to build an alternative had left them without the means of discipline. Godly pastors waxed gloomy as they saw their congregations fall away to the sects, and the sects in turn fall asunder. Indeed, probably the two major concerns of 1650s pamphleteering were disciplinary. In a church order that lacked legal sanctions, how might the sectarian threat be confronted, and how might ministers use exclusion from the sacrament of communion to discipline the ungodly?

The common clerical cry that this was 'the dregs of time' showed how far the world had fallen from the hopes of 1641. The support of many presbyterians, the largest single group after the covert 'episcopal men', for royalist plans and plotting in the 1650s did not owe everything to their sense of guilt for the king's death. It stemmed as well from the anguish of a profession endangered. The sermon to the second annual meeting of the Sons of the Clergy, meeting in St Paul's Cathedral in 1655, took as its theme contempt for the clergy. And if millions of words poured from the presses to confront sectarianism, then millions more lamented the reduction of the sacrament of communion to the unpalatable alternatives of total cessation or the admission of all 'promiscuously'.

Some stalwarts did strive to maintain their standards, but the social cost might be high. Thus, the minister of Gateshead, Durham, was accused of having excluded all but eight of a congregation of 1000. In response, angry parishioners often joined sectaries in refusing tithes, on the grounds that they had been denied their due. Surviving churchwardens' accounts suggest that the overwhelming majority of ministers abandoned the ideas of regular, grace-affirming celebrations for the godly, and either ceased the communion entirely or returned to the traditional practice of parochial celebration at the great festivals of Christmas, Easter and Whitsun. The confusion, and the withdrawal from any attempt at discipline, contributed enormously to a ministerial crisis of confidence.

And the clergy responded. On the one hand, denominational lines hardened. Baptist ministers formed regional associations, amongst the presbyterians the leadership of the London provincial assembly gained acceptance, while 120 Independent ministers conferred at the Savoy palace in London in 1658. And on the other hand, clergy of all denominations could see the need to repair the fragmentation arising from parliament's failure to institute a state church in the 1640s. In at least seventeen counties there appeared 'associations' of ministers. Usually non-denominational, and following the course mapped out by Richard Baxter in Worcestershire, these aimed to institutionalise the old godly device of combination lectures to sustain the clergy and reach out to the people, but they sought as well both to provide some local means to ordain new clergy, and to confront the problems of antinomianism and the sacrament.

The ministerial response involved more than organisation. Several associations, and surviving presbyterian classes too, rediscovered the turn-of-the-century conclusion that the way to the individual was through a general catechising – an approach to reformation that seemed to have been lost in the enthusiasms and divisions of the 1640s. Printed catechisms proliferated in the 50s, and the Westminster Assembly's *Shorter Catechism* (1645) attracted strong support in Cromwell's parliaments. The laments in successive parliaments at disunity and decay suggest a broader recognition of the ineffectiveness of the pulpit, to which so much trust had been pinned. The Worcestershire association in 1656 made a striking confession of the failure of preaching, for so long trumpeted as 'the effectual means to salvation': 'We find by sad experience, that the people understand not our public teaching, though we study to speak as plain as we can, and that after many years preaching, even of these same fundamentals, too many can scarce tell anything that we have said.'

Catechising and counselling might win the people, and by the end of the decade Baxter was convinced he had worked wonders in Kidderminster. But such techniques were dauntingly laborious, and despite all the hopes, and the outpourings of words, England remained obstinately unawakened. Baxter toiled to improve the work of evangelism with his *Reformed Pastor* (1656) and his hugely successful *Call to the Unconverted* (1658); but elsewhere energies were diffused in argument. John Evelyn in 1656 noted that preaching on the southern outskirts of London was only on 'high and speculative points and strains ... there was nothing practical preached, or that pressed reformation of life'. The London presbyterian Zachary Crofton, a more sympathetic witness, warned his readers, 'You have been too long pleased and puffed up with high flown doctrines ... heady disorderly knowledge, uttered in free but very confused discourses.' The publications of the 1650s bear out such complaints, and testify to the dilemma of the godly. It was no wonder that Oliver's repeated calls for national fasts lamented the prevailing ingratitude to the Lord – ingratitude manifested in the often bitter disunity of the godly and the unrepentance of the rest.

Nayler thus inflamed nerves already rubbed raw by too many affronts to the old order. Stoning to death was one popular suggestion for retribution, as MPs waxed hysterical about the dangers of toleration. 'If this be liberty, God defend me from such liberty,' cried that simple old puritan, Major-General Philip Skippon, hero of Turnham Green.

The issue was both legally and theologically taxing. The Instrument guaranteed freedom to all protestants save the immoral and breakers of the peace, and several of Skippon's colleagues on the council recognised that Nayler was neither of these. Furthermore, Nayler's teachings on the inner light were uncomfortably close to the 'glorious truth', as one councillor put it, which any protestant could accept. But in a house thinned by purge and growing weariness, the 'merciful men' were out-numbered as well as nervous. The urbane Lambert, with an author's interest in the Instrument, defended liberty of conscience and pointed to the constitutional implications of any parliamentary action. But a narrow majority sought an escape by appropriating to the new single chamber the judicial power of the old House of Lords. They proceeded to vote Nayler guilty of 'horrid blasphemy' – an offence they found as hard to define as they did the authority by which they decreed that he be branded, bored through the tongue and twice flogged.

Cromwell's response was muted, for he had no wish to offend a parliament that had yet to vote supply; probably more important, he too believed that Nayler had blasphemed appallingly. Evidently seeking only to limit any future encroachments on freedom of conscience, he waited until the first part of Nayler's punishment had been inflicted and then on 25 December wrote temperately to ask for parliament's 'grounds and reasons'. As averse as the protector to a confrontation, the perplexed house let the matter slip by. But Nayler's case had done more than underline the continuing lack of support for toleration. It had also exposed the difficulties of interpreting the Instrument. When the protector faced a parliament trying to regain powers the Instrument had sought to curtail there was, as one member pointed out, 'No judge upon earth' between them.

Arbitrariness seemed all around, at Westminster now as well as in the localities. The arguments for some clarification of the status quo therefore appealed increasingly to the officers as well as to civilian 'courtiers' and to country gentry. Ironically, the major-generals themselves began the work when, encouraged by the Christmas absence of the less godly, Desborough bluntly called for statutory confirmation of the decimation tax. His aim was not simply to render discriminatory taxation permanent. Some major-generals referred to the need to reassure the 'honest party' in the country who saw in decimation the only evidence that Oliver was not leading the godly back to Egypt. Decimation would manifest the purity of the cause. The long deferential silence of the early months of the parliament was at last broken when Cromwell's unsaintly son-in-law John Claypole, and Cromwell's former-royalist confidant Lord Broghill, opened the attack on the soldiers whom they had long opposed at Whitehall. If there was once again a court, then courtiers might head an 'opposition', as they had in the 1620s.

The new year brought one of the many struggles for the mind and heart of Oliver Cromwell. At the opening of the parliament he had given a disarming endorsement to the major-generals, 'a little poor invention . . . to have a little inspection upon the people'. But he was clearly taken aback by Desborough's parliamentary initiative, and the protests it provoked persuaded him that either providence or necessity was speaking and he should stand aside. His tact was rewarded, and a major grant of £400 000 for the Spanish war followed immediately on the defeat on 28 January 1657 of the decimation bill. The vote ensured Oliver's detachment from the major-generals, and the slow withering of their rule.

Abandonment of partisan pursuits opened the way to other solutions. The uncertainties of elective succession under the Instrument were underlined that January by the discovery of Sindercombe's plot, an unholy alliance of ex-army Levellers and royalists, all hoping to profit from the protector's assassination. Constitutional crisis, and experience of the major-generals, made the issue doubly urgent, and a move to reconstitute the government in hereditary rule and 'ancient constitution' quickly gathered momentum. On 23 February Sir Christopher Packe, a former lord mayor of London, proposed a broad platform that included a revived upper house of parliament and the crown for Oliver. The conservative gentry and merchants in the house responded eagerly, led by the Surrey member Sir Richard Onslow. Probably the most important supporter was Broghill, who was convinced that only the crown would enable the protector to sheathe the sword fully. He was followed by lawyers such as Whitelocke, who longed to see the common law reign supreme again, and who were prepared to overlook the recent failings of monarchy. All were spurred on by the realisation that otherwise Oliver's successor would be the strongest man in the army – and, personable though he was, the young and ambitious Lambert was a frightening prospect.

The hostility of sections of the army to these developments was predictable. The triumph of the gentry must endanger freedom of conscience, and also the hard-won position of the officers themselves. Lambert in his palace at Wimbledon, Colonel Pride married to Lord Chandos's daughter, Captain Adam Baynes the purchaser of Holdenby House, all might lose their prominence. Furthermore, in the eyes of Fleetwood, Desborough and many other officers, God had condemned English kingship in 1648–9. Lambert had contemplated monarchy in 1653, but there was a world of difference between an Oliver crowned by the officers and an Oliver enthroned by parliamentary gentry desperate to distance him from Lambert and his comrades. The leading officers therefore seconded their rather awkward speeches at Whitehall and Westminster with nudges to their alarmed juniors in London and whispers to the gathered churches.

The proposals that emerged in the house as the Humble Petition and Advice after long debates in March 1657 seemed almost to encapsulate the parliamentary war aims of 1642. A limited monarchy, with the great officers of state and councillors approved by a bi-cameral parliament, taxation by parliamentary consent, a reduction in the army necessitated by the ending of monthly assessments, and new limitations on the exuberant conscience: there were many who would have supported such a programme between 1642 and 1648. The wagers ran strongly for Oliver's acceptance.

Oliver hesitated. Much has been made of the officers' role in blocking kingship, but as General Monck later correctly pointed out, an officer had only to be dismissed to be deprived of his capacity to do mischief. Furthermore, Cromwell always justly trusted in his comrades' regard for himself and for the unity of the army. Despite secretary Thurloe's alarm lest the 'grandees' (Lambert, Fleetwood, Desborough) try to split the army, the height of their threats now was to offer to resign. The junior officers for their part listened thoughtfully as Oliver reminded them that this parliament had been none of his doing, and reminded them too of the inadequacies of an Instrument that had failed to protect Nayler – 'The case of James Nayler might happen to be your own case.' Why then did he reject the crown?

There were parts of the package to which he could object. £1.3 million per annum was offered to him as revenue, though his annual expenditures were close to £2.5 million. Cromwell also had, as the curious ceremonial of his court suggests, genuine reservations about the exaltation of his own position, and had paused long before appointing his forceful younger son Henry to a carefully restricted office in Ireland. Nevertheless, such reservations could be overcome by his anxiety to clothe the sword in decent constitutional garb. Ceremony became more lavish, and the protector soon allowed his elder son Richard to emerge from obscurity. On the financial side, negotiations during April persuaded parliament to increase the projected revenue by £600 000 per annum for three years. Furthermore, Cromwell was more than a little attracted by the religious clauses of the Petition, that promised to do more than the Instrument had done to restrain the likes of Biddle and Nayler. Perhaps surprisingly, in view of his tolerationist reputation and his council's occasional efforts to protect individual Quakers from persecution, Oliver greeted the new constitution as 'the greatest provision that was ever made' for liberty for 'the people of God'.

Most important of all, Cromwell had joined the countless other gentlemen who had grown uncertain about God's purposes. He confessed to parliament in April that the Barebone's episode had been 'a story of my own weakness and folly'. Indeed, he concluded, he had often been unable to tell 'what my business was . . . save comparing it with a good constable to keep the peace of the parish'. Kingship was hardly incompatible with that minimal vision. Worn out by the cares of office, Oliver wavered that spring as the crown seemed to offer an easier path. His weeks of illness testify to his indecision, as does the tortured syntax of speeches in which, as so often, he raked over the past in order to discern God's will.

Providence did not clearly tell in favour of kingship. Although the parliamentary majority pressed the crown on him, there were none of the addresses from the country for which he might have hoped if he still saw the voice of the godly people as the voice of God. The continuing divisions of the godly throughout the 1650s had shown that England was not yet walking in God's ways; now the army, the only gathered church Cromwell had known, as well as Independent and Baptist congregations in the country, and John Owen closer to hand, indicated their disquiet. Partisanship was still rife. The churches of Gloucestershire lamented 'the major-generals' being voted down, under whom the Lord's people had comfortable protection'; in the West Riding of Yorkshire, the 'army friends' saw the crown as a shibboleth identifying enemies of the cause. Such voices served as a sounding-board for a conscience already shaken by the failure at Hispaniola.

Even without the crown, a settlement which insisted that government run 'according to the laws of these nations' might not be valueless. Once he had rejected kingship, the protector seized on the chance to regularise his position. The revised Humble Petition and Advice allowed him to nominate a new upper house of parliament, whose value even the officers could see after Nayler's case; and it made his position effectively hereditary by allowing him to name his successor. Parliament then underlined the return to parliamentary ways by passing a spate of mundane legislation, and at last ratified the protector's contentious ordinances. On 26 June 1657 the Speaker of parliament filled the place of the defunct Archbishop of Canterbury as Oliver was installed as protector a second time, with all the trappings of kingship but the crown. The government's new reliance on parliamentary sanction was clearly symbolised. As MPs adjourned until the following January many expected the drift towards a parliamentary monarchy to continue. Both the structure and the tone of political life in the later protectorate suggest a reaction. To match the two-chamber parliament, the protector's council was now called the 'privy council'. Equally revealingly, courtly ceremonial became more ornate and Oliver's daughters married, amidst unsabbatarian dancing, into noble families, one to his confidant Lord Fauconberg, another to the heir of the Earl of Warwick.

Yet the new constitution inaugurated few significant political shifts. Cromwell's careful balancing of interests can be seen in his appointments. The council changed little. Secretary Thurloe, a moderate, a great intelligence gatherer, but hardly a major politician, came in alone; not until the end of the year did Oliver succumb to the hereditary principle by admitting his elder son Richard. The only departure was Lambert, cashiered in July for his opposition and probably also for his ambition. The military contingent survived, still checking if not quite balancing Oliver's old friends St John and Nathaniel Fiennes, both now judges, and new supporters like Wolseley, Broghill and Fauconberg, who comprised his civilian entourage.

The split between the soldiers and the civilians was by no means total. Charles Howard and Edward Montague, members of noble families and both colonels, acted with the 'courtiers', as did General Monck from Scotland; conversely, the civilian Sir Gilbert Pickering aligned with the soldiers on the council. Nevertheless, the division was widely recognised. That Oliver did not resolve it owed more to his sense of comradeship and his conviction that the soldiers' seats around his chair were their due, as custodians of the godly 'interest', than to unease about the army. The silence that greeted the dismissal of the popular Lambert would have dispelled any doubts.

Equally revealing are the appointments to the new second chamber of parliament, over which the protector brooded throughout late 1657. The sixty-three nominees included seven conformist peers, five sons of peers, four baronets, one Scottish and one Irish peer, and about a dozen substantial country gentlemen. These were balanced by seventeen serving regimental officers, including the thoroughly plebeian colonels Hewson, Pride and Barkstead. Not only was the second chamber to interpose between protector and parliament and avert another Nayler case, it was also to square the circle, by allowing Oliver to institutionalise the interest of the army within the conventional political system.

In the localities the slight impact of the ostensibly civilian constitution is as apparent. In March 1657 the Hertfordshire JPs took over the remaining decimation funds for use on such worthy causes as bridge repair, and the following year a Berkshire JP sent a militia officer for trial for disarming an alleged dissident. In Surrey Onslow's influence grew, while in Somerset the remnant of John Pyne's unpopular regime of the 1640s was dismantled. But such developments were offset by the withdrawal of gentry frustrated by Cromwell's rejection of the crown – in Essex fewer titled gentlemen acted at quarter sessions in 1657–8 than in 1655. Generally, the commissions of the peace issued in 1657 made only minor changes, and left undisturbed many of the religious radicals of the Barebone's parliament. The partisan machine in Kent survived, while the Cumberland commission consisted of one knight, two esquires, three merchants, a handful of yeomen and an army officer. There were too many of 'Cromwell's hangmen', as the Cheshire magnate Sir George Booth fulminated. Indeed, most commissions of the peace included more officers than had those of 1652: there were fourteen, of whom six were mere captains, in the West Riding of Yorkshire. These officers had by now established themselves locally, and the protector's failure to attract new support enabled them to survive on the bench. But the protector may not have been displeased. Convinced that 'we have lived rather under the name and notion of law than under the thing', he still sought to blend godly reform with settlement.

But political conditions in 1657 were not favourable to the Cromwellian synthesis. The protector's hopes of confining the war with Spain, on which he had embarked so optimistically in 1655, to the New World had proved vain. Even within Europe the war was expanding, since British assertions of the right to search neutral shipping risked driving the Dutch into alliance with Spain. Aware of the risks of isolation, Cromwell at last heeded the long-standing French offer of an alliance, and in March 1657 bound himself to send 6000 troops to aid against Spain in Flanders; the return on the alliance was to be the cession to Britain of the Spanish Netherlands towns of Dunkirk and Mardyke. The charge that the protector was 'not guilty of too much knowledge' in foreign affairs finds some support in Thurloe's sour comment that most of the council had opposed the Dunkirk venture on the grounds of cost. Yet even the new commitment to France addressed some vital interests. Dunkirk privateers devastated English shipping; and while it might not be the step on the road to Vienna and Rome for which Oliver still probably yearned, Dunkirk's capture would deter Spain from backing any future royalist attempt on England. The argument that the balance of power required support for Spain rather than France depends too much on hindsight.

Not unrealistic it may have been, but expensive it certainly was. Although France would pay for the troops on campaign, England had to equip and transport them, and the treasury was empty. Naval activity had added £500 000 per annum to the government's expenditure since 1655: annual military expenditures during the Spanish war in fact exceeded the total annual outlays on royal government in the 1630s. The reduction of the monthly assessment required by the revised Humble Petition and Advice, from £60 000 to £35 000, left the tax able to bear less than half the military and naval burden. In its effort to spare the landed taxpayer parliament had granted an additional tax, the old royal standby of a levy on new building in London, which it had fondly hoped would raise £300 000 per annum: but by the end of 1658 it had yielded only £41 000. The desperate council spent countless days in 1657–8 hunting for revenues and savings, while the troops were increasingly driven to resort to free quarter – a move hardly calculated to please the public, or the soldiers. Relations with the country were further strained as deteriorating harvests in the later 1650s increased resentment for the excise, and for the war's accompaniments of losses of shipping and trade.

The demands of war preoccupied the protector and his council. Not only did they dull reforming energies; they also compounded the protector's habitual slowness in matters of political strategy. Not until December, little over a month before the new parliamentary session, were the nominations of members of the second chamber complete, leaving little time for anyone concerned to think about their functions. Unpreparedness was also manifest in the council's inability to explain its crying financial needs to parliament.

Unforeseen consequences of the Humble Petition and Advice created more serious problems. Oliver's opening speech on 20 January 1658 was a godly anthem to 'peace and righteousness' in the land, an anthem of praise too to the last session for harmonising 'all interests'. Fiennes, lord commissioner of the seal, then sang to a patriotic tune, descanting at even greater length on Spain's bid for universal monarchy, on the ancient constitution and the virtues of the golden mean, before tucking in a brief appeal for money. But the protector had fewer friends in the Commons now to respond. He had elevated eloquent civilians like Broghill and Onslow as well as officers to his new second chamber; and the revised constitution allowed the members excluded by the council in 1656 to return.

The 1658 session ended in disaster, though not because the Cromwellians were numerically overwhelmed. Rather, the breakdown reflected the weakness of the parliamentary process, with its assumptions of political community, in face of genuine ideological division. In Hesilrig and Scot the commonwealthsmen had heroic parliamentary tacticians – Hesilrig proclaimed, accurately enough, that he could speak for hours on the virtues of the Rump. Recognising the suspicions of the Commons for an institutional rival, they seized on the 'other house' in order to embarrass the protector they hated. They aimed to excite radical disaffection in the army and City, perhaps with the immediate goal of subordinating the protector more fully to parliament, probably in the hope of eventually reviving the Rump – though 1659 was to show that goodwill between Rump and army was no more likely than it had been in 1652–3.

The commonwealthsmen now possessed more ideological substance than they had when in power. Harrington's appeals to republican military glory had taken hold among some of the officers, while the commercial expansion of the 1650s had given life to a different cast of republicanism that looked back longingly to the Commonwealth and saw in its navigation acts the key to a new future. Perhaps more compelling to snobbish country gentlemen than echoes of Harrington, or the commonwealthsmen's partisan contrasts of the glories of the Rump with present gloom, was the inclusion amongst the thirty or so who attended the 'other house' of the 'cobbler' Colonel Hewson and the 'drayman' Pride. Many conformists had thought it only natural that Oliver should create peers. Even to a sympathetic observer like the protector's steward, John Maidstone, this hardly seemed a House of Lords.

As he had done so often before, Cromwell responded to parliamentary crisis with a harangue on honesty and responsibility. On 25 January he lectured his deadlocked parliament on the threat posed by royalist plotting in wartime, in face of which an uncaring parliament left the hungry soldiers to freeze in the streets; and once more he declared his commitment to the army. But he also voiced a heartfelt conviction that the achievements of his rule warranted a settlement, if only 'the nation would be content with rule'. The weary note seems to echo that sounded in 1640 by *Salmacida Spolia*, the last royal masque. But the wranglers proved unstoppable, as they had then. On 4 February the protector rode furiously to Westminster in a commandeered coach, dissolving the parliament over the anxious protests of his son-in-law General Fleetwood, whom he not unjustly brushed aside as a 'milksop'.

The protector acted so precipitately because it seemed, as it had in the winter of 1654–5, that dissidents in parliament and army were about to combine. City radicals were preparing to petition both parliament and army under the umbrella Vane had patched together of the 'good old cause'. The danger was surely not that they would win the day at Westminster, but that they would breach the unity of an army whose material sufferings reinforced the ideological misgivings of many officers. And from unity Cromwell continued to draw solace. The protector, still lord general, made his usual long speech to the officers on the history of their common cause, and extracted from them their usual resolve to 'live and die' with him. He then sought out doubters, and dismissed the major of his own regiment, Packer, and his five captains, all Baptists. That he should have broken with comrades from the early days of the Eastern Association suggests the exhaustion of his hopes. His body was exhausted too, weakened by years of ill health and cares: observers agreed that the protector was near emotional and physical breakdown.

Circumstances now appeared to favour the royalists. The major-generals and the Quakers had between them intensified country resentments, and Charles Stuart could look not only to the crown's old supporters and to Spain but also to former 'presbyterians' like Waller, and even Fairfax. He looked too to the City of London, where the apprentices had grown restive under the moralist discipline that had brought the suppression of bear-baiting and theatres, and a tightened censorship since 1655. Economic dislocation in the Spanish war had increased the citizens' impatience, and the excise fuelled the flames. The success of men who had been purged in the 1640s in gaining election for the City in 1654 and 1656 hinted at the sympathies of the more respectable.

But though Thurloe's intelligence reports predicted dire things, the royalists were no better placed to rise than in 1655. Indeed, the passage of time had seen many drift into acquiescence: one royalist facing decimation had concluded, as providentially as any puritan, 'Afflictions are God's messengers to bring us nearer him.' Not coincidentally, the classic royalist–Anglican literary product of these years is Izaak Walton's *Compleat Angler* (1653). Going fishing offered as in most times an escape from care; but it also offered a clear conscience. As former enemies intermingled – the marriage in 1657 between the disreputable young Duke of Buckingham and Fairfax's daughter is only the most notorious of such contacts – the more astute of Charles Stuart's advisers placed their hopes in an assassin's bullet, or the internal collapse of the regime. Thurloe's intelligence work increased the demoralisation by exploiting divisions amongst the royalists themselves. A wave of arrests in March 1658, followed by ostentatious troop movements through the City, reinforced the implications of the English capture of Ostend in the Spanish Netherlands. The protectorate was unlikely to be upset by force.

But however physically secure, Cromwell was not free from crisis. He had told parliament in 1657 that the deficit then ran at about £500 000 per annum; the shortfall of the taxes granted in 1657 had ensured that there had been little improvement. The pay of the troops was six months or more in arrears, and though naval officials tried to reassure creditors by repaying in strict sequence they could only buy supplies for ready cash. The ghosts of the councillors of the 1620s must have smiled when within weeks of the dissolution of the parliament in 1658 there were rumours that the desperate council was about to call another. Yet the financial crisis was not as bad as it might seem. The debt at Oliver's death stood at the equivalent of about one year's revenue, in relative terms perhaps a third of that of the French crown.

But like Charles and the Rump before him, Oliver could not persuade people to lend. In the summer the council was 'forced to go a-begging' to individual London aldermen for loans for the upkeep of newly captured Dunkirk, to little effect. Although the City fathers always favoured stability and did not relish the prospect of collapse and anarchy, they had little cause to commit themselves to as bad a debtor as the protector, least of all in the current war-generated depression. The wheel had come almost full circle. Charles I had depended on a narrow coterie of lenders, and Cromwell now could only rely on Martin Noel, whose web of credit was unfortunately no stronger than his predecessors'. Furthermore, the reluctance of financiers to pay the high price demanded in negotiations in 1657 for a return to customs farming meant that there were no customs farmers to call on. Indeed, the paralysis of successive regimes facing small wars and minor debts underlines how limited was the freedom of action of any government before the financial revolution of the end of the century.

The council desperately sought a solution through the summer of 1658 in an endless series of meetings and committees. Desborough and the military party, citing new royalist conspiracy, urged a return to partisanship, and penal taxation of the disaffected. The outrage of the 'civilians', and probably Cromwell's own weariness, blocked this and other 'as well non-legal as contra-legal ways of raising money', as Henry Cromwell in Ireland called them. But there were no obvious alternatives. The divided council was now literally living on borrowed time, for in April it again ordered that the next six months' assessment be paid in advance to prevent the extension of free quarter, 'which otherwise will inevitably follow'. Equally inevitable, therefore, was another parliament. But Desborough and his allies were no more ready than they had been in 1657 to concede the crown that seemed likely to be the price of any major grant.

The protector tried to the end to continue his balancing act. The appointment of a new commander of his own regiment was seen as a test case, and to the dismay of the civilians Oliver that summer turned to Boteler, perhaps the most unpopular of all the major-generals. Equally revealingly, a majority of the 'junto' he established in June to plan for a new parliament was military. But their prolonged inability to act persuaded Thurloe at least that Oliver would abandon his characteristic 'waiting posture'. Expectations ran high that the parliament intended for later in the year would again offer the crown. Wearied of his government's paralysis and desperate for money, Oliver might not refuse this time. Grand juries in several counties gave voice to their hopes that summer in a volley of loyal addresses – a tribute to the protector that was both unusual and significant.

The hopes were fruitless. Although the majority in the Commons in the next parliament proved favourable to the house of Cromwell, Oliver was dead. He died on 3 September 1658, the anniversary of Dunbar and Worcester, although few joined the poets in celebrating the symbolism of that fact. In the Essex countryside Ralph Josselin noted, 'Cromwell died, people not much minding it.' His rule had generated little enthusiasm, though perhaps equally little contempt: as hostile an observer as Clarendon could acknowledge that 'brave bad man'. After all, the soldiers and sailors had made England the most respected military power in Europe, and the contrast with that record was to embarrass Charles II.

More generally, Cromwell had astonished the world, and gratified some republican political theorists, by showing that a strong state could be built, as it seemed, from scratch. Fortified by his belief in God's providence, he had coped with that doctrine of necessity that had caused his predecessors, Charles I and the Long Parliament, such unease. He would have impressed those earlier students of power, the Roman Tacitus and the Italian Machiavelli. But Oliver prided himself on his efforts not only as an Englishman but as a Christian. He had, as he repeatedly insisted, ensured freedom of worship for the godly and brought good men into public life. Others too recognised this, and not merely in retrospect. Even in 1656 Richard Baxter could 'bless God for the change that I see in this country', while the gathered church at Broadmead, Bristol, looked back after the Restoration to 'those halcyon days of prosperity, liberty and peace'. The majority view was, in that regard, less favourable.

|13|

Republicans, royalists and others, 1658–1660

The eighteen months following Oliver's death form what can fairly be termed one of the defining moments of the English polity. They are often dismissed as merely a stage in England's inexorable return to its natural home in monarchy, and derided for a chaos that is too often exaggerated; yet the last months of the republic provide an unprecedented gauge of the nation's political commitments. More than that, these months were crucial in shaping those commitments.

However widespread the discontent and disaffection, the 1650s had evinced little devotion to the house of Stuart. The phenomenal sales of *Eikon Basilike* might seem to have tapped a well-spring, but if so it was for a vision of politics that was pious and monarchical as much as it was Stuart. As the republic's propagandists eagerly noted, the 'king of Scots'' invasion in 1651 had been unmistakably Scottish. Flight from Worcester to the Catholic courts of Europe did little to strengthen Charles Stuart's native appeal. This was, after all, a time when the rhetoric of 'freeborn Englishman' ran widely, and when a self-consciously national culture was being shaped by a flood of republished Jacobean dramas, and invoked by Walton's *Angler*. While would-be royalists who might have triumphed at Cromwell's death remembered bitterly a decade of frustrations, loyalists trumpeted the capture of Dunkirk. As Charles's key advisers, Edward Hyde and Edward Nicholas, noted gloomily in their penurious exile, the future was to play for.

Oliver's death was bound to disturb the unstable equilibrium of politics in the protectorate, since instability and equilibrium alike had centred on the old protector's person. The flood of addresses of congratulation to Richard on his succession, from some twenty-eight counties, spoke of the hopes for normalcy under one who had had so little hand in the arbitrary measures of the 1650s, and was so little identified with the warriors' cause of the 1640s. The civilians on the council backed him eagerly, despite the greater capacities of his younger brother Henry, because he represented the principle of primogeniture and thus promised stability. But to some, Richard did not signal merely a return to what could pass for a traditional order. In his *Holy Commonwealth* of 1659, Richard Baxter saw in the young protector a second Constantine, the godly ruler of whom mainstream puritans had so long dreamed. Gracious, civilian in his attachments, and yet godly in a conservative style very different from his father's, Richard seemed indeed to embody something more mundane, but almost as desirable as the Constantinian legend. Hopes revived for the programme of limited rule and church order on which the presbyterian party and the remnants of the middle group had so nearly come together at Newport in 1648, and again in 1657.

But the divisions that had ended in revolution in 1648 and frustration in 1657 had not been resolved. Indeed, the kingship crisis had brought them further into the open, and Oliver was no longer there to bridge them. The officers around London who congratulated Richard saluted the 'good old cause' as they urged him to protect godly men and godly churches; and as they assured him that with them he could advance the cause of reform they testified to their continuing belief that they were still the heirs of 1647, citizens in arms, 'no mere mercenary army'. Richard reassured them skilfully, and mortgaged more of the future by promising a pay rise; but his advisers were painfully at odds. While Fauconberg muttered to Henry Cromwell of a strike against army malcontents, Fleetwood was manifestly sympathetic to the radical saints. Richard showed himself his father's son as he moved quickly to confront the dissidents, and at a great meeting on 18 October he assured the officers of his good faith.

Richard's pilgrimage to the army might have worked. He was able to fudge the crucial question of control over the sword by promoting Fleetwood to lieutenant-general and operational command over the whole army while retaining in his own hand the power to issue commissions. But the enduring problem of the army's pay remained. The soldiers closer to London could be quieted with a few weeks' cash; but every regiment, in every posting, knew that its only chance of securing payments in a near-bankrupt order was through the constant presence of officers at Whitehall to lobby. Had Richard been able to dispatch the officers to their commands he might have established a new environment; as it was, the men who had offered his father comradeship and spiritual support were left clustered around his capital as an unrivalled pressure group.

Since the absence of lenders left a parliament the only alternative to a return to arbitrary measures the officers were the more watchful. They had learned repeatedly since 1647 that they could expect little from those who had not fought and bled for the cause. The local addresses to the Protector were not the only sign that civilian opinion was mobilising. The late 1650s abound in efforts at ecclesiastical reunification. The most famous of these is the Independents' conference at the Savoy in London in late 1658, that yielded a declaration of faith and practice anxiously distancing the congregations from the sects and the Quakers. Others set about the Quakers more forcibly, while clerical attempts to restore discipline through county associations reappeared; and there was no mistaking the resurgence of parochial Anglicanism. Assize judges on two different circuits advised unhappy parishioners that they were not obliged to pay tithes to ministers who withheld the sacraments. On this issue Richard's council aligned itself with the non-sectarian godly, dismissing the two judges, ordering the payment of tithes, and observing pointedly that the old church was no more. Such a gesture sat oddly with the elaborate ceremonial of Oliver's funeral on 23 November. Although this elicited little response from the public, and disquieting cynicism from the soldiery, the procession was unmistakably monarchical.

Another straw in the wind was the council's decision to abandon a relic of the Instrument of Government when in December it summoned a parliament. The council may have felt it had little option but to retain the British format (as usual a clutch of officials and officers took over the Scottish and Irish seats); but it reverted to the traditional, and haphazard, franchise and apportionment for the English and Welsh constituencies. The council may have calculated that the small boroughs were more easily influenced, or that the gentry would be reassured; but it must have disquieted those who still hoped for reform. Another reversion to the old ways came in the opening ceremonial on 27 January. Abandoning his father's homespun oratory, Richard delivered a polished plea for unity and goodwill and then allowed that old middle-grouper Nathaniel Fiennes, lord commissioner of the seal, to amplify the platitudes of government.

The country gentry had begun to come together, but the discontented too sensed an opportunity. The number of royalists in the City became common talk, while commonwealthsmen flexed their muscles in the press and in the new parliament. Outside parliament, echoes of 1647 could be heard. Junior officers, their honour and professional identity tied to the welfare of their unpaid men, grew more resentful as enforced borrowing depleted their credit, and blamed their common suffering on the corruption of a regime prepared to deal with the ungodly who hoped to put new constraints on conscience. It was here that the absence of an Oliver, who could speak their language and persuade them to endure, might prove crucial.

The overriding pressures were financial. Yet the taxes required to eliminate the government's deficit of £0.3 million per annum, to begin to reduce its debt of £2.5 million, and to propitiate the soldiery for their mounting arrears, were by no means unthinkable. Admittedly, the Commons contained country gentlemen, always averse to taxation; and the previous autumn's harvest had not been good. But other economic pointers were mixed. In February Richard dispatched a fleet under Montague to dissuade the Dutch from intervening in the Baltic war between Sweden and Denmark, but any dislocation from that had yet to be felt. The Spanish war was still disrupting trade, but the damage was localised – Dorchester in 1658 laid in extra stocks to set the poor on work, and there were loud complaints in London; but the economy of Norfolk boomed for much of 1658–9. The 1650s had furthermore brought considerable post-war economic expansion, with rents in general recovering, considerable rebuilding of damaged towns, and real wages rising. The dozens of coffee-houses established in London by 1659, the blue chinaware now newly manufactured in Bristol, the advertising that began to appear in the newspapers, all testify to consumer prosperity. Had the goodwill been there, the money was there to tap.

Goodwill vanished as it had at the end of the protector's second parliament. It is often assumed that those impassioned commonwealthsmen, Hesilrig, Vane and Scot, deliberately talked Richard's parliament and protectorate to death, confident that the soldiers would recall them to power (as they duly did). Such intransigence seems unlikely, for these were all determined parliamentarians, deeply suspicious of soldiers in politics. But they were given an opportunity to spin out of control by the council's disastrous decision to ask the new parliament to ratify the constitution. As the Engagement had shown in 1650–1, to demand explicit approval was to provoke doubts that might otherwise have been dulled in silent acquiescence. The commonwealthsmen, and any who would, now spent weeks scrutinizing rule by 'single person', the 'other house', and the Scottish and Irish representation. The commonwealthsmen remained a tiny minority, and they seem to have hoped by their challenges not to wreck the parliament but to win over the many young and inexperienced MPs. Nevertheless, the radical petition that had provoked Oliver to the previous February's dissolution was now brushed aside unceremoniously, the frame of the modified Humble Petition and Advice was wearily, if tacitly, accepted, and by the early spring the conformist majority was getting down to business.

The officers could not postpone their men's pay until the debating had ended. Anyway, they sensed conspiracy as the Commons once more tried to define and contain 'heresy', relieved suffering royalists, and slighted military men who had taken extraordinary measures. Accordingly, the first formal move of the newly reconstituted general council of officers, a petition on 6 April for sanctions against royalists and pay for the soldiers, openly invoked 'the good old cause'. It galvanised the Commons. Paradoxically, the real potential for a Cromwellian order now appeared, as alarmed commonwealthsmen abandoned their parliamentary time-wasting and joined with future cavaliers and the large conformist middle to avert catastrophe and settle the revenues.

But the army's politics also had its own momentum. Republican ideology might be spreading, but older and more urgent ways of thinking still held their appeal. Radicals in the spring of 1659 repeatedly condemned the Cromwellian interlude as 'harlotry', as 'whoredom', and the 'grandees' at Fleetwood's imposing residence of Wallingford House grew to fear abandonment by their resentful subordinates. On 14 April Desborough urged the general council of officers to vindicate the cause by declaring formal support for the regicide. The attempt, though abortive, to graft a political programme on to the professional grievances of the soldiers was familiar, and unnerving. Four days later the Commons resolved that the general council should only meet with the approval of protector and parliament, and that every officer must renounce the use of force on parliament. But they disclaimed any intention of confrontation, and tried to sweeten the pill with an undertaking to address the soldiers' arrears.

Richard, who had earlier worked hard to contain the officers' anger, determined to exploit the Commons' votes. But it was one thing to dissolve the general council, quite another to try to break the army politically, and perhaps materially, by ordering the officers back to their commands on the pretext that the Commons were addressing their grievances. On 20 April the Commons hinted at how insubstantial such an address might be when they debated the establishment of a militia before they had funded the soldiers' arrears. The nervous 'grandees' immediately demanded that Richard dissolve parliament. Richard thought he could outface them: he had received addresses of loyalty from the City and its militia, and he was confident of some of his father's old comrades among the colonels – Whalley, Goffe, Ingoldsby. But most of the junior officers took their troops over to join the generals' rendezvous at St James's, leaving the humiliated protector with a handful of men. The final crisis had come quickly, and it ended quickly. On 22 April Richard dissolved the parliament. Just over a month later, on 24 May, he himself resigned, his efforts to secure aid from Henry in Ireland and Monck in Scotland having failed in face of the obvious divisions in their armies. An angry Henry in Ireland followed Richard into oblivion, though Monck managed to extricate himself from the fall of the house of Cromwell.

The expulsion of Richard's parliament and the end of the protectorate was a time of awakening for the radicals. The 'good old cause' that Vane had left artfully vague back in 1656 now assumed substance as pamphleteers competed to make it theirs. Cries for a gamut of law reforms, religious freedom for the saints, power for 'the good party', new elections, pay for the army, rang out; and driving all of them was the over-riding imperative to vindicate the hopes of regeneration that had been sacrificed to the pride of one man in 1653. The characteristic republican hopes of action, even of opportunity, resurfaced: as one of the Gawdy family of Norfolk put it, it would soon be 'a brave world for men of merit'. But the officers' means were prosaic, for they had nothing to offer against those who extolled the Commonwealth as the way to a true commonwealth and soldiers' pay. Despite their frustrations with the Rump six years earlier, despite Fleetwood's desultory effort to preserve Richard's protectorate, and despite too the triumphant return of Lambert, once the maker of constitutions, to his command, on 6 May the general council wrote to Speaker Lenthall recalling the Rump. Eventually over a hundred members followed him to Westminster.

The return of the surviving Rumpers was as much a climacteric as had been the first installation of the Rump in the revolutionary winter of 1648–9. The radical minority exulted and agitated, but others put those outpourings alongside the breach in continuity, and feared the worst. 'How likely it may be that they should prove a scourge to the nation,' Rev. Henry Newcome reflected sourly in Cheshire on the new men. Another godly minister, Ralph Josselin, reported that his Essex neighbours could only 'gaze' at what he himself took to be the crude self-interest of the alliance of soldiers and commonwealthsmen. Participation in local government quickly dropped as the Rump turned to its radical supporters, and as even Quakers found their way into some county magistracies. The slow reattachment of a powerful segment of the traditional political elite that had characterised the late protectorate had come to an end.

However much the 'honest party' hoped for a new order, memory dominated the politics of the restored Rump. It lost no time in asserting its exclusiveness against the voluble and combative William Prynne, who once more tried to contest his exclusion at Pride's Purge. Resentment for the commander who had interrupted them led the Rumpers to dismiss around 160 Cromwellian officers, and to reinstate some Oliver had purged. Though gratitude might have been expected for those who had brought them back, the Rumpers remembered all too well the eruptions of the military. They were no more willing than Richard had been to accord the army full institutional independence, and insisted on ultimate civilian authority: commissions would come from the Speaker, and dismissals could as well. When the Rump, desperate for money, fearful of raising the assessment, revived plans for reconstituting the armed forces as a militia – a move that might gratify classical republicans as well as country gentry – the officers equally quickly recovered their own resentments of 1652–3.

It was not that this parliamentary government was vulnerable to the charges of lethargy and corruption levelled in 1653. Members set to work busily on a host of committees, to examine the revenue, to reform the courts and provision for the ministry, to review the protectorate's foreign commitments, to use or sell off the state's resources, from palaces to forests. And they declared their intention of dissolving within a year. There lay the rub, for the Rump moved as slowly as it had after Worcester to prepare for a successor, or to frame a constitution. Outside parliament the cries for a reformed order grew louder. Lambert and the officers pressed for a selected Senate, to balance the people's elected representatives and entrench the army's interest. Harrington shaped ever pithier versions of his classical citizens' republic; his former ally and publisher, John Streater, saw in the dynamism and the riches of commercial expansion the means to reconcile an active citizenry and a professional army; resurgent Levellers called for a written constitution and entrenched protections; and Quakers and Fifth-Monarchists, convinced that the time was nigh, deluged the presses with prophecies of rule by the Lamb or by the saints. But already some of the Rumpers were becoming gloomy, and in mid-May the Cornish MP Colonel Robert Bennet squelched the optimism of a friend with the observation, 'Cromwell's pride was trampled with greater.' Not surprisingly, royalists thought they saw their opportunity in the frustrations and confusions.

Royalism had changed significantly since Oliver in 1655 had condemned it for its inveteracy and interbreeding. The officers during Richard's parliament had similarly imagined their old enemy ranged against them; but years of surveillance and failure had taken the heart out of such half-baked cavalier groupings as the Sealed Knot. The real threat now was of a renewal of the presbyterian-royalist alliance of 1647–8. The fall of the protectorate, the radical outpouring that accompanied it, and most of all the noisy hopes of the Quakers, generated a powerful presbyterian reaction that extended far beyond the printed vituperations of Prynne. Assessments were duly collected, and government secured a large measure of compliance in town and countryside. But the most astute of the royalist agents, John Viscount Mordaunt, recognised the intensity of the conservative anxieties that the presbyterian clergy were fuelling, with their cries of the 'church in danger'; looking beyond the usual suspects he helped weave together a broad conspiracy for a series of regional risings that summer. As so often, ill-discipline and fear prevailed; only in the northwest was there trouble. But the ability of the Cheshire presbyterian magnate Sir George Booth to lead about 4000 into the field for 'a free parliament' and to seize parts of Cheshire, Lancashire and north Wales, points to the extent of disaffection. Booth's hopes that others too would rise, and divide the army, were disappointed, and his isolated forces were crushed by Lambert on 19 August; but the political impact of his rebellion was considerable.

Victory once more affirmed the army's sense of itself and its partisan entitlement. Quartered around Derby on their return from Cheshire the officers prepared a petition for a sweeping purge of all local officials who had remained inactive during the crisis, and for the entrenchment of Fleetwood and Lambert in their commands. Hesilrig, who loathed soldiers who challenged his vision of parliamentary supremacy, and who wrongly held Lambert responsible for the petition, sought vainly to have him sent to the Tower. In the end the house on 23 September contented itself with reprimanding the petitioners, but Hesilrig's hard line had drawn in the generals. These countered by demanding the punishment of all those who misrepresented the Derby petition, and by demanding more insistently the jurisdictional independence of the army: no officer should be dismissed save by court-martial. Their implicit aim was not merely the honour and just deserts of the army, but its ratification as an estate within the commonwealth, the final custodian of the cause.

Such an aim had been implicit in all the army's pressure on Oliver Protector; to urge it need not have brought disaster, even in a regime as devoted to the principle of parliamentary sovereignty as this. But when the Rumpers learned that the grandees were circulating other units for support for their petition, and that agitators were again appearing in some regiments, they assumed a coup was coming. Listening to Hesilrig rather than the more conciliatory Vane, on 11 October they asserted the constitutional inviolability of the Commonwealth, and struck at the officers, by abrogating all measures and grants of the protectorate. The following day they dismissed Lambert and several other officers, and demoted Fleetwood. But though they posted a guard around parliament, they could see the writing on the wall, for they also declared it treason to levy taxes without parliamentary authorisation.

The high drama of Lambert's show-down on 12 October with the regiments surrounding Westminster could not conceal the emptiness of the army's hold on what was left of power. Fleetwood nervously invoked providence as he wrote to Monck in Scotland justifying the barring-out of the Rumpers; but providence, as Oliver had found, was no guide to a future state. As the officers searched for such a guide their hopes ran still to a remodelled republic, the most plausible alternative to the cries of Quakers and Fifth-Monarchists. There were two main approaches: one akin to the Levellers' scheme, with power flowing from the people to an elected but limited unicameral body; the other, in some version of Harrington's system, with the tyranny of an elective lower house blocked by a select second chamber, whose own corruption might or might not be averted by the rotation of members. The officers of course disagreed with Harrington on the merits of rotation; and John Milton, who was also now drawn into the desperate search for an expedient to blend elitism with active citizenship, agreed with them, as he showed most ringingly in his *Readie and Easie Way* of February–March 1660.

To many onlookers the likely outcome was not a Leveller or classical republic but power in the hands of John Lambert. That outcome might not have been the mere brigandage his enemies, and subsequent historians, have assumed. The old order had manifestly collapsed. Lambert, steeped as he was in republican ideas and history, may have calculated that the time was ripe for the hero to renew the state. And what Renaissance prince had more style and panache, was more the hero, than he?

Not surprisingly, the grandees at Wallingford House could agree neither on the form of a commonwealth, nor the path to it. The committee of safety they established as the executive was manifestly a stopgap: Lambert, Fleetwood and Desborough, with a handful of officials and what might pass for representatives of London and the most radical Scottish (Johnston of Wariston) and Irish army (Ludlow) interests. This distillation of the 'good old cause' looked uncomfortably like the dregs. The growing confusion of the republican centre was matched by alienation of the periphery. As godly officers held prayer-meetings to lament the pervading suspicion and fragmentation, their sympathisers dwindled, reluctant to support a coup bent on preserving the generals' commissions and thus contradicting the very principle of self-denial. Meanwhile, the country swung into opposition.

Until the summer, the habitual acquiescence in face of authority had offered still a chance for a non-Stuart form to root itself. Tax yields remained high – the county of Norfolk's payments on the assessment for the period 1657–60 showed a £38 surplus at the end. Apart from Booth's, the royalist risings failed miserably, and Charles Stuart's advisers waxed despondent. In their resignation some royalists even attended Harrington's coffee-house discussion circle, the Rota, that autumn, thinking, 'As to human foresight, there was no possibility of the king's return.' As late as the following January, the colonial assembly of Barbados protested their loyalty to 'England successively as it now is or shall for the future be fixed or settled.'

The Barbadians were far away across the dark Atlantic. Closer to home, the autumn's upheavals destroyed the political capacity of republicanism. Indeed, they so undermined government itself that Restoration polemicists were soon able to vilify the entire history of the republic. When the officers on their return reversed the Rump's purges, chains of command and administrative procedures weakened further. The consequences may have been most grievous in the impoverished navy, which was at war. That winter privateers grew more active, and the dislocation of trade intensified when political crisis encouraged a flight of short-term capital. Underemployed apprentices in London rabbled the soldiers repeatedly as the weather worsened, and when the soldiers retaliated they added new crimes to the City's litany of complaints.

As the identity, let alone the legitimacy, of the supreme power became unclear, the scrupulous and the timid flinched from acting in its name. Participation in both central and local courts dropped sharply. By the end of the year legal process was faltering, with consequences in scattered brigandage – not all of which was the work of hungry soldiers. The Rump's 12 October declaration against unparliamentary taxation gave a different cast to the disorders, for it encouraged overtly constitutionalist resistance; and in Norwich and in the West Riding the excise was duly challenged. Militia commissioners acting under warrants of the displaced Rump met in Cornwall at the end of October to raise money, but went home, convinced that they lacked authority.

Under such stresses the army crumbled. The political commitment of the rank-and-file had dwindled through the 1650s as professionalisation advanced. What piecemeal purges and distant postings had left undone, cynicism about the doings of superiors now achieved. Driven to resort to free quarter, the baffled soldiers were subject to the anger of householders, whose material discontents were fuelled by new political and religious resentments. Disorganisation was intensified by developments within the army. The crisis of the summer had brought additional and ill-managed recruitment, while the increased turnover among the officers, and the blatant competition of place-seekers, disrupted ties to units. Demoralisation destroyed the remnants of the army's republic. Hesilrig used the crisis of morale early in December to open the first breach in the army's treasured unity, as he won the neglected and resentful garrison of Portsmouth to declare once more for the Rump, all that could pass now for civilian authority. The remnants of the fleet, equally resentful, took up the call and blockaded London, intensifying the hardship and the crisis.

As republican polemicists became fewer and fainter, the swing away from public espousal of the Commonwealth gathered pace. The City's municipal elections on 21 December produced a common council that called for a 'free parliament', a coded term for a reversal of Pride's Purge. The corporation then proceeded to an ominous expansion of the City militia. In Dublin the Baptist army officers, perplexed by what they heard of England, their troops close to starving, fell easily to a coup by the 'old protestants' (the pre-war settlers) Henry Cromwell had cultivated. Even the charismatic Lambert's soldiers were reported to have offered to make a ring for the officers to fight in. It was a small step for a badly shaken Fleetwood, who was nonplussed by the threats of a general tax-payers' strike, to hand the reins of government back to Speaker Lenthall, and a re-restored Rump, on Christmas Eve. Fleetwood's despairing judgment, that God had 'spitt in their faces', shows the consistency of the true providentialist; it also reveals a fundamental political incomprehension.

The cause and the effect of fragmentation in England was the increasing prominence of the commander in Scotland, George Monck. It was Monck's opposition to the grandees that gave dissidents elsewhere the courage to act; and it was the distractions on every hand that gave Monck the space to prepare his moves. The basis of his power, as that of Lambert, was of course military. But his troops remained better paid than their comrades to the south, for the Rump had sent funds north to prevent the summer's crisis spreading. Furthermore, to the end of the year Scottish taxes continued to flow into Monck's treasury – his careful propitiation of Scotland's nobility had made them his eager collaborators as they sought to regain what they had lost in that country's own 1640s revolution. Nevertheless, it took time and effort to shape the army in Scotland to new purposes. When Monck had wished to support Richard Cromwell in the late spring he found that his subordinates would not let him. The fulsome declaration of allegiance to the Rump he then issued enabled him to survive the purge of Cromwellians, but he was not able to protect his forces from extensive and partisan remodelling. The crucial transformation came after Monck's first major act of resistance.

Monck's own principles seemed 'dark' at the time, and not much light has fallen since. A brilliant professional soldier, he had served various masters, and prized the subordination of the soldier to civilian authority:

accordingly, he despised Lambert. He was also a determined, if deliberately uncouth, presbyterian and defender of the ministry. While the radical upsurge of the summer unsettled him, the grandees' expulsion of the Rump, coming at a time of Quaker demonstrations, and Quaker penetration of his own forces, infuriated him. Whether that conjunction drove him to act, or provided him the occasion and justification for acting, we shall never know. But he declared his dislike of Lambert's 12 October coup, encouraged the City to withstand the committee of safety, and proceeded to purge and reconstitute his forces with systematic attention to detail.

The outcome of the last phase of the republic hinged on whether the much larger forces at Lambert's disposal could win over or break Monck's before Monck exploited the disaffection in England. Monck's waiting game decided the issue. Lambert could not gather sufficient men until mid-November, and could never gather sufficient supplies; meanwhile, Monck consolidated his political control over both officers and men, marshalled his supplies, and slowly moved towards the border. While his troops waited in relative comfort in quarters at Coldstream on the Tweed, Lambert's, unpaid, often unshod, levied free quarter at Newcastle and shivered. Lambert's officers meanwhile were distracted by the disarray in their rear, and flinched from an open assault on their comrades in front. News of the collapse of the committee of safety and the re-restoration of the Rump at last pulled Lambert south again on 27 December, but it was too late even for his legendary dash. Lord Fairfax, his old neighbour and commander, came out of retirement on the 30th to raise the Yorkshire gentry. As Fairfax's forces seized York for a parliament, Lambert's disintegrated just to the north. On 2 January 1660 Monck crossed the border to march south unopposed, accepting the enthusiastic addresses of gentry, town corporations and ordinary countryfolk as he went.

The outcome of the final defeat of the New Model Army, the arbiter of so much of the past fifteen years' history, was by no means foreordained. Fleetwood had handed power back to the Rump, and Hesilrig at least was eager to wield it. It is easy to focus on the divisions, on the triumphant Hesilrig who refused to enter parliament on 29 December until Vane had left. But, the capacity of the Rumpers for action once their enemies were out of the way – or rather, their capacity for action to help them get out of the way – is apparent in its prompt decision to raise the assessment drastically in order to pay off the increasingly mutinous soldiers. And the Rump was not merely intent on peaceful resignation when it instructed Monck to purge the English army. On 9 February it disingenuously ordered the general, who was in the midst of sending two-thirds of the captains into obscurity with the grandees, to dismantle the City's defences and disband the common council. Its hope must have been that this would destroy him politically at the same time as it neutralised the London conservative leaders. For two days his wife and his senior officers, who urged resistance to the Rump, contended with discipline for Monck's allegiance; or perhaps Monck simply flinched from stepping into the unknown. Then on the 11th he set himself against Westminster, triggering one of the great spontaneous celebrations in English history, 'the roasting of the rump', when rump steaks were roasted in derision across London and then through the provinces.

There is little sign that Monck was yet committed to the restoration of the house of Stuart that he eventually engineered. But he was a canny opportunist, and he paid close heed to the demonstrations, and to the dozens of petitions for a free parliament and an established church. On 21 February his soldiers secured the return to Westminster of the MPs excluded in December 1648. These were scarcely 'royalists' in the conventional sense: many retained their liking for the old 'presbyterian' aims of 1648, with a monarchy and a church firmly limited by the political nation. And to confirm them in their principles, Monck lectured them on the dangers of a restored monarchy and on the virtues of a presbyterian church order. His actions at this point are impenetrable. He may have been seeking to reassure surviving republicans in the army. But it is just as likely that his hesitation and apparent confusion were emblematic of the uncertainties besetting a nation that was still unstable and fragmented. Nevertheless, however 'presbyterian' the returning members, they saw the return of Charles Stuart as the only way out of chaos. And, as the army had recognised in 1647–8, to impose conditions on a king returning to a capital desperate to receive him was a daunting task.

Monck's uneasy course in February–March 1660 helps put other responses in perspective. It is easy to turn from 'the roasting of the rump' to the outpourings of loyal joy in the late spring and summer, when the king came back, and to assume inevitability. It is easy to assume too from the speed and consistency with which the derisively anatomical epithet, 'the Rump', was applied to the Commonwealth that the organic values of the pre-war world were back in all their force. The corollary is to make a lonely hero, or purblind bigot, of John Milton as that March he prepared for publication an expanded edition of his *Readie and Easie Way*.

Universal the execration of the Rump clearly was. But the need for a more complicated story is suggested both by Monck's conduct, and by the hopes for a moderated monarchy entertained by the 'presbyterians' in the last brief flourish of the expanded Long Parliament, as well as in the Convention Parliament that quickly succeeded it on 25 April. As they celebrated the Restoration, the good folk of Nottingham were that summer entertained with a play, *Robin Hood and his Merry Crew of Soldiers*, that spun together the Sherwood myth with recent history. The nostalgia with which this 'cavalier' concoction treated aspirations towards a republican life of action points to the survival of dreams of community and political capacity beyond the royal court, even as the king enjoyed his own once more.

Afterword

As he watched the Restoration, James Harrington is reported to have observed that England would be a commonwealth again in seven years. His prediction of course failed; but his conviction that the changed balance of material resources precluded stable monarchy found some warrant in Charles II's financial straits and frequent recourse to parliament for rescue. Harrington recognised that a broad political community was rooted deeply in the landscape. And though monarchy was in 1660 restored to great rejoicing, the community as well as the king had learned more than one lesson from the experience of the 1640s and '50s. As the marquess of Halifax, one of the leading figures of Charles II's reign, reflected, 'the liberty of the late times gave men so much light, and diffused it so universally amongst the people, that they are not now to be dealt with, as they might have been in an age of less inquiry'.

Change and continuity is a not unfamiliar verdict on any age, and it can surely be passed on the Restoration. Just as formal republicanism expired while the political values on which it had drawn lived on, so monarchy was and was not what monarchy once had been. The events of 1659 bred in the political nation a deeper devotion to monarchical legitimacy than ever before. By the end of that year military rule and Quakers seemed the unpalatable alternative to Stuart monarchy, and the Restoration was therefore unconditional. There were unforeseen consequences to the fears of the gentry in the Convention, and of their more royalist successors in the Cavalier Parliament. Because of those fears, and the refurbishment of the crown they worked, parliamentary ways only survived by a narrow margin. While one anxiety was laid to rest, another was raised.

The impression of unfinished business is strengthened by the dilemmas of the later seventeenth century. The temporary repudiation of royal debts in 1672 in the 'Stop of the Exchequer', and Charles II's periodic recourse to a French dole, show that rulers still lived from hand to mouth. Not until the 1680s' increase in customs revenues, and still more the financial revolution of the 1690s, could governments act abroad without incurring crisis at home. Indeed, only in the process of working out that financial revolution were the constitutional issues broached in 1641 decided.

The restored monarchy of Charles II was different from the monarchy of Charles I in a crucial regard. The state, on which avant-garde theorists had earlier speculated, had now emerged. Many would have been appalled at such a return on a civil war they thought had aimed to put restraints on power. There was a regular army, reduced but not disbanded at the Restoration; the navy nearly doubled in size between 1650 and 1655, and never again returned to its 1650 level (which had itself been nearly twice that of the fleet of 1640); and the tax bite of the 1650s and beyond dwarfed that of the 1630s. Patrimonial monarchy as the early seventeenth century had imagined it, with the crown living off its own, was no more. Hobbes was doubtless gratified by the clarification.

But the new state was not Leviathan. The reduction in the army hints at the survival in the localities of familiar ways of self-regulation and self-control, even while the retention of the navy allowed the projection of power into the Atlantic world. Leviathan failed to take hold conceptually too. Instead, the ideology of the republicans helped shape the new age, as the closed, corporate image of the body politic was steadily displaced by the rhetoric of national interest. That rhetoric not only better accommodated the dissensions left by 'the broken times', as they were so often called, it also addressed the changes in society and tastes that accompanied the new colonial imports. The Navigation Acts established a framework that steadily filled with *stuff*. As consumer attitudes and values became unmistakable, the bodily metaphor, with its disparagement of the merely gustatory, began to feel outmoded.

The eager purchase of sugar, tobacco pipes, coffee, the blue china of Bristol, was not just a response to supply. It was also a mark of confidence. Without question, the vital development for most people was neither political nor ideological but the easing of the socio-economic ills that had wracked England since perhaps the 1580s. By the mid-1650s grain prices were dropping, while wage-rates had risen in the post-war rebuilding; by the end of the decade a reduction in the rates of emigration that had run at an historic high in the '50s gave further evidence that a corner had been turned.

This is not to suggest the dawning of an era of good feelings. Memories of upheaval and challenge, in a time of multiplying comforts, occasioned something of a social reaction. Regulation of the markets in the interest of the consumer ceased as an element of national policy; the game laws, and soon a whole range of laws protecting property, became ever more draconian; and 'fleering' (crudely contemptuous behaviour towards the meaner sort) grew popular amongst some of the gentry. Falling grain prices gave an incentive to landowners to exploit their lands, when wartime seizures of stock and plough animals, and the enormous burden of taxes, had already weakened many smallholders. The polarisation of the rural populace into the landed few and the landless many proceeded apace.

If local communities were being transformed, the national community too was subject to change. Anti-Catholicism helped to identify England in an earlier generation, and it had been central to the parliamentarian cause; but the Catholic threat failed to materialise, though chaos had seemed to invite it. Preaching to the house of Commons on 5 November 1678, on the anniversary of the Gunpowder Plot of 1605 and at the height of the great scare of the 'Popish Plot', John Tillotson, a future Archbishop of Canterbury but also a relative by marriage of Oliver Cromwell, could not affirm that the pope was Antichrist. He saw in Catholicism primarily a political threat. Amongst his audience, the aged Colonel Birch was virtually the only MP who during the ensuing heated debates spoke in the once-familiar tones of strenuous protestantism. To Birch's colleagues, popery meant absolutism, secular evils, something un-English, but not the apocalypse. Even Birch later cast himself for his funeral monument as a Roman patriot rather than as one of God's Englishmen.

Birch was far from alone in donning the toga, for memorials to English models of Roman virtue abound in the epitaphs and monuments of the later seventeenth century. From Restoration England emerged Milton's great poems and Bunyan's *Pilgrim's Progress*, the heroic artefacts of zeal; Restoration culture was therefore hardly confined in a Roman mould. But the loneliness of Milton's and Bunyan's heroes reflects on the world of their writers. The work of godly edification over several generations ensured that dissent was able to face down Restoration persecution; but it had not turned England into Jerusalem. The monuments in Roman garb certainly declare a passionate commitment among the elite to ideals of the active life – and might have given pause to any proponent of a Baroque absolutism who took the trouble to observe them. But they also indicate that, though the campaign to reform the manners of the poor might ebb and flow, the struggle for godly rule was over.

Central to Roman virtue were moderation, stoicism, the tempering of the passions – values far distant from the forceful piety of the saints. The reaction against the old marks of godliness, defined now as 'enthusiasm' and 'fanaticism', is one of the most unmistakable features of the Restoration. It spanned the spectrum, from the coarse ribaldry and invective directed by the revellers in 1660 against all the ways of the godly, to enduring changes in epistemology and expression.

1660 has attained almost as much fame from the formation in that year of the Royal Society as it has from the restoration of monarchy. In that world, which so loudly declared the restoration of harmony, contest was all around. No less than the cult of Roman virtue, science in the seventeenth century doubled as an ideology for use against zealots. Thomas Sprat, in his propagandist *History of the Royal Society* (1667), urged the scientific approach as an antidote to 'enthusiasm'. To the chemist Robert

Boyle, a prime argument for science was its capacity to destroy radical sectarian claims for the cohabitation of the material and the spiritual, the spirit in the flesh. The sources of knowledge appealed to by saints and controversialists had yielded only confusion: sense-impressions, empirical data, might generate a polite and detached consensus. The reaction against unprovable claims to certainty, and the high-flown language in which they were couched, was of course part of a Europe-wide drift; and when Hobbes in *Leviathan* denounced those who indulged in 'insignificant speech' he had in view the Aristotelian philosophers whom his friends in Paris also ridiculed. But he aimed as well at the sectarians who claimed religious inspiration for their utterances. Sprat similarly, in his *History*, saw the same two groups as abusers of 'rhetoric'.

The conviction gained ground that language itself had been perverted. The consequences of such discovery are apparent in the distance between the florid style of Lancelot Andrewes, James I's favourite preacher, and the spare argument of John Tillotson after the Restoration. Once again, controversy and the new philosophy joined hands. From Francis Bacon onwards, scientists had lamented the obscurantism inherent in the Renaissance delight in multiplicity of meanings, and the fashion for metaphors and word play. In *Leviathan*, Hobbes insisted that words were simply names for objects. The Royal Society's adoption of Bacon's motto 'nullius in verba' (nothing in words) proclaimed its conviction that belief ought to rest upon evidence rather than persuasion, and that 'rhetoric' impeded understanding. Such claims contrasted sharply with the godly conviction that understanding lay in unfolding 'the Word' of scripture.

The corollary of the revaluation of language was a significant change in religious expression. However time-serving his politics, Bulstrode Whitelocke was undeniably one of the godly; yet in the later stages of the Commonwealth he had in his dismay at the divisions amongst the saints already turned towards private rather than public worship. The Quakers, chastened by the Nayler episode and by the events of 1659–60, withdrew into the quietism and restraint that has become characteristic of them. Others made no bones about their distaste for expressions of religious feeling. The intensity with which poets such as Donne and Herbert, or even the dourly Calvinist Fulke Greville, had explored their faith in the first half of the century is absent in polite circles in the second. John Dryden was almost alone in making public a personal statement of faith; and that testament, his poem *Religio Laici* of 1682, is chiefly remarkable for its lack of spirituality. Whatever the stature of *Paradise Lost*, piety and morality had become the order of the day, and 'zeal' an insult.

1649 was a political revolution, though the regime then established failed to put down roots. A more lasting revolution was the shift in taste and sensibility that came with the collapse of puritanism. As the sense grew that conviction had been lost and a cause perverted, a radical dissident warned the army as early as 1654: 'Consider how the people of God are scorned and reproached, and the name of God blasphemed daily for your sakes. It's now the common word, when any one speaks of a false dissembler and treacherous faith-breaker, "There's a saint," say they.' And before Oliver's death one of Richard Baxter's female correspondents, apologising for troubling him rather than going to her own minister, observed that to her neighbours, and to 'most of the gentry of England', a woman's private conferences with a minister were worse than 'gaming or mixed dancing or bare breasts'. The great best-seller of the Restoration was Samuel Butler's *Hudibras* (1663), which definitively identified puritanism with hypocrisy.

Puritanism in power nurtured the seeds of its own destruction. Puritans who declared that they were fighting the Lord's battles and setting themselves against what Cromwell called 'self-ends' found themselves in place and power. Whatever the general probity of its administrators, this revolution, like every other, attracted fellow-travellers. Even as conscientious a public servant as major-general Berry could worry that if any of the assassination plots against Oliver 'should take . . . what will come of our preferments?' Contemporaries thought it quite proper that those who ruled should be rewarded for so doing; but puritans had made a virtue of self-denial for too long to be given the benefit of the doubt when they prospered while stopping others from going about their enjoyments. Few would have had much sympathy for the low-born regicide Colonel Barkstead, Lieutenant of the Tower of London, who early in 1654 wanted more money since he must live 'suitable to his place'. In 1659 there were moves to impeach for corruption Philip Jones, who had turned his suzerainty over much of Wales into a profitable concern.

The drive for reform had petered out, and 'the glorious cause of the people of God' had come to look too much like self-seeking under a shell of piety. There were certainly grounds for the caricature so often drawn of hypocrites: thus, an officer pleading for Desborough's favour in 1655 used the revealing arguments that he did not wear costly clothes, did not powder his hair and had never been in a barber's shop. The maypoles and the frolicking at the Restoration command sympathy, while the ease and wit of the 'merry monarch' still appeal. Nevertheless, we may register too the power of another vision of the polity as Milton in *The Readie and Easie Way*, his last-minute battle-cry for a virtuous commonwealth, contemplated 'the perpetual bowings and cringings of an abject people' under monarchy.

Of course, godly republicans of Milton's persuasion were not the only losers in the game. As they surveyed the devastation of lives and landscapes, Scots and Irish lamented their sufferings under the English, not monarchy. But Milton, like most of his countrymen, had never had much sympathy for their aspirations.

Bibliographical essay

The basic aids for serious students of the period are now wearing thin. No detailed analytic bibliography has appeared in twenty years, no thorough thematic source collection for far longer. But to compensate, scholarly publications both proliferate and grow more imaginative. The following suggestions can only point to some of the more helpful of these.

General

The best brief political survey is B. Coward, *The Stuart Age* (2nd edn, London, 1994); M. Kishlansky, *A Monarchy Transformed* (London, 1996), though livelier and more up to date, is briefer and less balanced. For social history, J. Sharpe, *Early Modern England* (2nd edn, 1997), ranges more broadly, thematically and chronologically than K. Wrightson, *English Society 1580–1680* (London, 1982), which is more noteworthy for argument.

The political background

The most provocative and influential challenge to received understandings of English history has undoubtedly come from recent work on the British problem. Essential reading here are: J.G.A. Pocock, 'The Limits and Divisions of British History', *American Historical Review* 1981; the essays in B. Bradshaw and J. Morrill, eds, *The British Problem* (New York, 1996); in S. Ellis and S. Barber, *Conquest and Union* (London, 1995); and in A. Grant and K. Stringer, *Uniting the Kingdom?* (London, 1995). More systematic is B.P. Levack, *The Formation of the British State* (Oxford, 1987).

Scholarship on England proper is now in what might be called a post-revisionist phase, and interest has shifted from skirmishes over the presuppositions of parliamentary history. This has allowed many aspects of public life to come into clearer focus. P. Collinson, *De Republica Anglorum* (Cambridge, 1990), challenges prevailing assumptions of the socio-political identity of the English political community. Kingship has been reopened to view above all by J. Wormald's British scrutiny, 'James VI and I: two kings or one', *History* (1983), volume 68 and by J. Richards, '"His Nowe Majestie" and the English Monarchy', *Past and Present* (1986). The court too has been illuminated, by the essays in L. Peck, ed., *The Mental World of the Stuart Court* (Cambridge, 1991), and in R.M. Smuts, ed., *The Stuart Court and Europe* (Cambridge, 1996). Smuts's detailed study of *Court Culture and the Origins of a Royalist Tradition* (Philadelphia, 1987), and the essays in D. Starkey, ed., *The English Court: From the Wars of the Roses to the Civil War* (London, 1987), are also helpful.

The financial supports of government appear in M. Braddick's important survey, *The Nerves of State* (Manchester, 1996); they can also be glimpsed in the essays in R. Hoyle, ed., *The Estates of the English Crown* (Cambridge, 1992), and in R. Ashton, *The City and the Court* (Cambridge, 1979). Government in crisis is the concern of the essays in M. Fissel, ed., *War and Government in Britain, 1598–1650* (Manchester, 1991). The best work on royal government itself is still G.E. Aylmer, *The King's Servants* (revised edn, London, 1974), though J.F. Merritt, ed., *The Political World of Thomas Wentworth, Earl of Strafford* (Cambridge, 1996), contains much of value.

As befits the articulator of relationships of nation and neighbourhood alike, the law has been studied for its involvement in politics and government, as a system of thought, and as a frame for the local community. For the first, W.J. Jones, *Politics and the Bench* (London, 1971) and J.S. Cockburn, *A History of English Assizes 1558–1714* (Cambridge, 1972) are still crucial. For the second, J.H. Baker, *The Legal Profession and the Common Law* (London, 1986), and for the third, C.B. Herrup, *The Common Peace* (Cambridge, 1987) and J.A. Sharpe, *Crime in Early Modern England* (London, 1984), are fundamental.

Some of the most impressive recent work has been on political thought. The best introduction is to be found in the massive *Cambridge History of Political Thought 1450–1700*, ed. J.H. Burns (Cambridge, 1991). Undoubtedly the most influential study is J.G.A. Pocock, *The Ancient Constitution and the Feudal Law* (Cambridge, 1987), but this has been challenged by G. Burgess, *The Politics of the Ancient Constitution* (London, 1993). Burgess's *Absolute Monarchy and the Stuart Constitution* (New Haven, 1996) debates particularly with J. Sommerville, *Politics and Ideology in England 1603–1642* (London, 1986). R. Tuck, *Philosophy and Government 1572–1651* (Cambridge, 1993), forcefully ties natural law theories to politics. Useful studies of individuals are S. White on *Sir Edward Coke and 'the Grievances of the Commonwealth'*

1621–1628 (Chapel Hill, 1979); P. Christianson *Discourse on History, Law and Governance in Public Career of John Selden, 1610–1635* (Toronto, 1996); and M. Mendle, *Henry Parker and the English Civil War* (Cambridge, 1995). The essays by B. Worden in D. Wootton, ed., *Republicanism, Liberty and Commercial Society, 1649–1776* (Stanford, 1994), are vital for an understanding of English republicanism. For the crystallising sense of English nationhood, see R. Helgerson, *Forms of Nationhood* (Chicago, 1992), and for aristocratic ideals, see M.E. James, 'English Politics and the Concept of Honour, 1558–1642', in his *Society, Politics and Culture* (Cambridge, 1986). The essays in D. Woolf and J. Morrill, eds, *Public Duty and Private Conscience in Seventeenth-century England* (Oxford, 1993), are also important for ideology.

Studies of local government and local politics are legion. A. Fletcher, *Reform in the Provinces* (New Haven, 1986), is the most helpful survey; the same author's *A County Community in Peace and War: Sussex 1603–1660* (London, 1975), is, with A. Hughes, *Politics, Society and Civil War in Warwickshire, 1620–1660* (Cambridge, 1987), the best of the county studies. B. Quintrell, 'Government in Perspective: Lancashire and the Privy Council, 1570–1640', *Transactions of the Historic Society of Lancashire and Cheshire* (1982), is still the best case study of relations of centre and locality. J. Kent, *The English Village Constable 1580–1642* (Oxford, 1986), surveys the bottom layer of local government. J. Morrill, *Revolt of the Provinces* (2nd edn, London, 1980) has been the most influential account of localism, but it needs to be read with C. Holmes, 'The County Community in Stuart History and Historiography', in R. Cust and A. Hughes, ed., *The English Civil War* (London, 1997). The essays in J. Barry, ed., *The Tudor and Stuart Town* (London, 1990) are very helpful. The best introduction to early-modern London is A.L. Beier and R. Finlay, eds, *London 1500–1700* (London, 1986). A later period in London's history still needs to be approached through V. Pearl, *London and the Outbreak of the Puritan Revolution* (Oxford, 1961).

Undoubtedly the most important work on subterranean stresses in local communities is D. Underdown, *Revel, Riot and Rebellion* (Oxford, 1985). Approaching similar topics from a very different angle are the essays in B. Reay, ed., *Popular Culture in Seventeenth-century England* (London, 1985), and T. Harris, ed., *Popular Culture in England, c.1500–1850* (London, 1995). A study that situates the urban community in a changing world is D.H. Sacks, *The Widening Gate: Bristol and the Atlantic Economy* (Berkeley, 1991).

For introductions to the history of other areas, see T.W. Moody, *et al.*, eds, *The New History of Ireland*, vol. 3 (Oxford, 1976); N. Canny, *From Reformation to Restoration: Ireland 1534–1660* (Dublin, 1987); J. Wormald, *Court, Kirk and Community: Scotland 1470–1625* (London, 1981); and A. McInnes, *Clanship, Commerce and the House of Stuart* (Glasgow, 1996).

Patterns of belief

The work of P. Collinson provides the essential entry into an understanding of early-modern protestantism: in particular, see his *Birthpangs of Protestant England* (London, 1988), *The Religion of Protestants* (Oxford, 1982), and the essays in his *Godly People* (London, 1983); these should be supplemented with the essays in A. Fletcher and P. Roberts, eds, *Religion, Culture and Society in Early Modern Britain* (Cambridge, 1994). K. Fincham, ed., *The Early Stuart Church* (London, 1993), is by far the best introduction to the church as a whole, and its essay by J. Maltby on the prayer book is of the highest importance. K. Fincham, *Prelate as Pastor* (Oxford, 1990), is valuable on the performance of the church's governors, and T. Webster, *Godly Clergy in Early Stuart England* (Cambridge, 1997), on the performance of its pastors. I. Green, *The Christian's ABC* (Oxford, 1996), provides the definitive account of catechising. P. Lake, 'Anti-popery: the structure of a prejudice', in R. Cust and A. Hughes, eds, *Conflict in Early Stuart England* (London, 1989), is the fundamental study of England's defining phobia. And W. Lamont, *Godly Rule, 1603–1660* (London, 1969), is still valuable on apocalypticism, as is K. Firth, *The Apocalyptic Tradition in Reformation Britain* (Oxford, 1978). The ecclesiastical disputes are contested today in N. Tyacke, *Anti-Calvinists* (Oxford, 1987), J. Davies, *The Caroline Captivity of the Church* (Oxford, 1992), and P. White, *Predestination, Policy and Polemic* (Cambridge, 1991). A useful introduction is to be found in the essays by White, Tyacke and P. Lake in *Past and Present* (1987). A. Milton's study of arguments about Rome, *Catholic and Reformed* (Cambridge, 1995), provides a fresh perspective.

Away from the mainstream, J. Bossy, *The English Catholic Community* (Oxford, 1976); C. Haigh, 'From Monopoly to Minority: Catholicism in Early Modern England', *Transactions of the Royal Historical Society* (1981), volume 31, and J.C.H. Aveling, *The Handle and the Axe* (London, 1976), provide very different analyses of the Catholic experience and its meaning.

The reformation of manners has been forcefully debated since the opening foray of K. Wrightson and D. Levine, *Poverty and Piety in an English Village* (revised edn, Oxford, 1995). Their work has been contested by M. Spufford, in A. Fletcher and J. Stevenson, eds, *Order and Disorder in Early Modern England* (Cambridge, 1985), and more thoroughly by M. Ingram, in P. Griffiths, *et al.*, ed., *The Experience of Authority* (Basingstoke, 1996).

The problem of witchcraft has generated perhaps the liveliest historiography in the field. The most important work has been K. Thomas, *Religion and the Decline of Magic* (London, 1971), and perhaps the most useful introduction in J. Barry, ed., *Witchcraft in Early Modern Europe* (Cambridge, 1996). But much of value on the social and gender contexts can be found in A. Macfarlane, *Witchcraft in Tudor and Stuart England*

(London, 1970); B.P. Levack, *The Witch Hunt in Early Modern Europe* (2nd edn, London, 1995); and C. Larner, *Witchcraft and Religion* (Oxford, 1984). The most thorough approach is J. Sharpe, *Instruments of Darkness: Witchcraft in England 1550–1750* (London, 1996), and the most challenging S. Clark, *Thinking with Demons* (Oxford, 1998), although fortunately Clark's 'Inversion, Misrule and the Meaning of Witchcraft', *Past and Present* (1980), no. 87, provides an introduction.

Works that explore an area on which high and low culture met include: B. Capp, *English Almanacs 1500–1800* (Ithaca, 1979); A. Geneva, *Astrology and the Seventeenth-century Mind* (Manchester, 1995); and D. Cressy, *Bonfires and Bells* (Berkeley, 1989).

Society and economy

The essential introduction to the economy is C. Clay, *Economic Expansion and Social Change* (2 vols, Cambridge, 1984), and to population history the massive work of E. Wrigley and R. Schofield, *The Population History of England* (London, 1981). Equally massive and impressive are the relevant volumes (4 and 5) of J. Thirsk, ed., *Agrarian History of England and Wales* (Cambridge, 1967, 1987). On the textile industry, B. Supple, *Commercial Crisis and Change* (Cambridge, 1959), should still be read, while J. Thirsk, *Economic Policy and Projects* (Oxford, 1979) is essential reading on improvement and consumer industries.

Social change is central to K. Wrightson, *English Society 1580–1680*; J. Barry, ed., *The Middling Sort of People* (London, 1994); M. McIntosh, *A Community Transformed* (Cambridge, 1991); K. Wrightson and D. Levine, *The Making of an Industrial Society* (Oxford, 1991); Griffiths, *et al.*, ed., *The Experience of Authority*; and A. Fletcher and J. Stevenson, *Order and Disorder*.

The contexts of women's lives has been another area of significant new research and synthesis. The best survey is now S. Mendelson and P. Crawford, *Women in Early Modern England* (Oxford, 1998), but J. Eales, *Women in Early Modern England* (London, 1998), is a useful introduction. More focused, but still a fine introduction, is P. Crawford, *Women and Religion in Early Modern England* (London, 1993). For the most thorough analysis of sex and gender roles, see A. Fletcher, *Gender, Sex, and Subordination in England 1500–1800* (New Haven, 1995); for a closer and more analytic focus on the underpinnings of prejudice, see M. Sommerville, *Sex and Subjection* (London, 1995); more discursive treatments of a similar theme are M. Ezell, *The Patriarch's Wife* (Chapel Hill, 1987), and K.U. Henderson and B.F. McManus, *Half Humankind* (Urbana, 1985). B. Lewalski, *Women Writing in Jacobean England* (Cambridge, Mass, 1993), uses women's writings to explore responses to constraint, and the essays in J. Kermode and G. Walker, *Women, Crime* and the Courts (London, 1994), study responses of a different kind; so too does L. Gowing, Dangerous Words: Women, Words and Sex in Early Modern London (Oxford, 1996). The essays in M. Prior, Women in English Society 1500–1800 (London, 1985), treat various aspects of women's experience.

The literature on specific social groups includes L. Stone, The Crisis of the Aristocracy 1558–1641 (Oxford, 1967), which is still valuable on social practices, and F. Heal and C. Holmes, The Gentry in England and Wales 1500–1700 (Basingstoke, 1994), which is extremely helpful and wide-ranging. More closely focused are V. Larminie, Wealth, Kinship and Culture: the Newdigates and their World (Woodbridge, 1995), and J.T. Cliffe, The Puritan Gentry (London, 1984). There are two excellent studies of branches of the legal profession: W. Prest, The Rise of the Barristers (Oxford, 1986) and C. Brooks, Petty-foggers and Vipers of the Commonwealth (Cambridge, 1986).

R. Houlbrooke, The English Family 1450–1750 (London, 1984), is a helpful introduction to a more intimate world, while L. Stone, Family, Sex and Marriage in England 1500–1800 (London, 1977) provides more partisan entertainments. L. Pollock, Forgotten Children: Parent–Child Relations from 1500 to 1900 (Cambridge, 1983) and V. Fildes, Women as Mothers in Pre-Industrial England (London, 1990), place a more precise focus on family relations, while P. Griffiths, Youth and Authority (Oxford, 1996), analyses some of the strains. M. Macdonald, Mystical Bedlam (Cambridge, 1981) and (with T. Murphy) Sleepless Souls (Oxford, 1990), explores the stresses that could lead to madness and suicide. S. Amussen, An Ordered Society (Oxford, 1988), maps the ideology of family and its intersection with the wider society. D. Cressy, Birth, Marriage and Death (Oxford, 1997), investigates the early-modern meanings of the human experience.

Finally, one work that cannot easily be categorised – P. Seaver, Wallington's World (Stanford, 1985), deftly reconstitutes one Londoner's world; and one work that opens a wider world: N. Canny, ed., The Origins of Empire (Oxford, 1998).

Towards a narrative history

The starting-point for serious study of the period might well be found in recent collections of essays. C. Russell, Unrevolutionary England (London, 1990), and K. Sharpe, ed., Faction and Parliament (London, 1985) make a powerful revisionist case against conflict. That can be juxtaposed with J.H. Hexter, ed., Parliament and Liberty from Elizabeth to the English Civil War (Stanford, 1992), and G. Eley and W. Hunt, eds, Reviving the English Revolution (London, 1988). In between might fall R. Cust and A. Hughes, eds, Conflict in Early Stuart England (London, 1989), and their

The English Civil War (London, 1997). But the meaning of politics has changed in recent years, and S. Amussen and M. Kishlansky, eds, *Political Culture and Cultural Politics in Early Modern England* (Manchester, 1997), and K. Sharpe and P. Lake, eds, *Culture and Politics in Early Stuart England* (Stanford, 1993), bring interdisciplinary perspectives to bear on politics high and low.

In such perspectives some of the best new understandings of the reign of James might be found. Wormald's work on the British dimension in *History* (1983), volume 68, and M. Lee, *Great Britain's Solomon* (Urbana, 1990), are essential on James's Anglo-Scottish context, as is Fincham on the church history. But otherwise James's reign before his last years is thinly covered. L. Peck, *Court Patronage and Corruption in Early Stuart England* (London, 1990), and her *Mental World* volume (Cambridge, 1991), are central to an understanding of the court. T. Rabb, *Jacobean Gentleman: Sir Edwin Sandys* (Princeton, 1998) examines a central parliament-man, and R. Lockyer, *Buckingham* (London, 1981) unfolds that complex figure. Otherwise, students must still turn to A.G.R. Smith, ed., *The Reigns of James VI and I* (London, 1973), and to H. Tomlinson, *Before the English Civil War* (London, 1983).

The scholarship on politics in the 1620s is very lively. C. Russell, *Parliaments and English Politics 1621–1629* (Oxford, 1979) is the essential statement of the revisionist case. Important challenges have come from T. Cogswell, in *The Blessed Revolution: English Politics and the Coming of War 1621–1624* (Cambridge, 1989), and in his article, 'A Low Road to Extinction: parliament and supply', *Historical Journal* (1990), volume 33, from the Cust and Hughes collections mentioned above and from R. Cust, *The Forced Loan and English Politics* (Oxford, 1987). D. Hirst, *Representative of the People?* (Cambridge, 1975) and M. Kishlansky, *Parliamentary Selections* (Cambridge, 1986), give conflicting accounts of the electoral process, and they should be read with R. Cust's essay in Cust and Hughes, eds, *Conflict . . .* , and also with P. Lake, 'Thomas Scott', *Historical Journal* (1982), volume 25. C. Russell's essay on Pym in the 1620s in his *Unrevolutionary England* is invaluable, as is Tyacke's *Anti-Calvinists*, for an understanding of the ecclesiastical controversies of this decade. Tyacke is of course central too for the 1630s; J. Davies's *Caroline Captivity*, with its emphasis on royal as much as Laudian ritualism, should also be read.

The years of 'personal rule' in England have fared less well. The major work is K. Sharpe, *The Personal Rule of Charles I* (New Haven, 1992), but reviewers have generally found this too much an apologia. Merritt's collection on *Wentworth* has some valuable essays, and L. Reeve, *Charles I and the Road to Personal Rule* (Cambridge, 1989), explores the genesis of Charles's rule; but the major issues of domestic politics, such as ship money, need further address. Away from the English mainstream, K. Kupperman, *Providence Island 1630–1641* (Cambridge, 1993) is illuminating, as are

K.R. Andrews, *Ships, Money and Politics* (Cambridge, 1991), and R. Harding, *The Evolution of the Sailing Navy 1558–1815* (Basingstoke, 1995). But the best recent work on the 1630s has undoubtedly looked outside England. Central to an understanding of England in these years are A. McInnes, *Charles I and the Making of the Covenanting Movement* (Edinburgh, 1991); the essays in J. Morrill, ed., *The Scottish National Covenant in its British Context* (Edinburgh, 1990); D. Stevenson, *The Scottish Revolution 1637–1644* (Newton Abbot, 1973); and N. Canny, *The Upstart Earl* (Cambridge, 1982).

The transition to the crisis of the early 1640s is now a matter of lively debate. C. Russell's ambitious *Fall of the British Monarchies* (Oxford, 1991), and its briefer and more argumentative companion, *The Causes of the English Civil War* (Oxford, 1990), locate thoroughly short-term causes of crisis firmly in Scotland and Ireland. A. Hughes, *The Causes of the English Civil War* (London, 1991), provides a judicious assessment of the relation of England's earlier decades to the British catastrophe, while A. Fletcher, *The Outbreak of the English Civil War* (London, 1981), focuses firmly on the Long Parliament, and excels in its relation of centre to locality. A detailed application of such a centre/local perspective is J. Eales, *Puritans and Roundheads* (Cambridge, 1990). P. Donald, *An Uncounselled King* (Cambridge, 1990), provides a Scottish (and Hamiltonian) perspective on the crisis that led to the Bishops' Wars, while M. Fissel, *The Bishops' Wars* (Cambridge, 1994), skilfully dissects those follies. J. Morrill's essay on Pym in S. Amussen and M. Kishlansky, eds, *Political Culture* . . . , is a brilliant attack on J.H. Hexter, *The Reign of King Pym* (Cambridge, Mass., 1941), though the latter should still be read. M. Mendle, *Dangerous Positions* (Alabama, 1985), analyses some of the parliamentarian arguments, and D.L. Smith, *Constitutional Royalism and the Search for Settlement* (Cambridge, 1994), reconstructs a very different position; and on the latter, B. Wormald, *Clarendon* (Chicago, 1976), still impresses. B. Mac Cuarta, ed. *Ulster 1641* (revised edn, Belfast, 1997) and Canny's essay in J. Ohlmeyer, ed., *Ireland from Independence to Occupation* (Cambridge, 1995), are vital for the Irish Revolt.

The best study of allegiance in 1642 is M. Stoyle, *Loyalty and Locality* (Exeter, 1994). It should be read with D. Underdown, 'The Problem of Popular Allegiance', *Transactions of the Royal Historical Society* (1981), volume 31, and A. Hughes, 'King, Parliament and Localities', in R. Cust and A. Hughes, *The English Civil War*. D. Rollison, *The Local Origins of Modern Society: Gloucestershire 1500–1800* (London, 1992), fascinatingly relates socio-economic transformation in Gloucestershire to alignments; B. Manning, *The English People and the English Revolution* (2nd edn, London, 1991), argues the case for popular radicalism in the 1640s more tendentiously. An altogether more ambitious, but equally tendentious, application of Marxist categories to the continuing crisis is R. Brenner, *Merchants and Revolution* (Princeton, 1993); the long postscript fascinatingly seeks to relate revisionist arguments to theories of economic change. Studies that use a lighter touch to relate politics and cultures high and low are the volumes of essays by Christopher Hill, perhaps especially *A Nation of Change and Novelty* (London, 1990), and the more systematic work of D. Underdown, *A Freeborn People* (Oxford, 1996). The intersections of politics and a wider public are fascinatingly suggested in J. Raymond, *Making the News* (London, 1993); J. Raymond, *The Invention of the Newspaper: English Newsbooks 1641–1649* (Oxford, 1996); S. Achinstein, *Milton and the Revolutionary Reader* (Princeton, 1994); and N. Smith, *Literature and Revolution* (Oxford, 1994).

The military history of the war is still best studied through P. Young and R. Holmes, *The English Civil War* (London, 1978). C. Carlton, *Going to the Wars* (London, 1992), seeks to recapture the experience of campaigning; M. Bennett, *The Civil Wars in Britain and Ireland, 1635–1651* (Oxford, 1997), looks a little more broadly. R. Hutton, *The Royalist War Effort* (London, 1981), P.R. Newman, *The Old Service* (Manchester, 1993), are invaluable for the royalist cause, while C.A. Holmes, *The Eastern Association* (Cambridge, 1975), relates parliamentary to local and military developments. M. Kishlansky, *The Rise of the New Model Army* (Cambridge, 1979), argues the non-partisan genesis of that army, but has been challenged by I. Gentles's more judicious and substantial *The New Model Army* (Oxford, 1992). Kishlansky has been challenged too by A. Woolrych, *Soldiers and Statesmen* (Oxford, 1987), the essential study of the radicalising army of 1647. M. Tolmie, *The Triumph of the Saints* (Cambridge, 1977), studies the Independent churches that briefly allied with the Levellers. The counter-revolutionary cause can be followed through the detail of R. Ashton, *Counter-Revolution* (New Haven, 1994), and more briefly in several of the essays in J. Morrill, ed., *Reactions to the English Civil War 1642–1649* (London, 1982). Standing somewhere between the two extremes, and connecting honour with quite different ideologies, is the important essay by J. Adamson, 'The Baronial Context of the English Civil War', in Cust and Hughes, *English Civil War*. Other theatres should be studied in Ohlmeyer, ed., *Ireland from Independence to Occupation*, and D. Stevenson, *Revolution and Counter-Revolution in Scotland* (London, 1977), and *Scottish Covenanters and Irish Confederates* (Belfast, 1981).

Valuable studies of war and revolution in the localities are those by A. Hughes on Warwickshire; A.R. Warmington, *Civil War, Interregnum and Restoration in Gloucestershire, 1640–1672* (Woodbridge, Suffolk, 1997); J. Morrill, *Cheshire 1630–1660* (Oxford, 1974); R. Howell, *Newcastle upon Tyne and the Puritan Revolution* (Oxford, 1967); the essays in R.C. Richardson, ed., *Town and Countryside in the English Revolution* (Manchester, 1992); and Underdown's *Revel, Riot and Rebellion*.

The best analysis of the moment of revolution, and a model for the integration of different theatres of action, is D. Underdown, *Pride's Purge*

(Oxford, 1971). Equally impressive in its way is the vivid reconstruction in C.V. Wedgwood, *The Trial of Charles I* (London, 1964). Some of the forces pressing on the actors can be approached through a series of recent editions: S. Sedley, ed., *A Spark in the Ashes: The Pamphlets of John Warr* (London, 1992); B. Taft and J. R. McMichael, *The Writings of William Walwyn* (Athens, Ga., 1989); and C. Hill, *The Law of Freedom and other Writings: Winstanley* (London, 1983). A reformer of a very different kind is the subject of A. Cromartie, *Sir Matthew Hale* (Cambridge, 1995).

The world of the republic is best approached through the narrative and analysis of B. Worden, *The Rump Parliament* (Cambridge, 1974), and the parallel study of the Barebone's period, A. Woolrych, *Commonwealth to Protectorate* (Oxford, 1982). R. Hutton, *The British Republic 1649–1660* (London, 1990), provides a useful brief narrative. The essays in J. Morrill, ed., *Revolution and Restoration* (London 1992), try to put the decade in perspective, while D. Hirst, 'Locating the 1650s', *History* (1996), volume 81, attempts a longer focus. S. Kelsey, *Inventing a Republic* (Manchester, 1997), studies the Commonwealth's creation of an image of government, and S. Pincus, *Protestantism and Patriotism* (Cambridge, 1996), argues powerfully the partisan base of republican foreign policy. Another valuable study of foreign policy is R. Crabtree, 'The Idea of a Protestant Foreign Policy,' in I. Roots, ed., *Cromwell, A Profile* (London, 1973). R. Bliss, *Revolution and Empire* (Manchester, 1990), provides a valuable introduction to the politics of the Atlantic world. C. Durston, *The Family in the English Revolution* (Oxford, 1989), discusses a rather more intractable topic very thoroughly.

The religious history of the sects has been a field of considerable activity. The starting-point used to be C. Hill, *The World Turned Upside Down* (London, 1972), but Hill's picture of liberation is gravely challenged by J. Davis, 'Religion and the Struggle for Freedom in the English Revolution', *Historical Journal* (1992), volume 35. B. Reay and I. McGregor, *Radical Religion in the English Revolution* (Oxford, 1984), provide an introduction. More specialised are B.R. White, *The English Baptists of the Seventeenth Century* (London, 1983), and B. Reay, *The Quakers and the English Revolution* (London, 1985), and N. Smith, *A Collection of Ranter Writings* (London, 1983). J. Davis has questioned the existence of the Ranters in *Fear, Myth and History* (Cambridge, 1986), and excited a fascinating controversy in *Past and Present* (1990 and 1993), volumes 129 and 140. Equally fascinating issues are raised in C. Hill, W. Lamont and B. Reay, eds, *The World of the Muggletonians* (London, 1983). Invaluable for the Quakers are two biographies, H.L. Ingle, *First among Friends* (Oxford, 1994), and (far more than a biography), L. Damrosch, *The Sorrows of the Quaker Jesus* (Cambridge, Mass., 1996), an insightful study of James Nayler. P. Mack, *Visionary Women: Ecstatic Prophecy in Seventeenth-century England* (Berkeley, 1992), illuminates much more than the female prophets who are her subject. Developments in the parochial mainstream are suggested by J. Morrill, 'The Church 1642–1649', in his *Reactions to the English Civil War 1642–1649* (London, 1982); by two studies of Richard Baxter, one by N.H. Keeble (Oxford, 1982), and one by W. Lamont (London, 1979); and by D. Hirst, 'The Failure of Godly Rule', *Past and Present* (1991), no. 81.

The protector in several of his many guises is the subject of important essays in J. Morrill, ed., *Oliver Cromwell and the English Revolution* (London, 1990). But some of the most insightful writings on Cromwell are essays by B. Worden, 'Providence and Politics in Cromwellian England', in *Past and Present* (1985), no. 109, and 'Cromwell and Toleration', in G. Best, ed., *History, Society and the Churches* (Cambridge, 1985). Some of the protector's many words can be found in the valuable recent collection, I. Roots, ed., *The Speeches of Oliver Cromwell* (London, 1989). The most stimulating biography of Cromwell remains that by Christopher Hill, *God's Englishman* (London, 1970), but a sensible recent offering is B. Coward, *Cromwell* (London, 1991).

Five collections of essays focus helpfully on the crisis of mid-century: they are G. Aylmer, ed., *The Interregnum* (London, 1972); D. Pennington and K. Thomas, *Puritans and Revolutionaries* (Oxford, 1978); C. Jones *et al.*, eds, *Politics and People in Revolutionary England* (Oxford, 1986); I. Gentles, *et al.*, eds, *Soldiers, Writers and Statesmen of the English Revolution* (Cambridge, 1998); and J. Morrill, *et al.*, eds, *Public Duty and Private Conscience* (Oxford, 1993).

The essential works for Ireland and Scotland besides the Ohlmeyer collection are T. Barnard, *Cromwellian Ireland* (Oxford, 1975) and F. Dow, *Cromwellian Scotland* (Edinburgh, 1979). The road to Restoration can be followed in detail in R. Hutton, *The Restoration* (Oxford, 1985), and in A. Woolrych, 'Historical Introduction', to R. W. Ayers, ed., *The Complete Prose Works of John Milton, Vol. VII 1659–1660* (revised edn, New Haven, 1980).

Index

Index